MODERNITY, COMMUNITY, AND PLACE IN BRIAN FRIEL'S DRAMA

Irish Studies

Kathleen Costello-Sullivan, *Series Editor*

For a full list of titles in this series,
visit https://press.syr.edu/supressbook-series/irish-studies/.

MODERNITY, COMMUNITY, & PLACE IN BRIAN FRIEL'S DRAMA

SECOND EDITION

RICHARD RANKIN RUSSELL

SYRACUSE
UNIVERSITY
PRESS

As always, my most heartfelt thanks go to my family: my wife and best friend, Hannah, and my two sons, Connor and Aidan, who make me laugh and sustain me daily. *Soli deo Gloria* or, in the Irish, *Chun gloire Dé.*

A native of West Tennessee, **Richard Rankin Russell** is professor of modern and contemporary British and Irish literature at Baylor University in Texas, where he directs the graduate program in English. He directed the Beall Poetry Festival at Baylor for eight years: www.baylor.edu/beall. He has served as Literature Representative for the American Conference for Irish Studies. His publications include three edited collections—*Martin McDonagh: A Casebook* (Routledge, 2007; pb. 2013), *Peter Fallon: Poet, Publisher, Translator, Editor* (Irish Academic Press, 2013), *Bernard MacLaverty: New Critical Readings* (Bloomsbury, 2014). Including the first edition of this study on Friel, he has published five monographs: *Bernard MacLaverty* (Bucknell University Press, 2009), *Poetry and Peace: Michael Longley, Seamus Heaney, and Northern Ireland* (University of Notre Dame Press, 2010), *Seamus Heaney's Regions* (University of Notre Dame Press, 2014), and *Seamus Heaney: An Introduction* (Edinburgh University Press, 2016). *Poetry and Peace* won both the South Atlantic Modern Language Association Book Prize and the South Central Modern Language Association Book Prize in 2011. *Seamus Heaney's Regions* won the Robert Penn Warren/Cleanth Brooks Award for the best book of literary criticism published in the United States in 2014 and was a *Foreword Reviews* 2014 INDIEFAB Book of the Year Award Finalist in History.

Contents

Preface and Acknowledgments
for the Second Edition

> Your mix of wistfulness and impish wit
> Both shy and sharp-eyed taking us all in.
> —Micheal O'Siadhail, *The Five Quintets*

Brian Friel, the subject of this study, so aptly described by Micheal O'Siadhail in the lines above, died on October 2, 2015, two years after my original study's publication. He liked my book, calling it "masterly" in a letter he wrote me after I sent him a copy. That was good enough for me. I have always felt the job of the critic is to promote and explain the work of writers whom we admire, not to call attention to ourselves and our own cleverness.

As much as I like and admire the dramas of Friel's immediate peers, the late Tom Murphy and Tom Kilroy, and of his earlier antecedents in Irish drama such as Synge, Yeats, and O'Casey, I remain convinced that Friel was the greatest Irish playwright of the last century, the greatest Irish playwright ever, and indeed, one of the best playwrights ever to write in the English language. His range of subjects, his variety of formal innovations, and above all, his sheer craft with words mark him as a playwright for the ages. In this regard, I was pleased to see the Irish drama and Friel scholar Scott Boltwood, after surveying the achievement of Synge, Yeats, and O'Casey, recently declare Friel as the "most important and successful Irish playwright of the twentieth century."[1] Furthermore, in his review of the five-volume *Collected Plays* published by Peter Fallon's Gallery Press in 2016, Fintan O'Toole, who identified Friel's best and most lasting plays as *Philadelphia, Here I Come!*, *Aristocrats*, *Faith Healer*, *Translations*, *Dancing at Lughnasa*, *Making History*, *Molly Sweeney*, and *The Home Place*, sagely noted, "That's a hard core of eight plays, and in truth there are very few dramatists in the English language with more than half a dozen works that seem likely to hold the stage beyond their own era."[2]

The outpouring of tributes after his death was stunning and ranged from actress extraordinaire Meryl Streep, who termed him "a tender dramatist, an insightful humanist, and a lovely man," to Northern Ireland–born actor Liam Neeson, who called Friel "Ireland's Chekhov" and a "master craftsman," to former director of the Abbey Theatre in Dublin and the Guthrie Theatre in Minneapolis, Joe Dowling, who described Friel as "the greatest Irish playwright of the twentieth century" and further noted, "There is no parallel. There is no other writer that had the same depth that Brian had in terms of analysis of Irish society, in terms of the way in which he created those amazing plays that got deeper and deeper as his career went on."[3] Besides the outpouring of tributes in the *Irish Times*, the "national" newspaper of Ireland, and along with the notices published in various American newspapers, the *New York Times* published an entire page-length obituary by Benedict Nightingale and a personal appreciation by its theater critic Ben Brantley, ample testimony to how well in general Friel's plays had been received on Broadway and off-Broadway (particularly at Manhattan's Irish Repertory Theatre) over the years.[4] The drama critic for the *Wall Street Journal*, Terry Teachout, penned a moving remembrance wherein he praised Friel's "vision of human nature" as "penetrating and profound" and concluded, "Genius is not a function of celebrity, and most of those who know his work agree that when the roll of the greatest playwrights of the 20th century is drawn up, Brian Friel's name will be upon it."[5]

In 2018, plans were announced to preserve the home in Glenties, County Donegal, of Friel's maternal grandparents and, for a time, of the five sisters immortalized in *Dancing at Lughnasa*, and transform it into a Brian Friel center. After having won a series of awards for his work, including three Tony Awards for *Lughnasa*, and election both as senator in the Republic of Ireland and as *Saoi*, or "Wise One," to the selective Irish artists' group Aosdána in 2006 (one of only seven living artists at a time to be permitted this title), Brian Friel's place in theater and cultural history is secure, and in coming years, his achievements will likely bulk even larger.

This current study retains the major chapters of the first edition but adds much new material, explained below. My original book title, *Modernity, Community, and Place in Brian Friel's Drama*, remains, but this new edition, including its evocative cover, privileges my recovery of Friel's emphasis on spirituality throughout his career.

This new, expanded edition remains the only study of Friel to focus so extensively on a select number of plays, rather than try to give readings of them all in a comprehensive overview. The only monograph on Friel's drama to appear since the first edition of my book has been Christopher Murray's *The Theatre of Brian Friel: Tradition and Modernity* (2014), and that book, too, surveys a number of Friel plays—some sixteen—albeit a smaller number than most other studies of Friel have done.[6] The helpful *Brian Friel: A Literary Companion*, containing a comprehensive chronology through the year of his death and featuring a series of topical entries, written by Mary Ellen Snodgrass, appeared in 2017. In 2018, Boltwood published his survey and evaluation of Friel criticism, another sign of the ongoing vigor of scholarly work on Friel.

I now supplement the original study with a new interchapter on Friel's first play that he kept in print, *The Enemy Within*, and I also include an additional new chapter on his move from short fiction to writing drama full-time. In addition, I have added interchapters on the 2016 Donmar Warehouse production of *Faith Healer* and on the Field Day Theatre Company's origins and artistic and cultural aims. This last interchapter is enhanced by my work in the Seamus Deane Papers at Emory University; grateful thanks to former Emory professor and curator of rare books, Kevin Young, who directed my attention to those papers in 2012 during my research for a book on Seamus Heaney. My archival research in the Friel papers at the National Library of Ireland in the summer of 2017 now is incorporated into my readings of both Friel's breakthrough play, *Philadelphia, Here I Come!*, and his best and most important drama, *Faith Healer*, and I additionally incorporate new research on Friel throughout where appropriate, including a substantial performance review of major productions of *Faith Healer* in my chapter on that profoundly disturbing yet strangely hopeful play.

Beyond all these new additions and revisions, I now also add a full final chapter on three of Friel's plays after *Dancing at Lughnasa*—a chapter that had to be largely excised in the first edition for reasons of space. Some of this final chapter, treating *Molly Sweeney*, *The Home Place*, and Friel's version of Ibsen's *Hedda Gabler*, was originally published in *Modern Drama* as "Home, Exile, and Unease in Brian Friel's Globalized Drama since 1990: *Molly Sweeney*, *The Home Place*, and *Hedda Gabler (after Ibsen)*," but I have substantially developed my original readings of these plays, particularly of Friel's *Hedda*, for this new edition. Grateful thanks to Martin Llewellyn, editorial coordinator for journals at the University of Toronto, for permission to reprint that material here and also to Elizabeth Bradburn at *Comparative Drama* for permission to reprint material from my essay "Brian Friel's Transformation from Short Fiction Writer to Dramatist," much of which forms the basis of the interchapter on his transition to drama from short fiction.

A series of students have helped me think through my readings of Friel again, especially those who took my graduate seminar at Baylor on British and European drama from 1879 to the present in the fall of 2018. My hearty gratitude goes to those students—Sorina Higgins, Clayton McReynolds, Daniel Smith, Molly Lewis, Kelly Sauskojus, and Christina Lambert—whose interpretations of these rich plays in their reading notebooks and their challenges to my reading of the plays has prompted me to rethink them and ponder them anew. Another former student, Makenzie Fitzgerald, who wrote a wonderful undergraduate honors thesis on Seamus Heaney under my direction at Baylor, has been an additional source of encouragement for my readings of Friel. I am grateful too for the work of my research assistant in the summer of 2019, Anna Beaudry, who tracked down recent Friel criticism for me. The chair of the Baylor English Department, Kevin Gardner, has been very supportive of my research, and I am grateful for his support and friendship, along with that of Joe Fulton, Maurice Hunt, Alex Engebretson, Sarah Ford, William Weaver, Ginger Hanchey, Josh King, Luke Ferretter, Mona Choucair, Julia Daniel, Thomas Kidd, Jeff Fish, and others at Baylor.

Many thanks to the estate of Brian Friel, represented by Leah Schmidt, for permission to quote from his draft play *Bannermen* and from his letters to Seamus Deane, along with the additional permission she gave to quote from the unpublished material in the Friel Papers at the National Library of Ireland. Grateful thanks to James Harte in the Manuscripts Department at the National Library of Ireland for permission to also quote from the unpublished material in the Friel Papers there. Additional thanks to Syracuse University Press's acquisitions editor, Deb Manion, for allowing me to revise and expand my first edition as a new paperback edition and for her patience over more than two years as I wrote two books on James Joyce since we first agreed that I would revise my original Friel study! Many thanks as well to Kelly Balenske, assistant editor at Syracuse, who has helped with copyediting and shepherding the book through to press, as well as Kay Steinmetz, editorial and production manager at the press, whose thoughtful and rigorous copyediting has made my prose more polished and readable. My research assistant Robert Brown provided the revised index for this edition. I am also grateful to the director of marketing, Alex Fleming, at the Donmar Warehouse in London for permission to reproduce for this book cover and for promotional purposes the evocative image from the 2016 Donmar production of *Faith Healer*. The Syracuse design team, led by senior designer Victoria M. Lane, produced a wonderful cover based on this image; my thanks to her and her team and to Syracuse's marketing coordinator, Lisa Kuerbis, for catalog copy and additional promotional work she did for this new edition. The late Seamus Deane gave permission for me to quote more than the limit allowed by Faber from his fine introduction to *Brian Friel: Plays 1* (Seamus Deane, "Introduction." In *Brian Friel: Plays 1*, 11–22. London:

Faber & Faber, 1996), and Peter Fallon gave me permission to quote extensively from Gallery Press's edition of *The Home Place* (Extracts from *The Home Place* [2005] reproduced by kind permission of the Estate of Brian Friel c/o The Gallery Press. www.gallerypress.com); my thanks to both of them. Finally, the poet Micheal O'Siadhail gave me permission to quote as an epigraph for this new edition the two lines from his lovely description of Friel in his magnificent volume *The Five Quintets*, published by Baylor University Press in 2018.

Original Acknowledgments

I am very grateful to the College of Arts and Sciences at Baylor University, which granted me both a summer sabbatical in 2010 and a research leave for the fall semester, 2010, during which the original edition of this book was completed. I am thankful for the friendship and encouragement, scholarly and otherwise, given to me by many past and present colleagues in the Baylor English Department, including James E. Barcus, Mike DePalma, Joe B. Fulton, Greg Garrett, Clement T. Goode, Maurice Hunt, and Josh King. I also am grateful to my chair in English, Dianna Vitanza, and the dean of arts and sciences, Lee Nordt, who have been very supportive of my scholarship over the years. My Baylor undergraduate and graduate students, particularly the undergraduate students in my Friel and Heaney course in spring 2009, and the graduate students in my spring 2011 course on Friel, Heaney, and Bernard MacLaverty have increased my appreciation for and understanding of Friel's drama. The readers for Syracuse University Press made a series of helpful suggestions that greatly improved the manuscript, especially the introduction. I am especially grateful for continuing encouragement from my mentor Weldon Thornton, Professor Emeritus at the University of North Carolina–Chapel Hill, and Bryan Giemza, also of UNC–Chapel Hill, for their continued personal and professional encouragement. Kimball King first introduced me to the plays of Brian Friel during graduate school at Chapel Hill. Peter Fallon has also enhanced my understanding of Friel's work. Anthony Roche has given helpful, detailed advice on revision and corrected errors of fact. His own work on Friel has been illuminating. Marilynn J. Richtarik of Georgia State University and Steve Watt of Indiana University have encouraged my work on Friel, as has Terry Teachout. The staff at MARBL, the Manuscripts, Archives, and Rare Book Library of Emory University was most helpful. Jennika Baines, the acquisitions editor of Syracuse University Press was a wonderful editor with whom to work, answering my questions in prompt and helpful ways. Jim MacKillop, the Irish Studies series editor for Syracuse, encouraged this project early on.

Permission has been granted from James Silas Rogers, editor of *New Hibernia Review*, to reprint part of an earlier version of my essay on *Translations*. Permission has been granted from Matthew Roudané, editor of *South Atlantic Review*, to reprint a portion of my essay on *The Freedom of the City*. Permission has been granted from Alan Ackerman, editor of *Modern Drama*, to reprint a portion of my essay on Friel's *Molly Sweeney*, *The Home Place*, and *Hedda Gabler* (*after Ibsen*). Brian Friel has graciously given me permission to quote from one of his letters and from his unpublished play *Bannermen*. This book speaks to my great admiration for his work.

Abbreviations

BFP1	*Brian Friel: Plays 1*
BFP2	*Brian Friel: Plays 2*
DL	*Dancing at Lughnasa*
EW	*The Enemy Within*
HG	*Hedda Gabler*
HP	*The Home Place*

MODERNITY, COMMUNITY, AND PLACE IN BRIAN FRIEL'S DRAMA

Introduction

"I think I'm sort of a peasant at heart. I'm certainly not 'citified' and I never will be. There are certain atmospheres which I find totally alien to me and I'm much more at ease in a rural setting."

—Brian Friel, "In Interview with Graham
Morrison (1965)"

"I would like to write a play that would capture the peculiar spiritual, and indeed material, flux that this country is in at the moment. This has got to be done . . . at a local, parochial level, and hopefully this will have meaning for other people in other countries."

—Friel, "The Future of Irish Drama (1970)"

In 2002 Gerry Smyth noted in his important book *Space and the Irish Cultural Imagination* that an "interest in Irish space and place surged rather than diminished in the latter decades of the twentieth century," suggesting that such an interest "emerged from the confused matrix of spatial affiliation, alienation, and negotiation which came to form the basis of modern Irish cultural experience."[1] And yet, as Nessa Cronin lamented ten years later, "While Irish Studies scholars have variously written on the significance of place in Irish writing, there have been very few full-length studies that examine how and why a preoccupation with place is present in the Irish literary tradition."[2] The present study seeks to contribute to the growing body of work on studies of place within Irish writing and culture by exploring the impact of modernity on communities in the major dramas of Irish playwright Brian Friel and applying relevant theories

1

of place to this discussion. Friel has described his writing process in terms of self-exploration that also captures the flux and unease characteristic of his major plays' investigations into place: "You delve into a particular corner of yourself that's dark and uneasy, and you articulate the confusions and the unease of that particular period. When you do that, that's finished and you acquire other corners of unease and discontent."[3] These dramas explore and evoke the environmental, intellectual, spiritual, and cultural climate of specific periods of Irish history, particularly at times of massive change that create great uneasiness for his characters. In this regard, Seamus Deane has argued that "Friel's drama is concerned with the nervous collapse of a culture which has had to bear pressures beyond its capacity to sustain."[4] Learning to live in that unease by drawing on the best cultural traditions in Ireland while jettisoning pernicious elements of them and remaining cautiously open to the demands of the present, rather than attempting to dwell in a stable concept of "home," has been Friel's and his characters' greatest achievement.

While place in fiction and poetry has often been the subject of critical study—particularly in the subgenre of pastoral poetry and generally in American literature—the subject of place in drama, especially in non-American drama, is severely undertheorized. Thus this study seeks to articulate the complex nexus of place in Friel's work by specifically showing how his comprehensive dramatic theory of place emphasizes changes in the literal, fluid physical environment, including the land, seasons, and crops. His theory also encompasses more intellectual concerns about the impact of modernity on rural culture, often accelerated by technology, along with the imagined communities he strives to create between readers and script, actors and audience.

While many critics have noted in passing Friel's affinity for local culture and community, they have largely failed to discuss the profound implications of his varying environments—including rural and urban places; public, built spaces; and the personal spaces of the body and mind—and to integrate that interest with a comprehensive theory of his drama.[5] It might seem odd at first to pair drama, which is part of culture, with the environment, but nature and culture, as William Howarth has argued, are fundamentally related to each other: "[A]lthough we cast nature and culture as opposites, in fact they constantly mingle, like water and soil in a flowing stream."[6] The leading philosopher of place, the phenomenologist Edward Casey, has suggested that "the inherent emplacement of culture has been missed" during recent developments in both psychology and semiology, while reminding us that "[t]he very word *culture* meant 'place tilled' in Middle English, and the same word goes back to the Latin term *colere*, 'to inhabit, care for, till, worship.' To be cultural, to have a culture, is to inhabit a place sufficiently intensely to cultivate it—to be responsible for it, to respond to it, to attend to it caringly. Where else but in particular places can culture take root?"[7]

Friel himself has consistently drawn on agricultural terms when discussing culture and vice versa. For instance, one of his most famous short stories is "The Diviner" (a title later adopted by Richard Pine for his fine 1999 study of Friel). In his autobiographical essay "Self-Portrait (1972)," Friel borrows Seamus Heaney's analogy between the writer and the diviner in Heaney's poem "The Diviner" to explain how he draws inspiration from the local environment: "[T]here are only certain stretches of ground over which the writer's divining rod will come to life."[8] Another telling example of his understanding of the close relationship between nature and culture occurs in his best-known play, *Translations*, when Yolland, who has originally come to Ballybeg to help carry out the English Ordnance Survey, realizes that he is contributing to the loss of the Irish language and local culture and musingly casts this loss in terms of soil depletion: "Something is being eroded" (*BFP1* 420).

George O'Brien is undoubtedly right to argue that "language, culture's primary instrument, occupies a much more prominent place in Friel's theater than it did in the stories."[9] Certainly an entire strand of recent Friel criticism—by and large the dominant one—has correctly and profitably explored this crucial aspect of his work, as does the current study when relevant, because of its relative neglect until the 1980s. Yet analyses of language in Friel's major dramas have often ignored the natural, constructed, intellectual, and spiritual environments of those plays. For example, F. C. McGrath, in his introduction to his pioneering 1999 study, *Brian Friel's (Post) Colonial Drama*, argues against most earlier Friel criticism that downplayed his "orientation toward language and its relation to the illusions, myths, and narratives we construct to negotiate psychological and social experiences" and pledges to fully investigate Friel's "focus on language" throughout his work.[10] McGrath's argument that his book "culminates this strand of Friel criticism"[11] thus suggests that a new critical approach to Friel's work is needed now, one fulfilled by the current study. Thus I seek to explore the inextricability of various manifestations of environment with culture in Friel's major plays. I will show how his complex theory of drama has evolved as it plumbs the depths of a series of physical and metaphorical places: literal rural landscapes; the cityscape of Derry; the built environment of particular edifices; and sites of the body, mind, and human heart.[12]

Successive chapters analyze Friel's five best-known and most critically acclaimed major plays across roughly a quarter-century— *Philadelphia, Here I Come!* (1964), *The Freedom of the City* (1973), *Faith Healer* (1979), *Translations* (1980), and *Dancing at Lughnasa* (1990)—followed by a lengthy new concluding chapter that closely attends to Friel's concerns about modernity, community, place, and spirituality in three later plays, *Molly Sweeney* (1994), *The Home Place* (2005), and Friel's "version" of Ibsen's *Hedda Gabler* (2008). *Lughnasa* still looms so large in the Friel canon that it tends to obscure the considerable achievements of later Friel. My only major regret for the first edition of this study was that I contributed to this tendency by not including my chapter on these post-*Lughnasa* plays. As I have noted in the preface to this second edition, there are also a series of new interchapters that augment and supplement the original study and link the major themes and developments of Friel's career, including a new full-length chapter that explains the reasons why he moved from writing short fiction to drama by the end of the 1960s. Throughout, I contextualize Friel's place-centered theory of drama with analyses of rural poverty, spiritual impoverishment, memory, community, fertility, and epistemology. Besides the interchapter on Friel's transition away from the short story to drama, it is beyond the scope of this study to address Friel's short fiction; his fine achievements in that genre have been explored in several book-length studies of his work.[13]

My selection of these five major plays is driven in part by their innovation in form, memorable performances by leading actors in Ireland and abroad, and continuing popularity among Irish drama critics, students, and theatergoers. These five dramas, along with *Aristocrats* (1979), *Molly Sweeney*, and *The Home Place*, form the central core of Friel's work. As evidence of this nearly settled Friel "canon," I offer several assessments of critics' choices of his best dramas, both after his death at age eighty-six in 2015 and on his eightieth birthday, which were occasions for stock-taking. For those wanting to get a fuller sense of Friel's dramatic achievement, Gallery Press in Ireland and Faber and Faber in England published the *Collected Plays of Brian Friel*, containing original works and adaptations, across five volumes in 2016—some twenty-nine plays in all. This collection has now become the established edition of Friel and apparently includes all the plays and translations he wanted to keep in print.

What strikes one most about critics' selections of Friel's best plays is their relative consistency. The *Selected Plays*, first published in the United Kingdom by Faber in 1984 and in the United States under the same title by Catholic University of America Press in 1986, remains invaluable for containing most of these: *Philadelphia, Here I Come!*, *The Freedom of the City*, *Living Quarters*, *Aristocrats*, *Faith Healer*, and *Translations*. Around the one-year anniversary of Friel's death in early October of 2016, Peter Crawley offered a list of "seven key plays" by Friel, with running descriptions of each, five from the *Selected Plays*: *Philadelphia*, *Freedom*, *Aristocrats*, *Faith Healer*, *Translations*, *Lughnasa*, and *The Home Place*.[14] At that same time, Adrienne Leavy offered what she feels are the significant Friel plays that also are "representative of the range and diversity of his work": *Philadelphia*, *Freedom*, *Aristocrats*, *Faith Healer*, *Translations*, *The*

Communication Cord, Making History, Dancing at Lughnasa, and
The Home Place.[15] Several years earlier, Fintan O' Toole argued in
the "Friel @80" special supplement published in *The Irish Times*
on January 10, 2009, during the playwright's eightieth birthday
celebrations, that Friel's "best formal ideas" are expressed in four
of the major plays on which this study focuses: "splitting the main
character in two in *Philadelphia*; making a gripping play from four
monologues that tell contradictory versions of the same story in
Faith Healer; having two characters speak to each other while the
audience knows that they cannot understand each other's language
in the love scene in *Translations*; the sisters in *Lughnasa* 'dancing as
if language no longer existed.'"[16] And in 2006 Patrick Burke identified what he believes are Friel's masterworks, "partly defined as such
because of their near-complete congruence of substance with form
(always a concern with Friel)," in this order: *Faith Healer, Philadelphia, Here I Come!, Volunteers, Translations, Aristocrats, The Freedom of the City,* and *Dancing at Lughnasa.*[17] My study covers five of
these seven masterworks, and I also discuss a sixth one, *Aristocrats,*
in this introduction. Burke's list largely overlaps with the catalog of
Friel's finest dramas given in the "Friel @80" supplement: "*Philadelphia, Here I Come!, The Freedom of the City, Living Quarters, Aristocrats, Faith Healer, Translations, Dancing at Lughnasa,* and *The
Home Place.*"[18] My new final chapter for this second edition of my
study of Friel suggests that both *Molly Sweeney* and *The Home Place*
can lay some claim to joining *Aristocrats* and the five other masterful
original dramas analyzed in the body chapters. It also identifies the
considerable merits of Friel's version of *Hedda Gabler,* especially his
heightened sense of spirituality he incorporates into Ibsen's drama.
By treating eight of Friel's best plays rather than attempting a survey
of all his drama, as virtually every preceding book on Friel has done,
my revised and extended study offers the fullest and deepest readings
of each of these dramas to date.

Declan Kiberd has cannily observed that Friel's career "has
spanned the decades since the First Programme for Economic
Expansion in 1958 paved the way for investment by multinationals.

Like many northern nationalists, Friel has looked at this modernization with very mixed feelings, since the emergent southern élites seemed to be abandoning the commitment to nationalist *nostra*."[19] This rapid Irish economic acceleration—which has now spectacularly stopped with the abrupt descent of the country into recession after the construction-fueled boom of the "Celtic Tiger"—has compounded some of the damage inflicted on the country by proponents of Enlightenment rationalism over the last several hundred years. The communities in Friel's rich, dynamic places clash with and often show the falseness and inappropriateness of this dominant mode of modernity for human life even as they slowly are compromised from within and without by this rising tide. In this regard, Csilla Bertha has observed in her discussion of Friel as a postcolonial playwright that "[t]he discourse of modernity in Ireland (and other colonized countries) is complicated by its being related to foreign intervention claiming to bring enlightenment."[20] By "modernity" and "modernism" I mean that philosophical program that had developed a dogmatic emphasis on rationality thanks to Descartes (especially his *Discourse on Method*), in particular by the 1650s, and which dominated philosophy, science, and other areas of knowledge until the mid-twentieth century by pushing for a generalized account of everything through abstract intellectualizing that often jettisoned particularity and local culture.

The present study, in attempting to be faithful to the lived reality of human beings that neither reduces them to "atomic individualism" nor consigns them to simplistic categories based solely on their sex, race, or economic status, instead examines the rich, complex inhabitants of Friel's dramatic communities, including their spiritual lives, in order to understand how they live and move and have their being as emplaced individuals subject to the pressures of modernity.

My interchapter on Friel's *The Enemy Within*, for instance, explores Saint Columba's exile on Iona after leaving Ireland, an exile that has effectively rendered him alien to the Ireland he has left. Columba's rejection of the entrapping narratives of home, militarism, family, war, and the flesh enacts a kenotic spiritual process whereby he empties and decenters himself, becoming potentially receptive again to Christ's presence and work in his life.

Chapter 2 on *Philadelphia, Here I Come!* then shows how Gar O'Donnell's embrace of a disturbing and disabling strand of advanced modernity, based on speed and Hollywood culture, and his rejection of the often-stultifying rural rhythms of his home place combine to divorce him from any deep knowledge of himself, his community, and his culture. He is therefore susceptible to being "harvested" by his visiting aunt and uncle, who, though promising him American big-city excitement, will render him trapped in an archaic Ireland that no longer exists while he misses out on the modernizing Ireland of the late 1950s and early 1960s and beyond.

In my second interchapter I analyze how Friel's early interest in short fiction eventually led him away from that genre and into becoming a full-time dramatist, which was an essential maneuver for him in exploring modernity, community, and place. Although Friel criticized what he ostensibly saw as the vulgar medium of the drama and its live audiences in major essays and interviews from the 1960s, he actually was beginning to conceive of theater as a dynamic medium whereby he could create temporary spiritual communities at this time. As the decade proceeded, he fully committed himself to drama after having developed his dramatic theories onstage and through conversation and seminal essays.

My discussion of *The Freedom of the City* in chapter 4 draws on theories of the built and urban environment along with Jacques Derrida's concept of hauntology to articulate how that play, responding to contemporary events in Northern Ireland's recent conflict, inscribes a temporary community for the main characters trapped in the Derry Guildhall that we may enter into as attentive audience members.

The interchapter that now precedes my revised chapter on *Faith Healer* recalls the brilliant 2016 Donmar Warehouse production of that play, which featured three walls of rain between the audience and the actors and drew us in with its spatial intimacy. Gina McKee's performance as Grace Hardy and Stephen Dillane's as Frank Hardy were superb, but Ron Cook's turn as Teddy, Frank's Cockney manager, stole the show with its levity. This revival of the play expressed the deep spirituality at its heart, a spirituality captured by the production photo of a body floating in the air—waiting to be healed?—that adorns the cover of this present study.

In the sixth chapter, on *Faith Healer*, I show that Friel's masterpiece subtly explores how the central character Frank Hardy finally rejects the geopathologies of his repetitive litanies of place in his and other monologues in the play. He creates a homecoming of intimate immensity for himself as he walks onto the "stage" of his own murder in the conclusion, drawing audience and actors together in spiritual community.

My interchapter on the Field Day Theatre Company articulates the essentially mobile nature of drama envisioned by that company and how its traveling plays managed to imagine community— perhaps even across the religious divide in Northern Ireland, for instance. Although the company attempted to be apolitical and ecumenical in the religious representation of Catholics and Protestants on its board, the eventual emergence of Seamus Deane as the unofficial spokesman of the company and his insistence on understanding the political situation in Northern Ireland from a colonizer/colonized perspective led to suspicion in some quarters that the collective was too nationalist.

My analysis of *Translations* in chapter 8 contextualizes Friel's most famous drama in a rich Irish agrarian and intellectual matrix and demonstrates how its rejection of Enlightenment empiricism sits uneasily with its grudging admission that rural Irish culture must open itself to Western modernity. In an analogous egalitarian maneuver, Friel also critiques both violent English colonialism and bellicose Irish nationalism.

In my ninth chapter, on *Dancing at Lughnasa*, I explain how the four widening circles of place in that drama—the Mundy sisters' dancing bodies, the built environment of their cottage, the back hills outside Ballybeg, and Ryanga, Africa—whirl us up into the play's eternal present that older Michael recreates in his last monologue and renders memorialized and memorable to us.

In my final chapter, I read three of Friel's late plays—*Molly Sweeney*, *The Home Place*, and his adaptation of Ibsen's *Hedda Gabler*—through his continuing concern with the question of home and community, including spiritual community, given the pressures of globalization that became more dominant in the decade after *Lughnasa*. Characters such as Molly Sweeney find a new home in the populated world of her mind, where she partakes in a communion with the living and the dead. And other characters such as Christopher Gore in *The Home Place* make accommodations with a changing cultural landscape even as he realizes the dominance of his class in Ireland is nearly over. Finally, Friel shows in his portrayal of Hedda Gabler how she turns in upon herself in a restless death-frenzy, a pointed critique of self-obsessed modernity, while George and Thea move toward each other and begin establishing a collaborative, spiritual community as they reconstruct Eilert Loevborg's manuscript.

Before the first edition of this study, no critic writing on Friel had sufficiently answered what are fundamental questions at the heart of his artistic enterprise: Why are so many of his plays—and all but one of the major ones explored in this study (*The Freedom of the City*)—set at harvest time? What are the functions of mechanized culture in Friel's work? Why are there so many dead babies and only children in the plays? How was the notion of place and flux inherent in the Field Day Theatre Company integrally related to Friel's dramatic theory? What are his abiding philosophical interests and how do they inform his plays? How do we account for the conciliatory impulse often captured in seminal moments of his plays? And, finally, how does Friel's interest in the land and rural culture enable him to move beyond the simplicities sometimes expressed through nationalism or, for that matter, in reductive theories of postcolonialism?

Thus, while there is some analysis of Friel's ingenious use of stage space in his major plays, this study focuses more on rereading these dramas through theories about the interrelationship between people

and the land. These ideas are complemented by those on the phenomenology of place, particularly as articulated by Gaston Bachelard in
his classic work, *The Poetics of Space*, and by Edward Casey, particularly in his landmark study *Getting Back into Place*. Casey's outstanding body of work on the phenomenology of place, particularly
his concept of place as a dynamic, ongoing event, strongly influences
my analysis.

In our current state of globalization, such a study may seem out-
dated or passé, but as Arjun Appadurai has pointed out, Marshall
McLuhan's concept of the world as global village has "overestimated
the communitarian implications of the new media order," and our
lives and our world often seem placeless. Appadurai notes, "[W]ith
media, each time we are tempted to speak of the global village, we
must be reminded that media create communities with 'no sense of
place.'"[21] Brian Friel's insistence on the rituals of the drama in dialectic with an attentive evocation of place as an ongoing event, however,
can simultaneously anchor us and prepare us for the frenetic pressure
of the present that threatens to obliterate deliberately formed communities as it lures us into a constant contemporaneity. As Louis
Dupré has observed, "One of the most unsettling aspects of modern
life may well consist in a temporality conceived as being exclusively
oriented toward the future."[22]

At the same time, Friel's sense of place as an event also attempts
to privilege place and its natural rhythms over and against those
more rapid dislocations that his rural characters and their real-life
counterparts must have experienced with the initial and subsequent
stages of modernism in Ireland. Joe Cleary's formulation of an alternative model of modernity to that of the usual one—that imperialism's effect on rural, colonized cultures led to the advent of a later
modernity in such "backward" places—is one of the driving proposi-
tions behind this study. Cleary has convincingly argued that

Ireland did not have to wait—as is too frequently assumed—for the
arrival of industrialization or technological modernity to undergo
that traumatic sense of breakneck modernization, of rapid cultural

transformation and psychic alienation—the shock of the new—conventionally regarded as a constitutive or exemplary experience of the modern. In Ireland, modernization via colonization preceded modernization via industrialization; colonization was at least as devastating and destructive to any idea of stable organic society or to the continuity of tradition as the latter would ever be.[23]

Friel's *Translations* marks his recognition of this alternative modernity that Cleary articulates. In that drama, Friel critiques colonial policy in Ireland and simultaneously rejects a proto-republicanism that potentially devastates the communities it purports to protect. The play thus shows how his perennial theme of psychic dislocation was given new political impetus in a historic setting, contrasting his plays with contemporary settings like *Philadelphia, Here I Come!* and *The Freedom of the City*. Other dramas such as *Dancing at Lughnasa* suggest how devastating the advent of industrialism was to rural Ireland. In the major Friel plays analyzed here, stability only occurs in brief moments of community that are often shot through with misunderstanding—during Maire's and Yolland's recitation of place names to each other at the heart of *Translations*, for example—then disappear or are crushed by regressive ideologies.

If, as Una Chaudhuri has argued, modern drama "employs, as one of its foundational discourses a vague, culturally determined symbology of home,"[24] Friel's dramas constitute a significant contribution to such a symbology. Home, for Friel's characters, is almost never a matter of simple attachment to a place; rather, it functions as a complex and changing site of anxiety from which other homes, other locations, are often projected. As Fintan O'Toole has pointed out, the Irish phrases *sa mbaile* and *sa bhaile*, the equivalents of the English phrase "at home," "are never used in the narrow sense of home as a dwelling. They imply, instead, that wider sense of a place in the world, a feeling of belonging that is buried deep within the word's meaning."[25] Friel's characters—some Irish speakers themselves as in *Translations*, and others the descendants of Irish speakers—often feel uneasy in the world as they perceive old traditions waning. In some cases, they themselves help to curtail those traditions.

Voluntary exile and forcible eviction often drive the plots of Friel's dramas. Freely chosen emigration occurs in Gar O'Donnell's decision to leave Ballybeg in *Philadelphia, Here I Come!*, Frank Hardy's long absence from Ireland in *Faith Healer,* and Hugh O'Neill's departure from Ireland in *Making History* (1988, first produced in 1992). In other plays, physical dispossession is carried out: the murder of the temporary tenants of the Derry Guildhall in *The Freedom of the City* by the waiting British Army; the threatened removal of Ballybeg residents by the English soldiers/surveyors in *Translations*; the effective eviction of two of the Mundy sisters by the new knitwear factory in *Dancing at Lughnasa*; and the (understandably) forced departure of Dr. Richard Gore and his assistant Perkins by local nationalists in *The Home Place*. Technology's role in this displacement as part of an encroaching modernism is a recurring concern of this project, as are the fascinating ways in which technology sometimes enables attachment to place—for example, as seen in the radio the Mundy sisters name "Marconi" in *Dancing at Lughnasa*. Friel's major works have been written before what Chaudhuri claims is our current return "to a nomadic form of discourse" because of "the revolution in electronic communication" generated by rapid telephony and computerized messaging.[26] They constitute, then, an earlier chapter in the history of place, one which is marked by the introduction of other forms of mechanized culture—measuring devices, gramophones/ phonographs, cars, and airplanes—and the attendant complications for Friel's fictional inhabitants of rural Irish culture.

Friel's regional dramas highlight real and imagined moments of history to portray the intense change rural communities often experience at such times and to show how such metamorphosis is nearly constant in these communities. Thus, I want to stress that his theory of place is grounded not in stasis but in flux, which is central to understanding the concept of place itself. Edward Casey argues that "[a] place is more an *event* than *thing* to be assimilated to known categories" and, further, that "[a]s an event, it is unique, idiolocal.

Its peculiarity calls not for assumption into the already known . . . but for the imaginative constitution of terms respecting its idiolocality."[27] Friel's recognition that his chosen fictional and dramatic places are ongoing events thus has led him to imagine a whole plenum that attempts to reproduce this idiolocality in all its variety—language, community, nature, and epistemology.

"Flux" is a key word for Friel in his statements and essays of the 1960s. Indeed, flux is the major condition explored in the plays under consideration here, both through his use of fluidity inherent in the space of the stage and in the living, changing places depicted in the dramas. Over against the attitude held by directors like Joe Dowling and designers like Joe Vanek, who believe Friel's attitude toward stage design is dated, Richard Allen Cave has convincingly articulated that Friel learned from Tyrone Guthrie during his dramatic "apprenticeship" in Minneapolis in 1963 a "sensitive spatial awareness and its function within Guthrie's style of directing," which suggests that "an acute spatial awareness is the key to the visual dynamic of Friel's dramaturgy . . . with Friel we must think not in terms of scenery, but of scenography."[28] In the chapters that follow, I offer readings of such scenography by exploring the fluidity of Friel's staging—which reaches an apogee in the conclusion of *Faith Healer*, where he inscribes an intimate immensity in the concluding scene as Frank Hardy walks toward his killers in a seemingly endless fashion that expands the metatheatrical yard into the world.

Fintan O' Toole holds that "flux is at the heart of the [dramatic] form itself" for Friel, and Shaun Richards has argued that Friel's work "can be read as a series of increasingly complex engagements with that 'flux.'"[29] Friel identifies this sense of flux in one of the epigraphs to this introduction: "I would like to write a play that would capture the peculiar spiritual, and indeed material, flux that this country is in at the moment."[30] Friel's interest in cultural flux stems not only from his use of the fluidity of the stage itself but also through his formulation of flux as the proper subject of art based on art's relationship to society, which he explored in his 1967 lecture, "The Theatre of Hope and Despair."

Early in that lecture, Friel argues for the dynamism of the arts, using two agrarian metaphors to argue that the arts "grow and wither and expand and contract erratically and sporadically." He then notes shortly after this statement that "they are what they are at any given time and in any given place because of the condition and climate of thought that prevail at that time and in that place."[31] "The condition and climate of thought" suggests the image of a prevailing weather pattern in nature and suggests how Friel's theory of place embraces his foundational view of the arts and culture. If the physical environment around us is always in flux, so too, he argues here, are our intellectual and cultural environments. The arts and, for Friel, theater specifically must themselves accommodate and depict this fluctuation in order to register the changing local conditions of a given culture. He goes on to say about the arts that "[f]lux is their only constant; the crossroads their only home; impermanence their only yardstick."[32] Set in the context of Irish intellectual and cultural history, the second and third phrases of this last statement are especially provocative. Friel's sense of place does not seek to preserve the static rural ideal expressed by Irish Taoiseach Eamon de Valera of lads and lasses dancing at the crossroads, which he famously outlined in his St. Patrick's Day radio address to the nation in 1943.[33] Instead, Friel strives to show how flux is the essence of place. Moreover, his acceptance of a measuring device, even a metaphorical one here, is singular for a writer who usually associates measuring devices—whether the theodolites used by the British surveyors in the Ordnance Survey depicted in *Translations* or the craniometer employed by Dr. Richard Gore in *The Home Place*—with reductive modernity. Impermanence defies measurement, and therefore Friel seems to suggest here that the arts accomplish a task that reason cannot in their depiction of a particular time and place's mutability.

Friel finally links his discussion of flux as the proper subject of the arts in general to that of the dramatist, noting that "if he is of his time, his flux will be as integral but better camouflaged, his groping as earnest, his searching as sincere" as that of other artists.[34] His major dramas portray the intellectual, environmental, political, and cultural changes occurring in a particular community—usually in rural, northwestern Ireland/Northern Ireland, most often in County Donegal. As Sara Keating has remarked about Friel's interest in "the unsettled fluidity of human existence": "[D]espite secluding himself exclusively in the inspirational, isolated beauty of Donegal . . . his ceaselessly restless imagination still recognizes that the physical landscape, geography, is not a constant expression of reality, but a manifestation of the human spirit, and human identity: the very force of life in motion."[35]

The settings of the northwestern region of Ireland/Northern Ireland that anchor Friel's plays convey the relative impoverishment of his characters and their intense individuality as relatively diverse members of interdependent communities. Such communities are often characterized by their heterogeneity, not their homogeneity, as might be stereotypically presumed in such a relatively confined area. In Friel's 1986 interview with Laurence Finnegan, he clearly affirmed his view of cultural heterogeneity, including rural culture, when he sarcastically told Finnegan, "You have a much more acute and much more lucid sense of a culture than I have. . . . You can almost look at it the way you can look at, say, a satellite map of atmospheric conditions. I mean, you can look down on Ireland and say there is a large dense cloud of high culture moving towards the country or moving away from the country, and it's as explicit and as homogeneous as that for you, it seems."[36]

There are a whole host of characters and situations in Friel's mature work that reflect his consistent privileging of the variety inherent in culture. I think, for example, of the housekeeper Madge who acts as a surrogate mother to Gar in *Philadelphia, Here I Come!*. She and S.B., Gar's father, are then effectively replaced as parental figures by Gar's childless aunt and uncle with whom he will live in Philadelphia. The three different characters (all admittedly from the Catholic community) trapped in the Derry Guildhall in *The Freedom of the City* who briefly form an alternative, provisional community also come to mind. And then there is the strange "family" of Frank and Grace Hardy and Teddy in *Faith Healer* and the final horrifying community Frank forms with his killers. Consider too the English Yolland, who wants to become part of the Ballybeg community in *Translations*, and his lover, the Irish Maire, who wants to leave. Perhaps supremely, think of the single mother, Chris, raising Michael with her four maiden sisters in *Dancing at Lughnasa*, and also the sisters' brother, Father Jack, who seamlessly blends Catholic and rural African religious traditions in his new way of worshipping. Finally, landowner Christopher Gore in *The Home Place* has become a cultural hybrid; he is English-raised but delights in the rural Irish landscape and its inhabitants. Although most of the inhabitants are poor, rural, Irish or Northern Irish Catholics, these communities (with some exceptions, such as the island community in his 1971 play, *The Gentle Island*), are fundamentally heterogeneous and all the stronger for their variety. Moreover, in the major plays analyzed in this study, these communities often welcome sympathetic outsiders into their midst, becoming even more various and thus more humane. Friel's consistent depiction and privileging of such communities in his drama exemplifies Richard Barr's description of the movement in modern drama *"from concepts of community conceived in terms of homogeneity to concepts deriving from heterogeneity, from community based on commonality to community dependent on difference."*[37]

In "The Theater of Hope and Despair," Friel argues that the dramatist's function is to create community through intensely depicting individual lives onstage and on the page:

> They have the function to portray that one man's frustrations and hopes and anguishes and joys and miseries and pleasures with all the precision and accuracy and truth that they know; *and by so doing help to make a community of individuals.*[38]

Friel consistently creates communities onstage and between actors and audiences in his plays, even as those onstage communities crumble—much as the rural ones he saw declining in the Donegal he visited, then took up residence in, of the 1950s and 1960s. Two

pioneering Friel critics have argued for this dynamic interaction between cast and spectators in his work. For example, D. E. S. Maxwell
concludes the first monograph of Friel, published in 1973, by arguing
that "[b]oth his short stories and his plays supply the premises where
writer and audience collaborate."[39] And George O'Brien argues in the
context of his analysis of Friel's drama that "[o]ne of the most potent
secular institutions that promote the mutually illuminating intersec-
tion of the individual and the collective is the theatre."[40] What persists
is the community Friel has created with us, his readers and audience
members. It is up to us to remember how we felt during our reading or
watching of a Friel play and then to begin to think or even act in ways
that enhance the human and natural worlds we inhabit. This burden
has been placed on contemporary theater audiences, as Austin Quig-
ley, among other critics, has argued: "Such participation requires audience members to respond to the challenge of reconsidering their role
as audience as a first step in reconsidering the nature of the theatre
and the nature of the larger worlds in which they and it participate."[41]

Friel's work directly and repeatedly repudiates what Stephen
Toulmin has called "the modern cosmopolis, with its emphasis on
stability and *hierarchy*,"[42] by virtue of its particularity, uncertainty,
context, and potential for adaptability. If modernity since Descartes
has been characterized by such rigor in its quest for a generalized,
abstract model to describe human affairs and indeed all branches of
knowledge, which was adapted for use by the nation-state, then Friel
not only exposes the vacuous underpinnings of a sheerly rationalist
worldview but also points toward a way out of the impasse we have
gotten ourselves into by our slavish adherence to the rationalist man-
date. Toulmin's prediction in 1990 increasingly has become true—
that "life and thought in the third phase of Modernity will be shaped
as much by activities and institutions on non-national levels . . . as by
our inheritance from the centralized nation-state."[43] In response to
the dominance of the modern cosmopolis, Friel's imaginative works
show how communities, particularly local ones, often feature the
elasticity and adaptability necessary to enable us to live more practically and wisely.

At the same time, Friel recognizes the problems inherent in local community, which helps us realize that he is not simply affirming a supposedly innocent and untouched rural milieu in his dramas such as *Translations*. When asked in 1980 whether Yolland's impressions of Ballybeg as being "at its ease and with its own conviction and assurance" (*BFP1* 416) implied some sort of nostalgia for Celtic Ireland, Friel emphatically replied:

> I have no nostalgia for that time. I think one should look back on the process of history with some kind of coolness. . . . Several people commented that the opening scenes of the play were a portrait of some sort of idyllic, Forest of Arden life. But this is a complete illusion, since you have on stage the representatives of a certain community—one is dumb, one is lame and one is alcoholic, a physical maiming which is a public representation of their spiritual deprivation.[44]

The implications of this fairly well-known statement have not been sufficiently explored in criticism of *Translations* or other Friel plays. What he suggests here is that this remnant community is the very opposite of an Edenic one: even as they live carrying out the rituals and ceremonies of their ancestors, they are spiritually deprived and thus dislocated from their historic region.

Friel's *Aristocrats* is an especially fine example of his drama that shows the inability of a homogenous community to interact with a rural landscape and its attendant values. Even though this play does not form the subject of any of the main chapters of this study, it is worth briefly exploring to see how it exemplifies Friel's critique of one remnant of the rural Irish—the Ascendancy, here the Catholic O'Donnell family. The O'Donnell family lives in a traditional Big House, and their disconnection from local culture would be echoed in Friel's Protestant Gore family's similar alienation in *The Home Place*, despite its lead character's love for local culture.

Tom Hoffnung, who is researching the "Roman Catholic aristocracy—for want of a better term" (*BFP1* 281), indirectly suggests that the O'Donnells are living in a mausoleum, essentially dead while alive because they have so fully cut themselves off from the life of Ballybeg. Friel's diary notes from the time he created the play indicate as much: "The play that is visiting me brings with it each time an odour of musk-incipient decay, an era wilted, people confused and nervous."[45] The town turns out for Father's funeral late in the play but its inhabitants are clearly marking the end of an era. Casimir observes in a beguiling passage, likely part truth and part fiction, which overstates the importance of the O'Donnell family, that "Father would have been so pleased by that funeral today—no, not pleased—gratified. . . . down through the village street—his village, his Ballybeg—that's how he thought of it, you know, and in a sense it was his village. Did you know that it used to be called O'Donnellstown? . . . Every shop shut and every blind drawn; and men kneeling on their caps as the hearse passed; and Nanny sobbing her heart out when the coffin was being lowered" (309). Ironically, Eamon, whose rise signals the real ascendancy in the play—the rise of lower-class Catholics in the area (his grandmother served as a maid in Ballybeg Hall)—values the house more than any of the O'Donnell children. He observes, "Well I know it's [sic] real worth—in this area, in this county, in this country" (318). He perspicaciously asks, "Don't you know that all that is fawning and forelock-touching and Paddy and shabby and greasy peasant in the Irish character finds a house like this irresistible? That's why we were ideal for colonizing. Something in us needs this . . . aspiration" (318–19). Professor Hoffnung's attempts to chronicle the tiny Catholic ascendancy through his study of Ballybeg Hall and other Big Houses implies their imminent demise, as does the lack of progeny among the O'Donnell children, save Judith, whose baby is in the orphanage and whose possible future husband, Willie, does not want the child (318).

Garland Kimmer has argued convincingly that *Aristocrats* "suggests the way in which a family has lost touch with its actual, factual history and replaced it with a personal mythology that inflates the family's influence and significance."[46] As Kimmer further notes, because the O'Donnell family "effectively moved up the social ladder

by acting as the legal representatives and executors of English imperial society in Ireland," such actions "alienate[d] them from the peasants living, and occasionally starving, around them."[47] Cut off from
England and thus aspirations to become part of English society and
divorced from the life and culture of the local village, the O'Donnells
slowly turn in upon themselves, sinking in a morass of self-created
myth made poignant by their nearly utter impoverishment at the
play's conclusion. Friel's other rural communities, such as the peas-
antry in 1833 Donegal in *Translations*, are closer to the land and its
rhythms, but even they are shown to have constructed myths about
themselves, shown by Hugh's delusions of grandeur and, for most of
the play, his immersion in Greek and Roman classical culture.

There is another strand of Friel plays beyond the scope of this
study to analyze but worth mentioning for the discussion of rural
communities here: his translation of Chekhov's *The Three Sisters*
(1981), adaptations of Turgenev's *Fathers and Sons* (1987) and *A
Month in the Country* (1992), and adaptations of Chekhov in *Three
Plays After* (2002). In these works, we see a similar appreciation
for individuals islanded in the countryside and fighting boredom
and poverty, even as the sureties of their society are crumbling
around them.[48] In this regard, Friel's 1999 statement that he finds
"the late-nineteenth-century Russians so sympathetic" is revelatory:
"Maybe . . . the characters in the plays behave as if their old certainties were as sustaining as ever—even though they know in their
hearts that their society is in melt-down and the future has neither
a welcome nor even an accommodation for them. Maybe a bit like
people of my own generation in Ireland today."[49] In an editorial published in *The Irish Times* during the Friel celebrations of 2008, Fintan O'Toole quoted these same lines, noting that they suggest "the
richly ambiguous relationship of Friel's achievement to the Ireland
of his times. The great gesture of his work has been to carry on as if
the world from which he takes his artistic bearings were not in melt-
down, even while the work itself enacts that very implosion."[50] Such
a statement registers something of Friel's regret for the passing of an
Irish rural world and its positive values even as it charts that culture's

decline; "enacts" puts it too strongly, however, even though his plays make clear the perniciousness of other, negative aspects of that life.

The anthropologist Arjun Appadurai has offered a compelling model of how localities change through actual and imaginative work that affords us further insight into Friel's dramatized sense of place as dynamic. Appadurai has observed that "as local subjects carry on the continuing task of reproducing their neighborhood, the contingencies of history, environment, and imagination contain the potential for new contexts (material, social, and imaginative) to be produced. . . . Put another way . . . no human community, however apparently stable, static, bounded, or isolated, can usefully be regarded as cool or outside history."[51] Indeed, Friel's subjects are constantly creating history, as the title of his play, *Making History*, suggests. They are not excluded at all but rather are conscious agents of their tomorrows, even as they often struggle against disruptions to their ways and rhythms of life, as seen in plays such as *Translations*.

Friel's dramas similarly do not hope to freeze rural culture but to preserve and record something of its dynamism and positive qualities over time even as its communities decay. His diary entry for September 11, 1979, written when he was creating *Translations*, recognizes the flux of rural environments and the corresponding problem that this dynamism poses for any writer trying to capture it: "What is so deceptive and so distressing is that the terrain looks so firm and that I think I know it intimately. But the moment I move across it, the ground gives under me."[52]

In 1963 Friel vowed to write the "great Irish play," implicitly endorsing the artistic theory of rending the particular universal: "Such a play is one where the author can talk so truthfully and accurately about people in his own neighborhood and make it so that these folk could be living in Omagh, Omaha[,] or Omansk."[53] Despite the real problems in his local communities, Friel consistently shows how there were and are aspects of Irish rural culture worth preserving and whose waning presence haunts his dramas. Many aspects of his rural world dramatized onstage are stultifying, even horrifying. Friel himself, along with his major critics, have all argued that his interest in rural culture is not nostalgic and that reading the fiction and plays as attempts at dramatizing an Edenic Irish pastoralism is folly.

Anthony Roche, for example, has confirmed Friel's distaste for such readings, arguing,

> no one was more aware than Friel himself of the potential for the first play [*Philadelphia*] to be merely a tract about emigration and the second [*Translations*] to be a lament for the destruction of Gaelic civilization. . . . No one was more horrified when the success of *Translations* was attributed to its supposed validation of an ideal and idyllic Gaelic order.[54]

Moreover, Nicholas Grene, writing on both Friel and the Irish playwright Tom Murphy, notes their early work is "written against this sort of pastoral iconography of Ireland" found in John Ford's *The Quiet Man*, further suggesting that "[b]oth playwrights give a glum version of the West of Ireland scene so glamorized by Ford."[55] But crucially, he finally argues that "for all their common reaction against the rural Irish idyll, the differences between the playwrights, in theme, style and formal mode make of Murphy's plays true anti-pastorals, Friel's a version of pastoral only disguised as anti-pastoral."[56]

Friel often shows the dynamism of a specific rural culture that is penetrated by representatives—machine or human—of an outside culture. This process either strengthens or weakens the rural culture, which can be surprisingly adaptive. His depiction of a specific region with a particular dialect, culture, and topography of its own (and within that region, a specific parish) clearly differentiates his real and imagined northwestern parish and region on the island from the rest of Ireland, giving the lie to Tony Corbett's claim that Friel's fictional townland of "Ballybeg is an emblem of all Irish towns, and of Ireland itself."[57]

Perhaps to counter charges of rural nostalgia, Friel has written several plays that savagely indict repressive or hostile aspects of rural living, including *The Gentle Island, The Mundy Scheme* (1969), and *The Communication Cord* (1982). *The Gentle Island* remains a neglected play in the Friel canon (and sadly, it is not reproduced in *The Collected Plays of Brian Friel* published by Gallery Press and Faber and Faber) and introduces a crucial series of themes and situations developed in the later major dramas. D. E. S. Maxwell, an early interpreter of the play, argued correctly that "[i]ts purpose is not to elegize the past, to interpret social causes, to attribute any superior 'reality' to the simple life."[58] This play deplores the rural mores on the island of Inishkeen, particularly as articulated by Manus and Sarah. Manus's story of the "niggerman,"[59] and Sarah's savage attempt to kill the homosexual Shane because he had sex with her husband Philly in the wake of Manus's telling of this narrative, together offer a chilling glimpse of the potential in rural communities to savagely punish those different from the mainstream. Manus's own punishment and partial dismemberment for impregnating Rosie Dubh is another example of violent reprisal common to the island. Moreover, Shane's suggestion that "Inishkeen" is an "Apache name" that means "scalping island," and Joe's terming the character Bosco a "Bloody savage,"[60] anticipates the outsider Teddy's terming Frank Hardy's killers in *Faith Healer* "those bloody Irish Apaches" and the landlord's calling them "savage bloody men" (*BFP1* 366, 374). In a similar manner, Manus's negatively parochial retreat into island life anticipates the later character Manus's similar withdrawal toward the end of *Translations*, as we will see in chapter 8. Helen Lojek has convincingly argued that Shane's "newly-learned Irish—like Yolland's in *Translations*—suggests a blossoming human affection understandable in all languages."[61] But Peter, too, appreciates the island life despite its sporadic outbreaks of violence. He tells Manus during Act Two, in lines that anticipate Yolland's affection for the slower pace of life in Ballybeg and its seeming permanence, "it's the . . . calm, the stability, the self-possession. Everything has its own good pace. No panics, no feverish gropings. A dependable routine—that's what you have. . . . I envy you, Manus . . . everything's so damned constant. You're part of permanence. You're a fortunate man."[62] But his naivete (except for Manus and his family, all the islanders are leaving Inishkeen at the start of the play in hopes of jobs and a better life elsewhere) is quickly exposed by Manus, who says, "You wouldn't live here all the same."[63]

The rhetoric of *The Gentle Island* thus suggests the dire economic state not just of rural life for an island long ago "invaded by modernity," but also of the potentially stultifying life of the islanders, who are dependent on the mainland for excitement.[64] They turn quickly against outsiders and even locals, wielding violence against them casually and unexpectedly. Shane states that "we give support to his [Manus's] illusion that the place isn't a cemetery. But it is. And he knows it. The place and his way of life and everything he believes in and all he touches—dead, finished, spent."[65] His statement recalls the plan in the earlier *The Mundy Scheme* to turn the West of Ireland into a giant cemetery, which may have its origins in Friel's description of German war graves in the short story "The Saucer of Larks." But if the island is a site of death, life outside it is also precarious. The play's indictment of the boredom, economic fragility, and violence of rural life contrasts *Translations'* more balanced lament for the passing of an agrarian way of life and the attendant values that have already been compromised from within.

The Gentle Island was likely influenced by Friel's permanent move to Donegal's Inishowen Peninsula in the late 1960s and the terrible violence occurring at the same time just a few miles away in Londonderry/Derry. Indeed, the dual meaning of "Inishkeen," as pointed out by Friel's fellow Donegal playwright Frank McGuinness, can mean either "an island of lamentation or the Gentle Island."[66] The play seems to mourn both the loss of the island's "recognizable culture of its own"[67] and the burgeoning violence in the North: it is uncannily attuned to both the attenuation of rural culture and the rise of a dominant, similarly violent urban culture, proleptically anticipating this theme in *Translations*.

Furthermore, in response to critics who thought he was valorizing the Ballybeg of Gareth O'Donnell in his first major play, *Philadelphia, Here I Come!*, Friel wrote the savage drama *The Mundy Scheme*. And in response to critics who thought *Translations* was an exercise in nostalgia, Friel wrote the satiric farce *The Commu-nication Cord*. Interestingly, he has never written such a negative "response" play to *Dancing at Lughnasa*, although Anthony Roche has argued that "*Wonderful Tennessee* provides a more abstract and philosophic meditation on the themes which had so engrossed audiences in *Dancing at Lughnasa*."[68] *Tennessee*, like *Lughnasa*, argues for the continuing importance of myth in our lives—an especially important position for Friel in the increasingly materialistic Ireland of the 1990s. But each of these earlier "response plays" focuses on artificial expectations held by interloping Irish and especially Americans about the Irish countryside, not so much the rural culture in and of itself, whereas *The Gentle Island* and *Translations* would fault, in part, overly inward-looking aspects of rural culture.

Although the present study does not rely primarily on ecocritical theory, my readings of Friel's major dramas are indebted to several lines of ecocritical inquiry as outlined by the German theorist Hubert Zapf. The first of these is a

> content-oriented, sociopolitical form of ecocriticism in which literary and nonliterary texts are examined from criteria such as their attention to natural phenomena, their degree of environment awareness, their recognition of [ecological] diversity, their attitude to nonhuman forms of life, or their awareness of the interconnectedness between local and global ecological issues.[69]

In this regard, I will show just how precisely Friel depicts the natural world, its fragility, and its seasonal rhythms in his work. Most important in this regard will be my analysis of Friel's habit of setting his major plays at harvest time, which implies various connotations of gathering and reaping—such as life and death—for his inhabitants.

The effort by ecocriticism to analyze "the deep-rooted self-alienation of human beings within the civilizatory project of modernity which, in its anthropocentric illusion of autonomy, has tried to cut itself off from and erase its roots in the natural world" crystallizes an issue at the heart of Friel's work.[70] Other eco-critics similarly argue that one of the key premises of ecocriticism is that "the natural environment is always a shaping force of individual and group psychology and identity—and that this force can only be ignored or suppressed at a price."[71] It is difficult to ascribe any one overarching theme to Friel's fiction and drama, but his portrayal of human beings who often isolate themselves from family, community, and environment is a perennial concern for him. A startling passage from Friel's "Plays Peasant and Unpeasant" suggests this anxiety in its linkage of the relationship of rural inhabitants to the land and their heightened individualism: "To understand anything about the history or present health of Irish drama, one must first acknowledge the peasant mind, then recognize its two dominant elements: one is a passion for the land; the other a paranoiac individualism."[72] Seamus Deane, one of Friel's most perceptive critics, argues that his short fiction explores "the passage from a declining communal life to one in which the cult of the individual flourishes," noting further that "[t]he cult of the individual does not, paradoxically, lead to personal fulfillment. With its emphasis on internal freedom and its repudiation of the absorptive effects of a settled community, it most often makes a virtue of alienation and a fetish of integrity."[73] Such a "cult of the individual" is naturally an inheritance from the Enlightenment, as plays such as *Translations* and *Molly Sweeney* suggest through their philosophical underpinnings that are essentially communal and organic.

Friel's privileging of community, even those that are provisional, like the temporary one of the three characters trapped in the Derry Guildhall in *The Freedom of the City*, therefore accords with Charles Taylor's authoritative assessment of the necessity of the self's flourishing within community in *Sources of the Self*: "One is a self only among other selves. A self can never be described without reference to those who surround it."[74] However, "not only the philosophico-scientific tradition but also a powerful modern aspiration to freedom and individuality have conspired to produce an identity which seems to be a negation of this."[75] New selves can develop through characters' interaction with others, who function as the "webs of interlocution" that Taylor holds are the constitutive matrix for identity formation.[76] But all too often in Friel's drama, latent selves that are beginning to emerge—think of Frank Hardy's resolve to be free of his gift at the end of *Faith Healer*, or of Maire and Yolland's temporary linguistic "union" in *Translations*—are cut off from community, sometimes by the very defenders (Frank's murderers and the Donnelly twins, respectively) of that communal tradition.

Although Friel is supremely concerned with dramatizing the natural rhythms of flux in his drama, both in the living places he creates and in the fluid space of his stage, he realizes that there is a pernicious aspect to a particular type of flux—the modern project of radically reorienting our view of reality by an immersion in motion and speed that militates against our contemplative powers, a view epitomized by Gar O'Donnell's dislocation in *Philadelphia, Here I Come!*. As Peter Berger has observed in *Facing up to Modernity*,

> battalions of psychologists have been telling us for decades . . . the pace of modern living is detrimental to mental well-being and may also be harmful to physical health. Futurity means endless striving, restlessness, and a massive incapacity for repose. It is precisely this aspect of modernization that is perceived as dehumanizing in many non-Western cultures."[77]

Friel's rejection of this fundamentally modern project marks him as a holistic thinker who has long anticipated threats to human integrity and flourishing. Recent ecocritical theory argues that this burgeoning field itself is "part of a larger postclassical paradigm shift from causal and linear to complex, nonlinear forms of knowledge."[78] The interconnected webs of knowledge about local landscape and the local Irish place lore known as *dinnseanchas*, which feature in plays such as *Translations* and *Dancing at Lughnasa*, reveal the congruities that Friel's imagined dramatic worlds can share with rural Irish culture going back for generations. Such an epistemology made this way of life largely resistant to linear perspectives and modes of inquiry for a time. The rejection of perspectival instrumentation in *Translations*, for instance, abundantly demonstrates Friel's "complex, nonlinear" epistemology, as does Frank Hardy's occasional ability to become a conduit for a mysterious healing power in *Faith Healer* and the Mundy sisters' epistemology of the body in *Dancing at Lughnasa*.

Beginning with his short fiction, Friel has consistently depicted the pernicious effects of the dominant, rationalist strand of modernity on a premodern rural culture even as he cautiously suggests that that culture must open itself to modernity generally, or at least seek to humanize modernity, a project epitomized in the Irish hedge-school master Hugh's final speech about the new Anglicized place names in Donegal from *Translations*: "We must learn where we live. We must learn to make them our own. We must make them our new home" (*BFP1* 444).

Stephen Toulmin observes that modernity's account of rationality "rested on three pillars—certainty, systematicity, and the clean slate."[79] All three of these pillars have proven to be unattainable ideals. Friel's embrace of uncertainty, rejection of systems in favor of organic growth, and dedication to retrieving and retaining helpful aspects of tradition highlights the weaknesses of these three principles. In many ways, his worldview is much closer to the sixteenth-century humanists such as Montaigne, who focused on "the practical, local, transitory, and *context bound* issues" that were much closer to the concerns and needs of everyday life than the later and dominant rationalist attempt to articulate an abstract, overarching theory of everything—Toulmin's cosmopolis.[80] In fact, Friel's corpus of short fiction and drama anticipates Toulmin's argument in 1990 for the recovery of practical philosophy by emphasizing again the oral, the particular, the local, and the timely.[81]

Nicholas Daly argues that if industrial modernity "is predicated on the intellectual separation of people and machines," then "the corollary of this is a modernity that obsessively replays the meeting of the two."[82] Friel's largely rural characters encounter a whole range of machines: gramophones, radios, theodolites, a craniometer, automobiles, tractors, tape recorders, and airplanes. His plays often depict particular moments where modernity clashes with tradition, a clash signified both by Gar O'Donnell's quotations from Edmund

Burke's *Reflections on the Revolution in France* in *Philadelphia, Here I Come!* and the references to the French Revolution in *The Freedom of the City* and *Translations*. Friel approves of such characters as Hugh from *Translations* and O'Neill from *Making History*, who both realize that modernity's arrival in Ireland is inevitable and that Ireland must adapt while retaining the best aspects of traditional rural culture. The underappreciated *Making History*, not analyzed in this study, features as its central character Hugh O'Neill, a Janus-faced character who is concerned with preserving Gaelic civilization but who also has English roots and is open to certain aspects of modernity. *Dancing at Lughnasa* remains the Friel play most open to the charge of nostalgia, but even there, he portrays particular aspects of modernization in 1930s Ireland as a mixed blessing, privileging, for example, the radio that enables the sisters' dancing but rejecting the new knitwear factory.

In each of these plays, he shows the unsettling triumph of modernity over rural Irish culture, often with devastating consequences for his central characters. The most vicious proponents of modernity tear their victims apart in a frenzy during harvest season, the traditional time of plenty, suggesting how extreme proponents of modernity can crush their opponents mercilessly. For example, the character of Frank Hardy in *Faith Healer* is finally portrayed as walking toward a literal dismemberment by local Irish farmers with modern implements. In *Philadelphia*, Gar is "harvested" by his aunt and uncle, while the three protesters that emerge from the Guildhall at the end of *Freedom* are torn apart by murderous, piercing bullets fired by the British Army. Yolland's likely murder in *Translations* is another violent act in which a proponent of rural culture is destroyed, ironically in this case, by the would-be defenders of that culture, the Donnelly twins. In *Making History*, Hugh O'Neill suggests that when Maguire rises up against the English crown that "he'll be hacked to pieces" and thus the culture that he represents will be destroyed (*BFP2* 286). And in *Dancing at Lughnasa*, the Mundy sisters' Maenad-like dance of grief, along with the leaping in the back hills during the pagan festival of Lughnasa that leads to the burning of the young boy Sweeney, suggest how the modernization of the Irish Catholic Church isolated some of its most vulnerable parishioners with devastating results. Because of the modernizing pressure of the new knitwear factory that comes to Donegal in that play, two of the sisters are "harvested" when Rose and Agnes sacrifice themselves and leave for London, in part so the rest of the family will not starve to death. Finally, in Friel's version of *Hedda Gabler*, he heightens Ibsen's portrayal of Hedda's frenzied piano playing in the play's conclusion right before she kills herself, emphasizing modernity's tendency to isolate us into hellish, trapped spheres whereby we turn in on ourselves and eschew life-giving community.

What Daly has termed the "mechanization of daily life" is a crucial component of industrial modernity.[83] While Daly delineates a strand in literature and later in film that actually facilitates that process through introducing elements of speed, suspense, and mystery, Friel's fiction and drama are more varied in their responses to the machine. Some machines that appear in his work, such as the telephone Lily uses in the Guildhall in *The Freedom of the City*, along with the radio the Mundy sisters name "Marconi" and the gramophones Gerry Evans purports to sell in *Dancing at Lughnasa*, actually help facilitate community and happiness. We might say Friel even favors machines that contribute to the creation or enhancement of community through allowing their users, in the case of the gramophone or radio, greater abilities of communication with each other, but he rejects those mechanical, quantitative devices that replace our traditional powers of perception, such as the theodolite (a measuring device) and the bayonets of *Translations*, along with Dr. Gore's craniometer in *The Home Place*, or those that displace us from our connection to the land, such as the airplane Gar anticipates boarding the next morning at the end of *Philadelphia, Here I Come!*.

Friel's portrayal of Gar shows that although he feels that character had to physically leave the Ballybeg of the early 1960s, he has already largely left it in his mind because of his immersion in American movie culture and motion, hallmarks of his modernity. Gar's association with the airplane that will rocket him to his new life in

America and figuratively obliterate the old rhythms of his life in Bally-beg betokens both the pleasure and the peril of modernity's major invention—speed. Enda Duffy has argued that "with the advent of the new speed technologies" ushered in by various mechanical means of locomotion, but especially the car, "the very notion of life as the capacity for energetic movement, long the basis of scientific accounts for living organisms, took on a new valence. Human well-being was recast more vehemently as the capacity for active movement and the management of the organism's energy."[84] Gar's frenetic mental and somatic activities, along with the similar activities of other compelling Friel characters, are best understood as the inheritance of this modern emphasis on speed with often devastating consequences.

Moreover, Friel shows in *The Freedom of the City, Translations, Dancing at Lughnasa*, and *The Home Place* with various types of "evictions" that modernity itself can often jettison those who are unprepared for its arrival. While not ignoring the grinding mental, spiritual, and material poverty of the countryside, he critiques the mental, spiritual, and financial poverty often caused by industrialization in Irish society and suggests that establishing an equilibrium between rural culture and urban culture might mitigate some of modernity's excesses that have proven so destructive both to older, richer ways of conceiving the self and to organic community.

In their depictions of particular places and individuals shaped by them, Friel's dramas are ideally suited to portray such brief moments of community or reconciliation that are almost always thwarted. His society is intensely local and grounded in a shared sense of community, whether it be in the relatively large "village" of Derry or the more typical townland of Ballybeg. While *Translations* and *Lughnasa* evidence his continuing interest in rural places, Friel has expanded his theory of place through his exploration of the stage itself, particularly evident in the metatheatrical conclusion of *Faith Healer*; the built environment of the Derry Guildhall and the city of Derry in *The Freedom of the City*; the Mundy sisters' cottage in *Dancing at Lughnasa*; his depiction of the sisters' bodies in *Lughnasa*; and the imaginative space of our minds in his masterpiece,

Faith Healer. Place, for Friel, gradually grows more fluid, colored by imagination, and retrieved by the dazzling memory monologues of some of his most compelling characters—Frank Hardy in *Faith Healer*, Maire and Yolland in *Translations*, Michael in *Lughnasa*, Christopher Gore in *The Home Place*.

Finally, these characters establish relationships with other characters, with the audience, with readers, that can only be termed "spiritual." Richard Pine has pointed out that "almost inevitably" Friel has fulfilled "a liminal, shamanistic role as he sets about his task of divining the elements of ritual and translating them into drama."[85] Whether depicting Gar's great desire for spirituality in *Philadelphia, Here I Come!*, Frank Hardy's strange spiritual need to enter into community with his killers as he walks toward them in *Faith Healer*, the spiritual decline of Ballybeg in *Translations*, the need for paganism in *Lughnasa*, or the surprisingly spiritual ending to his version of Ibsen's *Hedda Gabler*, Friel consistently affirmed that human beings are not mere souls or mere bodies, but ensouled bodies dependent upon each other for making meaning through community. This study finally demonstrates his profound spirituality grounded in particular places and relationships—a faith that is unorthodox and elusive, yet nonetheless substantial and enduring and communal—an enduring response to the worst, most dehumanizing aspects of Enlightenment modernity that privilege the individual in isolation stripped bare of any metaphysical longings or comfort.

1

Interchapter

The Enemy Within: *Self and Spirituality in Exile*

Friel's 1962 drama, *The Enemy Within*, became the first play he kept in print. It explores the geographic, mental, and spiritual exile of Saint Columba, who left Ireland for the Scottish island of Iona in AD 536 and who seems surprisingly attuned to an early form of globalization through his vacillations between particular places. Late in the play, Columba shouts to his brother Eoghan and his son Aedh, who are trying to convince him to help conduct a rescue of Aedh's baby son from his wife Ita, who has taken the child to her family that is part of the pagan Antrim Picts: "Get out of my monastery! Get out of my island! Get out of my life! Go back to those damned mountains and seductive hills that have robbed me of my Christ! You soaked my sweat! You sucked my blood! You stole my manhood, my best years! What more do you demand of me, damned Ireland? My soul? My immortal soul? Damned, damned, damned Ireland!—(*His voice breaks*) Soft, green Ireland—beautiful, green Ireland—my lovely green Ireland. O my Ireland—" (*EW* 75). His striking vacillation between hate and love for Ireland here anticipates Gar O'Donnell's similar alternation between virulence and affection in *Philadelphia, Here I Come!*, which would be performed just two years later. Friel's Columba tells Brendan that Eoghan "came to save me. . . . To make me a real exile," admitting that he has grown so accustomed to life on Iona that a "homecoming" would render him alien in his own country (76).

Columba has been so emotionally and spiritually drained by this experience that he asks to be brought to the chapel where the novices are praying for him, "because I am empty" (*EW* 76). Such an emptying out, which sounds negative at first, is actually a crucial step in becoming spiritually receptive. He presumably wants his soul to be filled back up through the novices' intercession for him. The Greek word for this process is *kenosis*, and it has considerable, even divine, warrant in the New Testament: the Apostle Paul says about Christ, for example, in Philippians 2:7 that "Jesus made Himself nothing," or in another translation, "He emptied himself" (NIV). This entire passage suggests that Christians must become humble like Christ did. When Oswald returns from running away temporarily from the monastery, Columba seizes him and embraces him, perceiving this homecoming to be freighted with spiritual significance: "We were both asleep, Dochonna of Lough Conn! But we are awake now and ready to begin again—to begin again—to begin again!" (77). Such an exclamation is the lasting answer to Dochonna's earlier greeting of the saint at the beginning of Act Two, when Columba has returned to Iona after being involved in the battle with Hugh: "Welcome home, Columba! Welcome! Welcome!" (39).

Scott Boltwood has argued that because of the emphasis on Columba as a missionary crusader backed up by the use of force, "the play strategically encourages the perception of Columba as imperialist by [also] modeling his monastery upon the cosmopolitan metropole rather than the exile's encampment."[1] But how do we square this reading with Columba's kenosis at the conclusion of the play? The title would suggest, contra Boltwood's argument that the conclusion implies "Marx's farcical repetition of history, preparing the audience for the reversal of Ireland's fortunes" as Oswald will become "the colonizer of the future who will reverse history's tide to become the first English ruler of the Irish,"[2] that Columba has recognized his real enemy is within himself.

That enemy manifests itself in his love for his native Derry and Donegal, which is bound up with his militarism; with his real need to rid himself of the incessant call of his family, also connected to his bellicosity; and with his attempts to mortify his flesh unduly. Friel has affirmed much of this reading, noting in interview, "I took that quotation from the Bible, the 'enemy within,' as meaning literally Saint Columba's family. You have to get away from a corrupting influence."[3] Columba will likely teach Oswald this truth as they focus the monastery's life on appreciating Iona and its simple pleasures, not on engagements with Columba's family, Ireland, missionary crusades, or the wealth of the monastery. Thus, I agree with Elmer Andrews, who has argued that "The 'enemy within' is a force in Columba which resists Christian *disciplina*: it is also the mark of humanity, of sentient life. It is what denies monolith and stagnation. It is the irrepressible 'life-force' itself, the love of adventure and risk, relish of the physical world, the willingness to accept the 'challenge of a new territory. . . . '"[4] Yet I finally part company from Andrews when he argues that Columba "is still trapped in non-meaning" when he goes to the chapel to pray "because I am empty"; instead, while Columba certainly will have to start over repeatedly in his spiritual search, he has made the momentous decision to turn his back on the heretofore corrupting influences upon him, and that resulting integrity will enable his distinctive spirituality that is grounded in the flesh and his desire to know the kingdom of God on earth through community.[5]

While Eoghan and Aedh signify the corrupting call of family and militarism to Columba, the monk Caornan models an alluring but disturbing asceticism to the saint: Caornan mortifies his flesh with chains (is even buried in them) and evinces a desire to go the Orkney where "he would be all alone and there he could do penance for all the joy he found in the life here" (*EW* 45). This overemphasis on asceticism is perhaps epitomized by Columba's lament to Caornan early in Act One in response to Caornan's reverence of him: "As a builder of churches! As a builder of schools! As an organizer! But the inner man—the soul—chained irrevocably to the earth, to the green wooded earth of Ireland!" (21). Columba believes his struggle is against this world, and he communicates this conflict by articulating his longing for Ireland in a number of passages in the play.[6] After Brian appears to urge Columba to sanction his cousin Hugh's battle against the cousins Cumine, Columba even laments that "home is a millstone around my neck, Grillaan" (32).

Although Boltwood argues that Columba's life on Iona is better understood as migrancy, not exile, because "exile assumes the reunion of the sojourner with his home,"[7] Friel himself notes in his preface to the play that it focuses upon "a short period in St. Columba's thirty-four years of voluntary exile" (*EW* 7). Moreover, Boltwood has not considered the possibility that Columba may be returning to Christ through the radical de-centering of the self, a journey that has long been delayed because of Columba's great pride and acquisitive, materialist nature. Thus, Friel's Columba may well have become the "enemy within" the early Catholic Church in the play through his kenosis and desire to "begin again!" which is likely better understood as his new determination to stop spreading Catholicism in a violent, imperial manner, to become receptive to God's indwelling presence, and then to act accordingly, even joyfully, in refusing to continue his misguided struggle against this life. Columba now looks like he will embrace the kingdom of God on earth, a consistent theme in the rhetoric of the New Testament, by rejecting asceticism and embracing our enfleshed lives just as Christ did during His thirty-three years on earth. Grillaan has advised Columba in Act Two that his progress toward sanctity "is in the will and determination to start, and then to start again, and then to start again, so that their life is a series of beginnings" (*EW* 49). Grillaan has also advised that Columba follow the monastic Rule, which advocates a moderate diet and some sleep: "eat your two meals a day; sleep your five hours sleep; read your Office; celebrate your Mass; look after your administrative work. And beyond that—nothing. No more immersions in icy water, no more fasts or vigils or days of prayer. . . . Each man's cleansing, Columba, is of a different kind. Yours is in moderation in all things, in calm, reasoned moderation" (49). Friel has even said that Columba "was responsible for a hell of a lot of wars and butchery. I wanted to discover how he acquired sanctity. Sanctity in the sense of a man having tremendous integrity and the courage to back it up."[8] When asked how he acquired such integrity in this same interview, Friel immediately answered, "By turning his back on Ireland and on his family."[9] Columba's "turning his back" does not signify non-meaning, nor an embrace of an overly ascetic lifestyle; rather, it marks him as an independent religious figure with sanctity, courage, and the ability to resist excesses of the faith and the siren call of others to war.

In this sense, Friel's Columba finally may function as a figure of conscience who anticipates the eventual evolution of Irish Catholicism as a decentralized folk religion before the advent of the Devotional Revolution and the introduction of much more rigid Catholic doctrine in the second half of nineteenth-century Ireland. Contrasted with the stultifying Canon in *Philadelphia, Here I Come!* and the actively repressive Catholic priest of Ballybeg in *Dancing at Lughnasa*, this Columba remains receptive to surprise (the return of Oswald) and refuses to allow doctrine to overshadow grace (receiving Oswald gratefully after striking him earlier). Reading this play in tandem with *Philadelphia, Here I Come!* and particularly focusing on the figure of Columba and the Canon in *Philadelphia* enable our understanding of Friel's likely conviction of the contemporary spiritual paucity of the Catholic Church in contrast to its richness and integrity under Columba, once he turned his back on the beckoning, negative communities of his homeland, family, and the rigid, imperializing aspect of Catholicism at the time, and embraced positive community.

In his reading of Columba's recovered spirituality and the "profound emptiness," which is a "prelude to a new form of spiritual belief" by the priest Father Chris Carroll in Friel's *The Blind Mice* (1963) who has returned to Northern Ireland from five years' captivity by the Communist Chinese, Anthony Roche argues for our consistent appreciation of Frielian spirituality.[10] Citing Thomas Kilroy's observation of St. Columba and Father Chris, Roche points out that these priest figures are "early evidence of Brian Friel's 'lifelong treatment of the nature of spirituality,'" reflecting further that "there is a direct line of continuity between these early priest figures of the occluded Friel canon and their later shamanistic variants,

Frank Hardy[,] faith healer[,] and Father Jack practicing his Ryangan rituals."[11]

But what has this discussion to do with Friel's evolving sense of place and spirituality? As it turns out, a great deal: Friel's Columba finally shows how we can leave our homes permanently and yet become at ease in another place and with ourselves if we are willing to undergo something like kenosis and the resulting receptivity. Such a process, which need not be explicitly spiritual, leads inevitably away from the petty tyrannies of the self that can result in narcissism and back into the dynamic rhythms of community, whether within Columba's monastery or the local townland. Columba's real journey is not finally geographic, but a journey into the human heart and soul, the final "place" where, if we may not rest, we may at least be reacclimated to the promptings of our consciences and the call of community.

Moreover, when we consider that Columba is the patron saint of Derry, whose Irish name is Doire Colmcille, we should realize the appropriateness of Friel's dramatic meditation on this saint's life and hope that its trajectory might indirectly signify his hopes for the later passage of Northern Ireland from sectarian conflict toward peace. Evidence for such a reading comes in Grillaan's response to Columba's growing desire to help his cousin Hugh fight in Act One: "And his enemies—whoever they are this time—no doubt they have a churchman to bless their standards too, with the result that God is fighting for both causes. Isn't that the usual pattern?" (*EW* 32). Friel is almost certainly commenting here on sectarianism in Northern Ireland, which was a continuing feature of the province during its contemporary history and before when it was part of Ireland. Both Catholics and Protestants have argued that God sanctions their actions[12] with the result that any kind of spiritual authority calling for an end to the violence has often been muted. Columba's nickname, given him after he left fighting behind as the former "warrior-saint," is "the dove of the church." Friel's Columba, as Kilroy has pointed out, resists the "seductive, corrupting call" of his brother and nephew to help them fight—which Columba sees as "having come from Ireland herself, significantly a feminine Ireland, the Ireland of aisling poetry, a dream woman with a siren call to violent sacrifice." Thus he rejects nationalist and republican calls to fight for a United Ireland they trope as female, spilling male blood for her. Instead, by "abandoning blood relationships for those of the spirit" in adopting Oswald, who "turns up, a lost child found, a child of the surrogate family of the monastic community," Columba "offers a simple dramatic expression of the priestly vocation."[13] This pre-Troubles play thus proleptically suggests that representatives of even violent, religiously driven societies can turn away from conflict and toward peace by a refusal to dwell on territorial, seemingly originary claims to land or faith. Such actions will likely stem from deep internal reflection and a desire to be at least temporarily freed from the competing claims of class, homeland, sectarianism, and narcissism.

2

Mediascape, Harvest, and Crash

Philadelphia, Here I Come!
and Gar O'Donnell's Modernity

In *Philadelphia, Here I Come!*, a split stage and a split main character together portray the divided terrain of protagonist Gar O'Donnell's mind. Cut off from the land and most sustaining rural rituals, including those of Irish Catholicism, represented in the play by the ineffective, disengaged Canon, Gar longs for connection and love but only finds them in lonely fantasies that he repeatedly stages, with elements borrowed from American movies and popular culture. Caught between the frozen Irish past and an uncertain global present, Gar finally chooses to settle in Philadelphia with his mother's sister (Aunt Lizzy) and her husband. Already a creature of extreme mental vacillation, Gar's pending immersion into modern American urban life threatens to completely sever him from any sustaining matrix. While he has good reasons for leaving Ireland, including a lack of communication with his father, the rhetoric of the play suggests that Philadelphia will be a site of entrapment and that Aunt Lizzy and her husband will metaphorically devour him.

Moreover, the play's setting at a crucial time of modernization in Ireland implies that even as Gar embraces an unrealistic vision of America, he will miss the economic revolution that had just begun transforming Ireland in the late 1950s. Three questions that have been largely unaddressed in Friel criticism suggest the contours of my argument here: How and why is Gar's use of fanciful scenarios, ranging from Edmund Burke's *Reflections on the Revolution in France*

41

to popular culture, employed by Friel? Why is a crucial memory in the play—the day when Gar's aunt and uncle arrive in Ballybeg and also when his former love Kate Doogan gets married—set at harvest? And why does Gar's father, S. B. O'Donnell, tell him toward the end of the play that "you should sit at the back" of the plane in case "there was an accident or anything—it's the front that gets it hardest" (*BFP1* 94)?

First, Gar's recourse to flights of fancy, which are often based on a visual perception derived from film, is not the innocuous exercise it may seem upon a first reading or viewing of the play. Rather, it implies his interior orientation and the psychic damage that marks him as almost fully modern. The play privileges the oral tradition in several manifestations over a modern, mechanically visual outlook: Friel contrasts Gar's inherently filmic perception with the much more positive oral recitations of stories by both himself and his father and by some of the music, especially classical music, that Gar plays on his record player. Second, Gar's voluntary exclusion of himself from Kate's wedding, his fears of her fertility after marriage, and his aunt's lack of fertility that leads her to lure Gar to Philadelphia together betoken his divorce from the land. Finally, the abiding fear of Gar's plane crashing signifies Friel's concern to depict the crashing of representatives of rural culture into industrial modernism more generally. Thus, the play carefully shows how Gar himself and his rural culture—and to a greater degree, the culture that he is partially immersed in already and into which he will soon be catapulted—divorce him from community, militate against contemplation, and effectively dehumanize him.

If place is always an event, as I argued, drawing on Edward Casey's theory of place in the introduction to this study, then *Philadelphia, Here I Come!*, with the imagined American metropolis forming the essential part of the play's exclamatory title, stages a double event—the ongoing life in Gar's Irish village that he will leave behind and the life he imagines he will live in Philadelphia. Friel's breakthrough play surveys the mental deracination of Gar O'Donnell through a careful examination of isolation and dislocation endemic to both

Ballybeg and Philadelphia and, indeed, to Western culture after the Enlightenment. Only through grasping this realization in the play can we understand how places condition our every choice. Furthermore, keeping in mind Casey's dictum that place is an event enables us to understand that Gar's vacillation about emigrating, and then his final decision to go, constitute only the latest development in the event of place that Friel so thoughtfully stages. While Gar has largely "gone through the motions" of living in Ballybeg, he has done so as part of a place that is itself going through changes largely unrecognized by him. He will become part of a constrictive site of Irish American memory in Philadelphia, ironically the birthplace of American independence, even as the city around him hums and thrums.

Seamus Deane argues that "Gar O'Donnell is, in many ways, a recognizably modern case of alienation. He has all the narcissism that goes with the condition of being driven back in upon the resources of the self."[1] And, we might add, Gar has none of the saving advantages of true community that would rescue him from this rampant narcissism. His narcissism is different in kind from that evidenced in one of Friel's short stories that clearly influenced the play, "The Potato Gatherers."[2] Whereas Joe and Philly (the latter name explicitly links story and play together) engage in flights of fancy, they do so not as a matter of course but as a way to stave off fatigue from their hard labor during the day. Gar, however, so regularly fantasizes that he cannot even be said to revert to such dreams—they are a matter of course for him. They certainly originate from everyone's deep need to feel valued, but their specific content suggests a relatively unexplored aspect of the play—the pernicious influence of what Richard Weaver has termed the "Great Stereopticon"—the press, movies, and radio.

Writing in 1948, Weaver argued in his classic work, *Ideas Have Consequences*, that "[t]he great changes affecting the literature of our time began with those subterranean forces which erupted in the French Revolution."[3] According to Weaver, because of such doctrines as the "ethical optimism propounded by the Earl of Shaftesbury," traditional virtues of education and self-restraint were shunted aside and man was now thought to have a "natural moral sense which can be relied on not only to recognize virtue but to delight in it. The important consequence for literature was the sanctioning of impulse, which now became the subject of endless and varied exploitation."[4] With the rise in the belief that all men are naturally good—a view that the body of Friel's work utterly rejects—satirical comedy largely disappeared and became sentimental, another convention that Weaver critiques, as does Friel. After the Romantic poets enshrined the "impulse of revolt against conventions and institutions," literary motifs appeared that depicted "intensive explorations of the individual consciousness, with self-laceration and self-pity."[5] Friel's Gar O'Donnell thus acts out of a received post–French Revolution and post-Romantic intellectual and ethical tradition, one that leads him repeatedly inward to escape reality. Such an egotism makes him particularly susceptible to modernity's onrushing nature.

Commentary on the play generally refuses to acknowledge Gar as an inheritor of this tradition, or at least to trace out the full implications of his continued repetitions of a phrase from Edmund Burke's *Reflections on the Revolution in France*. Early in Episode One, under repeated questioning from Private Gar, Public Gar breaks off his description of his father's line of goods to exclaim, "Yahoooooo! It is now sixteen or seventeen years since I saw the Queen of France, then the Dauphiness, at Versailles" (*BFP1* 36). Gar likely read Burke as part of the prose course on the English syllabus for the Leaving Certificate examinations when he was 17 or 18. Deane argues that "Friel uses Burke here . . . to [suggest] . . . that the Ballybeg which Gar O'Donnell is trying to leave is indeed the remnant of a past civilization and that the new world, however vulgar it may seem, is that of Philadelphia and the Irish Americans."[6] But Deane is on shakier ground when he argues that Gar believes that by leaving his home, he is "forsaking the capacity to feel deeply."[7] Gar is so caught up in himself and the busyness he imposes on himself in Ballybeg through his actions and fantasies that he sometimes seems incapable of feeling in the present. In fact, it is only by dwelling in the past, when he views the newspaper clipping about his parents' wedding in 1937 (37–38), for example, or when he recalls the fishing trip on Lough na Cloc Cor with his father (82–83, 89, 94–95), that he generates significant emotions.

Overall, Gar's recourse to this tag line about the Queen of France reveals that Deane is right insofar as his argument goes—Gar realizes the Burke phrase signifies he will be leaving rural Ballybeg's remnant civilization behind. But more interestingly, Gar simultaneously uses the phrase as a sort of oral brochure for imagined travel to anarchic France (and implicitly to supposedly barbaric and wild America), which is consistent with the theme of travel portrayed in the scenarios he often scripts for himself from movies and radio. Spurgeon Thompson, following Deane's argument in *Strange Country: Modernity and Nationhood in Irish Writing since 1790* on how Burke's book is a foundational work for describing the contrast between tradition and modernity, has held that "the *Reflections* gains much of its strength from its affinity to travelogues," and thus the book enables Burke to represent the events in the French Revolution as inherently barbaric and Other to the rational English and Europeans.[8] The sense of wonder borrowed from Burke's description of the Queen of France and the Dauphiness at Versailles in the passage that Gar so often invokes, however, masks his abiding fascination with the wild and anarchic energies of Revolutionary France and, by extension, America. That spirit is signified in the play by Gar exclaiming wildly, "Yahoooooo!" before he launches into the Burke quotation for the first time (*BFP1* 36). Shortly thereafter, he curses to himself right after recalling his mother's death and immediately before reciting Burke again (38). In this latter passage, Gar becomes something of a barbarian himself after this recitation, removing the staid Mendelssohn record from his phonograph and calling, in the voice of Private Gar, for something lively, then switching into an American accent as *"Celidhe Band music"* begins and dancing madly around the room (ibid.). In so doing, Gar imagines himself as triply French, Irish, and American, a mad mixture of nationalities that reveals his longing for a more heterogeneous culture than the one in which he currently lives and the desire to play a starring role in that culture.

What we might call Gar's "cinematic imagination" is both potentially liberating and crippling since it enables him to temporarily, then finally permanently, escape the quotidian realities of life in Ballybeg; yet it also prevents him from the possibility of experiencing the more organic evolution of a mature self grounded in contemplation over time. Thomas Kilroy has argued that the theatricality of Gar's role in the play "is cinematic" and that "[t]hroughout the play he is the star and the director, where he plays all the lead parts and redirects the life around him in farcical scenarios."[9]

Moreover, Arjun Appadurai's use of the term "mediascape" to describe one of the contemporary "five dimensions of global flows"[10] helps us to understand Gar's tendency to narrate his life through media. Appadurai's concept of mediascape suggests how attitudes such as Gar's would increasingly become dominant, not marginal, as the twentieth century progressed and forms of media and their capabilities proliferated. Gar's media-influenced imagination uncannily anticipates Appadurai's contention over thirty years later in 1996 about global audiences' perception through their immersion and participation in mediascapes: "The lines between the realistic and the fictional landscapes they see are blurred, so that the farther away these audiences are from the direct experiences of metropolitan life, the more likely they are to construct imagined worlds that are chimerical, aesthetic, even fantastic objects, particularly if assessed by the criteria of some other perspective, some other imagined world."[11] Trapped in the hinterlands of Ireland and cut off from "the direct experiences of metropolitan life"—yet sufficiently exposed to various media, especially American cinema, to drink in their images—Gar weaves a series of fantastic stories inflected by media, "protonarratives of possible lives, fantasies that could become prolegomena to the desire for acquisition and movement."[12] Such "protonarratives" prepare him for and lead him toward his pending (and likely crippling) American exile.

Gar's clear immersion in American popular culture suggests a pervasive unease within himself that compounds his rampant, post-Romantic egotism. Like many young men of his age in 1960s Ireland,

Gar is obsessed with the radio and the silver screen, and his fantasies often echo scripts from radio shows or movies. Late in the play,
during his conversation with Kate, Gar even projects himself as a
future filmmaker, saying, "I'll come home when I make my first million, driving a Cadillac and smoking cigars and taking movie-films"
(*BFP1* 78). As we will see, Gar is already "filming" his last night in
Ballybeg in his mind as the play concludes in an attempt to preserve
it. In this earlier passage, however, Gar imagines himself as a returning hero driving an American luxury car and presumably videotap-
ing the reactions of the townland's inhabitants upon the return of
the native boy made good in America. He sees his time in America as
potentially disconnecting him from the village because of his material means.

However, one of his first imaginings in the play occurs when he
pretends to be a football player taking a free kick for, presumably,
the Irish national team, an exercise that displays Gar's yearning to be
connected to his nation. Employing a commentator's voice from an
imagined radio broadcast, Gar simultaneously enacts this dream of
becoming an Irish national hero but also effectively jettisons his vocation as helper in his father's shop by kicking his own shop coat that
functions as the football: "O'Donnell is now moving back, taking a
slow, calculating look at the goal. . . . He's now in position, running
up, and—(PUBLIC *kicks the shop coat into the air*)" (*BFP1* 31). If, as
Martin McLoone has argued, "broadcasting has been a primary site
for the mediation, promotion and maintenance of collective identity"
in the twentieth century,[13] Gar's imaginative recreation of himself as
the Irish national football hero in a radio broadcast consciously links
himself to the country he is about to leave. Here, as elsewhere, he
pictures himself as the hero on whom the hopes of everyone hinge.

But what of the elderly father, S.B., he will leave behind? Gar could
be a real hero by staying and helping his father and eventually taking
over the shop. An anxious S.B. wonders aloud to Madge in one of
the last scenes of the play, "Madge, I'll manage rightly, Madge, eh?,"
after which he then virtually repeats this pitiful plea a few lines later
(*BFP1* 96). Gar clearly feels he is dying in the stultifying atmosphere

of his father's shop and in Ballybeg generally and that he must leave to grow and be free. Certainly the isolation that he feels in early 1960s Ballybeg, despite the presence of Madge, his father, neighbors, and friends, is partly responsible for his desire to leave. Following the period 1951–1961, the time of the "vanishing Irish," in which 412,000 or roughly 10 percent of the Irish nation emigrated, "[o]ne person in three in the west of Ireland was described as 'chronically isolated.'"[14] Gar's absence will almost surely lead to a slow emotional death for his father and probably the further decline of the shop.

Although it is common to assume that the early 1960s, during which *Philadelphia* is presumably set, was a time when Ireland experienced sea changes in its culture (and certainly many radical developments occurred then), Brian Fallon has made a strong case that, in Ireland, "[t]he Fifties were in every way a watershed, in which an entire epoch ended and the modern one emerged."[15] While there was a general drift toward change in Ireland in the 1950s, the period 1958–63, as Terence Brown has argued, "represented a major turning point in Irish fortunes" and correctly "is seen as the period when a new Ireland began to come to life" because of the First Programme for Economic Expansion, introduced by T. K. Whitaker in 1958, followed by the second such program, which began in 1963.[16] If the play is set in the present, the period 1963–64, Ireland has already tremendously metamorphosed in the preceding five years, which makes Gar's decision all the more ironic. He believes he is leaving staid, stultifying Ireland behind, but actually he will miss out on the effects of this radical and rapid economic transformation.

Friel's Gar O'Donnell, 25 years old during the play, clearly comes of age as an adolescent during the 1950s and is caught up in the general movement of Irish culture toward America in that decade. While Irish culture had been greatly influenced by European culture in the 1930s and 1940s, Fallon argues that, by the 1950s, "[i]ncreasingly, Irish culture faced westward rather than toward the Continent, while American writers, stage and screen actors such as Burgess Meredith, folk singers such as Burl Ives, and leading journalists were regular visitors, usually via the recently created Shannon

Airport."[17] American culture was increasingly urban, metropolitan, and anxious to move away from its rural past. Is it any wonder that Friel's Gar, steeped as he is in American popular culture, wants to leave rural Ireland for the bright lights and big city of Philadelphia?

Although Friel has said that "*Philadelphia* was an analysis of a kind of love: the love between a father and a son and between a son and his birthplace,"[18] the latter part of this equation has been relatively unexplored in criticism of this drama. Indeed, it seems relatively missing from the play until, perhaps, the conclusion. For instance, Public Gar argues to Kate, "I've stuck around this hole far too long. I'm telling you: it's a bloody quagmire, a backwater, a dead-end!" (*BFP1* 79). Although Gar's anger here springs partly from the sheer boredom of his life in rural Ballybeg, it is also somewhat feigned and meant to disguise his continued love for Kate and his despair at her having gotten married to someone else. Gar clearly does have great affection for Ballybeg, as he still does for Kate, but he believes he must escape before he too becomes effectively dead.

One persistent way in which Gar often displays real disdain for his birthplace and surroundings manifests in his adoption of an American cowboy persona that signifies his desire for wide-open spaces. For example, at one point early in the play he cannot tell his father how many coils of barbed-wire had arrived that evening, finally rejecting the whole notion of fences, which he sees as Irish and provincial, and embracing what he believes is the open American frontier through Private Gar's use of a cowboy accent (*BFP1* 34). Taking on the rugged, individual persona of an American cowboy and privileging the American West's vast spaces enables Gar to begin the necessary process of separating himself from the intensely local community and relatively hemmed-in landscape he is part of in Ballybeg. Ironically, though, once in Philadelphia, he will be confined in a series of spaces that are far away from the American West: the little bedroom in his aunt and uncle's apartment; the apartment itself; the hotel where he will work; and Philadelphia, a city that could prove constricting to him with its welter of tall buildings towering over him.

Gar's persistent adaptation of an American cowboy accent connoting unlimited literal and metaphorical horizons of his mind accords with a similar property of film itself that Walter Benjamin has identified. Although film often offers us close-ups of our ordinary milieu—Benjamin notes that film also "manages to assure us of an immense and unexpected field of action" because its nature also explodes the quotidian world around us and allows us to "calmly and adventurously go traveling. With the close-up, space expands; with slow motion, movement is extended." Finally citing Rudolf Arnheim, Benjamin argues that "slow motion not only presents familiar qualities of movement but reveals in them entirely unknown ones 'which, far from looking like retarded rapid movements, give the effect of singularly gliding, floating, supernatural motions.'"[19] Gar has thus traveled mentally for years by watching films; now with expanded mental horizons, he will travel literally.

But what he sees as freedom through his filmic gaze is negated through film's mechanical qualities. Even though Gar feels that identifying with American antiheroes from popular films makes him singular, unique, the reproduction of film by mechanical means and distribution to mass audiences of course has presented similar opportunities for such identification with people throughout the world for decades, which suggests that Gar is merely aping a common image—reacting, not acting with any agency of his own.

Just as John Osborne had proposed a new antihero for the British stage in Jimmy Porter some eight years before in *Look Back in Anger*, in this drama Friel advances his own *enfant terrible*, Gar. Christopher Murray argues that his "uncertainty and agnosticism define Gar as the new anti-hero in Irish drama."[20] And certainly, besides imagining himself as an Irish football star, Gar plays this subversive role in most of his other reveries, such as the one just discussed where he is "Garry the Kid," a moniker that surely draws on the name of the outlaw Billy the Kid (*BFP1* 34).

Martin McLoone has discussed how American films appealed to Europeans much more than British films in the twentieth century because, in the words of Geoffrey Nowell-Smith, "British cinema appeared 'restrictive and stifling, subservient to middle-class artistic models and to middle[-] and upper-class values.'" Thus, "[i]t is hardly surprising that in these circumstances . . . the classless, democratic appeal of American popular culture would appear positively liberating" to Europeans and perhaps especially to Irish audiences who "willingly embrace[d] the cultural products of America from within a stifling, conservative (and heavily censored) official national culture."[21]

In a telling tirade, Gar exclaims to Kate toward the end of Episode One: "There's nothing about Ballybeg that I don't know already. I hate the place . . . ! Hate it! Hate it!" (*BFP1* 79), displaying both his knowledge of his environment and culture but, more significant, his rejection of them. If, as Wendell Berry has argued, true regionalism has as its motive "the awareness that local life is intricately dependent, for its quality but also for its continuance, upon local knowledge,"[22] then Gar's rejection, by and large, of local life and the understanding of that life for a "knowledge" of American film and popular culture marks him as particularly dislocated—both from his home place and from his anticipated home in Philadelphia, where his life working in a hotel will be in no way comparable to the glamour of America he has seen onscreen. Friel pointed out the unreality of New York City using the language of American film in an interview only a year after *Philadelphia* was produced, even while, like Gar, he admitted how "exciting" he found it: "Somebody once said that when you're walking along underneath these vast skyscrapers, you feel that they're great Hollywood sets and that if you walk round to the back of them you'll see they're being held up by props and that they're only a front. And it's this unreality about the place which I find very exciting."[23]

Although there have been many later studies on the pernicious effects of popular entertainment on the self, such as Neil Postman's classic analysis *Amusing Ourselves to Death*, Richard Weaver's discussion of this phenomenon remains valuable both because of its trenchant observations and because its publication some sixteen years before *Philadelphia* was produced demonstrates just how saturated American life had become with popular culture by the late 1940s, to the point that Weaver felt obliged to react against its pernicious effects. Ireland by the early 1960s was similarly saturated and had been for decades: Terence Brown has pointed out that not only was radio listening widespread in Ireland by the 1930s, people in the country, towns, and cities were "addicted in the 1930s . . . to the Hollywood film. In village hall and city cinema in Ireland the 1930s was the decade of an enthusiastic discovery of celluloid dreams from California."[24] And Diarmaid Ferriter has noted that while in the 1930s and 1940s, "there was widespread participation in native pastimes, Irish audiences also yearned for the faraway hills, and remained avid cinema-goers. In 1943, 22 million cinema tickets were purchased."[25]

Weaver focuses on the tradition of the leading man and woman in American movie culture in a biting critique that helps us understand how Friel's Gar has been led to play the hero and the antihero often in his fantasies, but also, perhaps more interestingly, how his returned, now Irish American aunt plays the heroine. Weaver objects to the "egotistic, selfish, and self-flaunting hero" and also to the "flippant, vacuous-minded, and also egotistic heroine."[26] By having watched so many American movies, Gar and his aunt mimic the leading man and lady depicted onscreen: Gar acts as hero and his aunt functions as heroine in a movie script they are themselves now writing. Each plays out his or her role in a prescribed, overly self-conscious manner, as if they know very well how their mimicry avoids real emotions.

Even more debilitating for Gar, his fascination with movies actually prevents him from meditating on the past, even though the play closes with his attempt to "film" the events of the previous night and that morning in his mind. Weaver points out how the press, the motion picture, and the radio encourage a constant simultaneity that militates against contemplation. "For by keeping the time element continuously present," Weaver holds, "they discourage composition and so promote . . . fragmentation." By so doing, movies and other electronic and even print media produce a "constant stream of sensation [that] . . . discourages the pulling-together of events from past time into a whole for contemplation. Thus, absence of reflection keeps the individual from being aware of his former selves, and it is highly questionable whether anyone can be a member of a metaphysical community who does not preserve such memory."[27] Although Gar O'Donnell plays many imagined roles in *Philadelphia*, these roles largely keep him unaware of his former selves, except for his flashbacks to the boat trip with his father on the lake and to his relationship with Kate. Mostly unable to apprehend his development over time, he is caught in a web of simultaneity that largely prevents him from meditating on the implications of the pending move for his selfhood.

Gar's immersion in movies has undoubtedly conditioned him to privilege himself over his local community because the Hollywood movies of the time modeled such behavior for him. As Luke Gibbons has argued, "Hollywood's challenge to the centrality of the family in the national romance of Irish life derived primarily from its emotional individualism and privatization of desire, particularly as idealized in the cult of romantic love."[28] This challenge to the family's centrality is repeatedly staged in the play. For instance, in Episode One, Public and Private Gar stage a scene with an imagined woman in Philadelphia at the hotel where he will work. Public Gar plays the part of himself as a dashing city man who offers to walk a gorgeous lady "played" by Private Gar toward her home, which she instantly accepts (*BFP1* 46). Besides his clear fascination for urban culture, what stands out about this snippet is Gar's desire to find instant love with a woman who immediately responds to his advances, a projection that stems from his many viewings of Hollywood romance onscreen.

Even more important for understanding Gar's concept of love—familial and romantic—is the way in which he has already been conditioned to such a cult of romantic love by the housekeeper Madge's repeated descriptions of the relationship between Gar's mother and father. For instance, early in Episode One, as Public Gar prays the rosary for his mother, Private Gar recalls Madge's romantic stories about his mother: "She was small, Madge says, and wild, and young, Madge says, from a place called Bailtefree beyond the mountains" (*BFP1* 37). The repeated refrain of "Madge says" shows how Gar has become dependent on Madge's stories in order to remember his mother; moreover, Madge may well have embellished these stories for his sake to give him an ideal image of a mother who died three days after he was born. Also, the parataxis employed in such a passage and the breathless manner in which this memory is relayed suggests its mythical, unexamined quality. Its juxtaposition with the various passages from the rosary finally implies a conflated continuity with Gar's residual Catholic faith and his faith in the memory of his mother. Finally, by recalling more of Madge's oral history—that his father was a gentleman who could not take his eyes off his mother—Gar successfully remakes his parents into a Hollywood-type couple in instant and constant love based merely on looks and clothing (ibid.).

At the beginning of Episode Two, Gar again recasts (the movie jargon is deliberate) his father as a gentleman, this time as a Chinese spy (*BFP1* 57). This exotic Asian identity quickly morphs, however, into an explicitly American one in which Private Gar imagines his father as a tall, athletic, blond-headed man who is handsome, a description quickly supplemented by Public Gar, who interjects that a beautiful woman in a gown often accompanies him (ibid.). Clearly, Gar has now reimagined his parents as a movie star couple, complete with jewels and fine clothing, the trappings of material success magnified out of all proportion to reality. This vision must be a result of Gar's immersion in Hollywood movies with their emphasis on "the cult of romantic love" that Gibbons identifies above.

More examples of Gar's obsession with movie-generated, highly individualized notions of love occur at the beginning of Episode Three during a complex passage that offers three "scenes" of Gar in a relationship with a glamorous woman, then as a single and mysterious character, and finally as part of his own father's relationship with his mother. As he imagines his father dreaming and himself walking down a fantastic series of Philadelphia streets, he imagines a beautiful blonde next to him (*BFP1* 81); then he quickly embraces bachelorhood, falling into a reverie about taking long, lonely walks (81–82). Reading himself through another type common to American film, variously figured as "the man with no name" or the loner (epitomized by the actor Clint Eastwood), Gar nevertheless romanticizes himself while rejecting romantic love. Endlessly fascinated by his projections, he transforms his fear of loneliness in America into an appealing quality that draws every eye to him. Finally, he incorporates himself into the narrative of his older father marrying his young mother (we find out she was 19 and Gar's father was 40) by imagining meeting a beautiful 19-year-old girl, granddaughter of Russian royalty, and falling deeply in love with her (82). Effectively suturing the wound of his mother's early death when he was three days old with the golden thread of an imagined exotic love, Gar simultaneously recovers what he believes was the "magic" of his father and mother's early relationship and adopts that idealized love for his own imagined relationship with another beautiful woman. In this hermetically sealed world of illusion, Gar becomes his own father and remakes S.B.'s dull life into one of intrigue and great passion for himself to live. Tellingly, he misses giving out his decade of the rosary during his blissful reverie, suggesting how fully his fantasy world, not Catholicism, occupies his devotion.

Intriguingly, in two of these three "movie scenes" imagined by Gar, he visualizes these fantasies while praying Catholic litanies, suggesting that while Gar continues to publicly profess his vanishing faith, he secretly venerates these secular images instead and meditates upon them increasingly. More and more he invests them with his imagination and gives credence to them while mouthing his prayers by rote. Gar's underground profession of faith in American popular culture connotes yet another break from his Irish agrarian culture with its emphasis on community and Catholic cohesion. This cohesion was increasingly under strain as the 1950s wore on, especially after Irish Minister for Health Noel Brown resigned in 1951 when attacked by the Catholic hierarchy for proposing free maternity care and free health care for all children in the state up to age 16.[29] If, as

Kevin Whelan has argued, "In post-famine Ireland, religious affiliation increasingly became a surrogate for national identity as the
effective agent of communal solidarity,"[30] Gar's outward adherence
to Catholicism maintains his nominal allegiance to both faith and
country, but his inward allegiance to American culture foreshadows
his imminent break from both Catholicism and Ireland.

Partly because of its presentation in darkened theaters, cinema
asks of us, almost demands of us, something like devotion and veneration. Its incorporation of striking sonic and visual effects demands
even more from its audiences; indeed, it can be likened to a religious
experience, with audience members expected to stay quiet and to
singularly focus their senses upon the screen. In this regard, Luke
Gibbons has even declared that, by the late 1950s, "the true rival of
Catholicism was not Protestantism, or even communism, but cinema itself, especially in view of its powerful seductive appeal to the
senses and obsessive forms of identification."[31] Of course, much of
the mystery of the Catholic Mass was removed by the new dispensa-
tion of Vatican II, which opened in 1962 and closed in 1965, neatly
encapsulating the time just before the events *Philadelphia* stages and
the period just after those events. Mass was now conducted in the
vernacular language instead of Latin. The priest now would face his
congregants and turn his back to the mystery of the Host, effecting
a more intimate immediacy with his flock but also removing some of
the Mass's traditional, ritualized drama that might have competed
with film for congregations' attention.[32]

Gar's attitude in the play toward the Canon, the official representative of the Catholic Church in Ireland, suggests that Irish cinema and popular culture generally have won his heart and devotion
even as he laments the Canon's ineffectuality. The Canon's habitual,
repetitive conversation with Gar's father annoys Gar to no end and
indicates that, despite his personal warmth and affection for Gar and
his family, the Canon stands for Friel's sense of the sterility of the
Irish Catholic Church at the time, persistently involved in people's
affairs in a superficial manner but refusing to deeply engage them
beyond traditional pietistic language. Toward the end of the first part

of Episode Three, as the Canon watches Gar and his father play draughts, Private Gar lambastes the Canon for his refusal to translate man's search for meaning into Christian terms: "[Y]ou could translate all this loneliness, this groping, this dreadful bloody buffoonery into Christian terms that will make life bearable for us all. And yet you don't say a word. Why, Canon? Why, arid Canon? Isn't this your job—to translate?" (*BFP1* 88). Literal translations, would, of course, occupy Friel's attention fully in the later play of that name, but here, he has his lead character refer to the act of translating to show the inability of the Church at the time to cope with the confusion and uneasiness endemic to the human condition because of the Holocaust in Europe, the dropping of the atomic bomb in Japan, and the economic revolution in Ireland. When Gar almost immediately after this indictment of the Church sings a popular song ("Give Me Your Answer, Do," which would become the title of another Friel play) and then launches into another one ("I Had You Cornered," 88–89), we realize how he now finds meaning in the discourse that preaches the bliss of nearly instant, romantic love instead of the strictures of the Irish Catholic Church. Finally, Gar's flight to America with the "Sweeneys"—which is the last name of his aunt and uncle—implies that the old Irish myth of the leaping Sweeney and the modern myth of American prosperity and anonymity together lead Gar to make the leap to America. The combination of the newer myth with the ancient one thus triumph over what C. S. Lewis called the "true myth" of the Christian narrative, epitomized by a Canon who will not speak Christian truth to a vacuous culture, as Gar laments.

In a 1964 interview with Peter Lennon, Friel compared Gar's attitude toward Catholicism with that of Saint Columba in *The Enemy Within*. He told Lennon that "Gareth was leaving home not only in a local sense but in a spiritual sense too. . . . I took that quotation from the Bible, the 'enemy within,' as meaning literally Saint Columba's family. You have to get away from a corrupting influence. I think in Ireland we feed on each other a lot; we batten on each other."[33] Friel implicitly conflates Gar's family with both the Irish Catholic Church and Ireland as well here, possibly suggesting that they form a sort of devouring trinity that Gar must escape in order to achieve a life for himself. I do not wish to play down the probable necessity of Gar's escape from family, Church, and country, but would point out again how his emigration is grounded thoroughly in his immersion in false and pernicious ideals perpetuated by the American popular culture he has consistently absorbed over the last decade or so of his life. Friel recognized the entrapping nature of that culture, remarking in an interview conducted in 1966 while *Philadelphia* was still running on Broadway, that "[w]hatever you flee from in one place, you'll probably find the same things somewhere else."[34]

The flashback scene with Gar's Aunt Lizzy and Uncle Con provides a cinching example of Friel's depiction of the destructive influence of American popular culture on both that country's inhabitants and on those elsewhere even as he reveals the often-stultifying nature of Irish culture at the time. Gar's drunken aunt quickly becomes maudlin on her return to Ballybeg and repeatedly attempts to dramatize the story of Gar's mother's wedding, even as she interrupts herself and is interrupted by her husband and their friend Ben Burton. In the process, she adds a layer of mystery and yearning to Gar's image of his mother that has been created by Madge's near-mythic tales of her over the years. And in her final pleading for Gar to be her son, Aunt Lizzy enacts a maternal/filial version of the cult of romantic love common to American film at that time, a maneuver that comports well with Gar's abstracted ideas about his mother and his notions of love in general.

Even though we are led to expect from Gar a description of his former girlfriend Kathy's wedding that same harvest day of his aunt and uncle's visit, instead Private Gar recalls in cinematic fashion, "you couldn't take your eyes off Aunt Lizzy, your mother's sister . . . remember?" (*BFP1* 60). Thus, Gar's flashback here effectively leads him into a double-remove from his present voluntary exclusion of himself from Kathy's wedding. Lizzy acts both the role of the seemingly glamorous returned Irish emigrant and the role of witnessing sister at Gar's mother's funeral, a double act that eventually compels Gar to follow her to America. His aunt effectively builds suspense, as any good film must, by setting a dramatic scene of Maire either crying or laughing at the altar and then by promising to reveal what her sister Agnes said that day (60–61). But this tantalizing glimpse is the most Gar will get out of her, as she stumbles from one memory to another in Ireland, and then showing herself incapable of being an accurate transmitter of past knowledge in America. She even reveals how thoroughly immersed she herself has become in American popular culture, calling her husband at one point "Rudolph Valentino" (62).

Gar's close connection to his home place, already under long and repeated assault through his years of exposure to American pop culture, is further challenged in this scene by his aunt's simultaneous recreation of his mother's wedding day in Ballybeg and her embrace of American materialism, along with Ben Burton's casual treatment of all places as the same. Lizzy urgently tells Gar that they have a comfortable apartment with air conditioning, color television, Irish records, and $15,000 in federal bonds (*BFP1* 65). She has given her allegiance to comfort with a veneer of Irishness and a patina of the rural with their backyard, its cherry tree, and animals such as squirrels and owls (ibid.). Desperate to show her connection to her adopted country and to lure Gar there as well, she offers a mishmash of comfort and Irish American culture to him. Perhaps an even more effective ploy for her may be Burton's seemingly throwaway response when she urges him to tell Gar whether he should come to America or not: "It's just another place to live, Elise: Ireland—America— what's the difference?" (64). Nearly sixty years later, the differences between the two countries are increasingly blurred not only by the proliferation of pop culture in both but also by the advance of electronic communications. But in 1964, despite the huge changes going on in the Irish economy and the Irish Catholic Church, Ireland was certainly very different from America.

Burton's remark is reinforced by Gar's former schoolmaster, Boyle, when he drops by the house earlier the night Gar prepares to leave. Boyle calls America "a vast restless place that doesn't give a curse about the past," saying further, "[i]mpermanence and anonymity—it offers great attractions" (*BFP1* 52). Even though Boyle

abstracts America into a monolithic entity of transitory forgetfulness, the very fact that a representative of educational culture makes
such a claim forcefully strikes Gar. Elsewhere in the play, toward the
end of his conversation with Kate, he repeats Boyle's phrases about
America's impermanence and anonymity to her even as he fears those
qualities and is secretly mourning his loss of her (79).

Lizzy's "performance" as presumptive mother finally wins over
Gar. She is portrayed as self-consciously reenacting a conversation in
America with her husband, during which she schemes to become his
mother's replacement by luring him with material inducements and
excessive emotionalism. For Gar, accustomed to the material sameness and drabness of his father's shop and home, "exotic" American
material culture—as epitomized by air conditioning and cars—
appeals strongly to his desire for prosperity. And similarly, because
he mistakes S.B.'s reticence and silences as signs that his father does
not love him, he knowingly falls for this staged outburst of emotion
by his aunt.

On this autumn day of fertility rituals—in the fields where the
crops are being gathered and in the church where Kate Doogan's
wedding is being held—Gar's Aunt Lizzy enacts her own ritualized
drama of infertility, pleading with Gar to become her son. She recognizes the relative infertility of herself and her sisters, noting of
Gar that he is the only child any of the five sisters had and tearfully
relating their plan to get him to emigrate to America by offering him
material possessions (*BFP1* 65). Tellingly, she continues by employing a harvest metaphor: "[M]aybe it was sorta bribery—I dunno—
but he would have everything we ever *gathered*" (ibid.; my emphasis).
Lizzy and Con have tried to fill their life in America with possessions, but she still feels an ache at the core that can only be filled
with a child—even, apparently, a grown one like Gar. As a displaced
couple from rural Ireland, it is perhaps natural for them to employ an
agricultural term like "gathered," but Friel uses the verb to establish
a series of resonances with other mentions in the play of that particular day during harvest season. He also shows how Gar himself
is being harvested by his aunt and uncle, cut down, as it were, and

proleptically bundled into their store of goods back in America even as they offer him those goods.

Gar has become a commodity coveted especially by his Aunt Lizzy and, as such, his allowing himself to be "harvested" by her and his uncle suggests just how far removed he is from his rural community, which values the harvest as providing food for the winter. Instead, we realize when Lizzy mentions the snowy Christmases they have, complete with a Christmas tree, and then laments their loneliness (*BFP1* 65) that Gar's presence will help his aunt and uncle through the lonely times of winter. They will "feed" off of him as he completes a perfect family holiday tableau—snow, Christmas tree, and child. Therefore, even though Friel himself, as noted above, argues that Gar had to leave Ireland because "we feed on each other a lot," he nevertheless suggests that Gar will be fed on metaphorically by his aunt and uncle once in America. Tellingly, in the same interview where he shows his distaste for this "feeding" process, Friel almost immediately states, "[b]ut the corruption I'm talking about, a man finds anywhere around him—in Dublin or in Winesburg, Ohio," which suggests how Gar can easily be corrupted by his aunt and uncle once in Philadelphia.[35]

Gar's embarrassment in this scene at being told how he has been coveted by his aunt and uncle, and his extreme discomfort when his aunt hugs him after he asks to go to America, does not, however, prevent him from offering to go. When she calls him "my son" twice and repeats his name thrice and embraces him, she is gathering him into her own sort of artifice of eternity along with her dead sisters (*BFP1* 66). Shortly before this maudlin scene ensues, Aunt Lizzy laments the death of her sisters and surprisingly includes herself in this litany of names (64). Even though Con helpfully reminds her that she is not dead and she angrily reproaches him, her old self effectively died after she left Ireland. Living in the past, surrounded with material goods gathered from America, she hopes against hope that Gar's presence will revivify the memories of her close family life from long ago. Gar himself repeats this mantra of five sisters dead earlier in the play (55), echoing the schoolmaster Boyle's repetition of it (53, 54), a recitation that is surely conflated in his mind with his Aunt Lizzy's iteration of their names during their harvest visit. He seemingly thus desires to become a hopeful consolation to the remaining sister and to sacrifice his own happiness to hers. Whatever life Gar leads in Philadelphia in the imagined afterlife of the play, his American fantasies of playing the outlaw or the leading man against the backdrop of wide-open spaces will run aground on the realistic shoals of contemporary urban American life.

The harvesting and gathering of Gar that fateful September 8th is explicitly contrasted with both the ongoing agricultural harvest at the time and with Kate Doogan's wedding. Gar refuses to go to the wedding, but his father, as a fully integrated member of the community, does attend. In such a rural area, the whole community would gather at local weddings, just as they would gather together to bring in the crops at harvest time. But Gar cuts himself off from this gathering and instead is reaped, shortly to be gathered, by his aunt and uncle. Friel's purposeful setting of Kate's wedding during harvest time is another double act never recognized by critics of the play, one that is understandably occluded by Gar's constant performance of a double act between the two sides of himself. There are no depictions of the harvest in *Philadelphia*, as there will be in *Translations*, but at the least the play shows that it is a good day for harvesting, as Gar himself recognizes after recalling his failure to ask Kate's father for her hand in marriage. As he puts the photograph of her that precipitated this reverie back on the shelf in his bedroom, Private Gar imagines a newspaper headline about the wedding, reciting in a weary fashion: "Mrs Doctor Francis King. September 8th. *In harvest sunshine*" (*BFP1* 44; my emphasis). Later, shortly before Gar recalls his aunt and uncle's visit to Ballybeg with Ben Burton, he again conflates their visit, Kate's wedding, and the harvest. "Reading" the wedding invitation aloud to himself from memory, Gar uses the memory of the arrival of Aunt Lizzy and her party to avoid thinking of Kate again: "They arrived in the afternoon; remember? A *beautiful quiet harvest day*, the sun shining, not a breath of wind; and you were on your best behavior" (60; my emphasis).

Harvests and potential or actual weddings are often conflated in Friel—as we will see in my discussions of *Faith Healer, Translations,* and *Dancing at Lughnasa*—as is the ancient reason for their enactment, fertility. The motif of fertility runs throughout *Philadelphia* and revolves around both the absence of children and their imminent presence. Gar himself is an only child, and his other aunts, all now dead except for Lizzy, were childless, which is much the same situation of the uncannily similar family of sisters in *Lughnasa* (both groups of sisters represent Friel's own mother and her sisters). But Kate's wedding promises to result in a large family—at least in Gar's mind—which he implicitly contrasts with the paucity of children that the five sisters had. Kate's potential fertility and Gar's own desire to have fourteen children at two points in the play was certainly consistent with fertility rates in Ireland during the 1960s.[36] Mary E. Daly has noted that in that decade, "the crude birthrate in both parts of Ireland was greater than in any other European country except Portugal." And examining fertility rates within marriage reveals an even more astonishing figure: "By 1959 the number of births per one thousand married women, aged 15–44, was more than twice as high in the Irish Republic as in England and Wales."[37] Ireland could afford such high birthrates because of its simultaneously high emigration rate. The play thus links Gar's pending departure (and his divorce from rural Irish culture) with the infertility of his mother's sisters and the projected metaphorical infertility of Gar's father after Gar leaves, casting these events in stark relief with Kate's presumably fertile marriage.

Philadelphia was first produced on September 28, 1964, some five months after Friel's short story "Everything Neat and Tidy" was published, and it shares that story's emphasis on movement as a terribly distracting and uncomfortable symptom of modernism and the central character's fear of literally crashing his means of locomotion.[38] Gar is constantly in motion, disconnected from the land, and constantly distracted—not just through his recourse to music and film but also through his desire to soon be literally in fast motion on an airplane. Friel's decision to split Gar into Private and Public Gars renders him a spectacular example of physical vacillation, which is only heightened by Private Gar's uneasy energy.

In his discussion of the change wrought in leisure time by industrialism, the American agrarian writer Donald Davidson makes several points startlingly relevant to Gar's division, particularly his articulation of how "the separation of our lives into two distinct parts, of which one is all labor—too often mechanical and deadening—and the other all play, undertaken as a nervous relief" makes our lives unharmonious.[39] Public Gar, of course, represents labor, while Private Gar represents play, and such a division—such a wall reared between work and leisure—harms both vocation and play, resulting in a profound dissonance. Davidson finally argues that "[w]e cannot separate our being into contradictory halves without a certain amount of spiritual damage."[40] Gar's division signifies his spiritual damage, which is, of course, compounded by his disconnection from the harvest and any remnant pagan practices inherent in rural culture that Friel would later depict in *Dancing at Lughnasa*. He is also disconnected from the Catholic Church, which, as we have seen, is represented with spectacular inefficacy by the Canon.

Gar's character thus symbolizes that of modern man in general, who conforms to and defers to what Weldon Thornton has termed our "matter-in-motion" worldview that we have inherited from the Enlightenment. The allegiance given to this worldview suggests a pervasive unease in modern man, as Thornton points out: "[T]he matter-in-motion worldview that modern Western culture implicitly defers to does not enable us to sustain or justify any conception of consciousness, to give any account of psyche, and so the typical modernist lives in constant unease and defensiveness about the reality of the very basis of his or her being."[41] The busyness of Gar O'Donnell and, as we will see later in my discussion of *Translations*, the similar busyness of characters such as Lancey and Yolland's father, characterizes modernism's trajectory toward acceleration in general, whereas the caution and introspection of characters like Hugh O'Neill in *Making History* or Yolland in *Translations* signify the playwright's privileging of a thoughtful cultural vacillation, coupled with a penetrating knowledge of different cultures. Gar's daily movements are characterized by literally always being in motion, an implicit reflection of the credence he gives to this modernist worldview.

Franklin L. Baumer has argued, citing W. R. Greg, an English author writing in 1875, that "[t]he most salient characteristic of life in this latter portion of the 19th century is its SPEED . . . and speed, though exciting, aborted leisure, which alone permitted men to reflect on the value and purpose of what they saw and did."[42] By the early 1960s, Irish life had also accelerated in little and large ways, and, as I have argued earlier in this chapter, was undergoing dramatic economic changes with the proposals led by T. K. Whitaker. Gar's own restlessness typifies this condition, but his desire to move even faster by adopting what he sees as exotic forms of locomotion promises further negative consequences. Gar's desire to return to the village "driving a Cadillac" (*BFP1* 78), also suggests how he will be wed not to Kate but to speed in his American future. Cars, like the Cadillac Gar longs to drive in his cinematic fantasy that he relays to Kate, have been, especially in America, symbols of rebellion, "represented as offering access to the chronotype of the 'open road,' and as promising the ascendancy of the individual."[43] Thus, Gar's vision of himself riding in a car while filming signifies his conviction that while he will be thoroughly a creature of motion by then, he can slow that motion down when necessary—surely a delusion—while maintaining and enhancing his individuality.

But Gar more often identifies himself with the speed of the airplane he will take to America, a telling characteristic of his immersion in modernity and longing for more acceleration. As Nicholas Daly has argued, the new railway system in Victorian Britain "stood as both agent and icon of the acceleration of the pace of daily life, annihilating an older experience of time and space, and making new demands on the sensorium of the traveler."[44] The following advent of jet travel, which began in Ireland by 1958, the same year as Whitaker's economic reforms were proposed, multiplied such acceleration and demands on an unprecedented scale. Gar has likely never traveled even by train, and thus the changes wrought in him as he proceeds from riding in the mail van—which he plans to catch to Strabane, County Tyrone, his last morning in Ireland—to flying will be nearly incalculable. Friel clearly wants to highlight and criticize the plane's ability to whisk us around the world and dislocate us in the process. Although Gar only imagines getting on the jet plane in the play, Friel concludes his 1975 screenplay of *Philadelphia* with a lingering shot of the plane sitting on the tarmac as Gar, played by the inimitable Donal McCann, hesitates at the top of the stairs before the plane's open door, which could symbolize a mouth, linking it to his aunt and uncle's future "devouring" of him.[45]

Gar's hesitation likely stems from his genuine love for Ballybeg despite the mixture of stultifying boredom, duplicity, and genuine community that he experiences there—perhaps epitomized by his long conversation with his friends Ned, Tom, and Joe. His friends talk about football and women and falsely portray themselves as great athletes and lovers in a valiant effort to avoid the truth of Gar's pending departure. Their frenetic talk thus disguises their own jealousy—voiced briefly by Joe early in this passage—that Gar is leaving Ballybeg and going to America (*BFP1* 70). After hearing their romanticized story of a night on the beach with two Dublin women, Private Gar quietly tells us the correct narrative, featuring their timidity toward the women and their utter boredom, which leads them to try to take the trousers off Jimmy Crerand, who defies them (73). Such false braggadocio is a common currency for male teenagers in any time or place, but the friends' actual affection for Gar is revealed toward the end of this scene when Ned takes off his leather belt with the large brass buckle on it and offers it shyly to Gar, ostensibly to protect himself from any "Yankees" that might attack him, but actually to demonstrate his friendship (75). Public Gar is moved but can only mutter a repeated "thanks" to his friend. Joe's final revelation that they came by the house because Madge promised them supper does not so much undercut the emotion that wells up in Gar here but increases it as he realizes she has asked them out of great love for him (76).

Gar finally longs for the literal acceleration promised by the airplane because of what he perceives as the slow pace of life in Ballybeg, at one point telling Kate after his tirade about how much he hates Ballybeg that "the sooner that old plane whips me away, the better I'll like it!" (*BFP1* 79). Indeed, the plane he will be on to America is mentioned a number of times in the play, signifying Gar's desire to be whisked away, caught up in an even greater acceleration. Twice, early in Episode One, Gar even projects himself using the plane as a way of showing his disdain for his old life in Ballybeg. In his first fantasy, this is how he sees himself:

> PRIVATE: Up in that big bugger of a jet, with its snout pointing straight for the States, and its tail belching smoke over Ireland; and you sitting up at the front (PUBLIC *acts this*) with your competent fingers poised over the controls; and then away down below in the Atlantic you see a bloody bugger of an Irish boat out fishing for bloody pollock and—
> (PUBLIC *nose-dives, engines screaming, machine guns stuttering.*)
> PUBLIC: Rat-tat-tat-tat-tat-tat-tat-tat-tat-tat. (*BFP1* 31)

This projection is prompted by Gar's recollection of just having salted some pollock for his father's shop and his distaste for the task. He seems to believe here that he will be in charge of his life—signified by his being at the controls of the plane—once he is airborne. Further, he hopes that the speed and motion of that life will effectively annihilate his connection to local Irish culture, which is tellingly represented by fishing, a poignant memory of which he will exhume late in the play in a desperate effort to connect to his father.

We cannot discount the intense pleasure that Gar's imagined and soon-to-be-actual immersion in speed offers him. In a qualified way, Friel himself has observed his attraction to the pace of life in New York City, noting, "The pace of life is exciting—for a time."[46] As Enda Duffy has suggested, "The new experience of speed as individual pleasure" ushered in by modernist locomotive devices, such as the car and airplane, created a need for an "adrenaline aesthetics [that] works to delineate a pleasure that is effected first on the body and its sensorium."[47] Substituting the pleasure generated by this "adrenaline aesthetics" helps Gar to defer the loss of the more traditional pleasures of friendship and family, particularly the relationship with Madge and his father, until nearly the end of the play. It is only when his father voices his fears of the velocity Gar's airplane will experience once in the air that Gar is jolted from his adrenaline aesthetics back into the slower pleasures of his former rural life, which he desperately tries to recapture by narrating the story of fishing with his father once upon a time.

If Gar is a metaphorical fighter pilot destroying his old culture and worldview in this scene, shortly afterward he portrays himself, equally unrealistically, as expectorating out of the plane's window onto his father and Madge and others in Ballybeg (*BFP1* 33). Note that this fantastic imagining of the airplane scales it down drastically in size and also slows it tremendously, allowing Gar to spit down on his townland in disgust. He has already moved from a desire for speed and destruction to a yearning for relative slowness that will allow him to vent his contempt, an analogous fantasy to that of his driving the Cadillac and one that is equally incredulous.

Most telling, though, for understanding Friel's use of the plane is a conversation that occurs late in the play when Gar's father S.B. mentions he has been listening to the weather forecast and that "it—it—it—it would be a fair enough day for going up in thon plane" (*BFP1* 94). S.B.'s stutter and use of a common Northern dialect word for "that" (*thon*) signifies his uneasiness with Gar's flight, which clearly symbolizes modernity to him. He then says, "And I was meaning to tell you that you should sit at the back. . . . So *he* [the Canon] was saying too . . . you know there—if there was an accident or anything—it's the front gets it hardest—" (ibid.). Friel's works often stage the metaphorical crashing of modernity into rural, remnant cultures in Ireland; the whole of *Philadelphia*, as I have argued here, depicts this figurative crash and its effects on Gar. But this late passage in the play also stages a fear of a literal crash—Gar's airplane falling out of the sky and slamming into the ground or, more likely, the ocean.[48] Such a fall connotes S.B.'s fear of an additional, literal acceleration and accompanying chaos, a telling figuration of late modernity. For Nicholas Daly, the crash between human flesh and steel images industrial modernity's meeting of humans and machines, as the pending crash of Johnny Barr's rapidly accelerating automobile at the end of Friel's short story, "Everything Neat and Tidy," signifies.[49]

Thus, perhaps S.B.'s only act of imagination in the play situates Gar on a continuum of the twentieth century's extreme change and acceleration, which Franklin Baumer terms the victory of "becoming" over "being."[50] After World War I and its assault on European innocence, cynicism crept into the European mind, but so did a rage for constant change, the "Time-mind," which Wyndham Lewis argued "focuses on the dynamic aspects of reality, forcing people into a 'trance of action,' hurrying them along, as the Futurists wanted them to do, at ever greater speeds, but without fixed goals, since reality was, on this view, a becoming, a history, an unending dialectical process."[51] Even though "the history of the psyche is that of incessant change,"[52] and despite the economic and other changes occurring in Gar's Ballybeg of the early 1960s, these latter changes signify a restrained openness toward modernity, a flux Friel privileges over and against the much faster, goalless simultaneity that Gar craves and late modernity promises. Friel's Gar occupies a situation somewhere between Lewis's "Time-mind" and our current computer-driven information culture, of which George Steiner said that it is "probably the most comprehensive and consequential since *Homo Sapiens*' development of language itself. There is, to put it in shorthand, a new locale for man after von Neumann or Turing."[53] I use "situation" rather than Steiner's "locale" because Gar's condition is really placeless, or about to become so.

However, as a sign that he recognizes how his life is accelerating, Gar, almost immediately after this exchange about the potential air crash, desperately tries to connect to his father and local rural culture through telling him the story about their fishing trip on the lake, a narrative that implicitly attempts to wipe out his earlier fantasy of shooting an Irish fishing boat from the plane he will soon ride. This story likely echoes a similar one articulated in Friel's 1972 autobiographical essay "Self-Portrait," in which he recalls a childhood memory of walking home from a fishing trip with his father in rural County Donegal, then realizes this "memory" actually never happened. Nevertheless, he says, "to me it is a truth. And because I acknowledge its peculiar veracity, it becomes a layer in my topsoil; it becomes part of me; ultimately it becomes me."[54] Much as the arboreal description of memory at the end of Friel's short story, "Among the Ruins," is cast in ecological terms, this memory is too.[55]

Gar has actually already told this story twice before this scene, but only in private because it is such an intimate memory. The first time he tells it occurs at the end of the rosary recitation in Episode Three, as Private Gar stands up and looks down at S.B., recalling in a long monologue that he had "put your jacket round my shoulders because there had been a shower of rain. . . . between us at the moment there was this great happiness, this great joy—you must have felt it too—although nothing was being said— . . . and young as I was I felt, I knew, that this was precious, . . . and then, then for no reason at all except that you were happy too, you began to sing" (BFP1 83). The song he recalls S.B. singing, "All Round My Hat," is a song of real emotion, love, and longing, unlike the more popular songs Gar has sung or danced to in the play. Tellingly, even though father and son do not speak for a long time during this remembered exchange, they still express their love to each other, unlike their present situation in which they speak tritely and cannot communicate their love.

The second time Gar relates the story, he employs a storytelling voice in an attempt to mesmerize himself and convince himself of the happiness of that memory, but the story is much shorter than its first iteration and ends in great anger, with Gar lamenting as he borrows and profanes a phrase from the rosary: "Have pity on us, he says; have goddam pity on every goddam bloody man jack of us" (BFP1 89). Private Gar, moved by the Mendelssohn music he is listening to, falls into reverie and recalls, "It says that once upon a time a boy and his father sat in a blue boat on a lake on an afternoon in May, and on that afternoon a great beauty happened, a beauty that has haunted the boy ever since, because he wonders now did it really take place or did he imagine it" (ibid.). He concludes by mourning, "There are only the two of us, he says; each of us is all the other has; and why can we not even look at each other?" (ibid.). He feels left out of the intimacy his father enjoys playing draughts with the Canon and narrates this story privately in a desperate attempt to rekindle a loving memory between them that is significantly agrarian in nature.

But when he tells it to his father a few pages later, he tries to disguise the urgency in his voice and drops the storytelling tone, even as he reveals the "great beauty" that occurred between them that day. He begins *"with pretended carelessness,"* by seeming to muse, "D'you know what kept coming into my mind the day?" Then he quickly says, "The fishing we used to do on Lough na Cloc Cor" (*BFP1* 94). It takes S.B. several moments, but after additional prompting by Gar that cannot elicit the memory from him, Gar exclaims, "It doesn't matter who owned it [the blue boat]. It doesn't even matter that it was blue. But d'you remember one afternoon in May—we were up there—the two of us—and it must have rained because you put your jacket round my shoulders and gave me your hat—" (95). This memory, crucially set in spring, ripples with potential for Gar and his father's relationship, unlike the significant, immediately past events of the play set during harvest—Kate's wedding and the visit by Gar's aunt and uncle. Public Gar goes on to remark that "we—that you were happy. D'you remember? D'you remember?" But S.B. fails to do so, crushing Gar's hope for a final connection with his father and finally leaving him to rush into the shop away from his father, who in turn fumbles to recall the color of the boat and the specific song he is alleged to have sung, completely missing out on the point of the memory: a father's loving protection of his son.

As Declan Kiberd has argued, Gar's inability to recognize his father's hidden emotional depths constitutes a significant failure of imagination on his part:

> What makes Gar's plight tragic is not so much this inarticulacy as
> his failure to allow for a similar emotional complexity in his father,
> a failure to realize in full the hidden, undiscovered private self of
> his father, and that all the words uttered by Private on Gar's behalf
> might just as easily have been uttered on behalf of the father.[56]

Surely S.B. too has had longings for years, and as the scene proceeds,
a major example of these longings appears, one that intertwines his
silent love for Gar with his past dream that his son would take over
the shop for him one day.

When Gar has left, S.B. recounts his powerful memory of Gar,
which also occurred when Gar was 10 years old, a critical point of
agreement between their stories. When Gar was 10, he clearly loved
his father and was loved by him in communicable ways, unlike now
when each loves the other but is mired in silence and repression.
Interestingly, however, S.B.'s memory is not agrarian, but bourgeois, having to do with Gar's desire to stay home from school
and work in his father's shop: "D'you mind the trouble we had
keeping him at school just after he turned ten. D'you mind nothing
would do him but he'd get behind the counter. And he had this wee
sailor suit on him this morning—" (*BFP1* 96). Even though Madge
swears Gar never had a sailor suit, much as S.B. is convinced when
talking to Gar previously that they never went out in a blue boat
together, the truth of the memory, the happiness between them,
remains for S.B., as it does for Gar in the story he has just told his
father: "[A]nd this wee sailor suit as smart looking on him, and—
and—and at the heel of the hunt I had to go with him myself, the
two of us, hand in hand, as happy as larks—we were that happy,
Madge—and him dancing and chatting beside me—mind?—you
couldn't get a word in edge-ways with all the chatting he used to go
through . . ." (97). Only the reader or audience member can connect
the central truth of these two memories encapsulating their past
happiness together that S.B. and Gar share despite their inability to
communicate with each other.

Friel imagined his breakthrough play in terms of a V, signifying how the manic energies of Private Gar in the opening and middle scenes of the play gradually taper to great loneliness. He wrote the following description of this diminishing action inside of a large V in his early draft notes for the play: "His extravagance, exuberance, ebullience will taper down to painful watchfulness as the night goes on. He can't fight their apparent calm poverty. Who really cares for him but his father[?]."[57] We could certainly add the surrogate mother-figure Madge to this short list of those who truly care for Gar. But partly because of his father's and even Madge's inability to vocalize their affection for him, Gar will leave. Their "apparent calm poverty" also likely signifies their lack of a deeper spiritual existence that Gar finds missing in the Canon.

Despite the great irony of S.B. vocalizing his affection for his son only when Gar has left the room, the play seems to end more happily in terms of a memory that can be accurately preserved and repeatedly rewound mentally, with Gar watching Madge shuffle off to bed and "filming" this scene in his mind. Private Gar gazes rapturously at his real mother figure, the woman who has helped raise him along with S.B., and says, "Watch her carefully, every movement, every gesture, every little peculiarity: keep the camera whirring; for this is a film you'll run over and over again—Madge Going to Bed On My Last Night at Home . . . Madge . . ." (*BFP1* 99). Although this imagined movie scene promises real accuracy and intimacy for Gar in the future, there are significant problems with his visual outlook here that contrast the ironic, but more positive happiness implicit in the "truth of fiction" that Friel stages in Gar's earlier oral stories about fishing with his father and S.B.'s story of Gar in the shop and then walking with him to school afterward.

First, Gar has essentially become an emigrant in this final scene and fallen prey to the peculiarities of memory common to the Irish abroad. Seamus Deane has commented on the position of Irish exiles and the way in which they are "always, in their conception of the land they left, archaic; they have not participated in and are frequently ill

informed about the changes that have taken place in their absence."[58]
We have already witnessed this kind of archaic memory in the returned
exile Aunt Lizzy earlier in the play. Lizzy is understandably out of
touch with life in Ballybeg and does not even know the identity of
Senator Doogan, Kate's father (*BFP1* 62). A few moments earlier, she
wonders if the chapel where her sister, Gar's mother, got married is
still standing, again showing she has lost most of her local knowledge
of the village and has not kept up with news or gossip (61). As Deane
remarks further, such exiles are "more susceptible to stereotypic representations of their culture, because the stereotype is the most effective and affixing form of memory and delusion."[59] Lizzy Sweeney is
a walking, talking stereotype of the Irish emigrant and models such
behavior to Gar, who, although he dislikes her brashness and crudity,
believes she leads an exciting life in America. Moreover, as Anthony
Roche points out, Gar is torn "between two surrogate mothers: the
Madge of Ballybeg and the Lizzy/Elise of Philadelphia."[60] The seemingly more exciting mother, Lizzy/Elise, wins Gar because of her
willingness to evidence her "love" for Gar with the smorgasbord of
material things she will give him once in the big city. The irony here
is that by leaving an Ireland on the brink of experiencing both a new
and dynamic economy and relationship to modernity, Gar will render
himself archaic, trapped in a frozen, stereotypical image of Ireland,
in contrast to his actual country that will be greatly changed by the
time he returns from Philadelphia.

Gar's "filming" this last scene in his mind suggests another
problem with memory preservation created by even a simulation of
machine perception. Reading this moment in the context of other
filmic flashbacks by Gar earlier in the play, Roche has argued that

> [t]he film metaphor here is explicitly to *silent* movies as the final
> textualized element of *Philadelphia, Here I Come!* indicates: the
> card which interrupts the action in silent film and Brechtian drama
> to draw attention in the latter case to the *process* of what is being
> enacted. The psyche is being technologized here as in *Krapp's
> Last Tape*."[61]

As much of this chapter has tried to show, however, Gar's psyche has long been "technologized" by his immersion in mediascapes, particularly cinema. This final moment actually marks a disturbing apotheosis for Gar's filmic perception because even though he clearly recognizes and remarks upon his "filming" of this scene, he actually believes that the emotion of this memory will be more powerful than the emotions of the "memory" he had of fishing with his father and that he powerfully, though haltingly, expressed through something resembling traditional Irish storytelling, in which words and cadences enchant the audience and make them attentive. Gar is a diminished *seanchaí*, or Irish storyteller, though with a limited audience and inability to enchant anyone, even himself, with his narrative abilities.

Furthermore, Gar's refusal now to preserve memory in this traditional way and his acceptance of "filming" memories signifies his immersion in late modernity and adoption of a more mechanical mode of visual perception, which promises more accuracy than oral storytelling but is bound to destroy this memory's sacral uniqueness. As Benjamin reminds us, "for the first time in world history, mechanical reproduction emancipates the work of art from its parasitical dependence on ritual."[62] Although Gar himself is "filming" Madge's nightly ritual, he has decisively rejected the basis of Friel's drama in ritual and embraced mechanical culture. Every time he "replays" this memory in America, the "copies" he trots out will destroy the uniqueness of the subject and actually effect a distance, not an intimacy, from his emplaced Irish culture. Gar has moved sufficiently far away from his Irish agrarian culture to embrace a stereotype of American, urban culture, which in turn promises to make him look back, not so much in anger now, although this can be a very angry play, but in bewilderment and nostalgia at a local culture from which he has effectively exiled himself. Kevin Whelan, writing on post-Famine culture in Ireland, distinguishes between "two modes of memory: an individualist, self-obsessed, disabling one, which internalizes damage as melancholia, and a culturally induced enabling form, which seeks wider explanations and political strategies."[63] Gar O'Donnell's final "film" of *Philadelphia, Here I Come!* suggests his self-obsession will continually disable him in his American future and render him a permanent melancholic, a condition that ironizes the hope of the play's title, and one that exiles him from a modernizing Ireland in the late 1950s as it began to escape its endemic poverty and the iron grip of the Catholic Church.

3

Interchapter
Why Friel Left Short Fiction for Drama

In 1965, Irish playwright Brian Friel emphatically told Graham Morrison, "I don't concentrate on the theatre at all. I live on short stories. [P]lay-writing . . . began as a self-indulgence and then eventually I got caught up more and more in it. But the short story is the basis of all the work I do."[1] By 1968, however, Friel had virtually stopped writing stories. Until now, no critic has sufficiently explained why Friel moved from writing short fiction and drama to solely writing drama by the end of the 1960s, although one critic, citing Friel's statement about playwriting as "self-indulgence," has recently wrongly argued that Faber and Faber's inability to secure publishing rights to Friel's short fiction and its publication instead by smaller firms in the 1960s and 1970s "may have altered not only the Irish 'canon,' but even the actual generic choices of a writer."[2] The more accepted narrative that has gradually emerged in criticism of Friel's work, however, suggests that he not only found the formulaic requirements for short fiction in the *New Yorker*, which published many of his stories, stifling but also realized that his short fiction was too imitative of that written by the two Irish masters of the form at the time, Sean O'Faolain and Frank O'Connor.[3] But there are several other equally important

This interchapter includes material reprinted from "Brian Friel's Transformation from Short Fiction Writer to Dramatist," *Comparative Drama* 46, no. 4 (2012): 451–74.

reasons for Friel's gradual commitment to drama and rejection of short fiction. They include his experimentation with other genres such as radio drama and journalism, which may have helped him realize that he was better suited for a more fluid, experimental genre than short fiction, and perception—expressed in his major essays on theater—that only drama, with its ability to enchant audiences, would allow him to depict his consistent theme of flux while also appealing to a potential community within the theater. Finally, Friel's interest in politics almost ineluctably kept him in the dramatic arena as the conflict in Northern Ireland lengthened and deepened through the 1970s and 1980s.

For a time, he seems to have wondered if radio drama would be the subgenre most suited to his desire to create community through exploring the intellectual, social, spiritual, geographic, and political milieu of his region of Northern Ireland. As I have argued elsewhere, Nobel Laureate Seamus Heaney, also raised in the North like Friel, used the platform of BBC Northern Ireland to "create sonically an imagined regional community of the sort described by Benedict Anderson [in *Imagined Communities*], a new province, where the contributions of both Catholics and Protestants would be honoured."[4] While more reticent about his aim in this regard than Heaney was, Friel was nonetheless long interested in drawing together disparate members of the community in Northern Ireland. He realized early in his career that radio exercised a special hold on the minds of the Irish and had the sort of mesmerizing effect he would later base his ritualized theory of theater upon, a theory meta-dramatically explored in his masterpiece, *Faith Healer*. Heaney recalled the intensity with which he and his family members listened to the radio in the 1940s and 1950s: "If an angel had passed or a mighty wind had arisen or tongues of flames descended, the occasion could not have been more prepared for or more expectant."[5] Even when television became more popular in the 1960s, Rex Cathcart has shown that Northern Irish audiences "remained loyal to the older medium" in part because "television long lacked any significant local component whereas radio continued to supply a regional service."[6]

Friel may have been drawn to radio drama additionally by what Dermot Rattigan terms its "'sightlessness,' the basis of its unique appeal, which promotes an imaginative visualization on the part of its listeners."[7] Moreover, because of his interest in the incantatory qualities of theater through vocal power in many of his plays, Friel probably also discerned how this technology, as Rattigan argues, "could be classified as a technological genre of oral literature."[8] And although "the storyteller (or sound drama) is physically absent from the listener's presence, . . . [he] is curiously present in the listener's imagination."[9] But I believe that Friel finally realized that radio drama's so-called sightlessness inhibited community from developing during the performance of a play among its audience members, who of course cannot see or hear each other and their reactions to the play. Moreover, the persistent reception in Britain and Ireland of radio drama as "relief and entertainment," lighter fare than the preceding and succeeding newscasts or serious political analysis, likely also led Friel away from the subgenre toward the stage, which he felt was better suited for his serious dramas of environment.[10] And yet he believed that because there was no real "theatrical tradition" in Ireland, as he told Eavan Boland in 1973, "we don't know whether we should attend theatre, or go and be entertained by it, or go as a kind of package tour to it."[11] As we will see, Friel had no illusions about stage drama and in fact was rather biased against it, even as he moved toward fully becoming a stage playwright.

Friel's interest in radio drama was also part of an outgrowth of his facility with short stories, with both the attendant benefits and drawbacks that each of those mediums has for effecting community and creating a sense of place. Richard Pine believes that for Friel, "Radio drama offered a method of developing the technique of the short story by voicing its various personalities and making explicit the main preoccupations."[12] But Pine quickly argues that in one of Friel's two 1958 radio plays, *To This Hard House*, he displays a "stilted language and rhythm of speech . . . [that] indicate that . . . he could not confidently convey all the short-story narrator's sense either of the personality of place or of the observations permitted to the narrator himself."[13] Further, both this play and Friel's other radio play from 1958, *A Sort of Freedom*, "have relatively weak closures because the author had so far failed to adapt the literary closure of the story into a dramatic conclusion."[14] More recently, while admitting Friel's weaknesses in staging action in these early radio plays, Scott Boltwood has argued for a rereading of them in the context not of Friel's later drama but in the realistic if somewhat formulaic context of the Ulster theater tradition that dealt generally with either rural privations or the vagaries of urban working-class life.[15] As Friel became more innovative in his mature drama, beginning with 1964's *Philadelphia, Here I Come!*, he must have realized that breaking away from writing dramas to be broadcast on BBC Northern Ireland Radio would enable him to experiment formally for the stage.

Friel was also beginning to realize how the essential privacy of radio listening worked against both the portrayal of the organic communities that were the constant subjects of his work and his attempts to form community among his audience members and between audience members and actors. Even though Rattigan argues that radio "alone has the unique ability to communicate directly with each individual while broadcasting to *all* listeners," he nonetheless includes a damning quotation from Donald McWhinnie, a BBC radio drama producer in 1959, during the time in which Friel was writing radio dramas: "radio at its best is a private experience."[16] Anticipating Rattigan's claim for radio drama's simultaneous private and public appeal, Ulf Dantanus has suggested in his discussion of Friel's radio dramas that "while speaking to large numbers of anonymous listeners you can still remain intimately confidential with one individual, making the traffic seem to function from one source, the writer, to one recipient, the listener. The role performed by the listener is much closer to that of the reader, and there is a sense in which 'writing for radio is much closer to writing for the printed page than it is to writing for television or the theatre.'"[17] After analyzing Friel's radio plays *A Sort of Freedom*, *To This Hard House*, *A Doubtful Paradise*, *The Blind Mice* (first performed as a stage play), *The Founder Members*, *The Loves of Cass McGuire* (later performed as a stage play), and the television play *Three Fathers, Three Sons,* however, Dantanus rightly concludes that the subgenre of the radio play finally was discarded by Friel in part because on the radio, "the ability to create the atmosphere and mood of a place are . . . curtailed" and for Friel, "it would never be enough to create an 'illusion' or 'impression' of place" because "a securely rooted locale is one of the corner-stones of Friel's work."[18] Dantanus adds that like Chekhov, whose plays also would not work on the radio, Friel's interest in "the intricate emotional relationships between characters," along with "an overall ironic and even tragic attitude to life" are inhibited by the medium of radio.[19] The salient features of Friel's stage plays—a specific sense of fluctuating place and community—could be hurt by the radio medium but enhanced by their performance onstage. And yet, as Kelly Matthews has shown in her examination of BBC Belfast drama producer Ronald Mason's influence on Friel, "In their economy of language, structural integrity, pacing, and distinct characterization, Friel's later works for the stage display the best attributes of successful radio drama."[20]

Although he left radio drama, Friel continued to experiment in other genres, turning next to journalism. George O'Brien speculates that Friel's *Irish Press* columns from April 1962 to August 1963 represent "the beginning of the end of Friel the short-story writer."[21] O'Brien calls them "trial pieces" in which Friel "improved his command of his methods and his material," and more important for our purposes here, he argues that they "culminated in his recognition and acceptance of the theatre as the form most suited to his expressive needs, a form as far removed from these 'I'-driven articles as possible."[22] Boltwood, who devotes a long opening chapter of his book on Friel to the *Irish Press* essays, argues that in contrast to his later essays, this substantial body of work (there are fifty-nine columns) "reveal[s] a more reckless and unguarded writer."[23] Boltwood perceives the columns as "fictions with their own literary strategies" that reveal a more complex Friel "than suggested by the sum of his canonical prose work."[24] According to Boltwood, Friel largely plays down the importance of his well-known "apprenticeship" with Tyrone

Guthrie in Minnesota at this time and also points out that "he stops writing entirely for six of the next seven weeks" for the first time during his sixteenth months of writing the columns, finally writing only more column after his return to Ireland.[25] Boltwood concludes his masterful analysis of fifteen of these columns by arguing that the columns reflect the alienation and dislocation Friel experienced in America as an outsider, but in the last column written in America, structured as a brief play entitled "The Phone Call," "we witness the emergence of a dramatist who is confident and ready to abandon this weekly distraction from his artistic pursuits. . . . Thus, Friel may have ended his partnership with *The Irish Press* to preserve and exploit the artistic developments suggested by 'The Phone Call.'"[26] Friel also likely tired of the formal compression of the newspaper column and desired to work in a more expansive medium that called upon the reader's imagination to engage more fully with his words.

Fintan O'Toole has argued that Friel's "decision to stop writing prose and start writing plays reflected, surely, a much wider loss of faith in the traditional narrative" common in Europe after the horrors of World War Two, the Holocaust, and the atomic bomb in which "narrative itself came to be seen as, at best inadequate, at worst a lie. Theatre . . . offered the hope of restoring some authority to the act of telling stories."[27] But O'Toole misses the point of both Friel's short fiction and his drama concerning fictive authority: Friel is very well aware, of course, that narrative can lie and often does. Yet he consistently privileges the authority of the imagination through narrative often colored through memory or imagined memory. There are many examples of such fictional "truth" in Friel; perhaps the best known one concerns the way in which Friel privileges the fictional elements he imbued *Translations* with instead of depending slavishly on actual history.

So the question of the authority of fiction, broadly speaking, is a red herring in understanding Friel's work and not dependent on a particular genre, as O'Toole wrongly suggests. A real reason Friel moved into drama exclusively is that he found it more amenable to experimentation than the particular vein of the Irish short story that he had been writing in. In his discussion of the arts in general in his 1967 lecture, "The Theatre of Hope and Despair," he speaks of the arts' ability to settle into a pattern, articulate their message, then reject the audience they have won and move on:

> Once they realize that they have been so long in one site that they have come to be looked on as a distinct movement . . . they take fright, attack . . . the apparent permanence . . . that they themselves have created, reject the offer of hospitality, and move to a new location.[28]

Note the continued recourse Friel has to metaphors of place here that he employs to privilege flux and reject permanence, the latter of which he always hesitates to endorse, whether it refers to place or to the nature of art.

Most important, Friel's growing desire to write about community and to connect to a wider community through his work is crucial to understanding why he moved into drama full-time. In this regard, D. E. S. Maxwell, author of the first full-length study of Friel, wrongly suggests (without offering any proof) that "both his short stories and his plays supply the creative premises where writer and audience collaborate."[29] And Seamus Deane, who has otherwise written well and thoughtfully on Friel's short fiction, likewise misperceives Friel's relationship to audience in his short fiction. Deane argues that the short story, more than any other genre, "acknowledges and even exploits the existence of an audience."[30] Citing Walter Benjamin on the Russian writer Leskov, Deane suggests that the folktale and the short story, despite their many differences, "at least share the conviction that the audience and the teller have a common cultural identity," noting further that

> in Ireland, this is intensified by the further appeal to a regional familiarity, recognizable in Joyce's evocation of Dublin, O'Connor's of Cork, and Friel's of Donegal-Derry. The tone subsequently produced has a great charm for the reader, since it allows him entry

to the story on the ground of an assumed common knowledge and experience. Such a tone defines the distance between writer and reader by the pretence of abolishing it.[31]

And yet Friel noted in 1965 about the short story that "you can delude yourself that the people who read it think exactly as you think and are highly appreciative. It never occurs to you that it's being read by people in dentists' waiting rooms or waiting for a train."[32] Because many of Friel's short stories were first published in the *New Yorker*, his immediate audience for those stories was Manhattan urbanite readers who were attuned to different cultural antennae than his readers in more rural Ireland would have been. Thus, his statement here and others elsewhere explicitly contradict Deane's position that short fiction enacts a communal experience between reader and audience.

Even given his interest in appealing to Irish rural audiences, Friel realized that short fiction was inherently anticommunal. Because of his great respect for and appreciation of Frank O'Connor cited above, Friel likely knew and approved of O'Connor's claim in *The Lonely Voice* that because of the typical short story's focus on marginalized characters, "there is in the short story at its most characteristic something we do not often find in the novel—an intense awareness of human loneliness. . . . The short story remains by its very nature remote from the community—romantic, individualistic, and intransigent."[33] He thus realized by the mid-1960s that his interest in finding and creating community had to find a more appropriate genre than the essentially private genre of the short story.[34] As one of the best commentators on his short stories, Elmer Andrews, has argued, Friel's move from short story to drama "might be seen as a move from what O'Faolain characterizes as one of the most personal and private of literary forms . . . to what we might regard as one of the most objective and public."[35]

Boltwood terms Friel's five essays published between 1964 and 1984 as characterized by a "circumspect auteur," in contrast to the more daring writer he believes emerges in the *Irish Press* columns,[36] but unfortunately, he does not engage with these essays, which contain provocative, seminal statements by Friel on the role of the playwright. Relatively little attention has been paid to how these essays and interviews from the 1960s and 1970s illuminate Friel's growing attraction to drama, despite his seeming aversion to it. One critic who has dealt with these essays, however, dismisses them as unhelpful for understanding Friel's drama beginning in the 1970s. F. C. McGrath wrongly argues that Friel's assertion in "The Theatre of Hope and Despair" reflects "unexamined formalist assumptions that were commonplace in the 1950s and 1960s . . . [and] can account for plays like *The Loves of Cass McGuire* or *Philadelphia, Here I Come!*, but they are of limited use when applied to a play like *The Freedom of the City*."[37] McGrath mischaracterizes these essays as formalist when they actually advocate a revolutionary stance on the part of the dramatist, as we shall see.

Friel's comments on the advantages and disadvantages of the short story versus the drama in interviews from the 1960s and early 1970s seem to reveal a gradual evolution in his attitude toward the two genres. Throughout the essays and the interviews I discuss here, he adamantly claims to be more interested in the short story, defending it as a higher art form than the more "vulgar" theater. Interestingly and hilariously, one of his exemplars in the short story genre, Frank O'Connor, in his review of Friel's breakthrough play, *Philadelphia, Here I Come!*, "lamented the fact that Friel—the writer of delicate, Chekhovian short stories—had fallen among the vulgarians of the theatre."[38] But as the 1960s proceed and Friel spends more and more time attacking the theater and discussing how to reach a dramatic audience, he evinces more of an interest in drama and in developing his dramatic theories, even gaining more respect for the audience, whom he at first terms a "mob," then later a mob that "is more receptive to intellectual concepts."[39] Friel's long-standing interest in manipulating the collective mind of the theater audience is a perfect theoretical correlative to the weight he places on the heterogeneous community as subject of his drama.[40] What better genre could there be to communicate his ideal of community?

Actually, Friel seems to have made the decision to become a dramatist by around 1960, the year, as he notes in his "Self-Portrait," that he left teaching: "By then I had had some pale success with short stories and radio plays. . . . And it was about that time that I had to make a decision."[41] He goes on to discuss how many future playwrights were immersed in the theater from an early age. And he then recalls that he suddenly found himself at age thirty "embarked on a theatrical career and almost totally ignorant of the mechanics of play-writing and play-production apart from an intuitive knowledge."[42] Because of this ignorance of what seems to be his chosen craft by 1960, he notes that he then went to his now-famous "apprenticeship" with Tyrone Guthrie in Minnesota by 1963.

Several statements here are worth our attention in attempting to understand why Friel became a playwright and stopped writing short stories. The first is that he really believes in retrospect that he had decided to become a playwright—despite his continued writing of short stories—by 1960, and certainly by 1963, when his interest in drama and conviction of his necessity for immersing himself in that genre led him and his family to the Guthrie Theater in America. This decision should make us realize that in the interviews that followed over the succeeding years, Friel is posturing to a certain degree about his lack of interest in the theater; perhaps he was so devoted to the theater even then that he was afraid of being mocked for his earnestness—hence the aspersions he casts on the genre and especially on theatrical audiences. He also uses these interviews and autobiographical pieces to sound and develop his own theories about drama to determine whether his calling had sufficient integrity for him to fully devote himself to it.

Second, Friel's interest in the theater was sufficiently seriously confirmed by his time at the Guthrie that he subsequently likened his calling as a dramatist to a "theoretical priesthood," a fascinating statement given his horrified remembrance of his own training for the priesthood in the late 1940s at St. Patrick's College, Maynooth, for two and a half years, which he finally left without taking orders.[43] Friel never lost his sense of vocational calling for the theater in which he sees himself as a sort of an aesthetic priest devoted to unveiling mysteries and power beyond his full ken. He sees himself not as Joyce saw himself in writing his *Dubliners* in the early 1900s—as an aesthetic priest transmuting the bread of everyday life for his audience to feed upon—but as a humble acolyte to private mysteries that he then publicly transmits through words, actions, and music to audiences that he desperately wants to transform into a community, even a temporary one lasting for the duration of one performance of one play.

In "The Giant of Monaghan," an uncollected but revealing account from 1964 about his time spent observing Guthrie, Friel makes clear that he aspires to the sort of unity between playwright and actors made possible through the dramatist's inspiration. He suggests that because of Guthrie's "infectious excitement" in such times of inspiration,

> director and cast worked in such intimate communication, so intensely, so vibrantly, so fluidly, that the distinction between director and directed seemed to disappear; they were in perfect unison, conductor and orchestra, inspiring and complementing each, informing and being informed, so that the scene suddenly matured in meaning and significance and beauty, and there was captured a realization of something much deeper and more satisfying than the conscious mind of the author had ever known.[44]

Anthony Roche has argued that this passage is echoed in the concluding speech by Michael in *Dancing at Lughnasa* that privileges movement over language "as if this ritual, this wordless ceremony, was now the way to speak, to whisper private and sacred things, to be in touch with some otherness" (*BFP2* 107–8).[45] Roche suggests that "ritual" is "the word that best describes the way both men came to view the nature of theatre, and which is briefly evoked by Friel's comment that what he witnessed at the Guthrie was a 'theoretical priesthood.'"[46]

At this point in his burgeoning career as a playwright, Friel thus realized that only the incantatory power of the dramatist best expressed by the ritual at the heart of drama could potentially unite disparate audience members into a temporarily coherent whole— something that the distant author of short fiction could never do with his reading audience scattered as they are across time and place. In a seminal essay on Friel, Seamus Deane has identified this process as the way in which Friel transforms the stage "into a 'magic circle,' a place into which the audience is being given a privileged insight."[47]

But typically for Friel, who often undercuts the perceived seriousness of one attitude with another that parodies that stance, he satirizes himself and other dramatists in much more demeaning religious language than he uses in "The Giant of Monaghan" and "Self-Portrait." For example, in "The Theatre of Hope and Despair," he terms the playwright "a propagandist" who is "fired by a messianic zeal."[48] Does Friel really believe that the dramatist is a propagandist/ preacher? Yes and no. His is not the raucous voice of the carnival barker or tent evangelist. But he quietly and insistently claims that when dramatists depict in "mean, gruesome detail only one portion of our existence . . . , they are crying out for recognition of the existence of something less ignoble, something more worthy. They are asking us to recognize that even in confusion and disillusion, strength and courage can exist, and that out of them can come a redemption of the human spirit."[49] Such a spiritual aim would seem to sit uneasily with Friel's early conception of the audience as mob, but his drama works steadily toward a spiritual aesthetic based on the ritualistic origins of theater in pagan ceremonies that is meant to involve audience participation in an amorphous but nonetheless real way. As we will see later in this study, two highlights of Friel's spiritual theater are *Faith Healer* and *Dancing at Lughnasa*.

In his 1965 interview with Graham Morrison, Friel points out the difference in audience for the short fiction writer versus the playwright in terms of a public audience who responds in terms of emotion, not intellect: "The theatre is altogether so different from a short story anyhow. You get a group of people sitting in an audience and . . . they are a corporate group who act in the same way a mob reacts—emotionally and spontaneously. . . . The end purpose is to move them, and you will move them, in a theatre, anyhow, not through their head but through their heart."[50] Crucially, although he likens them to a mob, Friel already perceives the audience as "a corporate group," not the series of individuals who silently read short stories.

Two years after the Morrison interview, in "The Theatre of Hope and Despair," Friel again lambasts the theater even as he crucially stresses its communal aspect. After rejecting the technique of the short story writer or novelist, who conduct private and personal conversations with their readers, he claims,

> But the dramatist functions through the group; not a personal conversation but a public address. His technique is [that] . . . of the preacher and the politician. . . . If he cannot get the attention of that collective mind, hold it, persuade it, mesmerize it, manipulate it, he has lost everything.[51]

I cite this passage at such length because it remains one of Friel's fullest articulations of his intent as a dramatist. He understood early in his career that drama, out of all the genres, is the most communal and thus that it was most suited for portraying his plays about local, organic communities because through it, he could most clearly communicate his ideas to the greatest number of people. He says as much in his 1970 interview with Desmond Rushe when he states, "A lot of modern music is like a lot of modern poetry—it has become intensely personal, and communication is diminished by this. A lot of these men aren't communicating with us anymore."[52] Joe Dowling, who has directed a number of Friel's plays, confirms Friel's interest in clear communication with his audience, noting that "while many lesser writers make obfuscation a virtue and confuse their audiences with contradictory signals, Friel is always clear in both meaning and form. He writes to communicate with the audience rather than alienating them and holding them at bay."[53]

By the time of his interview with Rushe, in response to his question, "You have gone over completely from the short story to playwriting?," Friel readily responds, "I keep seeing close relationships between them, but I hope I haven't left short-story writing. It's a form I like very well. It's not as vulgar a form as the theatre, which is really a vulgar form of communication."[54] But later within this very interview, Friel argues that audiences are not going to the theater "any longer simply for entertainment. They want to be engaged mentally, and if the dramatist does this, he is succeeding. The theatre is becoming more and more an intellectual exercise."[55] When Rushe immediately asks him, "Is the audience becoming more intellectual, then?," Friel muses, in an explicit qualification of his statement about the theater audience as a mob in the Morrison interview five years earlier, "Mass intellect is a very different thing to individual intellect. The group of people we call an audience is something like a mob, and they're incapable of individual thought. But at the same time this mob has a different kind of attitude to the one they had twenty or thirty years ago. They are more receptive to intellectual concepts."[56] Of course, any active theater audience engages in a series of complex acts. As Susan Bennett has articulated in her pioneering book, *Theatre Audiences: A Theory of Production and Reception*, an audience is constantly interpreting what is occurring before their eyes: "the audience inevitably proceeds through the construction of hypotheses about the fictional world which are subsequently substantiated, revised, or negated."[57] This complex process may be more complicated and rapid in the context of productions of major Friel plays beginning with *Philadelphia, Here I Come!*, since such plays constantly seek innovation, unlike the stock Ulster theater of realism or light comedy out of which Friel's early work emerged.

And yet even if Friel believed by 1970 that audiences "were more receptive to intellectual concepts," they were likely not conscious of this attitude. Dennis Kennedy, arguing against Herbert Blau's contention that "what is universal in performance is the consciousness of performance," holds more simply and compellingly that "it is the living presence of the spectators that most matters and provides commonality to the event. . . . They become an audience by virtue of their cooperative attendance, nothing more."[58] Friel stakes everything on this living presence, and even though he is conservative in his attitude toward most directors, whom he feels usually do violence to the script,[59] he nonetheless implicitly believes in the mutual exchange between live actors and live audiences that transforms his drama into living art.

A mob, of course, is united in its violent attitude, rendered at least briefly homogeneous in this way; but Friel always seeks to portray heterogeneous communities onstage that gradually grow more different and strange before our eyes. In the process, he seeks to enchant diverse audiences and readers into a community that preserves their differences but unites them through his subtle deployments of rhetoric and imagery. Director Tim Etchells has articulated the paradoxical unity of theater audiences that is shot through with both individuality and provisionality:

> Watching the best theatre and performance we are together and alone. Together in the sense that we're aware of the temporary and shifting bonds that link us both to the stage and to our fellow watchers, plugged into the group around and in front of us, the communal situation, sensing the laughter, attentiveness, tension or unease that grip us collectively. . . . Sat watching we spread-out, osmose, make connections. But at the same time, even as we do so, we feel our separateness, our difference from those around us, from those on-stage. Even as we shift and flow within the group, we're aware that our place in its emerging consensus, its temporary community, is partial and provisional—that in any case the group itself—there in the theatre, as elsewhere, in our cities and streets, in the relations between nations, peoples and states—is always as much a fraught and necessary question, a longing and a problem, as it is any kind of certainty.[60]

Friel repeatedly privileges this conception of audience in his drama, for in play after play, there is a moment of connection onstage between disparate characters that is meant to unite the audience as well; shortly thereafter, that unity dissipates and the actors separate, as will the temporary community of the audience after the conclusion of the play.[61]

As longtime theater practitioner Blau has argued, the audience "is not so much a mere congregation of people as a body of thought and desire. It does not exist before the play but is initiated or precipitated by it; it is not an entity to begin with but a consciousness constructed. The audience is what happens when, performing the signs and passwords of a play, something postulates itself and unfolds in response."[62] Richard Barr argues in assessing this remarkable insight that "the audience is thus at once creative in and created by performance relations."[63] Appropriately for a playwright who has dedicated his career to depicting communities in flux onstage, Friel long ago realized the fluid and shifting nature of audience consciousness and how a dramatic performance initiates that embryonic community. When he notes that an actor "sees himself penetrating that character and being suffused by it . . . so that what will finally emerge will be neither quite what the author wrote, nor what the actor is, but a new identity that draws from the essences of both," he affirms the mediating, dynamic role of the actor and by extrapolation, the role of the audience in assessing a play.[64]

In the early 1970s, Friel was still pondering audience engagement and seemed at first to be veering back toward an endorsement of privileging emotional appeals over intellectual ones in "Plays Peasant and Unpeasant." For example, he seemingly approves of the riots in the early Abbey Theatre in Dublin when he observes, "But it must be admitted that theatre riots are not what they were in Synge's or O'Casey's early days when actors had to have police protection. . . . Admittedly, there are subtler methods of expressing strong disagreement than spitting on your author and hurling chairs at your players. . . . But the robust technique was at least indication of a rude involvement, and was certainly the most convenient and most natural weapon for a peasant society."[65] He argues later in the essay, however, in an important statement that captures the trajectory of his own attitude toward audience and indeed toward his own plays, that "what the future of Irish drama will be must depend on the slow process of development of the Irish mind, and it will shape and be shaped by political events."[66] Later essays and interviews correspondingly show Friel becoming slowly, even grudgingly to accept that the Irish mind in the theater audience can equally be aroused through intellectual appeals as well as through the emotional ones.

Dennis Kennedy has observed that "Of all the questions raised by the study of audiences, spectator arousal is the most difficult to assess."[67] As Kennedy suggests, theatrical modernism "promoted elite or specialized audiences who were intellectually and emotionally committed but sufficiently quiescent so as not to disturb the show."[68] This promotion of audience restraint stemmed from the arousal of consistently unruly audiences up through the mid-nineteenth century. Friel sought to walk a fine line between theatrical elitism and sheer populist theater in appealing increasingly to the audience's intellect, although, of course, he never jettisons emotion, as the various heterogeneous communities in his major plays that are often formed, then crumble quickly, movingly demonstrate.

By 1986, Friel would brag about theater's vulgarity and his ability to enchant heterogeneous audiences into one unit. He observes then that "I'm attracted to everything that's vulgar and cheap about theatre, and a lot of theatre is vulgar and cheap. It's very attractive: it's quite easy but it's also attractive. To force an audience into a single receiving and perceptive unit is a very easy thing to do. It's like, if you are a conjuror you can do certain tricks. . . . It's a very easy thing once you have forged those 500 disparate people into one receiving entity."[69] His dramatic character who most closely epitomizes these interrelated claims is Francis Hardy, the Faith Healer in Friel's play of the same name. "Frank," as he is commonly known, is described in the opening stage directions as a sort of vulgar conjurer. He wears an overcoat that is "shabby, stained, slept-in. Underneath he is wearing a dark suit that is polished with use; narrow across the shoulders; sleeves and legs too short. A soiled white shirt. A creased tie. Vivid green socks" (*BFP1* 331). His outfit bespeaks his tawdriness and pitiful attempts to inspire respect in his audiences. Moreover, Hardy's performances with their mixture of failure and cure give the lie to Friel's claim that conjuring an audience into a single unit is "very easy." Sometimes, everything comes together magically and it works, creating audience havoc in the process. As Frank recalls in his spectral afterlife, "Because occasionally, just occasionally, the miracle would happen. And then—panic—panic—panic! Their ripping apart! The explosion of their careful calculations!" (337). The hope that Frank Hardy represents remained the hope of Friel as he turned away from short fiction: to enchant his audiences and mesmerize them into a temporary community of admittedly disparate individuals that surges and sizzles then dissipates after a performance.

Despite his protestations at the tendency of theater audiences toward simplicity and vulgarity that we have seen above, Friel finally wanted a broader audience than he could reach in short fiction. In 1999, he argued for the public role of the dramatist as enchanter of audience in remarks that chime with his remarks in 1967 in "The Theatre of Hope and Despair": "The playwright's words . . . are written for public utterance. They are used as the story-teller uses them, to hold an audience in his embrace and within that vocal sound."[70] Friel thus learned from his immersion in short fiction to listen to and articulate private visions and then, from his immersion in drama, to give them public utterance.

Despite the manifold attractions of drama that eventually led him to stop writing short stories, Friel never really did leave the short story behind, as the structure of many of his plays attests. *Faith Healer*, for instance, is basically composed of four short stories told dramatically from three different characters' point of view. Indeed, his continuing reversion to what is thought of as "the monologue" (think of the actual monologues in *Faith Healer* or the young Michael's long statements in *Dancing at Lughnasa*, for example) suggests his storytelling impulse continuing to exert influence on his dramatic writing. And conversely, the earlier short stories are shot through with dialogue, often thought to be primarily the concern of the dramatist. We might say, then, that if dramatic elements such as long stretches of dialogue crop up repeatedly in the short fiction, giving us a glimpse of the playwright in embryo, so too do the narrative monologues of the short fiction remain persistently lodged in the major plays, giving us the uncanny sense when we read those dramas of the revenant presence of the short story writer. As Fintan O'Toole suggested in his 2008 *Irish Times* column celebrating Friel's fifty-year career at that point, "he smuggled the short story back in to his theatre and made it strange and haunting."[71]

4

Raising and Remembering
the Dead of the Troubles

The Imagined Ghostly Community
of The Freedom of the City

> We call up our ghosts not to lay them but in the hope of having
> the genuine dialogue with them we didn't have when we had
> the opportunity.
> > —Brian Friel, "Self-Portrait (1972)"

> No justice . . . seems possible or thinkable without the principle
> of some *responsibility*, beyond all living present, within that
> which disjoins the living present, before the ghosts of those
> who are not yet born or who are already dead.
> > —Jacques Derrida, *Specters of Marx*

Friel's major creative period began with his interest in the Northern
Irish political crisis, which is manifested in his 1973 play *The Freedom of the City*. F. C. McGrath has argued that this play stands out
in the playwright's corpus because it "marked a new level of awareness about language, and it is Friel's awareness of the intimate relations among language, discourse, illusion, myth, politics, and history
that distinguishes his mature work from his early work."[1] Moreover,
as Seamus Deane argued in a 1982 BBC Northern Ireland Radio
interview, "[i]t [Friel's corpus] is recognizably of a piece, but I think
that there is a deep division in his work which I date from about
the year 1972 and which I think . . . has to do with the effect, the
absorption by him of the political crisis in the North."[2] Friel's move

to the Republic of Ireland in 1969 potentially gave him the necessary distance to dramatize this crisis.

At the same time, as he indirectly makes clear in a 1966 interview with John Fairleigh, given when he was still living in Derry, Friel realized that Gar's emigration in *Philadelphia* was not for him:

> Of course I feel the frustration and the resentment of a Catholic in the North of Ireland and sometimes get very angry and can't think calmly about the country at all. But I am committed to it, for good or evil. Whatever you flee from in one place, you'll probably find the same things somewhere else.[3]

Thus, we must see Friel's permanent move to Donegal in 1969 not as an emigration from Northern Ireland to the Republic of Ireland but as a move from one part of the "North of Ireland" to another. He never recognized the border between Northern Ireland and Ireland and perceived the island as one country. We can also sense that his commitment to the problems in Northern Ireland did not wane even with his move to Donegal. His engagement with the Troubles stemmed from his consistent concern with the political and cultural problems endemic in his chosen region of northwestern Ireland/ Northern Ireland.[4]

Friel long recognized the essentially performative politics of Northern Ireland manifested in its parades and political ceremonies. This aspect of Northern Irish politics has also been articulated by John P. Harrington and Elizabeth Mitchell, who have observed that "Northern Ireland's charged atmosphere of sectarian division encourages a considerable amount of dramatic political performance within, and about, its borders. . . . Paramilitary violence . . . has been part of larger symbolic performances designed to preserve and consolidate contested political beliefs."[5] Moreover, given the performative but fixed and repetitious nature of politics and culture in the North, Friel likely realized that he could provide a fluid option to that fixity of representation by offering a drama that featured characters moving toward each other and engaging in dynamic interactions

before their lives are snuffed out. As we will see in my discussion of
the Field Day Theatre at the beginning of my interchapter on that
theater movement, Field Day later gave Friel a public platform for
dramatic alternatives to political performances in the North during
a particularly difficult time. While it has some problems with documentary immediacy, *The Freedom of the City* constitutes his first
relatively successful attempt to present a compelling political drama
of community that attracts our sympathy. The truthful fiction of
these relationships contrasts the falsely unifying narratives that swirl
around his three major characters, Lily, Skinner, and Michael.

Friel consistently argued that he perceived Derry as more like a
town than a city because of the intimate relations among its citizens.[6]
And Seamus Deane has suggested that "[t]he town of Ballybeg . . .
has fused within it the socially depressed and politically dislocated
world of Derry and the haunting attraction of the lonely landscapes
and traditional mores of rural Donegal."[7] Despite its urban setting,
then, *The Freedom of the City*'s focus on a form of eviction also
unites it with Friel's rural plays of voluntary exile, such as *Philadelphia, Here I Come!*, and his dramas of threatened eviction, such as
the later *Translations* and *Making History*. Here, the evictors are
British Army soldiers, backed up by Saracens and other machines
of war. They lie in wait for the Catholic civil rights marchers who
have taken refuge in the Guildhall after their march is disrupted and
are lauded by nationalists as martyrs and denigrated by the British
Army and unionists as terrorists. The specific cultural and political ramifications of the Londonderry/Derry Guildhall show how a
built place influences these characters' decisions as well as those of
the factions with various agendas waiting outside the hall. Friel's
three main Catholic characters are thus doubly dislocated from a
secure, rooted place—trapped in the Guildhall, the symbol at the
time of Protestant unionist domination in Londonderry/Derry, and
marginalized within that city through their abysmal housing. Moreover, the degree of separation from the natural world shown by these
three characters in *Freedom* recalls Gar's dislocation from Ballybeg
in *Philadelphia*. But finally the play goes beyond Gar's deracination

to show their modern, fundamental alienation from each other and from the local Protestant community, greater Northern Ireland, and, by extension, Ireland and Britain.

Friel's portrayal of a photographer running onstage to take pictures of the victims in the opening moments of the play suggests his continuing interest in portraying the clash between hard-edged modernity, symbolized by dehumanizing, even crushing machines (the British Army tanks), and largely unprepared, hapless humans. Thus he implies that despite its users' best intentions, this particular medium, like the use of film in *Philadelphia*, cannot do justice to real, embodied lives. Interestingly, he also depicts a positive aspect of machine culture through the trapped characters' use of devices in the Guildhall, such as the telephone.

Brian Rotman has noted that "when two media interact and give rise to a new subjectivity," ghosts are produced, perhaps explaining "why embodied performance, always an assemblage of interacting media, is ghost-friendly, why theater's staging of a speaking *I* is such a fecund and paradigmatic source of ghosts."[8] Friel's adroit stagecraft enables us to see these three ghosts of the Troubles, who reenact their last moments through their vocal iterations of their distinctive lives.

More audaciously, he suggests how they are intimately linked with their physical and intellectual environment in Londonderry/Derry and in the Guildhall. Their "performance," then, springs from their attachment to place in profound ways that have never been recognized in readings of this drama. As Alice Rayner has argued, "Haunted space collapses temporal linearity among past, present, and future. . . . In theatrical space, performance does not inter the past so much as raise the dead, in a ghostly repetition that is the same insofar as it is mortal. That is, it raises the dead from within the paradoxical space of sameness and repetition, sameness and difference."[9] *The Freedom of the City* successfully raises and resurrects these three dead characters from the repetitious weight of both modern British empiricism and Irish nationalism. Derrida's theory of hauntology will illuminate both our growing knowledge of these characters and their knowledge of each other, enabling us to engage with them through something approximating a temporary human community in the localized place of the Derry Guildhall.

Friel's imagined community of Lily, Skinner, and Michael are caught between the mythologizing impulses of Irish tradition, symbolized by the Catholic Church and the republican balladeers, and the harsh, empirical trajectory of modernity, symbolized by the British characters of the trial judge, the sociologist Professor Dodds, the ballistics expert Professor Cuppley, and the forensics expert Dr. Winbourne, each of whom reduces their humanity through their focus on fragments and numbers. Finally, the fragile, evanescent community depicted among the play's three poor Catholic characters is continuous with those found in Friel's Ballybeg plays. In *Freedom*, however, Friel emphasizes the community's potential before it is snuffed out perhaps more positively than in any of his previous plays. As we will see, at a telling moment in the play, that potential as well as the hopes for the civil rights movement in Northern Ireland are fascinatingly represented as similar to the aims of the French Revolution, and this depiction contrasts with the more negative representations of the French Revolution in *Philadelphia, Here I Come!* and *Translations*. Through this comparison, Friel suggests that had the old regime of Protestant bigotry in contemporary Northern Ireland fallen quickly (and, crucially, bloodlessly), a new period of cultural understanding might have emerged. The unfair manipulation of the image of the unarmed protesters in the Guildhall by the British Army and its assorted proxies such as the judge, along with the propaganda disseminated by the Catholic Church and the nationalist balladeer, together show how representatives of a negative form of modernity and tradition, respectively, can each crush human community under their frightening weight. Thus the play dramatizes the clash between these pernicious manifestations of modernity and tradition and shows how this victory for British representatives of empirical modernity creates opportunities for the losers and supposed defenders of tradition like the Irish Republican Army (IRA) to retreat into regressive ideologies.

Friel's hopeful narrative of community freedom contrasts the ironic "Freedom of the City" that the anarchic Skinner bestows on the mother and housewife Lily. He imaginatively recreates the lives of three intensely individualized, innocent fictional victims in a tragic and at times humorous story that resonates more truly than does either the nationalist narrative about the event or the "official" British history that has been written about it since then (including the report from the Widgery Tribunal). Thus, the specific truths in Friel's fictional narrative of freedom will linger long after the various abstractions of Irish nationalism and British imperialism fade. As Elmer Andrews has noted in his assessment of the central three characters, "The play is on the side of the concrete and specific: abstraction is the real enemy."[10] Friel himself has consistently argued for the superiority of imagined, specific fictional truth over that of received, abstract historical narratives. For example, in his important essay "Plays Peasant and Unpeasant," written in 1972, the same year he was working on *The Freedom of the City*, he lauded the twentieth-century Irish playwrights such as Synge and the early O'Casey for being "dramatists [that] were revolutionary in the broadest sense of that word; and [we recognized] that subjective truth—the artist's truth—was dangerously independent of Church and State."[11]

My understanding of these three characters' communal narrative is based upon their fully realized freedom as individuals in the community that they temporarily form in the Guildhall. Friel, as we have already seen, often features interdependent communities in his drama. In his discussion of the realistic communities in County Donegal, Ireland, which Friel bases his own fictional communities upon, Ulf Dantanus points out that "[t]he community, while allowing for a fair amount of personal freedom and individuality is inevitably cemented by common considerations and values."[12] Friel's conception of Derry as a large town suggests that there are still possibilities within it for small communities like the provisional one his Catholic characters form in the Guildhall, a place from which, ironically, they would normally be excluded because of their faith. As in *Philadelphia*, despite Friel's protestations that Gar had to leave Ballybeg, and as in the later play *Translations*, *The Freedom of the City* rejects Enlightenment-based, atomic individualism (and, here, republican mythologizing) as deleterious to the organic world of local communities. The play suggests true freedom for individuals is only possible in the context of community, even as this provisional fictional community is destroyed upon its members' exit from the Guildhall. While Helen Fulton argues that the three protesters "demonstrate the triumph of the ideology of bourgeois individualism, where the disempowered are encouraged to 'take responsibility' for their own disempowerment,"[13] she misunderstands Friel's own rejection of solipsistic Western individualism in favor of interdependent communities. In privileging the imagined story of the protesters inside the Guildhall over the stories told in court and the various false narratives being constructed by nationalists and representatives of the Catholic Church, on the one hand, and the judge, the ballistics expert, Professor Dodds, and British soldiers on the other, Friel values imaginative life as evoked in community, even in such hybrid communities as that formed by the three very different individuals in this play. In the process, we are allowed the privilege of seeing how, like their contemporary real-life analogues in any contemporary city, these three main characters acquire agency and "enculture the city, rather than responding passively to its deterministic power."[14]

❧

The Freedom of the City functions in many ways as an extended meditation on place and displacement within and outside of Derry. Although Friel himself considers Derry a large town because of the intimate knowledge many of its citizens had of each other during the time he lived there, it functions as a major city in northwestern Ireland/Northern Ireland because it, like other cities, "accumulates and embodies the heritage of a region, and combines in some measure and kind with the cultural heritage of larger units, national, racial, religious, human."[15] The Catholic citizens that comprise roughly 70 percent of the city traditionally have looked toward rural Donegal for their identity, as did Friel himself in his increasingly frequent trips into Donegal in the 1960s. Richard Pine has pointed out the tension and separation for the Catholic inhabitants of the hillside Creggan estate epitomized by the walled center city of Derry: "This hill outside the city was excluded from the world of the apprentices' protected guilds, for whom Derry was built . . . and each element of an equation, town and country, which should have been reciprocally interactive and interdependent, became mutually polarized and exclusive."[16] The unemployment rate in Derry City in February 1967 was 20.1 percent versus a rate in the rest of Northern Ireland of 8.1 percent,[17] and there was widespread discrimination against Catholics in housing and employment. Northern Ireland's Prime Minister Terence O'Neill proposed reforms, including the removal of the city's gerrymandered housing authority; a new, more fairly allocated housing system; and the appointment of an Ombudsman, on November 22, 1968. The announcement came after peaceful civil rights marchers had been attacked by police in the city in August 1968. After another group of marchers were even more viciously attacked by loyalists and off-duty so-called B Specials at Burntollet Bridge outside the city in early January 1969, the city was ready to explode with nationalist anger.[18] O'Neill finally stepped down on April 28, 1969 when a number of explosions attributed to republicans in Northern Ireland convinced many citizens that the civil rights movement was merely a front for the Irish Republican Army (later investigations revealed that these bombs were planted by Protestant loyalists who wanted to destroy O'Neill).

Ironically for Friel's play, which highlights the biased findings of the British Widgery Tribunal about the events that became known as "Bloody Sunday," the Cameron Commission set up by O'Neill to determine the fault for the 1968 disturbances linked to the civil rights marches released its objective report on September 12, 1969. This report "was well disposed towards the civil-rights movement, generally absolving it from accusations that it was a cover for republicanism," condemning the Royal Ulster Constabulary of "'grave misconduct' and 'malicious damage' in Catholic areas in Derry" and showing the civil rights marchers' claims of bias and discrimination to be well-founded.[19] But despite all of the largely Catholic civil rights marchers' demands being met by O'Neill's reforms, and despite the very fair-minded Cameron Commission's report, the continual provocations of Catholics by loyalists finally led to overwhelming nationalist outrage, which reached a fever pitch with the August 12, 1969 Apprentice Boys march on the walls of Londonderry/Derry, looking down on the Catholic Creggan and Bogside housing estates. According to their tradition, the Apprentice Boys tossed pennies down onto the Bogside residents, which, according to Marianne Elliott, "symbolized hundreds of years of Protestant contempt, and the area exploded."[20] Riots were fought against the police for three days and then spread throughout the province. The contemporary "Troubles" had begun.

Thus, the places of Friel's play—the polarized city of Londonderry/Derry and the exclusive unionist dominion of the Guildhall— are part and parcel of the mindset of his marginalized Catholic characters and also of their real-life counterparts. After thoroughly documenting the widespread discrimination against Catholics in the North of Ireland, Elliott has argued in her magisterial study, *The Catholics of Ulster*, "[f]or several centuries Catholics have felt no sense of ownership of Ulster and their rejection even of the name 'Ulster' since partition was part and parcel of an extraordinary nihilism and communal fatalism which thankfully appears to be coming to an end."[21] Northern Irish Catholics, particularly after the Troubles began, thus felt doubly deracinated—not just isolated within majority Protestant Ulster but now also cut off from overwhelmingly Catholic Ireland. And if they were revolted by IRA violence within their own communities, their disapproval could often only be whispered, further separating them from some segments of their culture.

Friel himself and his characters are often displaced, longing for homes of their own, but the three main characters in *The Freedom of the City*, along with those in *Faith Healer*, are the most dislocated in his dramatic canon. Their marginalization is represented both by Friel's ingenious use of the stage space and by his evocation of their hidden lives in then-gerrymandered Londonderry/Derry. In the first instance, Richard Allen Cave has shown how while the stage looks realistic, "within a traditional box set representing the Mayor of Derry's parlour in the Guildhall," it is actually "exposed as a theatrical construct within surrounding black spaces (the margins of a spectator's sightlines), where in sharply angled spotlights characters appear who inhabit different narratives and time frames from that being enacted in the main playing space."[22] Thus, "[a] realist play is circumscribed by another in the Expressionist political mode; the values, tone, dramatic conventions and expectations of the first are challenged, judged, forcibly changed and determined by the second. . . . The result of this theatrical *tour de force* is not confusion but a searing awareness of the power of ideologies to shape distinct perceptions of events and to transform those biased perspectives in time ineluctably into myth, when the context is one of political struggle."[23] Anthony Roche has also read Friel's use of the stage space in a Brechtian manner, arguing from Michel de Certeau's theories of space and narrative in *The Practice of Everyday Life* that the dominance of the mayor's parlour "gives an illusion of solidity and fixity of place that the play works to undermine" through the characters' exits and entrances, which signify changes in locale and time, and elaborate lighting techniques.[24] And yet these incisive and insightful accounts of Friel's sophisticated use of stage space in the play must also be coupled with a deeper understanding of his dramatic meditation on the interaction between the place of the Protestant-dominated, elite Guildhall and the marginalized conditions of Derry Catholics at this time.

The three central characters' refuge in the Guildhall, accomplished through happenstance in the play, nevertheless carries a political charge because it can be seen as an unlikely, accidental extension of the increasing practice of "squatting" in the province, especially in Derry City, at the time. This practice, used to protest council homes being unfairly allocated, received much publicity when Austin Currie, a Nationalist Member of Parliament for East Tyrone "squatted in a council house in Caledon village to highlight the injustice of its allocation to the young secretary of a local unionist candidate, when large Catholic families, living in squalor, had been repeatedly refused council housing."[25] The distorting narratives generated in *The Freedom of the City* suggest the explosive nature of what Friel's characters have done in occupying the Guildhall by making that restricted space their temporary place to live.[26] For example, early in the play, the Judge voices the widespread possibility in some British and Protestant circles that "[t]he facts we garner over the coming days may indicate that the deceased were callous terrorists who had planned to seize the Guildhall weeks before the events of February 10th [the date of the fictional civil rights march in the play]" (*BFP1* 109). And Liam O'Kelly, a television newsman for the Irish state television broadcaster RTÉ, unethically reports that "fifty armed gunmen have taken possession of the Guildhall here below me and have barricaded themselves in" (117).

Like all types of buildings that signify absolutism in their "architecture of power and display—long, straight avenues crowned by a triumphal arch or leading to a majestic building symbolizing the power of the State, the Empire or the Church,"[27] the Guildhall commands respectful awe with its neo-Gothic architecture and Tudor overtones on the exterior and its marble, oak paneling, and stained-glass windows inside. Its importance for the play cannot be overstated: Friel even used "The Mayors [*sic*] Parlour" as the play's working title for a time.[28] Once his three major characters are inside the Guildhall and look around the Mayor's parlour where they are trapped, Lily muses, "This room's bigger than my whole place." And in response to Skinner's sarcastic question, "Have you no gold taps and tiled walls?" Lily says soberly, "There's one tap and one toilet below in the yard—and they're for eight families" (*BFP1* 120). The opulence of the Guildhall thus constantly bespeaks the marginalization of its three temporary, poverty-stricken inhabitants. Long the bastion of the gerrymandered local unionist government in the city, the Guildhall has since more positively served as the premiere of Friel's *Translations* in 1980 and, more recently, as the home of the long-running, recently concluded Saville Inquiry into the events of Bloody Sunday; it also has been a venue for the Derry *Feis*, or cultural celebration of all things Irish.

But in 1972, it was a forbidding and foreboding structure, especially for the city's marginalized Catholics.

Ulick O'Connor has termed the Guildhall as "the nearest equivalent in Derry to a pre-revolution Bastille. . . . Thus when three people in Friel's play . . . burst into the Mayoral Room in the Guildhall as a place of refuge, it is as if a trio of *sans culottes* were to have taken shelter in one of Louis XVI's drawing rooms."[29] Indeed, during Liam O'Kelly's first television report, he notes that "small groups are gathering at street corners within the ghetto area to celebrate, as one of them put it to me, 'the fall of the Bastille'" (*BFP1* 118). Gar's repeated references to the French Revolution in *Philadelphia, Here I Come!* suggest that he has become fully caught up in pernicious aspects of modernity such as extreme vacillation and movement. But here, the "occupation" of the Guildhall by these three Catholic characters in the context of the French Revolution is perceived by members of their community as ushering in a new age of democracy and equality, even though this hope has flickered out by the end of the play.

The Guildhall had already been the scene of demonstrations by the Derry Housing Action Committee (DHAC) in the spring of 1968, led by the leftist radical Eamonn McCann, "in order to provoke retaliation from unionist authorities and to radicalize the nationalist community."[30] Such temporary occupations of the Guildhall would have helped the British authorities as portrayed in Friel's play to consider his three main characters as potential anarchists, but presumably not terrorists. Only a few months after the events of Bloody Sunday, in June 1972, the Guildhall was badly damaged twice by bombs placed within it. Thus, both before Friel's characters' imagined "occupation" of this culturally and politically significant building and after, it was the site of verbal and physical violence. His fictionalized account of these three protesters in 1970, after the 1968 demonstrations by DHAC and before the 1972 events of Bloody Sunday and the bombings of the Guildhall, thus constructs an imagined space that quickly becomes an inhabited place of temporary community located between Irish nationalist aggression and the bloody, official British response to both the nonviolent movement of the Northern Irish Civil Rights Association (NICRA) and the violent extremism of the Irish Republican Army.

On January 30, 1972, the British Army's First Battalion Parachute Regiment was sent into the city of Londonderry/Derry in Northern Ireland to quell an illegal demonstration by members of NICRA against internment without trial. British soldiers shot thirteen protesters dead; a fourteenth protester later died of his wounds. Bloody Sunday had two immediate effects: an upsurge in Irish Republican Army and other paramilitary violence across the province for many years, and an abiding Catholic distrust of the British Army that had originally been brought in to safeguard them from Protestant attacks. Many Northern Catholics now desired a united Ireland and an end to the Protestant Stormont regime that had ruled Northern Ireland from 1922 until 1972. Their second wish was satisfied when the Stormont parliament was prorogued soon after Bloody Sunday. Direct rule was then instituted from London, and the British Army became entrenched in Northern Ireland. Throughout the 1970s, 1980s, and well into the 1990s, the "Troubles" engulfed Northern Ireland.

Friel faced great indirect pressure to write creative literature on the conflict since this subject was already being explored by other prominent Northern Irish authors, like Seamus Heaney and Michael Longley, and by a variety of lesser-known but still prominent playwrights from the province during the early 1970s.[31] Additionally, his nationalistic sentiments were firmly on the side of the Catholic civil rights movement in the province. However, he maintained a studied bewilderment about his inability to write about the Troubles in interviews from this period. For example, in the BBC Northern Ireland Radio interview he gave to fellow playwright John Boyd in August of 1970, Friel said that he would not write another play like *The Mundy Scheme*, a play with "that kind of here and now relevance." Boyd then asked him point-blank, "Does that rule out a political play on the troubles in the North? You've been asked that question, I know, before." Friel's response is studiously evasive:

I don't want to rule out any possible theme. It's a likely theme of course, and indeed in many ways, it's an obvious theme. And it does have a kind of international relevance because of the drift to the Left over the world and because of the student disturbances and, for all these good reasons. But, in some strange way, I shy away from it. I don't understand it.[32]

It may seem that Friel was being disingenuous with Boyd since *Freedom of the City* would appear only three years later and since he was working on the play that eventually became *Freedom* at the same time he gave this interview to Boyd. Indeed, as Roche has pointed out, Friel's first notes for the play that would become *Freedom* "date from 29 April to 15 September 1970 and reveal that the central narrative incident of three Civil Rights marchers taking over and transforming the Guildhall was already in place."[33]

Friel noted in an interview he gave to Eavan Boland in 1973 that he had been writing a different play before Bloody Sunday happened, which was originally entitled *John Butt's Bothy*, set in the eighteenth century and constructed around evictions.[34] For Friel, the embryonic *Bothy* and *Freedom* shared common themes of evictions and poverty, not political violence.[35] As Friel went on to tell Boland, his fear was that *Freedom* would be understood as an up-to-the-minute commentary on the events of Bloody Sunday and would thus be regarded as reportage or propaganda, not art:

> This play raises the old problem of writing about events which are still happening. . . . *The trouble about this particular play in many ways is that people are going to find something immediate in it, some kind of reportage.* And I don't think that's in it at all. . . . This is a play which is about poverty.[36]

As we will see in my chapter on *Faith Healer*, Friel explores both emotional and spiritual poverty through his onstage community. Here, he investigates material and what we might term "geographic" poverty caused in the Catholic community in Northern Ireland in part by Protestant oppression. Because the play was produced only a year after the events of Bloody Sunday and features three innocent Catholic civilians being gunned down by the British Army, many people saw it as a thinly disguised commentary on the aftermath of that event and the findings of the Widgery Tribunal, which investigated the killings.[37] But in fact, although the conclusion of this chapter focuses on the outcome of the recent Saville Inquiry as a dramatic performance, the play actually oscillates between two actual events, the Burntollet civil rights march of January 4, 1969, when marchers were stoned by followers of Ian Paisley, the bigoted Protestant preacher,[38] and Bloody Sunday and its aftermath, as explorations of the main characters' lives alternate with the running trial of the British Army soldiers who murdered them and who are finally exonerated.

The play is saved further from its moments of documentary immediacy and from being nationalist propaganda by its suggestion that even the photographer, and certainly the British Army and the nationalist community, distort the diverse humanity of the three civilians who are murdered after leaving the Guildhall. The photographer's picture-taking promises to record the "truth" but instead may distort it at the victims' expense; the British Army and the judge of the tribunal view them as terrorists; and the nationalist community, it is suggested, is already turning them into martyrs. Other forces in the play misrepresent their actions as well, such as the Catholic Church, but Friel seems most concerned with critiquing the official British government response to the violence and the unofficial, folkloric response on the part of Northern Irish nationalists. Friel's drama depicts the final hours of these three characters and individualizes them in an intensely realized, communal narrative riposte to monolithic identities on both sides of the conflict.

Before any dialogue occurs, *The Freedom of the City* opens with a scene of a photographer taking pictures, perhaps in an attempt to capture the complex humanity of some of the dead protesters. He is depicted as *"crouching for fear of being shot,"* and running *"on from the right and very hastily and very nervously"* photographing

"*the corpses, taking three or four pictures of each*" (*BFP1* 107).
When I first wrote on *The Freedom of the City*,[39] I believed that
Friel's inclusion of the photographer taking pictures that day was
simply an instance of how his documentary immediacy weakened
the play. I now see that while this use of the photographer does
add a veneer of authenticity by including a representation of the
aftermath of events, Friel also recognizes the cost of this documentary immediacy and thus suggests how this use of machine culture
can actually militate against the humanity it purports to preserve,
even protect. His inclusion of two different reproductions of photographic negatives that suggest photographs taken on Bloody Sunday
in the original program for the play indicates his awareness of this
danger. These negatives uncannily give a ghostly aura to the onstage
protesters with their stark black-and-white images, reinforcing their
spectrality.[40]

Susan Sontag has argued in *On Photography* that photographs
replace true reality with selective images, and her later work, *Regarding the Pain of Others*, revisits that earlier claim in the context of
modern suffering, especially during war. Sontag's perspective on
photography is particularly valuable because she lived long enough
to appreciate contemporary videography and imaging but nonetheless sees the photograph as an indelible form of remembering. As she
argues, "Nonstop imagery (television, streaming video, movies) is
our surround, but when it comes to remembering, the photograph
has the deeper bite. Memory freeze-frames; its basic unit is the single
image. In an era of information overload, the photograph provides
a quick way of apprehending something and a compact form for
memorizing it."[41] Recall Gar's efforts to "keep the camera whirring;
for this is a film you'll run over and over again" at the end of *Philadelphia, Here I Come!* (*BFP1* 99). There, Gar imagines filming his
last morning at home with a motion picture camera, suggesting that
this moment, too, will not be preserved. Here, however, at the beginning of *The Freedom of the City*, Friel depicts a photographer taking
pictures of the dead, presumably to show us how this moment will
be captured. But as the play gradually makes clear, this method, too,

has its limitations given the nature of the medium; the pressure of the moment itself; the dynamic humanity of the protesters, whose flux cannot be captured by still photographs; and photography's link to journalism's privileging of shock value.

If, as Sontag further holds, "[t]he photograph is like a quotation, or a maxim or a proverb,"[42] even evocative photographs, like those taken on Bloody Sunday by Gilles Peress and Fulvio Grimaldi,[43] could minimize the actual suffering by acting as a pithy visual shorthand. Still photographs cannot hope to do justice to human dynamism; and these particular shots, while conveying some of the agony of the protesters at the time, cannot show the continuity of their suffering that day nor the extended suffering of their parents and loved ones ever since. Moreover, because Friel's imagined photographer—probably a composite of several photographers there that day—is under the very real threat of being shot at, as Fulvio Grimaldi was that day after he took his pictures,[44] his photographs are understandably taken *"very hastily and very nervously"* and thus are not carefully composed or reverent toward their subjects.

Although Walter Benjamin's "The Work of Art in the Age of Mechanical Reproduction" is usually invoked in discussions of film, his remarks on still photography's limitations in expressing humanity are crucial to understanding Friel's critique of photography in *The Freedom of the City*. Benjamin argues that Atget's photographs of deserted Paris streets, taken around 1900, are essentially evidentiary because "he photographed them like scenes of crime." After Atget, therefore, "photographs become standard evidence for historical occurrences, and acquire a hidden political significance. They demand a specific kind of approach; free-floating contemplation is not appropriate to them. They stir the viewer; he feels challenged by them in a new way."[45] The pictures taken on Bloody Sunday, of course, have been used both in the court of public opinion and in the two legal inquiries—the Widgery Inquiry and the Saville Tribunal—conducted since the shootings. Several of the pictures taken that day recall Benjamin's description of Atget's photographs of deserted Paris streets that anticipate crime-scene pictures: the most telling, perhaps, in this regard, is one of the body of Bernard McGuigan lying on the pavement with blood pooled around his head in the foreground and an empty Bogside, "which ten minutes earlier had been thronged with an estimated 10,000–20,000 people."[46] Such pictures almost inevitably become politicized, a fact reflected in the rhetoric of the play on the part of the judge, soldiers, and others affiliated with the British state and those who support the protesters but view them as martyrs. Contemplation thus disappears, as Benjamin suggests above, because the photographs challenge the viewer's ocular perception so aggressively and therefore generate a corresponding loss of the subjects' humanity and uniqueness.

In her discussion of the famous picture of the Republican soldier in the Spanish Civil War whose image is captured by Robert Capa's camera just as he is hit by an enemy bullet, Sontag points out that we should not be surprised at the purposeful shock value of this and other images of atrocities because "[c]onscripted as part of journalism, images were expected to arrest attention, startle, surprise. . . . The hunt for more dramatic . . . images drives the photographic enterprise, and is part of the normality of a culture in which shock has become a leading stimulus of consumption and source of value."[47] I am not at all trying to deny the very real and helpful way in which the images taken by photographers such as Peress, Grimaldi, Colman Doyle, and others that fateful January day helped indict the British soldiers in the court of public opinion, if not in the court of law. But I am suggesting both because of the problems inherent in the medium and the way in which these pictures were repeatedly disseminated around the world that the humanity and differences among the Bloody Sunday victims became flattened and minimized.

By 2003, in the wake of the photographs taken of the aftermath of the terrorist attacks on the Twin Towers of New York City and during the early days of the Iraq War, Sontag could claim that "[t]he ultra-familiar, ultra-celebrated image—of an agony, of ruin—is an unavoidable feature of our camera-mediated knowledge of war."[48]

Brian Friel realized early in the era of the Troubles because so much of the coverage of the conflict was "camera-mediated" that the sheer repetition of images was bound to eventually produce a condition of forgetfulness in the public, as pictures of atrocity after atrocity essentially blended together and people became numb to even thoughtful photographs meant to evoke sympathy and empathy for the wounded and dead. Friel knew that only a living genre like drama could even hope to give a sense of the life behind such images—the flux that comprises human identity. As a play partly about the events and aftermath of what many Irish still believe to be a conspiracy between the British Army and the British legal system, *The Freedom of the City* enacts a more daring "conspiracy" of its own—against photography's purported aim to truthfully capture still moments of "life"—by setting up a community of temporarily free individuals who choose to interact with each other and the audience even as we know they are already dead. He thus revivifies the dead even as he portrays what Michael Parker suggestively observes are "the photographer's eerie white flashes [that] . . . drain the dead further."[49]

While the presence of the photographer in the play suggests the problems that this medium creates in remembering victims of violence, much worse are the empirical attitudes of more fully fleshed-out characters who also effectively deny the victims' humanity—the Judge, Professor Dodds, the British Army soldiers, and the ballistics expert. Collectively, these characters attempt to abnegate the rich and full lives of the temporary, local community that forms in the Guildhall that day.

The Judge's opening statement purports to be objective by employing a rhetoric of facts, but it is undermined by a telling admission:

> *This tribunal of inquiry,* appointed by her Majesty's Government, *is in no sense a court of justice.* Our only function is to form an objective view of the events which occurred in the City of Londonderry, Northern Ireland, on the tenth day of February 1970, when after a civil rights meeting British troops opened fire and three civilians lost their lives. It is essentially a fact-finding exercise; and

our concern and our only concern is with that period of time when these three people came together, seized possession of a civic building, and openly defied the security forces. (*BFP1* 109; my emphasis)

Whenever the Judge speaks in the play, his supposedly impartial marshalling of "the facts" is undercut by his bias against Friel's three main characters and in favor of the British soldiers.

After this opening speech by the Judge, an American sociologist, Philip Alexander Dodds, enters and offers an explanation of the "subculture of poverty" (*BFP1* 110, 133), which is broken into two parts by the appearance of British troops firing on the civil rights protesters. Dodds injects an academic, seemingly objective tone into the play that potentially counterbalances the Judge's obviously subjective tone; Dodds's discourse on poverty also strengthens Friel's claim that the play is mainly about poverty, not politics. But, as Maria Germanou has convincingly argued, "Initially Friel builds for Dodds a position of neutrality that he gradually deconstructs."[50] Professor Dodds outlines this subculture of poverty in terms of its transmission from generation to generation. He argues that this subculture has two dominant aspects: it is the means by which the poor adapt "to their marginal position in a society which is capitalistic, stratified into classes, and highly individuated; and it is also their method of reacting against that society" (110). In a somewhat condescending manner that neglects the particular personalities of these three characters and the specific physical and political environment of Derry explored earlier in this chapter, Dodds remarks that people in this culture are provincial and have little sense of history but can be inspired to break out of this condition the moment they become aware of other movements in the world by their counterparts.[51]

Along with the Judge and Dodds, the British Army soldiers, the ballistics expert Professor Cuppley, and the forensics expert Dr. Winbourne also hold what can be termed an "empirical epistemology" because of their overreliance on statistics and numbers to the neglect of the three main characters' richly limned humanity. And moreover, the play repeatedly suggests the unreliability of their supposedly objective perspectives. Bernard McKenna has argued that through their excessive use of the radio in "speaking a mechanized code language" that "the human voice of the British soldiers becomes an almost mechanical signal, virtually a part of the radio and receiver. Each speaks his password into a machine, clutching the machine to his cheek and ear, fusing himself with the machine. Within such a matrix, human frailties and vulnerabilities do not exist."[52] And Cuppley, linked to Professor Dodds and his penchant for abstracting human beings by his academic title, betrays a fascination with machine culture similar to that of the British soldiers, rendering his report to the Judge supposedly objective but tellingly incomplete. He tells the Judge, for example, that the bullets that killed the three main characters came from "a high-velocity rifle, using 7.62 mm ammunition; and from my point of view it's particularly untidy to work with because, if the victim has been hit several times in close proximity it's very difficult to identify the individual injuries" (*BFP1* 161–62). Because of these bullets' propensity to make "a gaping wound" and then bring "particles of bone and tissue with it which make the wound even bigger" (162), Cuppley cannot even give an accurate number of wounds for the three victims: he tells the Judge that "thirty-four was an approximation" and that "the serious mutilation in such a concentrated area made precise identification almost . . . guesswork" (ibid.). Finally, while Winbourne gives evidence of gunshot residue, he hesitates at first to conclude that Michael fired a gun, but he finally allows the judge to lead him to that conclusion (143).

We have already seen Friel's critique of Gar's fascination with machine speed in his portrayals of that character's imagining of himself on the airplane that will whisk him to America in *Philadelphia, Here I Come!*. Although Gar's record player connects him to an oral tradition that Friel privileges, and although Lily in *The Freedom of the City* uses the telephone to call her friend Betty Breen (*BFP1* 145) and Skinner plays waltz music on the radio (131) in order to draw closer to Lily, these more positive connections with machine culture serve mainly to highlight the various characters' estrangement from entering the upper echelon of society. Gar, for instance, seeks culture through classical music even while knowing he is effectively locked out of Kate Doogan's upper-class world. And Lily's telephone call to Betty marks her as a "tourist" trying out the luxury of a private telephone: she concludes her call with Betty by admitting, "No, the [public] kiosk's still broken. I'm ringing from the Mayor's parlour," and *"suddenly bangs down the receiver and covers her face with her hands,"* presumably in embarrassment (145). Finally, while Cuppley's extensive description of the bullet holes in the victims' bodies is empirical and meant to distance us from them, Friel also employs such a narrative to show how these characters who are largely locked out of mechanized culture are pierced by that culture in a striking way that anticipates a whole series of other wounded victims who "crash" into modernity and are killed or emigrate: Frank Hardy, who will be hacked to pieces after the conclusion of *Faith Healer*; the English Yolland in *Translations*, murdered by the Donnelly twins; and Rose and Agnes in *Dancing at Lughnasa*, who voluntarily emigrate to England when forced out of their hand-knitting jobs by the new knitwear factory that is opening near Ballybeg.

Immediately after Dodds's second monologue, he exits and Michael, Lily, and Skinner appear, blinded by gas, and enter the Guildhall. They end up occupying the building's parlour during the rest of the play, and their conversation illuminates their individuality. Friel poignantly suggests that none of the three protesters has fully realized his or her own potential. The real tragedy is that these are human beings about to be killed in the prime of their lives. The married Michael is 22; Skinner is 21; and Lily, while some twenty years older, is a full-time mother. Ulf Dantanus notes that "as human beings, [they] are never allowed a chance to realize themselves."[53] Along with the loss of their lives, another potential is snuffed out here—the ability to reflect on anything for longer than a moment. These characters do evince Professor Dodds's temporal orientation: they are task-oriented, and everything is a means to an end for them because of their economic poverty. Their resulting mental impoverishment is best summed up by Lily, who briefly realizes before she is killed "that life had eluded me because never once in my forty-three years had an experience, an event, even a small unimportant happening been isolated, and assessed, and articulated" (*BFP1* 150). These characters with their mental impoverishment thus are the opposite of Friel's Gar O'Donnell, who has ample time for reflection but thinks too much about himself and becomes an extreme narcissist.

Their desire for basic improvements in their living conditions compounds their diminished humanity, which unites them despite their disparate individual attitudes. Skinner is a cynical ne'er-do-well who thinks he sees through the rhetoric of the civil rights protesters. Michael, a pacifist, cannot stand Skinner and regards him as a hooligan. In the first act, Michael is prepared to walk outside and turn himself in, but Skinner tells him his theory does not have practical applications, and thus Michael, though claiming pacifism works, is scared enough to stay inside.

Lily is a mother of eleven who has gone on the march, as she tells Skinner, for "wan man—wan vote—that's what I want" (*BFP1* 154). After he tells her she already got that six months ago, she says she was marching to protest gerrymandering and for civil rights. He claims he does not believe her and then tells her why he thinks she has marched:

> Because you live with eleven kids and a sick husband in two rooms that aren't fit for animals. Because you exist on a state subsistence that's about enough to keep you alive but too small to fire your guts. Because you know your children are caught in the same morass. Because for the first time in your life you grumbled and someone else grumbled and someone else, and you heard each other, and became aware that there were hundreds, thousands, millions of us all over the world, and in a vague groping way you were outraged. . . . It's about us—the poor—the majority—stirring in our sleep. And if that's not what it's all about, then it has nothing to do with us. (Ibid.)

Skinner's account coheres perfectly with Dodds's academic explanation about escaping the subculture of poverty given earlier in the play: "[O]nce they become aware that their condition has counterparts elsewhere, from that moment they have broken out of their subculture" (111). Lily finally has the scales removed from her eyes when she hears Skinner's disquisition, and she agrees with him.

After she musingly says to him, "I suppose you're right," she tells the now-flippant Skinner that her child Declan is "a mongol. . . . And it's for him that I go on all the civil rights marches. Isn't that stupid? You and him (MICHAEL) and everybody else marching and protesting about sensible things like politics and stuff and me in the middle of you all, marching for Declan. Isn't that the stupidest thing you ever heard?" (*BFP1* 155). This moment lays considerable claim to being the moral center of the play, coming as it does in the midst of the three characters' discussion about the purpose of the civil rights movement as they briefly form a fragile community among themselves for a time. Declan anticipates a series of disabled characters in Friel's later work, such as McGarvey, whom Frank Hardy will try unsuccessfully to heal at the end of *Faith Healer*; Sarah, who has a terrible speech defect in *Translations*; and Rose, in *Dancing at Lughnasa*, who is clearly mentally disabled. But additionally, Declan's verbal presence in the midst of Lily's speech enables him to briefly become a part of this community of heterogeneous protesters that Friel's play privileges and thus make it more diverse. Marching for disabled rights seems far from the politics of the civil rights movement in late 1960s/early 1970s Northern Ireland, but Friel's inclusion of Declan through Lily gives that movement an even more heightened dignity and moral force. As evidence of the power of Lily's claim to be marching for Declan, when she finally asks again, "Isn't that the stupidest thing you ever heard?" even the irreverent Skinner quietly and powerfully affirms her, saying "No" (ibid.).

Friel's two perennial themes of potential and community coalesce in *Freedom* as the characters trapped in the Guildhall form a provisional community based on a shared humanity rife with potential for the Northern Irish political situation. This provisional community is Friel's answer to another group of provisionals that would swell in numbers after Bloody Sunday—the Provisional IRA. Despite the bickering between the cynical Skinner and the chirpingly optimistic, pacifist Michael, despite Lily's relative ignorance for most of the play, these three are a microcosm of the type of democratic society based on dialogue that could emerge in the province. British imperialism had formerly squelched attempts at a true democracy; subsequent events after this turning point in the Troubles would create entrenched attitudes reinforced with violence on both sides. There was a moment during Bloody Sunday, Friel suggests, when both sides had a chance to engage in constructive conversation, but that chance quickly passes in the play.[54]

Friel's approval of this temporary community of former strangers (including the hovering verbal presence of the disabled Declan) suggests its continuity with other such communities his dramas often depict that reject the fetish modernity has often made of individualism. In this regard, it is important to remember ecocritic Hubert Zapf's contention cited in the introduction to this study concerning "the deep-rooted self-alienation of human beings within the civilizatory project of modernity which, in its anthropocentric illusion of autonomy, has tried to cut itself off from and erase its roots in the natural world."[55] Friel's urban characters in *Freedom* would actually be more at home in a rural environment, and they are islanded in the city, separated from a potentially sustaining nature. Richard York notes that "Friel's Irish people live close to each other, and are forced into self-knowledge by the theatrical quality of their intimacy. And this, one may well feel, is a genuine part of Friel's fidelity to his own society."[56] And in reference to this specific group of three characters in *The Freedom of the City*, Christopher Murray approvingly suggests that these three characters "form a kind of fatherless family,"[57] while Terence Brown argues that their relationship to each other

alert[s] us to a dominant feature of his work as a whole—that is the inability of his characters to express themselves as social beings in any context other than the family or the local community. In *The Freedom of the City* we see indeed the local, distinctive identities of three Derry citizens . . . denied any mode of self expression in a

political system which finally takes their lives, reputation and very
individuality.[58]

Only through their particularly realized communities can Friel's characters truly acquire their identities. When these communities come in
contact with pernicious forces in the outside world, a resultant loss of
individuality, if not outright death, occurs for their members. Much
of Friel's best dramatic work offers a glimpse of the potential for true
individual freedom in the midst of the interdependent community
and then shows how that moment quickly dissipates.

This potential Friel explores in *The Freedom of the City* is probably best summarized by a scene early in the play when Skinner jokingly asks Michael to recite Kipling's "If," which he terms "a poem
to fit the place and the occasion" (*BFP1* 138). Although Ulf Dantanus characterizes this as a "reference to a well-known poem by a
spokesman of British imperialism,"[59] the larger significance of the
poem lies in its general theme of potential. The opening lines of the
poem that Skinner mock-recites to Michael are, "If you can keep
your head when all about you / Are losing theirs and blaming it on
you" (ibid.). Skinner *is* teasing Michael for his calmness but he is suggesting at the same time he does not realize the gravity of their situation. The British Army is obviously losing their collective heads over
the situation, as are the assembled nationalists. Skinner is gently and
sardonically urging the others to gain a fuller understanding about
their current position, but he is also already recognizing that they
are doomed. This recognition makes the suggestion of political and
cultural rapprochement all the more bittersweet since that chance
has passed these three by the instant they barricaded themselves in
the Guildhall.

The community that forms among the three central characters
is strikingly spontaneous and light-hearted, yet can be considered
deeply spiritual. Elmer Andrews terms Skinner "the anarchic, Dionysiac spirit who leads Lily beyond social constraint" and argues
that "[i]n the mayor's parlour Lily and Skinner momentarily achieve

a powerful communion through their dressing up and play-acting, their drinking and laughter."[60] Elizabeth Hale Winkler notes that Skinner and Lily's embryonic community is best characterized by "their very ability to communicate instinctively" and argues that the humor of these two characters is an "affirmation of life."[61] Most recently, Joseph Csicsila argues that "by sharing with one another their very day-to-day human concerns and struggles, they participate in spiritual sympathy with one another."[62] Although Michael largely refuses to play Skinner's games, he too affirms the newly formed community among the three characters, most powerfully when he insists upon all of them emerging from the Guildhall together. He tells Skinner, "We're all going out together" (*BFP1* 159), and later he gathers them together as they collectively march forward.

This shining glimpse of potential—of what could have been for these characters—thus becomes deeply ironic. It is a delayed but also proleptic irony since the characters are dead as the play begins but come to life again as their last moments in the Guildhall are portrayed. The final frozen tableau of them being shot is thus already history; Friel suggests that their deaths have become abstracted by the nationalist side and representatives of the Catholic Church, along with the British government, tribunal, and army. Certainly, the most ironic scene in the entire drama occurs when Skinner mockingly confers the freedom of the city upon Lily and Michael in the guise of mayor (*BFP1* 135–36). Their royal trappings are the closest they will ever get to this honor, for if they somehow were to get out of the situation alive, they would never even be allowed to set foot in the mayor's parlor, much less be awarded the freedom of the city. They have been trapped their whole lives by their poverty; now they are cornered by the British Army, which, again, was brought into the province originally to protect Catholics from Protestants. Friel highlights the poverty of the Bogside in Londonderry/Derry through intensely dramatizing three human beings who ironically discuss their lives of abject poverty surrounded by the opulence of the Guildhall. The final scene illustrates that these three poverty-stricken characters have now been "evicted" from the Guildhall by the representatives of the local government who helped consign them to such penurious conditions by denying Catholics decent housing and employment for so long.

Most important, these three characters have also become ensnared by two different accounts of the event—the British imperial narrative or the Irish nationalist story about their deaths. These narratives diminish their individual humanity and render them as abstractions that may be appropriated into either discourse. Friel steers a path between the Scylla of nationalist rhetoric, what Helen Fulton terms "a mythologizing discourse, recalling Ireland's prerepublican and prepartition history in terms of war, violence, and rebellion," and the Charybdis of official British rhetoric, part of what Fulton calls an "institutional discourse," in showing these three characters to be pawns used in the propaganda war by both sides.[63]

In "Plays Peasant and Unpeasant," Friel rejects both the influence of the Catholic Church in Ireland and the cult of Irish nationalism associated with Kathleen ni Houlihan, and in his play he similarly rejects the constricting narratives woven by that institution and by the republican balladeer. He argues that "during the period of unrest I can foresee that the two allegiances that have bound the Irish imagination—loyalty to the most authoritarian church in the world and devotion to a romantic ideal we call Kathleen—will be radically altered."[64] But in fact, in the course of *The Freedom of the City*, Friel shows how these two allegiances were still very strong in early 1970s Derry by showing how a history of the event is already being constructed both by the Irish nationalists in the city and by the Catholic Church in Northern Ireland and in the Republic. For example, a balladeer enters after a newsman leaves and leads some children in a rousing air that follows the tune of another song about a martyr, "John Brown's Body":

A hundred Irish heroes one February day
Took over Derry's Guildhall, beside old Derry's quay.
They defied the British army, they defied the RUC.
They showed the crumbling empire what good Irishmen

Could be.
Three cheers and then three cheers again for
Ireland one and free,
For civil rights and unity, Tone, Pearce [*sic*] and Connolly.
The Mayor of Derry City is an Irishman once more.
So let's celebrate our victory and let Irish whiskey pour. (*BFP1* 118)

The 100 civil rights marchers occupying the Guildhall in the balladeer's song double the newsman's number; he has claimed there are
50 protesters inside (117). Comparing the trapped protesters to the
eighteenth-century Irish rebel Wolfe Tone and especially to Patrick
Pearse and James Connolly, leaders of the Easter Rebellion against
the British in 1916, enables the nationalists to stitch together a nearly
two-hundred-year-old narrative that encompasses a series of martyrs for the cause of an independent Ireland. But these contemporary
protesters are clearly not committed to the use of violence to achieve
Catholic emancipation as were Tone, Pearse, and Connolly; neither
are they politically sophisticated and aware like the earlier leaders
were. And of course, they are not even leaders, merely protesters
caught up in events.

Scott Boltwood's characterization of the constricting aspect of
nationalist narratives is a useful summation of the process of myth-
making that Friel's balladeer is attempting:

> Like any genealogy, nationalism tolerates only a single line of
> descent through each generation in a legitimating myth of ideologi-
> cal paternity, and this process seeks to occlude the polymorphous
> narratives of diverse, if not unaligned, movements with an official
> history of an immutable bequest from one generation to the next.
> Such a reductive chronicle draws a direct line from the 1798 Upris-
> ing to Independence through Daniel O'Connell, Young Ireland,
> James Stephens, and Charles Stewart Parnell.[65]

Friel's balladeer thus tries to extend the "reductive chronicle" of Irish
nationalist history from 1798 through the contemporary conflict in

Northern Ireland by appropriating the "polymorphous narratives" of the three complexly human protesters.

Friel's condemnation of the Catholic Church's response to his three main characters' deaths is not as strident as his critique of Irish republicanism, but it is nonetheless substantive. For example, when the Priest first speaks in the play, he falsely claims that Lily, Michael, and Skinner acted as religious martyrs, stating, "They died for their beliefs. They died for their fellow citizens. . . . They sacrificed their lives so that you and I and thousands like us might be rid of that iniquitous yoke and might inherit a decent way of life" (*BFP1* 125). In his second speech, the Priest still refers to the three as "victims," but bizarrely claims they were "victims of this conspiracy" by (presumably) Irish republicans "to deliver this Christian country into the dark dungeons of Godless communism" (156). Certainly he is right that republicans will mischaracterize their murders as a sacrifice for the cause, as we have already seen, but the Priest's fear that Irish republicanism will attract more of his congregants to their "faith" than he will to the Church drives his second distortion of their deaths.

While Friel's nationalists claim 100 martyrs are inside, and the priest twice casts Lily, Michael, and Skinner as victims, the official government estimate suggests that "up to forty persons are involved" and more disturbingly that "[o]ur information is that they have access to arms" (*BFP1* 126). Thus, in the space of a few pages, Friel brilliantly critiques both the overblown rhetoric of the nationalists, which attempts to make martyrs out of Michael, Lily, and Skinner, and the "officialese" (official lies?) employed by the British government that baldly states they are "a band of terrorists" (ibid.).

Examples of the misleading rhetoric used by both sides abound in the play. Early in the first act, we hear voices of nationalists behind the battlements discuss conflicting numbers of those thought dead inside the Guildhall and attribute the death of "a baby in a pram" and "an old man" who has his head blown off to the British Army (*BFP1* 125). Later in this act, the brigadier lies to the judge when he claims the three protesters "emerged firing from the Guildhall" (134). This "official" claim is an outright lie, as we find out from the concluding scene of the play, when the three appear with their hands over their heads.

Reading *The Freedom of the City* through an overly deterministic political lens finally is a disabling critical maneuver, as Helen Fulton's analysis cited above demonstrates. Such a rigid reading neglects the hopeful promise of freedom in what is admittedly a very angry play and ignores art's role in briefly suggesting such a freedom. Seamus Deane has suggested that despite the undeniable political context of Friel's plays, he seeks "some consolatory or counterbalancing agency which will offer an alternative" to the failures of Irish politics.[66] Although Deane claims that this quest is unsuccessful, he argues further that in the process of this search, Friel recognizes "the peculiar role and function of art, especially the theatrical art, in a broken society."[67]

Friel's greatest allegiance is to his art, and that commitment finally allows *The Freedom of the City* to engage in a political protest against British mistreatment of Catholics in Northern Ireland by the early 1970s, yet for it to rise above received reality and create a shimmering new reality of potential for his central characters. This literary creation recalls Denis Donoghue's description of the power of literature to create new realities:

> [T]he imagination can transform the appearances and the seemings, such that a subjective reality appears to emerge, at least while the going is good. The imagination, the "violence within," as [Wallace] Stevens elsewhere called it, engages with reality, the "violence without" and allows the poet to feel that a new reality, subjective in its main character, has been produced.[68]

Donoghue's conception of the imaginative work of literature seems especially applicable to Friel's play, especially since this drama is explicitly engaged with reality, the "violence without," in a frightening way as the assembled British troops outside lie in wait for the central three characters. But within the Guildhall, Friel's imagination endows the three with temporary power and momentary hope. It is finally only through the strength of its form that the play speaks what Donoghue terms the "counter-statements" of literature that contradict the societal statements—"instructions, edicts, laws, definitions of reality"[69]—loudly proclaimed by opposing groups in the streets outside. In this sense, *The Freedom of the City* ultimately upholds literature's ethical dimension and suggests its superiority to the forceful presence of the waiting British army and to all the misleading rhetorics of power expressed in the play. In so doing, it demonstrates Friel's rich conception of community by showing how art creates precisely rendered communities of liberation in which individuals are truly free yet bound to other members of the group through interdependent relationships.

F. C. McGrath, however, fails to recognize the essence of the community of these three central characters that Friel privileges, arguing they are "drawn according to another code (that of literary realism) based on a fundamentally different epistemology that emphasizes and privileges their individuality rather than their institutional encoding."[70] He thus misreads Friel's anti-Enlightenment conception of the individual freely realized in community as mere literary realism. Although McGrath thinks that Friel vacillates in the play between modernist (his depiction of the central three characters) and postmodernist (the distorting institutional discourses) epistemologies, Friel's consistent epistemology throughout his work is antimaterialist, organic, holistic, and privileges the community over the individual, as this entire study shows.

Furthermore, the play itself creates a double community—the one just articulated among the three protesters in the Guildhall and the ones that form between readers of the play and characters and especially between theatergoers and the characters. This second series of communities is achieved in part through Friel's formal reliance on the monologue throughout the play, a maneuver that he would later take to new heights in the minimalist monologues of *Faith Healer* spoken by only four characters. Bernice Schrank posits that *Freedom* itself becomes the necessary "forum in which the questions raised by

Bloody Sunday and all it encompasses [are addressed]," going on to argue that "[t]hrough the repeated use of monologues, Friel implicates the theatre audience in the politics of the play, encouraging them to move from passive spectatorship to active engagement."[71] Michael Parker has attempted to present a more substantive articulation of how Friel's dramatic structure effects audience engagement through employing Russian theorist Mikhail Bakhtin's concept of the "dialogic,"[72] but his analysis largely implies how the audience is brought into imaginative sympathy with the characters rather than demonstrates it.

For a greater understanding of how Friel generates audience participation in this rich though imperfect play, we must turn to Jacques Derrida's theory of "hauntology" articulated in his *Specters of Marx: The State of the Debt, the Work of Mourning, and the New International.* Given the democratizing impulse behind the Northern Irish Civil Rights Association and the communal empathy that Friel's central characters establish with each other during their brief time together in the Derry Guildhall, Derrida's theory of hauntology enables us to acquire an epistemology of the dead that will help us more fully appreciate Friel's ghostly characters' community and our place in it while nonetheless realizing that just as we can never fully know the dead, we also can never fully know ourselves.

In the "Exordium" to *Specters of Marx*, Derrida muses that he would like to engender us "to learn to live *with* ghosts, in the upkeep, the conversation, the company, or the companionship, in the commerce without commerce of ghosts. To live otherwise, and better. No, not better, but more justly. But *with them*," noting finally that "this being-with specters would also be, not only but also, a *politics* of memory, of inheritance, and of generations."[73] I believe Friel's *Freedom* instantiates just such a conversation and companionship between his ghostly characters and his audience, creating a "politics of memory" that binds us together, the living and the dead. But how does the play create such a radical community?

William Watkin has argued that death creates a lasting condition of unknowability both toward the dead and ourselves, observing,

"When your friend is gone you must accept that you will never know them [*sic*] in full, and in interring their [*sic*] memory inside yourself you are forced, perhaps for the first time, to admit that you will never know yourself in full either, especially as one part of yourself is made up of the presence of the dead, unknowable other."[74] Such a condition of double unknowability certainly seems to preclude any formation of the type of communities of which I am speaking. Yet Watkin's reading of Derrida's prose-poem *Glas* and his *Gift of Death* suggest otherwise, because as we muse upon the dead other and incorporate it within ourselves,

> the other's being "in us" splits us. As Derrida makes clear, at the moment when we realize the other is truly other, at the moment of their [*sic*] perceived death, we absorb the other into our own being. This has two aporetic effects: the other ceases to be other as the "you" becomes part of the "I," and yet the "I" ceases to be itself. In the act of commemoration and mourning, the other becomes familiar; self becomes other. . . . [Thus] we do not give otherness to the other, instead, we receive otherness from them [*sic*].[75]

This process of exchange is exemplified in our reception of the main characters' deaths in *Freedom*.

Thus, we can now realize that while the opening description of the three bodies of Skinner, Lily, and Michael purposely distances them from us because of their immobility and posture in lying "*grotesquely across the front of the stage*" (BFP1 107),[76] their ritualistic movement toward us at the conclusion effects a movement in our own minds toward them even as we, in Watkin's phrase, "receive otherness from them." As the three exit the Guildhall, they are described as having "*their hands above their heads. They begin to move very slowly downstage in ritualistic procession*" (167). All their helplessness is signified in their raised hands and ritualistic, deathly walk; all our sympathy is generated by our apprehension that they are about to be "sacrificed," as many of Friel's other characters are at the conclusion of his plays.

Yet this ritual sacrifice is markedly different from others in Friel's major plays because it is here employed by him to show how distorting rhetoric colors our view of these characters' last moments. If, as Barbara G. Myerhoff holds, ritual's "repetitive character . . . provides a message of pattern and predictability," and that "[e]ven when dealing with change, new events are connected to preceding ones, incorporated into a stream of precedents so that they are recognized as growing out of tradition and experience,"[77] the twice-portrayed ritualized actions of Friel's main characters at the end of the play suggests how opposing factions have given their deaths a soothing narrative fatefulness that Friel shows to be false. Thus, their "sacrifice" enables the republican balladeer's, Catholic Church's, and television reporter Liam O'Kelly's romanticizing rhetoric as well as the bias of the Judge, the British Army, and others who would see them as terrorists. The relentless "logic" of both groups sees them as religious martyrs and terrorists, respectively, thus finally feels satisfaction in their deaths because of its seeming inevitability.

Immediately after Skinner closes the door, we are told in the subsequent part of the stage directions that Friel purposely shows to be "contaminated" by a distorted view of the protesters as religious martyrs that *"the auditorium is filled with thundering, triumphant organ music on open diapason. It is sustained for about fifteen seconds and then fades to background as LIAM O'KELLY of [Radio] Telefís Eireann enters left with microphone in hand. He talks into the microphone in soft, reverential tones"* (BFP1 167). O'Kelly's elegy for these dead is overly aestheticized, characterized by the organ music that we hear in the stage directions and described by O'Kelly in his account of the funeral Mass as Bach's "most beautiful, most triumphant and in a curious way most appropriate *Prelude and Fugue No. 552"* (ibid.).

We are given another glimpse of the three in the stage directions immediately following O'Kelly's remarks: *"The music stops suddenly. MICHAEL, LILY and SKINNER now stand across the front of the stage, looking straight out. The JUDGE appears on the battlements"* (BFP1 168). The Judge then launches into an indictment of the protesters and apologia for the security forces, a narrative that distorts with its pseudo-empiricism and seeming neutrality just as O'Kelly's narrative does with its aestheticism and romanticism.[78] After the Judge finishes, we are left with a haunting duotone stage: *"The entire stage is now black, except for a battery of spotlights beaming on the faces of the three. Pause. Then the air is filled with a fifteen-second burst of automatic fire. It stops. The three stand as before, staring out, their hands above their heads"* (168–69). Christopher Murray has said of this scene that "there are few things in the modern theatre more moving than this final image of defiance, which anticipates the end of Beckett's *Catastrophe* (1982)," concluding, "thus is the text of the Widgery Inquiry wholly discredited by Friel's own text and the sheer power of theatre."[79]

Again, as with the stage directions that immediately precede Liam O'Kelly's speech, these stage directions are misleading, but now only in part: Here, the spotlights seem to suggest that the cold logic of "truth" disseminated by the Judge and trial experts illuminates the lives of the characters, while in actuality, the last sentence of the stage directions suggests rightly that they are sacrificial, unarmed victims to this empiricist ideology as well as to that romantic ideology epitomized by O'Kelly, the balladeer, and the gathered mourning crowds. By depicting the nationalist balladeering and the British trial before the three characters ever emerge from the Guildhall, Friel enables the attentive reader or playgoer to realize that they were effectively martyred by nationalists and convicted by the British before the full story was known.

In these two concluding passages, we thus see how the unknowing that enters into us at the moment of the other's death itself becomes compounded by these obfuscating ideologies. Fittingly for Friel, who always privileges the living voice on the stage, these dead are best represented not by their visual appearances here but by their spontaneous, at times generous conversation with each other earlier in the play, echoing the validity of his observation about the Troubles in 1970: "Generosity of spirit is the quality we need most now."[80] Their voices, at times sharp and raucous, at others poignant and plangent, echo in our heads long after the play is over, sonically leading us into a community with them rife with ethical obligations.

Colin Davis has remarked in his discussion of Derrida's concept of hauntology, "Hauntology supplants its near-homonym ontology, replacing the priority of being and presence with the figure of the ghost as that which is neither present nor absent, neither dead nor alive."[81] Thus, "Attending to the ghost is an ethical injunction insofar as it occupies the place of the Levinasian Other: a wholly irrecuperable intrusion in our world, which is not comprehensible within our available intellectual frameworks, but whose otherness we are responsible for preserving."[82] Recalling and remembering Friel's ghosts of the Troubles in *The Freedom of the City* thus becomes the mental labor he expects from attentive audiences—whether theatergoers or readers. Listening and reading closely, remembering as exactly as possible—these are our collective tasks. The play's fictive characters from 1970 are no less pressing in their requests of us to remember than they would be were they literally real, although the possibility remains that they can be more easily dismissed than could their real-life analogues.

Employing Davis's reading of Derrida's theory of hauntology enables us to realize the liminal function of Friel's three revenants. As Davis remarks, "For Derrida, the ghost's secret is not a puzzle to be solved; it is the structural openness or address directed toward the living by the voices of the past or the not yet formulated possibilities of the future. The secret is not unspeakable because it is taboo, but because it cannot not (yet) be articulated in the languages available to us."[83] Friel's spectral secret in *The Freedom of the City* lies in his successful evocation of community through truthful language and gestures.

In an observation with direct bearing for our understanding of this haunted play, Alice Rayner beautifully articulates the relationship between the written text and its performance, drawing on a famous passage from Beckett's *Waiting for Godot*:

> A human body ghosts a text, and the ghost is encrypted there as a condensation of incorporation. Out of that invisible or transparent

body, incorporated by textuality, an exchange takes place in the emptiness of the theater, in the hollowness of the visible, inside-out surfaces of three-dimensional space. There, words become acts, and objects become speech that whispers, like ashes, like leaves, in the voices of the dead, like the sound of falling water, reflecting absence.[84]

If, as Rayner argues earlier, "a play text precedes performance as a disembodied demand for action and embodiment,"[85] we, the readers or theatergoers, similarly must "do justice" to both "events and writing" first "by interpreting the meaning of the textual demand—the hermeneutic gesture—then by transcribing that meaning into the fleshly forms of social praxis."[86]

If we properly, bodily respond to the ghostly community of Friel's drama, we must match our actions to that of the main characters. Anthony Roche observes that "what is at the heart of Friel's play, as it is of so much political mobilization in Northern Ireland, is that its three central characters were marchers, that they sought to establish a foundational space by walking."[87] Of all Friel's dramas, *The Freedom of the City* perhaps most urgently calls us to some sort of action and justice through its gesturing, speaking ghosts. The germ of the new Northern Ireland that is slowly emerging from the psychological and physical rubble of the past Troubles can be found in such truthfulness imagined in the heart of this rich play.

Friel was not sufficiently detached from the events of Bloody Sunday and from the Widgery Tribunal's report when he wrote *The Freedom of the City*, as he has acknowledged,[88] but his artistic imagination was powerful enough to create a consoling narrative of freedom that largely redeems his near-immediate response. The play's "true fiction" accords with a tendency of Friel that Seamus Deane has noticed: "Friel still adheres to his fascination with the human capacity for producing consoling fictions to make life more tolerable. Although he destroys these fictions he does not, with that, destroy the motives that produced them—motives which are rooted in the human being's wish for dignity as well as in his tendency to avoid reality."[89] Friel's fictionalized characters thus attain a dignity their real-life counterparts were never granted by the British soldiers who shot them that fateful January day in 1972 during Bloody Sunday.

Despite its emotionalism, its occasional incorporation of verbatim wording and other phrasing that veers uncomfortably close to that of the Widgery Report, and its rapid publication and production so soon after Bloody Sunday, *The Freedom of the City* deserves considerable acclaim for its balanced critique of both brutal British imperialism and violent, myth-imbued Irish republicanism. Friel's analysis and rejection of Irish republicanism is especially notable given his father's immersion in nationalist politics. Paddy Friel, the playwright's father, served three terms on the Derry Corporation as a Nationalist councilor from the South Ward (representing the Bogside, Creggan, and Brandywell), until the corporation was suspended in 1969 as a result of the Troubles.[90] As Scott Boltwood has argued, however, Friel has become "progressively disenchanted with any notion of a constricting national identity, or Irishness,"[91] and thus we must understand *this play* as marking Friel's increasing disillusion with Irish nationalism.

In regard to Friel's assessment of nationalist myth-making in the play, Elmer Andrews has argued that he criticizes "the recognizably Gaelic, Catholic, Nationalist idioms of myth, tradition, piety and martyrdom" by showing how these idioms "condemn that group to a demoralizing cycle of recurrence and eternal defeat," concluding by noting that "[i]n choosing to foreground a particular form of imaginative projection in a context of tragic waste, he is warning against, not reinforcing, a group's predisposition to recollect itself in terms of such gambits of despair."[92] Although Friel's sympathies lie with the families and friends of the protesters injured and slaughtered that day, his play anticipates Andrews's suggestion that constantly dwelling upon narratives of despair can be disabling for members of persecuted groups.[93] At the same time, the nationalist community in Northern Ireland has long felt it cannot have real peace and healing until its slain relatives and friends are cleared from the charges that they were armed instigators of the violence that occurred on that day.

The inquiry into the tragic deaths of Bloody Sunday by Lord Saville was told on the third day of the hearing on June 14, 1999 by Arthur Harvey QC, lawyer for several of the families of those injured and killed, that "it was entirely 'undesirable' that the ghost of the unsuccessful Widgery investigation, at which [British] soldiers were allowed anonymity, should be allowed to 'walk the corridors of the Saville Inquiry.'"[94] *The Freedom of the City* suggests the continuing political resonance of Friel's statement about exploring one's personal past that he made in 1972, the year before the play was performed: "We call up our ghosts not to lay them but in the hope of having the genuine dialogue with them we didn't have when we had the opportunity."[95] This drama enacts that dialogue, enabling us to eavesdrop on and temporarily become part of a fictional, provisional community of Catholic civil rights marchers who are drawn together for a short time to poignantly show us their humanity and individuality in a specific place, wherein they form an imagined community, outside the flattening narratives of British empiricism and Irish nationalism.

Patrick Maley's assessment of *Freedom*'s staging of various dissonances for audiences is particularly helpful in our apprehension of what Friel's play asks of current and future readers. Maley first audaciously posits that "more invested in its audience than it is in its antecedent events, the play asks audiences not simply to recognize that priests, republicans, reporters, soldiers, authorities, and others surrounding Bloody Sunday were capricious curators of history." While it is difficult to argue that the play is less invested in the events of Bloody Sunday than in its audience, particularly given Friel's admission of writing the play so soon after the release of the Widgery Report, Maley's second point is much more convincing (and notice how it is inextricably connected to the events of that day). He argues, "It demands that audience members weave that awareness into our individual and collective consciousness of the event, existing as an active posterity that is constantly crafting and re-crafting our understanding and relationship to history." Most interestingly, he finally posits that "the play locates its audience in the space of dissonance on which *Freedom* is built, fostering posterity within that unsettled space, and demanding that posterity renegotiate constantly its relationship to history."[96]

Friel's revenant drama, with its persistently pacing ghosts, suggests that a true assessment of the events is not irrecoverable and can be part of such a negotiation. Instead, this truth must be reached through a clear-eyed process that rejects both British government propaganda that sees the protesters as violent republicans and an Irish nationalist narrative that sometimes views the slain protesters as instant political martyrs, ignoring their richly complex humanity and that of many other innocent victims of the Troubles. Despite its despair and even because of it, *The Freedom of the City* gives us what Mark William Roche has called for, "moments of harmony within a world of contingency, which might represent a nonlinear, nonteleological, almost spatialized version of synthetic literature."[97] Thus, the play portrays an imagined potential for community in the midst of the Troubles that Northern Ireland continues to grope toward.

For many years, the official British history of the events of Bloody Sunday, given an imprimatur by the hastily convened and ill-founded conclusions of the Widgery Tribunal, resembled Paul Ricoeur's formulation of how rhetoric is employed by ideologues to create an "imposed memory" that "is armed with a history that is itself 'authorized,' the official history, the history publicly learned and celebrated."[98] Notice how Ricoeur suggests that such a history is itself at least metaphorically bellicose, which helps us understand better the "authorized" history of the actions of the overly aggressive, murderous British Army's First Battalion Parachute Regiment on January 30, 1972. But at 3:30 PM on June 15, 2010, in a statement viewed by a crowd of 6,000 people on a large-screen television set up outside the Londonderry/Derry Guildhall, British Prime Minister David Cameron announced to the House of Commons that the killings of the fourteen protesters on Bloody Sunday were "unjustified and unjustifiable." Cameron went on to apologize for the murders: "On behalf of the government and on behalf of the country, I am deeply sorry."[99] His announcement, however, was upstaged by a moment of drama that took place at 3:26 PM when a hand appeared in an aperture of a stained-glass window high up in the Guildhall and gave a "thumbs-up," which led to a loud cheer from the assembled crowd. The relatives of the fourteen dead had been given an advance copy of the Saville Report, and one of them then excitedly signaled the crowd.[100]

Thus, the city of Londonderry/Derry continues to surprise us, proving the truth of Lewis Mumford's claim that the city in general is inherently dramatic: "[E]very phase of the drama it stages shall have . . . the illumination of consciousness, the stamp of purpose, the colour of love. That magnification of all the dimensions of life, through emotional communion, rational communication, technological mastery, and above all, dramatic representation, has been the supreme office of the city in history."[101] That moment in June 2010 on the Guildhall Square contains all these elements—emotional communion (the tears of relief and joy), rational communication and technological mastery (the giant television screen), and dramatic representation (the thumbs-up gesture)—expressed within a local community united in the midst of a still-divided city.

Drawing on Ricoeur's concept of memory in *Memory, History, Forgetting*, Richard Kearney has argued that memorials have a transfiguring role to play that involves a "creative retrieval of the betrayed promises of the past, so that we may respond to our 'debt to the dead' and endeavor to give them a voice. . . . [T]o try to give a future to the past by remembering it in some right way, ethically and poetically."[102] *The Freedom of the City* works in precisely this way, as a sort of theatrical memorial that names the dead and enables them to reacquire their own distinctive voices.

By giving Lily, Skinner, and Michael their voices—and by extension, giving voices back to the dead of Bloody Sunday—Friel leads us into a metaphysical realm that, as Antonin Artaud puts it, "forces language to 'convey what it does not normally convey.'"[103] Drawing on Artaud's theories of drama in his *The Theatre and Its Double*, Virginie Roche-Tiengo argues that "nobody living should be able to hear Michael, Lily, and Skinner's ultimate confrontation with the absolute, the everlasting power of Thanatos," but Friel "restores theatre to what Artaud calls 'a religious, metaphysical position.'"[104] Thus, "we hear voices from the otherworld, and [we] witness motionless ghost-like bodies, the quintessence of everlasting remembrance and self-knowledge."[105] In this immensely privileged position of auditors of these voices from beyond the grave, we apprehend not only their humanity—their hopes and dreams—but their spirituality as well. Reincarnating them, as it were, before our eyes, Friel suggests how these embodied souls call and beckon to us, inviting us into their lives and afterlives. Through them, we have a communion with the dead, and we are given a responsibility to remember them into the future.

Beginning with this moment of dramatic hope in June of 2010, the anger, bitterness, and despair of Friel's play will eventually be laid to rest as the remembered and revivified victims of that terrible day have been given the justice and respect their families and friends awaited during thirty-eight long years. But just as important, the play calls us to keep their memory alive. Only in our continually cultivated memories can these dead (and those from other atrocities) be kept alive, kept in an emplaced, imagined, spiritual community, whereby their memory can be nourished by—and nourish—us.

5

Interchapter

Rain, Lies, and Healing: Faith Healer *at the Donmar Warehouse, London, July 29, 2016*

Rain—three walls of it—spattering, shimmering, shining. Or is it crystal beads? A look over the balcony reveals water all over the edge of the stage. Water, pouring rain, opened each of the four monologues of the 2016 Donmar Warehouse production of *Faith Healer* in London, June 23–August 20. Such deluges seem appropriate for a play whose subjects have such miserable lives in so many ways. And the rain's ability to obscure the stage until a given character emerges and starts speaking serves to suggest the veil of lies told by each character.

Let it also be said immediately that the spatial intimacy of the Donmar, heightened by the falling rain that pulls us audience members stage-ward, trying to peer through it, mightily contributes to this production's success.

The acting by Stephen Dillane, playing Frank Hardy, and Gina McKee, playing Grace, was very fine, as was the direction by Lyndsey Turner, but the star of this production was Ron Cook who played Frank's Cockney manager Teddy with aplomb, wryness, humor, and finally, great poignancy. Because Teddy's monologue follows that delivered by the broken-hearted Grace, audiences are usually desperate for levity and Cook delivers. How many bottles of Bass Beer, often featured in Joyce's *Ulysses*, however, can one man open?

As Dillane takes us humorously through the highs and lows of Frank's itinerant life as a faith healer, gradually we realize that for him, Grace is just as "fantastic" as Frank—and for much more human reasons. If Frank's sporadic healing ability, most memorably evoked by the recollection of his healing ten afflicted people that long-ago night in Llanbethian, Wales, is "fantastic," so is Grace's love for him and for the stillborn, "black-faced baby" she gives birth to in Kinlochbervie, Scotland, a baby Frank never explicitly acknowledges but implicitly recognizes. And Grace is "fantastic" as well for Teddy, as Ron Cook's delivery convinces us, in his love for her, even though he professes twice that it was a "professional relationship."

As we are gradually drawn into these characters' lives by their pleading appeals to us, this production reverses the three-sided rain-enclosure and breaks theater's fourth wall, leading us to laugh, love, and finally, ascertain the truth of these narratives. Thus, the conclusion of Frank's final monologue, uttered as his ghost steps through what can only be a proscenium arch—another three-sided space—into the second yard beyond the lounge bar that fateful night in Ballybeg, forever the last day of August, ushers us into an intimate yet immense space, something like Peter Brooks's "holy theater."

Ritual is always at the heart of Friel's drama, and in this belief, it goes back to the origins of drama itself. As Frank moves silently toward his killers, he also moves toward us, implicating us, in a way, in his vicious (offstage) murder. But simultaneously, as Dillane's quietly restrained but increasingly exultant intonation indicates, we are somehow made whole, complete, as we finally imagine Frank being torn apart by these violent, silent men. He speaks earlier, in his first monologue, of his faith healing audiences being "ripped apart" when they see or experience one of his healings.

Now, as he imagines his death making him whole, complete, he offers that possibility of wholeness to us in a community that can only be called spiritual.

The rain stops. The play stops. But the temporary community formed by the Donmar Warehouse production of *Faith Healer* lingers on, shimmering with possibility before us.

6

Faith Healer

Woundedness, Homecoming, and Wholeness

> I am sure that our writers find it distasteful or perhaps too
> remote from their imaginative reach to write about the troubles
> and in a way I envy them that fastidiousness or incapacity or
> whatever but for those of us who grew up with the situation,
> whose daily life and experience is pigmented with it, the ques-
> tion is not can or should we write about it, but how can we
> write about it.
> —Brian Friel, "Friel's Sense of Conflict"

When Fintan O'Toole interviewed Friel in 1982, he asked the playwright about the possibility of an autobiographical source for the
preponderance of dislocated characters in his work. Friel responded,
"There is certainly a sense of rootlessness and impermanence. It may
well be the inheritance of being a member of the Northern minority. . . . [Y]ou are certainly at home but in some sense exile is imposed
upon you."[1] Years later Richard Pine, one of Friel's most discerning
critics, was asked by an interviewer, "What are Friel's main thematic
preoccupations?" Pine's remark has great pertinence for the concerns
of this chapter: "Questioning the concept of home. He said to me
that he resists the concept of community, and [he] is not sure that he
can accept the idea of home, and that is a massive preoccupation."[2]

In his draft notes for *Faith Healer*, Friel's greatest and most chal-
lenging play, written beginning in 1975, he mused about the concept of home and how it is intertwined with faith, wondering, "Is
HOME the least likely environment for faith and the most needful

141

of healing? Why does faith die at home? And why do we return home to kill the faith we . . . have deliberately acquired elsewhere?"[3] This first question suggests why Frank, Teddy, and Grace never tour Ballybeg—perhaps because it is "the least likely environment for faith." Yet, it seems it is also "the most needful of healing," and thus, Frank finally returns home. But does he go home to "kill" his faith and to "cure" himself? To heal his home? Grace speculates in her monologue that while she and Teddy did not "want to come back to Ireland," Frank "insisted. He had been in bad shape for months and although he didn't say it . . . I knew that he had some sense that Ireland might somehow recharge him, maybe even restore him" (*BFP1* 351). But this is sheer speculation on her part, and Friel's draft notes suggest instead that Frank returns to Ireland not to be recharged and "restore[d]," but to kill his faith in healing others and thus die to his old egotistical self. Friel did not know at that time how to convey the import of Frank's death, but he did clearly know that he would confront McGarvey, the disabled character: "What happens when Frank goes out of that pub to confront that cripple?" Uncertain, he then wrote in his notes, "Is it an end? Is it a beginning?"[4] This chapter suggests Frank's death is both: he dies to dependence on others founded on his ability to heal and in so doing, actually becomes himself for the first time, born into a new life. That life is not the Christian afterlife, but an eternity of performing his life—particularly his final twenty-four hours—for readers and audiences time and again. Frank succeeds, that is, in staging his many failures and in resurrecting himself over and over, recreates for us his profound physical, then spiritual community he achieved with his killers, with Grace and Teddy that last night, and that he wants to share with us. Although he is dismembered by his killers, he nonetheless gives the other characters, us, and even, potentially, Northern Ireland a temporary sense of wholeness.

These themes of exile, homecoming, and community are all intertwined in *Faith Healer*. It would be too simple to make a reductive equation of Friel with his most disturbing and alluring character, Frank Hardy, the Faith Healer, but certainly parallels abound, and the political implications of the play in the context of the conflict in Northern Ireland have yet to be fully explored, as do its spiritual resonances, and this chapter finally tries to elucidate the peculiar spiritual communion Frank Hardy has with his killers, other characters, and perhaps with audience members as well.

The political valences of *Faith Healer* can be apprehended by recovering and clarifying the mythic analogues Friel establishes for Frank Hardy. Frank's actions cast him variously as a figure analogous to but not identical with Dionysus, Cuchulain, and Christ. His imminent dissection has an additional mythic reverberation of the Red Hand of Ulster, a culturally and politically conflicted symbol of the province. When asked about the analogy between faith healing and the waxing and waning of the artistic gift, Friel admits about *Faith Healer*, "I think as a play and as theatre it has got to succeed at its own level first. And if there are extensions into that kind of analogous situation . . . fine."[5] And yet there has been no convincing analogy drawn in the criticism on this rich play, beyond the obvious artistic analogy, to the Troubles.[6] Friel has admitted, however, in his lengthiest and most significant statement ever about the conflict in Northern Ireland, that writers who treat the Troubles engage in "an attempt to reveal the Northern situation in different ways, by elaborate metaphor, by historical analogy."[7] Thus my reading of *Faith Healer* by analogy, myth, and symbolism has been given considerable warrant by Friel himself.

There is some evidence for his view of the violence in Northern Ireland as inherently theatrical, despite his protestation, in the early 1970s, as we have seen in chapter 4's discussion of *The Freedom of the City*, that he was not interested in writing a play about the Troubles. In fact, Friel told Fintan O'Toole in 1982 that Northern Ireland colors everything he does, stating, "The experience is there, it's available. We didn't create it, and it has coloured all our lives and adjusted all our stances in some way. What the hell can we do but look at it?"[8] Indeed. And in gazing at Frank Hardy and listening to his final monologue, we are led not only to recognize Friel's condemnation of the intimate violence in contemporary Northern Ireland but also to perceive that tendency toward violence in our own hearts as we enter into a temporary spiritual community with Frank and the other characters, including his killers.

Friel's own life, to some degree, and certainly this drama exemplify what Una Chaudhuri has termed "geopathology," the mental dis-ease that often appears "as a series of ruptures and displacements in various orders of location, from the micro- to the macrospatial, from home to nature, with intermediary space concepts such as neighborhood, hometown, community, and country ranged in between."[9] In her analysis of Eugene O'Neill's *Long Day's Journey into Night*, Chaudhuri makes a provocative and compelling argument for my purposes here in showing the persistence of dislocation for Friel's three major characters in *Faith Healer*: "For the characters, acting (lies, dissimulation, self-deception) provides a way to *occupy* spaces without *inhabiting* them (a solution to the problem of home). . . . Performance succeeds, where addiction fails, in easing the symptoms of what I am calling geopathic disorders, the suffering caused by one's location."[10] Certainly, looking back to Private Gar's antic performances in *Philadelphia, Here I Come!* and Skinner's manic behavior in *The Freedom of the City*, we can see ample evidence of their geopathic disorders as each suffers in his surroundings.

But *Faith Healer* marks an apogee in Friel's portrayal of geopathology as well as a turn toward homecoming in the form of the place of ritualized theater set in his perennial location of Ballybeg. The long absences of Friel's characters from their homes in this play signify their geopathology. Their repeated performances through dissimulation assuage their problems with attachment to a particular place for a time. Frank Hardy's alcohol addiction is one of the major foci of the play, as Frank McGuinness has pointed out.[11] Hardy's habitual use of alcohol is clearly an attempt to ease the symptoms of his "geopathic disorders," but eventually it fails, as Chaudhuri observes in general about addiction as a coping mechanism for radical dislocation. Frank even admits toward the end of Act One that one of the reasons he returned to Ireland was that "the whiskey wasn't as efficient with the questions as it had been" (*BFP1* 338).

Finally, however, contra Chaudhuri, Frank tires of performance, of lies, of mendacity. In his final, but finally real performance, he walks onto the stage of his death, offering himself up to a horrific death wherein he finally *inhabits* a place (crucially through ritual), not merely *occupies* it, as he has done in the van and in a series of small towns in Wales and Scotland for years. As Seamus Deane has argued, "[I]t is this place, rather than those other places that have been chanted so ritually throughout, that ultimately matters. . . . Ballybeg is unavoidable. What makes it home, and therefore different, is that time and place converge there."[12] Pretense thus is jettisoned in favor of truthfulness. The spiritual connections generated between Frank and his killers, among all of the characters, and through us by extension, brief as they are, shimmer in our minds long after the play is over or this last scene is read. Frank's inhabitation of both Ballybeg and the figurative place of the theatrical stage at the play's conclusion suggests both his and Friel's surrender to the will of the respective audiences with whom they seek to form community.

Frank's final "performance" in the yard behind the pub—a yard that connotes strongly the stage of a theater—invokes ritualistic language to suggest our continuing need to express spirituality in connection with others through community, even the one briefly formed here between Frank and his killers. Through the use of sacred, ritualistic language at the end of Frank's second monologue, Friel manages to instantiate the particular, ordinary-seeming place of the enclosed yard behind the pub in Ballybeg with a sacral feeling. He accomplishes this transformation by rendering the moment akin to what Walter Benjamin calls "Messianic time," a simultaneity of past and future in an imminent present.[13] The ongoing existence of this moment of Frank's sacrifice thus rebuffs empirically measured notions of time such as clock and calendar (a rejection that is more fully articulated in Friel's next play, *Translations*), continually inviting readers and theatergoers into this sacred space to experience with Frank both his pending pain and the potential that that pain releases. As Theodor Adorno reminds us in *Minima Moralia*, "The art-form which has from earliest times laid the highest claims to spirituality, as representation of Ideas, drama, depends equally, by its innermost presuppositions, on an audience."[14]

Robert Tracy has shown how Friel's apprenticeship to Tyrone Guthrie in Minneapolis exposed him to Guthrie's strong interest in the ritualistic theories of J. G. Frazer. He further notes that Guthrie even wrote an essay titled "Theatre as Ritual," which stressed ritual sacrifice and drew an analogy between the death and resurrection of Dionysus in ancient Greece and the death and resurrection of Jesus Christ.[15] Just as important, Tracy argues that Friel's time in training at Maynooth, the Catholic seminary where he spent three years in the mid-1940s, steeped him in the deep knowledge of daily performing Christ's sacrifice in the Mass. As he studied divinity, Friel learned "to play the central part in a ritual that every Catholic priest re-enacts every day, commemorating by re-enacting the sacrifice that Christ performed on the cross. . . . That early training inevitably emphasized the nature of ritual as a magical commemorative act, regularly repeated and always the same."[16] As we will see, Frank Hardy's reenactment of the actions of Dionysus, the Irish mythological hero Cuchulain, and even, in a qualified way, of Jesus Christ enables Friel to offer this character as a symbol of both despair and hope for the contemporary situation in Northern Ireland.

Furthermore, *Faith Healer* makes clear Friel's own privileging of the theater as a sacred place, a replacement for the formerly otherworldly place created by the Catholic Church in Ireland. Robert Welch has observed that Catholic institutions in Ireland from the period roughly from 1860 to 1960 "were places to challenge the mind, the spirit, and the flesh; by asserting their otherness and their difference from the general tendency of twentieth century materialism and secularism they offered Irish society the rebuke of prayer, humility, obedience, and holiness." This "sacramentalist approach to life and to things"[17] that Welch argued the Irish Catholic Church fostered was also, of course, valuable in a period of rampant poverty in Ireland as a respite from grinding poverty and marginalization. Two of the most significant speeches in *Faith Healer* include Teddy's monologue about all the material misery he and Grace and Frank have endured over the years (*BFP1* 367) and his joy that last night in Ballybeg at the happiness in the pub, along with Frank's last monologue about the dematerialization of the "whole corporeal world" and his satisfaction in apprehending the spiritual nature of himself and the wedding guests who are about to kill him (*BFP1* 376). As we shall see, in these passages Friel creates an otherworldly place replete with ritual, signifying sacred meaning, which is identical with the theater itself and the play itself but, finally, not homogenous like ritual.

In one of the most insightful readings of ritual, Louis Dupré observes that despite the ability of both drama and ritual to cast us into a temporary apprehension of flowing, present time,

> theatrical performance differs from liturgical ritual in that during the [dramatic] action the outcome remains unknown—even though the spectators persistently expect it to be an appropriate one. The drama never homogenizes the various parts that compose it, as ritual does. Conflicts may be resolved, but their resolution does not suspend the agonistic quality of existence itself. . . . Though the uncertainty of its outcome distinguishes the drama, the orderly, stylized dramatic processes assure the spectators that they may count on a definite, albeit not definitive, conclusion.[18]

Friel's sure sense of the considerable continuities between ritual and drama, but also his recognition of their discontinuity, together enable him to create dramatic tension through his embrace of uncertainty, one of his favorite principles. We are given "a definite, not definitive, conclusion" because of the act of murder that will occur in the "future" of the play and the ramifications of that murder for the other characters and for us.

A number of commentators on *Faith Healer*, including Tracy, have pointed out the play's privileging of ritual without finally showing its full significance for our understanding of the play. Elmer Andrews, for example, notes that each of Friel's three characters "at times abandons rational communication for the comfort of ritual," arguing further that both Grace's and Frank's chanting of the Welsh and Scottish town names in their monologues "are expressive of the longing for transcendence, for a break with historical reality, a lyric space."[19] And Nicholas Grene, citing Friel himself saying that ritual is "the essence of drama. Drama is a RITE, and always religious in the purest sense," holds that *"Faith Healer* is not about ritual, whether Christian or pagan. . . . It is rather itself a theatrical ritual enacted for its audience."[20] But Andrews and Grene offer little in the way of analysis of this ritual: Grene merely cites the final puzzling scene, noting that "[t]his is open to multiple interpretation [*sic*]" and concluding that "it incorporates and brings to resolution the many themes that the play has enunciated."[21]

I believe that the ceremonial actions of this final scene suggest and reinscribe the necessity for ritual and, by extension, spirituality in our lives. Seamus Heaney has compellingly observed how "Friel's plays ultimately recognize this modern solitude of the person within the universe, and they search for minimally trustworthy bases upon which to situate a spiritually purposeful and value-engendering existence."[22] Heaney omits from this analysis, however, Friel's nearly constant emphasis on the individual's struggle with community. By portraying how drama is essentially communal, ritualistic, and religious, Friel demonstrates the singularity of the events of the play and of each performance or reading, yet through this particularity, suggests its universal authenticity and thus the potentially transformative power for its characters and us. Benjamin argues that "[i]t is significant that the existence of the work of art with reference to its aura is never entirely separated from its ritual function. In other words, the unique value of the 'authentic' work of art has its basis in ritual, the location of its original use value."[23] *Faith Healer*, in this sense, is perennially auratic, authentic, of unique significance each time it is read or performed. To employ Benjamin's language, it eludes reproduction of any type.

⁀

The two places relevant to our purposes in the play are Kinlochbervie, Scotland, where Frank and Gracie's baby was born dead, and the yard behind the pub back in Ballybeg, where Frank, Gracie, and Teddy return, significantly, during harvest, on August 31. If place is an event, as I argued citing Edward Casey in the introduction and in chapter one, Kinlochbervie as a remembered place is also ongoing, but as a site of tragedy in the three characters' minds. "Kinlochbervie" functions as a linguistic substitute for Frank and Grace's stillborn baby who is birthed there. It signifies a patina of sonically aesthetic wholeness coating two linked, ugly, violent separations—the death of the baby itself and Frank's desertion of Grace in her time of need. Grace muses, "I think it's a nice name, Kinlochbervie—a complete sound—a name you wouldn't forget easily" (*BFP1* 345). After this recollection, she recalls how Frank would be "always changing my surname," thus forgetting her publicly (ibid.). Clinging to the name of the village where the baby was born thus becomes a double act of inscribed remembrance—for the unnamed baby and for herself. Frank's and Grace's recitation of the various Welsh and Scottish town names serves to relax them before they tell of particularly unpleasant incidents, such as the baby's death and Frank's death, and also mesmerizes the audience. But in addition, these litanies bespeak separation and segregation, and their continuous nature signifies the way in which those particular places as events are ongoing sites of horror for the characters. Even Llanbethian, Wales, where Frank healed ten people in one night, is an unpleasant memory for Teddy, who is ditched by Frank and Grace as they run off to a hotel for a spree (360).

Surprisingly, perhaps, what also seems like a continuing, entrapping narrative, the finally told story of Frank's murder behind the pub during that fateful harvest season in Ballybeg, actually becomes a site of potential wherein ritual is restored metatheatrically to its proper place in the theater. Thus we are given a strange community of the murdered and his murderers in a living event that contrasts those places enshrined in the town name litanies. Even though Frank Hardy is portrayed as walking to his sure death, that last scene accrues a revivifying, poetic quality, essentially the reverse of the incident with Grace's delivery in Kinlochbervie, an event that promises life but delivers death. Frank, with his greater facility of words, more easily and fully enchants the audience with his painterly description of the ritualized place of his death compared to Grace, with her limited but powerful evocation of her delivery of her dead baby and the subsequent, similarly ritualistic, "little ceremony" with Teddy afterward (*BFP1* 364).

Richard Allen Cave has argued that "[t]he body is continually described in *Faith Healer* in ways that provoke (indeed at times haunt) the imagination of the audience."[24] Indeed, we are haunted by the terrifyingly graphic scene in the bloody van during Grace's delivery (*BFP1* 363). Interestingly, however, the most disturbing somatic image is one never described by Friel—the rending of Frank's body that we can only imagine in the wake of the play's conclusion. The process by which Friel creates the lingering spectral presences of Grace and Frank becomes a pagan, spiritual reversal of the Catholic concept of transubstantiation. Instead of the elements of the Eucharist becoming Christ's literal body and blood, the utter materiality of the Hardys' bodies and their squalid living conditions must be fully articulated so that these can gradually dematerialize in two significant sections of the play: when Teddy recalls that last night of Frank's life (367) and in the closing lines of the play (376).

In language that strikingly anticipates and captures his aim in *Faith Healer*, and that I also cited in the chapter on my hauntological discussion of *The Freedom of the City*, Friel has argued in his autobiographical essay "Self-Portrait" that "we call up our ghosts not to lay them but in the hope of having the genuine dialogue with them we didn't have when we had the opportunity."[25] If, as Colin Davis has argued, Derrida's concept of hauntology enables us to "interrogate our relation to the dead, examine the elusive identities of the living, and explore the boundaries between the thought and unthought," Friel's ghostly faith healer and his faithful wife Grace are specters that "gesture towards a still unformulated future,"[26] one rife with positive implications for Friel's sense of how spirituality still speaks to us and even for how an emerging Northern Ireland might still become a community.

Frank Hardy says in his opening monologue that he played Welsh and Scottish villages, not English ones, "because Teddy and Gracie were English and they believed, God help them, that the Celtic temperament was more receptive to us" (*BFP1* 332). But "the Celtic temperament" was generally *not* receptive to them; often they were lucky to have six people in the audience, as Grace notes in her monologue (350). Friel's concern runs much deeper than depicting some sort of Celtic spirituality that is on the wane; he wants to portray hope versus despair, belief versus disbelief, the potential power of the immaterial versus the material. *Faith Healer* is the drama that most fully enacts his theory of "the theatre of hope and despair" that I explore in the second interchapter to this study. Throughout the play, Frank Hardy wavers back and forth between hope and despair, between drunkenness and sobriety, between healing and charlatanism.

Frank is another antimodern character who is sacrificed in a mythic way. He points out in the opening lines of his monologue that the "identical," "derelict" Scottish and Welsh buildings they have met in over the years usually contain remnants of past rituals: "Maybe in a corner a withered sheaf of wheat from a harvest thanksgiving of years ago or a fragment of a Christmas decoration across a window—relicts of abandoned rituals. Because the people we moved among were beyond that kind of celebration" (*BFP1* 332). Frank concludes his opening monologue by recalling the toasts they drank that last night in Ballybeg with the wedding guests and publican, which celebrated human and natural fertility: "Toasts to the departed groom and his prowess. To the bride and her fertility. To the rich harvest—the corn, the wheat, the barley. Toasts to all Septembers and all harvests and to all things ripe and eager for the reaper. A Dionysian night. A Bacchanalian night. A frenzied, excessive Irish night when ritual was consciously and relentlessly debauched" (340). As these two passages show, Frank thinks the people they have moved among are beyond ritual—they even debauch it in the pub—but in that final night in Ballybeg, partly because of drink, partly because of Frank's boasting, ritual rears its violent head and Frank is hacked and beaten to death in a grotesque expression of ritual's residual presence in the local community.

Grace recalls that Frank had been in the habit of "picking fights with strangers—cornering someone in a pub and boasting that he could perform miracles and having people laugh at him" in the past year (*BFP1* 351). This last night in Ballybeg, then, seems in keeping with Frank's recent habit of "picking fights" as he purposely chooses the ultimate fight of his life by curing Donal's finger and lingering until he would be called upon to heal McGarvey, who is present in his wheelchair in Grace's monologue and in both of Frank's. Grace even remembers realizing that Frank would try to heal McGarvey before the end of the evening: "And I knew at once [after Frank cured Donal]—I knew it instinctively—that before the night was out he was going to measure himself against the cripple in the wheelchair. And he did. . . . And throughout the night the others had become crazed with drink and he had gone very still and sat with his eyes half-closed but never for a second taking them off the invalid" (352–53).

Frank's curing of Donal's finger coupled with his staring at McGarvey all night finally provokes the other four men into testing his faith healing. They have already prepared for his failure—and may not even let him try to heal McGarvey, although it is impossible to tell—by placing an axe, crowbar, mallet, and hay-fork in the back of a trailer outside in the yard where they call him at dawn (*BFP1* 375). Frank says he has been warned by the landlord to get out of there before the men come back, and whether or not this is a lie too, the representation of the landlord's supposed response suggests the violence that awaits Frank. He claims the landlord calls them "'savage bloody men'" who will "'kill you. I know them. They'll kill you'" (374). As he steps into the yard for this final encounter, he sees McGarvey and thinks how patient, young, and innocent he looks, with "[n]ot a hint of savagery" (375). McGarvey's lack of savagery heightens the audience's perception of the violence that the other four men must have used upon Frank, though this violence is never portrayed. Teddy, however, calls the four men who kill Frank "those bloody Irish Apaches," suggesting through his stereotypical view of the barbarity common to both the Irish and Native Americans the utter violence done to Frank that fateful night (366). That Frank is killed savagely seems clear. But why and to what purpose?

His frenzied killing suggests that he is another sacrificial victim, somewhat similar to the victims at the end of *Freedom* and Yolland in *Translations*. But unlike those earlier victims, Frank *wants* to be killed—to free himself from the nagging questions about his ability and about the power and persistence of ritual that have haunted him his whole life. The significance of his murder at harvest time also signifies a very different implication from Yolland's murder during harvest season in *Translations*, as we will see. Yolland's death suggests the loss of a potential rapprochement between the Irish and the English at a significant moment in Irish history. He is also a hybrid figure, whose interest in local culture generally acts as a temporary stay against modernity and industrialism. But Frank's death, while also symbolizing the death of local communities, is more potentially renewing than Yolland's murder. As Nicholas Grene has argued, Frank's death implies a mythic power of renewal on a national basis: "In *Faith Healer*, the circumstances of Frank Hardy's violent murder suggest glancingly the sacrificial death of the king who must be killed to renew the life of his country, a motif much more explicitly dramatized in *Wonderful Tennessee*."[27] And Robert Tracy claims that in this moment of sacrifice, "Friel goes back to the ritualistic origins of theatre to create at once a modern miracle play and a drama of sacrifice, a kind of commemorative passion play, in which Frank's role as Faith Healer brings him to accept the related role of sacrificial victim."[28] These readings get closer to the significance of the last scene and Frank's motives for offering himself to his killers than Ulf Dantanus's claim that Frank's oppressive childhood and the similarly oppressive society which he returns to that night in Ballybeg "could be seen as having demanded a sacrifice for his efforts to liberate himself from it."[29] Frank has transcended his local society and those he has visited in Wales and Scotland for so many years. His sacrifice thus seems more analogous to the death of the fisher king in renewing spiritually dry societies. His gift and his body die, but he remains

behind, a ghostly voice warning Ireland and all societies of the necessity to recognize the common spiritual unity even among enemies.

Richard Pine has stated flatly that "[e]xcept when (as in *Living
Quarters* or *Aristocrats*) he employs stage 'tricks' . . . Friel traffics in
ordinary sensations: we see no ghosts, we hear no voices, we are not
bewitched by faery,"[30] but this is an astonishingly untenable statement, given both the ghosts that are the major actors in *The Freedom of the City* and *Faith Healer* and Pine's own deep interest in
metaphysical issues within Friel's plays throughout his magisterial
book. Grene, however, has articulated "Friel's imaginative prefer-
ence for the revenant drama," pointing to the last passage of *Faith
Healer* in which everything corporeal dematerializes, and arguing
that Friel often quests "for this sort of truth beyond the body."[31] The
playwright's penchant for transcendence, despite the messy, sordid
realities of his three characters' lives in the play, finally reaches its
height in Frank's last monologue. Alice Rayner argues that of all the
genres, "theatre, in all of its aspects, uniquely insists on the reality
of ghosts," but immediately notes that "something is fundamentally
unassimilable about ghosts."[32] As we will see, this essentially spiritual truth that Friel's characters perform enables a triple community
to potentially be formed—among Frank and his killers, among the
audience and the actors of the play, and, most audaciously and only
symbolically, among divided factions in Northern Ireland. Without
applying this theory specifically to *Faith Healer*, Richard Kearney
has argued in one of the seminal articles on Friel that "[t]he festering
wound of the North is a constant reminder for Friel that the body
politic of the Irish nation is deeply hemorrhaged," and thus that "[a]n
amputated Ulster acts as a phantom limb haunting his work."[33] The
imminent rending of Frank Hardy's body at the conclusion of *Faith
Healer* signifies that his body, like Cuchulain's in Irish mythology,
symbolizes a divided Northern Ireland.

Frank Hardy and his killers therefore enter into a *communitas*
relationship with each other, in anthropologist Victor Turner's terms.
Turner defines *communitas* as "an unmediated relationship between
historical, idiosyncratic, concrete individuals."[34] Of the three types of

communitas that Turner identifies, the final moment of Friel's *Faith Healer* accords well with spontaneous *communitas*, a state in which there is "'a direct, immediate and total confrontation of human identities,' a deep rather than intense style of personal interaction. 'It has something *magical* about it. Subjectively, there is in it a feeling of endless power.'"[35] This is only a temporary state, unregulated by societal structures such as those that control so-called normative *communitas*. Crucially for Friel's play, which is shot through with falsehoods and deceptions, especially those uttered by Frank Hardy, when spontaneous *communitas* occurs a condition of honesty and unpretentiousness is created, and "[i]ndividuals who interact with one another" in this mode "become totally absorbed into a single, synchronized, fluid event," as Turner observes.[36]

Frank Hardy's language in this final scene bespeaks such an absorption, such a fluidity as he appreciates his own body and those of the men—all incarnated beings—then has a profound spiritual communion with them as their bodies seem to dematerialize:

> And as I walked I became possessed of a strange and trembling intimation: that the whole corporeal world—the cobbles, the trees, the sky, those four malign implements [the axe, crowbar, mallet, and hay-fork]—somehow they had shed their physical reality and had become mere imaginings, and that in all existence there was only myself and the wedding guests. And that intimation in turn gave way to a stronger sense: that even we had ceased to be physical and existed only in spirit, *only in the need we had for each other.* (BFP1 375–76; my emphasis)

Frank's sense of the initial dematerialization of everything around him except himself and the wedding guests, whose bodily presences are "all existence," suggests he must return to some incarnated sense of himself before he can have the spiritual kinship with his killers that follows. One of Friel's original passages of dialogue for Frank that did not make it into the final version captures his oscillating sense of himself as torn between body and spirit, rather than understanding both are united, and seeing only the spiritual as his essential self: "Sometimes I was totally, essentially me—a spiritual distillation. Other times I was a rag-and-bone man, a dirty physical hulk."[37] Here, in the conclusion as Frank walks toward the men and offers himself to them, he finally realizes his physicality and has an initial incarnated recognition of community with these farmers, whom he describes in his first monologue in utterly physical terms: "Good suits. White carnations. Dark, angular faces. Thick fingers and black nails" (*BFP1* 339). Frank, who has spent his whole "professional" life in dirty, sordid conditions, has always rejected them in favor of his soaring rhetoric and sense of himself as an aristocrat, above those whom he would cure. He has thus abstracted himself and his own body for years, which is another reason he cannot admit that Grace had the stillborn child in Kinlochbervie. To recognize that child would be an admission of his physical nature, which he has denied, as a sort of contemporary Gnostic. Now, however, he finally accepts his embodiment, and in doing so, can then proceed into a soul-communion with the farmers.

Soul and body are never sundered for Friel, and Frank's phrase— "that even we had ceased to be physical and existed only in spirit"— here stems from a profound recognition of his common spiritual relationship with the wedding guests who are about to kill him by mutilating his body. The satisfaction inherent in this formation of spontaneous *communitas*, created through Frank's ritualistic movements and words and through the final acceptance of his embodiment, generates in him a profound elation, as something akin to a religious experience unfolds. At the beginning of Part Four, the stage directions observe of Frank Hardy that *"there should be tenuous evidence of a slightly heightened pulse-rate, of something approximating to excitement in him, perhaps in the way his minds leaps without apparent connection from thought to thought"* (370). Frank's ghost is growing more agitated because he will shortly narrate the moments leading up to his death, but the agitation also conveys his anticipation of the temporary formation of community. At the end of this last section, Friel's stage directions tell us that Frank *"takes off his*

hat as if he were entering a church and holds it at his chest. He is
both awed and elated" (376). His recognition that "for the first time
I had a simple and genuine sense of home-coming" (ibid.), while he
did not experience this feeling upon his return to Ballybeg earlier
in the evening (338), demonstrates the profound significance of this
spiritual event.

The final act of Frank's offering himself to the waiting farmers is
a homecoming precisely because he is experiencing *communitas*, not
because he is back in Ireland, his original home. He is now inhabiting
a place in which his pretensions have been jettisoned and where he
now sees himself not as "an aristocrat" (*BFP1* 333), as he does when
he heals someone and is "whole in myself" (ibid.), but as equal to
others, another embodied soul. In a recognition of his solipsism aris-
ing from his feeling of being "an aristocrat" at such moments, Grace
has complained bitterly in her monologue about his "private power,"
about his "certainty that was accessible only to him" (343) shortly
before he would perform. As she recalls, "And then, for him, I didn't
exist. Many, many times I didn't exist for him. But before a performance this exclusion—no, it wasn't an exclusion, it was an erasion—
this erasion was absolute: he obliterated me" (344).[38] The "others" to
whom Frank does not feel superior are the four wedding guests and
their wheelchair-bound friend, McGarvey, his putative last audience
for his last "performance." And instead of feeling "whole in myself"
when healing someone, Frank experiences the reverse: instead, he
now feels gradually that he is connected to the farmers just as they
are about to ritually rend and tear his body.

In looking back over Frank's life from this point, we see how he
has passed through the first stage of Arnold van Gennep's "transition
rites," which include separation, margin, and reaggregation. As Victor Turner reads Gennep, the separation stage "comprises symbolic
behavior signifying the detachment of the individual or the group
from either an earlier fixed point in the social structure or from an
established set of cultural conditions."[39] Frank Hardy (and Grace
and Teddy, too, for that matter) went through separation when he
left Ireland for the life on the road as a performing faith healer. Then,

of course, his life on the road with Grace and Teddy marks his dwelling, literally and figuratively, on the margin as they visit a series of Welsh and Scottish villages and perform in the "kirks or meeting-houses or schools—all identical, all derelict" (*BFP1* 332). During this liminal period, Frank, like other liminars, "becomes ambiguous, neither here nor there, betwixt and between all fixed points of classification," as Turner puts it.[40] His mendacity is dominant, as he increasingly fluctuates among playing roles of the hurt lover, the charlatan, the showman, the dutiful son; and increasingly, he turns on Grace.

Finally, back in Ballybeg on this fateful harvest evening that slowly lengthens into morning just as August turns into September—a liminal time between night and day and between two months—Frank moves through the final part of his liminal stage. Besides experiencing these liminal passages of time, he passes through a threshold, "a wooden door" (*BFP1* 375), and then sees that "the wall facing me as I walked out was breached by an arched entrance" (ibid.). As he "walked across that yard, over those worn cobbles, towards the arched entrance," he sees "framed in it, you would think poised symmetrically, were the four wedding guests; and in front of them, in his wheelchair, McGarvey" (ibid.). Note the hypnotic language of the liminar here: the procession of adverbial clauses enchants us and focuses our attention on Frank's ritualistic walk and its inherently in-between qualities. Significantly, the five men sit framed in the archway, another threshold (the Latin *limen* literally means "threshold"). As Turner remarks elsewhere, liminal entities usually display behavior similar to that of Frank Hardy's humility and supplication here: "Their behavior is normally passive or humble; they must obey their instructors implicitly, and [they must] accept arbitrary punishment without complaint. It is as though they are being reduced or ground down to a uniform condition to be fashioned anew and endowed with additional powers to enable them to cope with their new station in life."[41]

Frank reaches the reaggregation stage only with his imminent death, in which "the passage is consummated and the ritual subject, the neophyte or initiand reenters the social structure, often, but not always at a higher status level. *Ritual degradation occurs* as well as elevation."[42] Frank is about to be ritually degraded and slowly torn apart with the assembled farm implements, but interestingly, before he will be murdered, he seeks out his murderers: "I walked across the yard towards them" (*BFP1* 375). He has always held himself aloof and had the people who sought healing approach him; now, he moves into *communitas* and thus equality with his last "audience."

But the applicability of van Gennep's and Turner's analysis of this tripartite process finally falters with Frank's murder: their stages are symbolic and describe situations where the liminar lives, not dies. What are we to make of Frank's literal enactments of this process? To discover why Frank must literally die we must turn to his successful, temporary healing of his relationship with Grace earlier in the night, recalled by Teddy in a little-analyzed passage that suggests Teddy too is temporarily healed. This double healing makes Frank realize that literal self-sacrifice might produce lasting healing in Teddy and Grace and perhaps others who are troubled emotionally or spiritually.

Toward the end of Teddy's monologue, the longest and most complete passage (except about Frank's last few hours, during which Teddy is passed out drunk), he mentions that as Grace sung an Irish song that night, he is transfixed by Frank's gaze, a gaze that always signals he is about to attempt a cure:

And the way he's gazing at me and the look he has on his face is exactly the way he looks into somebody he knows he's going to cure. . . . It's a look that says two things. It says: No need to speak—I know exactly what the trouble is. And at the same time it says: I am now going to cure you of that trouble. That's the look he gave me. He held me in that look for—what?—thirty seconds. And then he turned away from me and looked at her—sort of directed his look towards her so that I had to look at her too. And suddenly she is this terrific woman that of course I love very much, married to this man that I love very much—love maybe even more. (*BFP1* 368)

I quote this passage at such length because it is so seldom cited in criticism of the play, yet it is absolutely crucial in revealing to us Frank's intent to heal both Grace and Teddy and perhaps, by extension, a greater community of people that night. Teddy neglects to mention that Frank healed Donal's bent finger that night as both Frank and Grace do in their monologues. Teddy believes the important healing that occurs comes with Frank and Grace's being temporarily united in harmony, and the feeling engendered in Teddy is that he loves them both dearly and thus forms a complete community with them. Frank's penetrating gaze at Teddy, then at Grace, suggests that the happiness he has created that night in the pub leads him to decide his course of action that night—to attempt a more profound healing of his friends and the wedding guests through his sacrificial death.[43]

Frank has already sacrificed his pride a great deal that evening and sought to make Grace comfortable and at home in the pub, and as Teddy recalls that evening, he notes that "it was like as if I was seeing them as they were once, as they might have been all the time— like if there was never none of the bitterness and the fighting and the wettings and the bloody van and the smell of the primus stove and the bills and the booze and the dirty halls and that hassle that we never seemed to be able to rise above. Like away from all that, all that stuff cut out, this is what they could be" (*BFP1* 367). What Teddy sees that night is an idealized vision of Frank and Grace's union without the material sordidness of their existence. This moment strikingly anticipates the language of dematerialization at the end of the play when Frank experiences another emotional and spiritual reunion, now with the wedding guests, as he senses the vanishing of "the whole corporeal world . . . somehow they had shed their physical reality and had become mere imaginings" and that "even we had ceased to be physical and existed only in spirit; only in the need we had for each other" (376).

As we are told by Frank himself, he knows when he is going to cure people: Teddy's report that "the look he has on his face is exactly the way he looks into somebody he knows he's going to cure" signifies that Frank believes his death will heal both Teddy and Grace even as he knows later that night he will not be able to heal McGarvey. But Frank's death works no wonders for his two friends: Teddy is slowly drinking himself to death in the play, and Grace takes her own life. Nevertheless, these two crucial passages from the end of Teddy's monologue amply indicate a significant part of Frank's motivation for dying at the hands of the wedding guests the next morning.

Even though his death does not bring the healing for the other two characters that he had desired, the moment of love that Teddy feels for both Frank and Grace here and the community that is briefly created is a largely unrealized anchor in the play that, again, anticipates and complements the more profound formation of spiritual community in its conclusion. Friel himself has said that his early plays are studies of love, but so is *Faith Healer*. Frank's temporary healing of his own and Teddy and Grace's emotional deprivation that night is a significant and lasting gift to both of them that Teddy, at least, returns to fondly in his memory.[44]

More important, implies Friel, is Frank's belief, misguided though it may be, in his more lasting potential healing of the profound spiritual deprivation among the characters in the play and, by extension, his society in his final sacrifice through their formation of community. Although Seamus Heaney, in an otherwise illuminating essay on Friel, argues that Frank's "sacrifice is utterly un-transcendent; Frank expects no flow of grace or benefit for himself or the survivors,"[45] as we have just seen, Frank's sacrifice of his ego earlier in the evening has created happiness for himself, Grace, Teddy, and all the assembled wedding guests. Now, with Frank's giving of his body to his killers to rend and crush, he does fully expect something positive to occur—not physically for McGarvey, not for himself, but for the survivors, Teddy, Grace, and the wedding guests. Frank's movement from healing bodies in the past to healing relationships on this last night of his life (with the exception of his healing of Donal's finger) signifies his trajectory away from a lingering Enlightenment obsession with the physical and toward an antimodern embrace of the spiritual.

But ironically, the physical state of the crippled McGarvey signals the profound spiritual deprivation among the characters of the play. Frank mentions toward the end of his first monologue that he saw a picture of McGarvey in his wheelchair in his mind's eye "before Ned told us of the fall from the scaffolding and the paralysis" (*BFP1* 340). The manner of McGarvey's fall seems a throwaway detail, until we remember Friel's lament in "The Theatre of Hope and Despair" about the dramatists' battle "against the crippled civilization they find themselves in," noting further that modern dramatists "have whipped away all the *scaffolding*, all the *crutches* we depend on."[46] The language of disability from this essay lodges in and lingers in *Faith Healer* because Friel is using McGarvey's disability both as a sign of the spiritual deprivation of modern Ireland, and by extension that of the modern world, and to suggest how the play itself strips away "all the crutches we depend on" to reveal us to ourselves, an honesty that is a precondition for community. We now apprehend the spiritual deprivation of the maimed wedding guests signified physically through Donal's crooked finger and McGarvey's paralysis. Frank Hardy's great epiphany on his last night on earth concerns his recognition of the emotional and finally spiritual poverty of those around him and his belief that he can heal these deprivations. This belief drives his actions in the Ballybeg lounge bar and then later, outside in the pub's yard. As we will see, whether or not Frank's actions are beneficent does not matter if he can make us believe that they are and will be.[47]

But along with Frank's belief that sacrificing himself will somehow heal Grace, Teddy, and others around him, *Faith Healer* depicts the continuing influence of myth, even on contemporary societies that are thought to be beyond its influence, through the Greek myth of Dionysus, the Irish myth of Cuchulain, the Ulster myth of the Red Hand, and the New Testament narrative of Jesus Christ. Frank's final words, "At long last I was renouncing chance" (*BFP1* 376), demonstrate his awareness that he is choosing to give in to what seems a predetermined fate signified by the operating mythological substratum of the play. Frank even recalls that night at the end of his first monologue as "A Dionysian night. A Bacchanalian night. A frenzied, excessive Irish night when ritual was consciously and relentlessly debauched" (340). Friel thus suggests the residual power of agriculturally based mythology—particularly that of the Bacchanalian and Dionysian revels—to condition local culture despite growing urbanization and the dominance of scientific rationalism. It is impossible to know whether Friel had read Nietzsche's *The Birth of Tragedy* on the dismemberment of Dionysus by the Titans, but Nietzsche's language in chapter 10 of his study, coupled with our knowledge of Friel's rejection of the Enlightenment cult of the individual in favor of dynamic community, certainly augments our understanding of Frank Hardy's pending death by dismemberment and potential future rebirth as a type of Dionysus figure auguring the formation of community. If "the suffering of individuation . . . dismemberment . . . [is] the true Dionysiac suffering . . . we should therefore see the condition of individuation as the source and origin of all suffering and hence as something reprehensible."[48] Further, looking forward to Dionysus' rebirth, Nietzsche's comment that it marks "the end of individuation" and "casts a ray of joy across the face of the world, torn and fragmented into individuals,"[49] helps explain the powerful surge of joy audiences sometimes feel at the end of Friel's play but try to suppress since they know Frank is walking to his sure murder. Nietzsche finally sees in the deaths and rebirths of Dionysus the essence of "the *mystery doctrine of tragedy*: the basic understanding of the unity of all things, individuation seen as the primal source of evil, art as the joyful hope that the spell of individuation can be broken, as a presentiment of a restored oneness."[50] By having Frank Hardy's trajectory recall Nietzsche's account of the dismembered Dionysus, Friel reverses the traditional definition of tragedy and suggests that Frank's murder and future rebirth could break "the spell of individuation" and effect unity between himself and his murders and perhaps among others and, by extrapolation, show how dramatic art can create community in the theater as well.

Other myths driving the narrative of *Faith Healer* have been suggested: for example, Declan Kiberd cites Friel's debt to the Irish legend of Deirdre of the Sorrows in its plot, which suggests Friel's recognition of the pervasiveness of myth generally and the ways it is recycled in the lives of individuals.[51] Frank's suicide is thus precipitated in part by his recognition that he is enacting the myth of Deirdre of the Sorrows in having fled the North of Ireland with his "Deirdre," Grace, and now, having returned, is essentially being betrayed unto death. And yet, who plays the role of King Conchubar, who wants Deirdre to be his wife, in the play? The only major authority figure is Grace's father, and he clearly does not lure Frank as a Naoise figure back to Ireland and then betray him. I have always felt that in addition to repeating, to some degree, the more obvious myth of Dionysus, Frank frustratingly enacts another, more obliquely rendered Irish myth: the story of Cuchulain, especially his death through Friel's physical depictions of him.

Frank Hardy shares many characteristics of Cuchulain, including his penchant for wandering. Like Cuchulain, he also is warned twice that night that he will be killed—by both Grace (*BFP1* 353) and the publican (374). In the last chapter of Lady Gregory's *Cuchulain of Muirthemne*, "The Death of Cuchulain," Cuchulain first recognizes his imminent death when his mother Dechtire gives him what should be wine in a cup but is instead blood. He says, "[M]y luck is turned against me, and my life is near its end, and I will not come back alive this time from facing the men of Ireland;" shortly thereafter, a young girl at a ford is washing out bloody clothing, and Cathbad the Druid warns Cuchulain to turn back from his sure death, but he refuses.[52] These parallels, significant in their own right, are only part of the identification with Cuchulain that Friel develops to show the political ramifications of Frank Hardy's sacrifice.[53]

John Wilson Foster's analysis of the Ulster Cycle and its reverberations in twentieth-century Irish writing is particularly helpful in this regard. As Foster remarks, Cuchulain "is not a god in the cycle; he seems rather to be both superhuman and subdivine, a demigod islanded between mortality and immorality."[54] Like Cuchulain, who occasionally has supernatural power or, more precisely, serves as a conduit for those powers, Frank Hardy experiences moments of seemingly real divine power, especially when he heals ten people one night in Llanbethian, Wales (*BFP1* 359, 370–71). And yet, like Cuchulain, who famously suffers moments of complete weakness when he cannot fight, Frank, more often than not, cannot actually heal people.

More startling for the political implications of the play—and I believe they are profound—Frank Hardy symbolically embodies the province of Ulster in both his fertility and infertility, his ability to heal and his failure to heal. As Foster notes, Cuchulain is "as much an embodiment of Ulster as he is an individual. . . . But on this level Cuchulain is also a figure of impotence: he combines in himself the fertilizing power of the romance hero with the infertility of the romance king and his kingdom. In its tidal pattern of wastage and renewal, the saga is of course in a very real though metaphoric sense about potency and impotence, fertility and infertility." As Foster has shown, Cuchulain's occasional impotence was "used as a metaphor for modern Ireland's condition under English rule" by cultural nationalists such as Standish James O'Grady, who in his essay "The Great Enchantment" claimed, "The political understanding of Ireland today is under a spell and its will paralyzed."[55]

In the context of his discussion of *Faith Healer*, Robert Welch has pointed out that "to be Irish is to be, in some degree at least, compelled into one of a number of narratives. And nowhere in Ireland is this more in evidence than in the North, where the story you subscribe to may end up being, literally, a matter of life and death."[56] The Cuchulain story becomes "a matter of life and death" for Frank Hardy, although he likely does not consciously subscribe to it. As I have noted earlier in this study, Friel lived for many years in County Donegal, the northernmost county on the entire island, and he refused to recognize the only six-county contemporary Northern Ireland; his long residence in Donegal and his rejection of the six-county province enabled him to at least figuratively reinscribe the ancient nine-county province of Ulster onto his imaginative map of Ireland. As the conflict in Northern Ireland continued in the late 1970s as Friel was writing *Faith Healer*, he may have seen in the figure of Frank Hardy as a figurative Cuchulain the embodiment of a province increasingly torn by sectarian strife. Without making my same specific point, Ruth Niel has suggested briefly that Friel's blending of hope and despair in the play "has far-reaching cultural and political implications, for its conception of man is of a being that is incurably broken, and this strides across the theological premises of the sectarian divide."[57] Frank, after all, is probably a lapsed Catholic from the Republic who has married a Protestant from a Big House in the North. In his portrayal of Frank's bickering and violent relationship with his wife, Friel may be metaphorically staging the conflict in the North and portraying the periodic attempts between the two sides to live in harmony as doomed and infertile, at least in the late 1970s in the run-up to one of the worst times in province history: the so-called blanket, "dirty," and finally hunger-strike protests by republican prisoners in the Maze Prison.[58]

Moreover, the figure of Cuchulain itself is culturally vexed, standing variously for the Republic of Ireland (symbolized by the Oliver Sheppard statue of the dying Cuchulain in the General Post Office in Dublin) and, more recently, for contemporary loyalist conceptions of Northern Ireland as surrounded by betraying enemies—both Britain and the Republic of Ireland. Cuchulain, after all, was repeatedly depicted as defending the "Gap of the North" from periodic invaders from the west and south, and loyalists have styled themselves as lonely defenders of their community and way of life.[59] As Foster reminds us, at the turn of the twentieth century, "Cuchulain's career . . . reminded the more discerning that Irish leaders, like Achilles, were fatally vulnerable in one respect. In the Irish case it is vulnerability to treachery and betrayal which gather their shape-changing forces around Cuchulain until he is hacked to pieces."[60] Friel grew increasingly disenchanted with Irish nationalism, as Scott Boltwood has convincingly shown.[61] Friel's characterization of Frank Hardy may symbolize the way he felt as the conflict in the North wore on—that Irish republicanism especially was increasingly inward-turning and murderous. Conversely, the proleptic hacking and carving of Frank's body also surely recalls that practiced by the murderous loyalist gang, the Shankill Butchers, in the mid- to late 1970s.[62] The final image of imminent butchery is thus culturally and politically multivalent and shows how violence was widespread throughout the island of Ireland in the twentieth century.

Finally, any discussion of the hacking-off of limbs in the context of Northern Irish myth and violence must call to mind the ancient image of the province itself, the Red Hand of Ulster. Photographer Declan O'Neill has shown that this image is nearly ubiquitous in Northern Ireland: it adorns the flags of Ulster and Northern Ireland, is used by loyalist paramilitaries, is featured on County Tyrone's uniforms for the Gaelic Athletic Association, marks certain burial plots, adorns some of the stained-glass windows in Belfast's City Hall, and was formerly the logo used by the Northern Ireland tourist board. The symbol is "constantly revised and eroded, [and] litters the architectural and social topography of Northern Ireland."[63]

The most popularly accepted origin of this conflicted symbol concerns a Viking party about to land on the shores of what is now Northern Ireland. The leader promises the first man to touch the land possession of the territory. An Irish mercenary on board named O'Neill cuts his hand off with a sword and throws it ashore, winning the land at a huge personal cost. Thus the symbol itself is bound up with the notion of contested territory and violence. The sacrificial violence about to be practiced upon Frank Hardy's body can thus be read as a symbol of simultaneous possession and loss, both for Frank personally, as he comes "home" finally and loses his life, and for contemporary Northern Ireland, where contested ideologies compete for the winning narrative of ownership through a compelling image of sacrifice.

Seamus Deane has helpfully argued about the connection between art and violence in the play: "The violent men who kill the faith healer are intimate with him, for their savage violence and his miraculous gift are no more than obverse versions of one another. Once again, Friel is intimating to his audience that there is an inescapable link between art and politics, the Irish version of which is the closeness between eloquence and violence."[64] One thinks in this regard of the similar strategy employed by Friel's countryman and close friend Seamus Heaney, who concludes his 1972 poem "The Tollund Man," which muses on the connection between tribal violence in ancient Jutland and contemporary Northern Ireland, by stating, "Out there in Jutland / In the old man-killing parishes / I will feel lost, / Unhappy and at home." And in 1975, Heaney would conclude "Punishment," collected in his volume *North*, by observing that he "understand[s] the exact / and tribal, intimate revenge" that is visited upon "betraying" Catholic women in Northern Ireland who were punished by the Irish Republican Army for consorting with British soldiers.[65] Thus, the conclusions of both poems illuminate the conclusion of Friel's play by conveying the writer's intimate recognition and understanding of sectarianism even as he rejects it but implicates all of us in violence.

For the violent rhetoric of the play expressed by Frank, Grace, and Teddy in turn suggests that we murder each other every day with our words. Writing about the transactional role of spectators in drama, Louis Dupré has convincingly argued that their identification with what transpires on stage leads them to hold the actor "responsible for the deeds he or she commits in that role. Thus the stage forcefully reminds them both [actors and audience] of their own need to project themselves in personae. Only in the eke-stasis of becoming what we are not does freedom allow us to become what we are."[66] Thus, our temporary identification with Frank's murderers enables us to recoil from their violence and reject it. While we may not physically kill as the wedding guests do, Friel adroitly shows how murderous rhetoric poisons potential connections among human beings. For example, Teddy verbally explodes when recalling his encounter with a man walking by outside of Grace's flat in London after Teddy had just found and retrieved the poster advertising Frank Hardy as a faith healer, which had been dumped on the street by Grace's landlord after her death. When the passerby accuses Teddy of theft, he angrily recalls, "And I caught him by the neck and I put my fist up to his face and I said to him, I said to him, 'You open your fucking mouth once more, mate, just once fucking more, and I'll fucking well make sausage meat of you!'" (*BFP1* 366). Earlier, when analyzing Frank's talent, Teddy laments, "that's all the stupid bastard had was brains! For Christ's sake, brains! And what did they do for him, I ask you, all those bloody brains? They bloody castrated him—that's what they done for him—bloody knackered him!" (357). Teddy's verbal violence in both these quotations not only linguistically anticipates Frank's final bloody death but also suggests how even those of us who do not consider ourselves physically violent can be verbally vicious and crush connections with others in this way.

This association with Cuchulain and its negative implications for contemporary Northern Ireland that I have outlined is counterbalanced, however, by Frank Hardy's mythic enactment of sacrifice that points toward that of Christ, whose sacrificial death and forgiveness is the model needed for feuding factions in Northern Ireland. My brilliant former student Lydia Cooper has shown that the four monologues of the play "mimic the gospel accounts of Christ, recounting and interpreting Frank's ministry, death, and message." And, "like the four gospel accounts, they contradict one another in many specifics: Grace's monologue reverses Frank's claim about their marital status, just as the Matthew and Luke genealogies contradict each other regarding Jesus's paternal lineage (Matt. 1:1–14, Luke 3:3–21)." Crucially, in a manner "similar to most orthodox interpretations of the discrepancies among the gospel accounts, the contradictions in the play suggest that the truth within the narrative supersedes the accuracy of its details."[67] The truth above all else conveyed by the play concerns our deep spiritual condition and connection to each other.

Frank has other similarities to Christ, which startle us once realized, and these likenesses are followed finally by his sacrificial death. For instance, like Christ, Frank has fervently loyal followers in Teddy and Grace, who literally cannot stop talking about him. Like Christ, Frank Hardy has miracles attributed to him. Like Christ, Frank is deeply suspicious of place and evinces an uneasiness in being at home. And like Christ, Frank freely offers himself as a sacrifice to be wounded, pierced, and murdered, when he could have simply walked away. Although I disagree with Margaret Strain that Frank himself is "freely accepting grace" in his final moments and thus "finds faith in a power which is the source of all gifts," she nevertheless is correct that "Frank approaches his death expectant, not despondent."[68] He is expectant because he believes his death will heal Teddy and Grace and perhaps the wedding guests too as we have seen already, but also because he knows now that "for the first time there was no atrophying terror; and the maddening questions were silent" (*BFP1* 376). Frank Hardy experiences no grace, and despite some striking similarities to Christ, he is, in the end, not a Christ figure. But his sacrifice and similarities point us toward Christ's healing power, even as his function as Cuchulain connotes his violence and his soon-to-be-torn body. Perhaps appropriately, Foster reminds us that Patrick Pearse considered the Irish epic *Táin Bó Cúailnge* ("The Cattle Raid of Cooley"), one of the central installments of the Ulster Cycle featuring Cuchulain, "like a retelling (or is it a foretelling) of the story of Calvary."[69]

Frank's recognition of "the need we had for each other" is a startling statement about the men who will soon kill him, but in it lie the seeds of forgiveness and reconciliation on both microcosmic and macrocosmic levels. The wounds inflicted upon his body by the wedding guests will not affect his soul. He has finally accepted, then transcended, his body and in so doing suggests that, despite violence on local and national levels, human beings share a common spiritual bond. Friel implies that if this bond is recognized more fully among the living, future conflicts, in Northern Ireland and worldwide, can be avoided. This implication is strengthened by a consideration of this play as constituting the outstanding example of Friel's conception of theater as a truthful, healing art.

Grene argues that despite all the emphasis on the sordid and material in the play, we feel in this final scene "that Friel has brought both Frank, and us in the audience, to a truth that transcends the mere lived contingencies of mortal life."[70] As Grene goes on to posit, "[I]n the very idea of faith healing, in the attempts to analyze Frank's vocation/art/trade, there is the concept of a healing perfection that would leave people transformed. Not only the healed but the healer."[71] I have already remarked upon Friel's recognition of the power of imaginative truth: *Faith Healer* bears this out, both for the characters in the play and for the audience members who have seen it. However, *Faith Healer* goes even further than Grene suggests, for it is finally a metaphor of Friel's conception of the playwright's role in creating spiritual hope.

Hope emerges in Frank's recognition of the common spiritual bond he shares with his killers in a yard outside the lounge bar in rural Ballybeg. If we consider the opening concern of this chapter with geopathology, we apprehend that Frank now chooses to inhabit a *place* of violence where he is comfortable and finally at home, whereas the places he has lived over the years in Scotland and Wales are merely *spaces* he has occupied. In the sacred, metatheatrical space of the walled yard with its arch behind the pub, Frank and his killers somehow all recognize and share a common spiritual unity shortly before his death. The hope of fully grasping this potential unity remains only in the audience's capacity for this recognition and presumable vow to reject the example of his killers.

Whether or not *Faith Healer* or any of Friel's plays succeeds in this goal depends on his ability to use words in an incantatory manner through the mouths of characters like Frank Hardy in his role as *seanchaí*. An early draft note for the play features Friel experimenting with such a voice, and he reminds himself, "This should be an Eamon Kelly type narrator, something between a seanachie and Job."[72] By listening intently to such voices, the audience can participate in the drama's pain and also experience hope. Anthony Roche has argued that the resonance of the communal art of the storyteller in Irish drama, especially in plays like *Faith Healer,* "redefines the spatial relationship between actors and an action up there on the stage, and an audience separate and down here. . . . The movement of the plot [in an Irish play] is more like the expansion or creation of a circle; the painful situation in which the on-stage characters are placed is deconstructed and made tolerable as audiences come to participate and share in it, as it extends to and is extended by them."[73] *Faith Healer* constitutes a supreme example of the way in which the audience becomes part of the play and shares in "the painful situation" of its characters.

We are reminded of the importance of audience in the opening stage directions of the play with the "*Three rows of chairs—not more than fifteen seats in all—*" that "*occupy one third of the acting area stage left*" (*BFP1* 331). Roche has convincingly suggested that the chairs, along with the poster advertising Frank Hardy, "indicate the extent to which the faith-healing performance described by all three characters is being re-enacted before us. This in turn makes the audience itself a crucial participant in the faith-healing, extending the drama from the confines of the stage across the footlights to embrace the entire auditorium."[74] These chairs also presumably represent the audiences that would have gathered to watch Frank heal people in the past, but their emptiness actually signifies their dual function. As Alice Rayner has noted, chairs have such a function because "an empty chair speaks of a future arrival or a loss; it anticipates the person who will sit; it remembers the person who did sit. . . . The pathos of an empty chair holds both memory of a loss and anticipation of return in all the particularity of a person, in character, in quality. . . . A chair, in short, is also a memorial device."[75] Because one-third of the stage is occupied by these empty chairs throughout Frank's first monologue, we are continually reminded not just of past audiences but of our present participation in the play, and of the potential for future audiences to form a temporary community with the actors. More remarkably, when those chairs disappear to be replaced by single ones in successive acts occupied by Grace (341), Teddy (353), and Frank's coat (370), they are symbolically filled by the presence of the current reading or viewing audience of the play who has been effectively hypnotized through Frank's opening monologue: we have become Frank's future audience, with ourselves filling these memorial devices. Thus, the chairs enable us to apprehend the ghostly presence of audiences past who gathered to watch the faith healer and the continuing orations of the ghostly Frank and Grace and the living Teddy.

Moreover, Frank's description early in the play of what happens to an audience when he would heal someone implies an analogy, by extension, to a theater audience that is figuratively ripped apart even as we are brought together and temporarily made whole when watching a powerful scene such as Frank walking toward his killers. Frank muses, "Because occasionally, just occasionally, the miracle would happen. And then—panic—panic—panic! *Their ripping apart!* The explosion of their careful calculations! The sudden flooding of dreadful, hopeless hope!" (*BFP1* 337; my emphasis). "Their ripping apart" anticipates the literal rending of Frank's body, but more intriguingly implies strongly that Friel wants his own reading and stage audiences to be torn apart emotionally by his poetically rendered ending about the imminent tearing of human flesh. When we watch or read *Faith Healer*, somehow, mysteriously, its miraculous bringing together of disparate characters in community in its conclusion floods our hearts with anticipation and hope even as we recoil from such brutality and wish for some sort of healing—for Frank, for Grace and Teddy (which is ill-founded), for Frank's killers, maybe even for Northern Irish society.

Dennis Kennedy has compellingly argued that "in the theatre what turns a stage fiction into more than a fiction is the connivance of an audience. Though the result is not reality-in-the-world, connivance moves fictional enactment to a state that lies beyond the imaginary and beyond the symbolic. The relationship between a willing, attentive audience and the performance is an agreement which approaches the quality of faith. A temporary agreement, to be sure, but a shared trust nonetheless."[76] More specifically, Friel's contemporary, the Irish playwright Thomas Kilroy, has argued that Friel's use of the monologue in his masterpiece seeks such a trust, noting, "To be theatrical a monologue has to possess its audience as a confidant."[77] Thus, we are active listeners, sharing as Friel unfolds his exploration of spiritual truth, not, as Elmer Andrews would have it, "the producers of the play's meaning."[78] There is ample evidence Friel shared such a view and, moreover, that *Faith Healer* is his most explicit dramatic statement of it. In 1966, after returning from viewing some wildly successful performances of *Philadelphia, Here I Come!* On Broadway, he stated flatly, "One writes for the audience, for a group of people of all ages and types who become an entity for a period of something over two hours; and you expect, you hope, you pray for certain reactions from that entity."[79] The procession of three verbs, itself a type of trinitarian language here, and then the use of "pray" itself suggest that Friel understands live theater as an act of joint faith entered into by actors and audience. Further, through the ideal performance of a play, and especially any play by Friel, most notably this play, this act of joint faith takes place in the specific space of a theater, which echoes the playwright's description of the place behind the lounge bar in his conclusion.

The style that Frank's narration assumes here at the end of his second monologue itself contributes to the formation of community with his killers and with us. I have to admit that I have always had trouble imagining this temporary community as genuine in any way, but Friel clearly endorses it. I have finally realized the rightness of Benedict Anderson's argument in this regard: "Communities are to be distinguished, not by their falsity/genuineness, but by the style in which they are imagined."[80] In this regard, two aspects of the "final style" of the play stand out because of the way they are intertwined with place: its repetition and its immensity, despite the intimacy of this ritual space.

Anthony Roche has observed that "[n]owhere in all of the manuscripts of Friel's plays contained in the National Library's Archive is there a greater transformation or a greater degree of structural modification and development between the firsts [*sic*] drafts and the final script of the play than with *Faith Healer*."[81] In the original draft of the fourteen-page act termed "Faith Healer" that was part of a three-act play titled *Bannermen* (1976, also containing the acts entitled "Faith Healer's Wife" and "The Game") Friel concluded what was then Frank Hardy's only monologue with three paragraphs after he walks into the yard where he will be killed. Only one of these paragraphs describes the yard:

I followed him out. The scene was as I knew it would be: an open place, trees, wind, the immobile grouping of men caught in the bleaching dawn, McGarvey's withered figure trapped in a wheelchair; the four stern and formal in their good suits in a staged semicircle behind him, Ned's hand on his shoulder.[82]

The language is suggestive, imagistic, metatheatrical. But its terseness does not suggest the spiritual openness eventually privileged by the greatly revised and expanded conclusion, an openness that we are invited to enter with Frank Hardy.

In contrast to this original sketch of the setting for Frank's murder, when Friel added a second monologue for Frank in *Faith Healer*, he expanded this final scene by a page and a half of carefully articulated passages that convey Frank's movement toward his killers in a timeless, ritualistic, intimately immense fashion.[83] Frank articulates a series of variations on multiple phrases, especially the two linked phrases "that yard" and "as I walked," whereas the original final three paragraphs never employ the word "yard" and "walked" appears only once. These repetitions start only after he passes through the first yard—"a tiny area, partially covered, dark, cluttered with barrels and boxes of empties and smelling of stale beer and toilets" (*BFP1* 374) to the ritualistic space of the second yard, clearly a symbolic theater. First, he tells us, "I found a wooden door. I passed through that and there was the other, the large yard. And I knew it at once" (375). Then, he immediately tells us, "I would like to describe that yard to you," but does not do so at first, building suspense by stating instead, "[i]t was a September morning, just after dawn. The sky was orange and everything glowed with a soft radiance—as if each detail of the scene had its own self-awareness and was satisfied with itself" (ibid.). Only now does Frank say, "The yard was a perfect square enclosed by the back of the building and three high walls. And the wall facing me *as I walked out* was breached by an arched entrance" (ibid.; my emphasis). After two more passages mentioning the implements his killers will use on him and the two birch trees, respectively, he again uses a form of "walk," noting, "The ground was cobbled but pleasant *to walk on* because the cobbles were smooth with use" (ibid.; my emphasis). This is a particularly effective sentence both because of its "inner" repetition of "cobbled" and "cobbles" but also through what we might term its "outer" repetition—the way in which the verb "walk" chimes with "as I walked out" in the earlier passage and sonically anticipates another form of itself in the very next line: "*And I walked across that yard*, over those worn cobbles, towards the arched entrance" (ibid.; my emphasis). This line rings additional echoes with the just-mentioned cobbles and with the earlier mention of "an arched entrance."

After Frank describes the wedding guests specifically, especially McGarvey, Friel again resorts to another paratactical phrase, which is quickly succeeded by a very similar one, both driven by the narrator's walking: "And although I knew that nothing was going to happen, nothing at all, *I walked across the yard* towards them. *And as I walked* I became possessed of a strange and trembling intimation" (*BFP1* 375–76; my emphases). Here follow the phrases about the dematerialization of the surroundings and even of the narrator's and wedding guests' bodies I analyzed earlier in this chapter. Why would Frank employ so much repetition here? Besides his penchant for using repetition to relax himself before a healing attempt, he is clearly trying to hypnotize us, the audience, in this passage. Once he feels we are under his spell, lulled by this repetition, he can begin his "magic trick" of making his surroundings vanish and expressing the spiritual connection he feels with the wedding guests.

Moreover, his focus on repeatedly picturing himself as walking imparts a spaciousness and immensity to the second yard, the symbolic stage of his sacrifice. Friel's poetic, repetitious language thus conveys his sense that he is crossing a vast expanse of ground to reach his killers. The "two mature birch trees" swaying in the wind (*BFP1* 375) add the sense of an immense forest to this intimate, metatheatrical space as well. Friel employs this linguistically created spaciousness to prepare us for the dematerialization passage and the increasing sense of spiritual connection between Frank, the wedding guests, and, finally, the audience. As we hear or read of

Frank's continued walking, our sense of the yard is enlarged and we feel included in this space and, shortly thereafter, also enveloped in Frank's profound sense of spirituality. Gaston Bachelard has argued that "[p]oetic space, because it is expressed, assumes values of expansion,"[84] and this poetic space in particular is shot through with dimensions of immensity because of Frank's particular powers of expression.

Immediately before the final two passages in the play, Friel's stage directions indicate that Frank is now entering the sacred space of ritual: "*He takes off his hat as if he were entering a church and holds it at his chest. He is both awed and elated. As he speaks the remaining lines he moves very slowly down stage*" (BFP1 376). Because Frank has successfully achieved one final performance, the transformation of the dirty pub yard into hallowed ground through his musing, expansive language, not only has he convinced us of this site's sacredness but also he himself now believes in its power and the efficacy of the ritual murder to come and thus "*is both awed and elated.*" He then steps into community with both his murderers and the audience members.

Paradoxically, Frank's creation of this enlarged space emphasizes the lessening of his burdensome healing powers. Bachelard again is helpful here, noting that "whatever the affectivity that colors a given space, whether sad or ponderous, once it is poetically expressed, the sadness is diminished, the ponderousness lightened."[85] We sense this growing feeling in the last two pages of the play, as an expansive geographic space becomes the site of Frank's gradual spiritual expansion and includes the wedding guests and us by extension in his burgeoning spirituality. The final paratactical "And" phrase that echoes with the others already delineated occurs in the third-to-the-last sentence of the play, which comes immediately after Frank is described as moving "*very slowly down stage*" toward the wedding guests: "And as I moved across that yard towards them and offered myself to them, then for the first time I had a simple and genuine sense of home-coming. Then for the first time there was no atrophying terror; and the maddening questions were silent. At long last I was renouncing chance" (*BFP1* 376). Through the continuity of his recurring parataxis and his repetitions in these final passages, the second yard behind the unnamed Ballybeg lounge bar has paradoxically become both an intimate site of ritual violence and the whole world.

In this regard, the original Broadway production of *Faith Healer* at the Longacre Theatre from April 5–22, 1979, was likely diminished by that space's immensity. Nicholas Grene notes that "reviews of a 1983 off-Broadway revival in the intimate Vineyard Theater suggested that *Faith Healer* was lost in the large Longacre Theatre." The performance space of the Longacre not only led to many inaudible lines by James Mason,[86] but I believe it also may not have allowed the audience to have the intimate connection with the characters necessary before Frank's repetitions toward the end of his last monologue imaginatively create a sense of vastness. Moreover, there may have been too much work required from the audience, as Friel has pointed out theatre critic Walter Kerr noted in his review at the time.[87] Finally, there were major casting problems that Friel has detailed in his essay "*Faith Healer* Comes to New York." While James Mason, who played Frank Hardy, was frequently brilliant, his wife, Clarissa Kaye, who played Grace, sobbed through rehearsals, "sleepwalked through her performance every night," and "was living in a kind of exile"; finally, Ed Flanders, who played Teddy, refused to be on stage with Kaye and "was replaced at the last minute by Donal Donnelly."[88]

Subsequent performances have fared much better, in part because of the strength of other actors than in the original Broadway production, and also because other directors have tended to choose smaller venues to allow for the actors to have a more intimate connection with audiences. For instance, Joe Dowling's direction at Boston's Colonial Theatre, February 26–March 10, 1980, and again at the Abbey Theatre in Dublin beginning August 28 of that same year and running for 29 performances, is often considered the quintessential production, not just because of Dowling's artistic production, but also because of the great Irish actor Donal McCann, who played Frank Hardy at both theaters. Kate Flynn played Grace, and John Kavanagh, Teddy. Fintan O'Toole, who has named *Faith Healer* as one of his top 100 modern Irish artworks, has observed that McCann gave "one of the great performances of modern Irish theatre" in the 1980 production at the Abbey, and elsewhere, he elaborated on this description, stating unequivocally,

> McCann's defining moment as Frank Hardy is, along with Siob-hán McKenna's Mommo in Tom Murphy's *Bailegangaire*, the most searing performance witnessed by Irish theatregoers of my generation. Very few actors have ever inhabited a stage in the way he did in that role, seeming to fill the entire expanse of the Abbey by himself. No other actor I've seen could make the auditorium feel cold as he walked out towards the audience, taking us physically into the presence of some ineffable, restless mystery that hovered between wonder and terror.[89]

McCann, who is better known to film audiences as Gabriel Conroy in director John Huston's last film, an adaptation of Joyce's "The Dead," apparently absolutely inhabited the character of Frank Hardy. O'Toole's description of McCann walking out "towards the audience" clearly references the last, chilling, mysterious scene where we are caught "between wonder and terror." Another attendee at that production, the esteemed Irish novelist Colm Toíbín, recalled after that when McCann's final monologue began, "I suddenly realized that he was speaking from the dead, that he was going to describe his own death," and somehow, "the space around McCann began to lift and shiver; the space began to transform itself until he did so too. The actor seemed both there speaking and, at the same time, to be part of some ghost world."[90] From these accounts, McCann portrayed the character of Frank Hardy so completely that he pulled off the trick of somehow, paradoxically, *embodying* this ghost!

McCann reprised the role in the Abbey's 1990 production, but for Nicholas Grene, that Dowling-directed version did not work nearly as well because of a change in the staging of the last scene. As Grene argues, "In the revival, the last stages of the final monologue were supported by back projected images of the yard, with Frank appearing actually to move off stage into the space he describes." For Grene, "it seemed like a failure of trust in the effect of the language and the actor that had worked to such magnificent effect in the earlier production."[91] Because Frank did not move toward the audience in that production, the audience members may not have entered into the sort of spiritual communion with him and his killers, and even with Grace and Teddy, that Friel desired.

In the 1994 Dowling-directed revival for the Long Wharf Theatre in New Haven, Connecticut, also starring McCann, that experiment with the final scene seems to have been dropped, and critics who attended the play spoke reverently of it and their connection to McCann's portrayal of Hardy. For instance, Ben Brantley, in his *New York Times* column marking Friel's death, has termed an evening performance of *Faith Healer* at the Long Wharf "one that still blazes in recollection for me, as religious experiences of art do." At that point, having seen only Friel's *Dancing at Lughnasa* in New York and London, Brantley had not yet come to appreciate or understand Friel's drama, but that night, he understood better its great "depth" and "the elusiveness of great art and the pain of the artist who creates it." While describing Judy Geeson as Grace and Ron Cook as Teddy "very fine," Brantley exhorts that McCann's performance was "extraordinary. Twisted of frame, with eyes that often seemed focused on something he couldn't quite make out in his peripheral vision, his Francis had the agonized presence of a dead man resurrected against his will and forced to take stock of his days among the living."[92]

The present author's first attendance at a performance of *Faith Healer* was the 2009 Broadway production, which communicated some of the play's intimate immensity by being staged at the cozy Booth Theatre, but there were significant problems with the casting, to my mind. Ralph Fiennes played Frank Hardy for laughs throughout his first monologue, complete with a bit of soft shoe, with the result that for audience members who did not know the play, Fiennes's somber reappearance in the fourth act to narrate Frank's pending death was jarring. Moreover, the great American actress Cherry Jones (winner of two Tony Awards) pitched her portrayal of Grace too high at the beginning of her monologue, and thus she could not become more histrionic and disturbed as the monologue progressed.[93] Ian McDiarmid, playing Teddy, stole the show. Finally, partly because of what I think of as Ralph Fiennes's normally wooden delivery, coupled with his earlier clownish first monologue, I could feel neither the tragedy of his imminent death as he walked toward us in the conclusion nor any spiritual communion with him.

For the current author, the two best performances of *Faith Healer* were the 2016 performance at the Donmar Warehouse I have described in the interchapter preceding the present one, and, perhaps surprisingly, the 2014 performance in Houston by the unforgettably named Stark Naked Theatre Company. Both productions drew the audience in through their intimacy, and at the Houston performance, I experienced one of the smallest "houses" I ever had. The small audience size occurred because the day I attended was Sunday, February 2—Super Bowl Sunday. Football is the state religion of Texas and suffice it to say, the theater was not crowded that afternoon. There were perhaps ten of us in the audience, but probably because of this small crowd and the intimacy of the playing space with its few shabby props, I found the performance extremely compelling.[94]

In such intimate theater spaces, Frank's concluding words stand out for their precision and resonance and come home to us with extraordinary force. Friel's revisions to the initial script of *Bannermen* heighten Frank's eerie phrasings. For example, in the original scene from Act One, Frank does not use the phrase "offered myself to them," as he would do in the antepenultimate sentence from *Faith Healer*. Instead, the original, penultimate paragraph runs, "And as I walked towards them, for the first time I had a simple and genuine sense of home-coming: for the first time there was no atrophying terror and the maddening questions were silent." A separate, final sentence, "At long last I was renouncing chance,"[95] then follows in *Bannermen* that is identical to the final sentence in *Faith Healer*. When Friel revised this passage for the end of Frank's final monologue, he inserted the phrase of self-offering, suggesting strongly that Frank's is a voluntary, conscious sacrifice. Notice too that the revised passage employs repetition once more to startling effect: "then for the first time" and "Then for the first time" (*BFP1* 376) emphasize Frank's epiphany that mingles the recognition of coming home with a lack of fear at his fate. This repetition also imparts a decisive tone that lingers into and echoes with the final sentence about renouncing chance.

Crucially, Frank Hardy follows the trajectory articulated by Heidegger in his *Poetry, Language, Thought*, as outlined by Richard Kearney in his seminal essay on Friel. Kearney observes that "man being-in-the-world becomes authentic when he ceases to abuse language as a strategic instrument for the manipulation of people and objects and responds to it instead as that which it truly is: the house of Being in which man may poetically dwell."[96] By the final scene of the play, Frank has ceased to wield words as weapons against Grace and others, even in castigating himself, and instead makes peace with language, dwelling in it through his repetitive, poetic descriptions of his last fateful walk on to the stage of his imminent death. Thus he moves from opening both his monologues with a repetitious litany of Welsh and Scottish town names, actual places, into living in language itself as he walks across the yard toward the wedding guests and McGarvey.

Such an inscription of words onto a particular space through an evocation of a lived, inhabited place, onstage in the yard of the lounge bar and night after night in performances of *Faith Healer*, offers a timeless arena in which we pause and linger, reveling in being while also marveling at the connection within this strange community briefly established between the victim and his imminent killers. Thomas Kilroy's suggestion that Friel elevates the play "out of conventional time and lodges it in artificial stage time where the improbable is possible,"[97] while intriguing, is finally misleading because of his emphasis on artificiality. Rather, *Faith Healer* frees us from modernity's time trap of irreversibility and the lure of futurity by returning us to the repetitions of ritualistic, religious time. Caught up in the incantatory words uttered by Frank Hardy in his final performance, we suffer his anguish and hope against hope that his sacrifice will somehow bring forth healing.

Friel's metatheatrical stage, his sacral space created by Frank Hardy at the end of the play, shimmers with spiritual life and enriches and expands us spiritually by our participation and contemplation of it. As Lydia Cooper has articulated so well, "The stage, then, becomes a metaphorical tent healing: '[o]ne night only'—over and over, night after night (*BFP1* 331). And at each performance, the audience enters into the narrative empathetically to create sense out of the denials, deletions, and disingenuous remarks, forging a 'sense of home-coming' in a world scarred by exile and loss (376)."[98]

Frank's (and Friel's) metatheatricality depends heavily upon a profound notion of premodern ritual. Louis Dupré has observed that the Enlightenment notion of time militates against the sort of continuity that ritual privileges. He points out that "the kind of historical awareness that has developed over the last two centuries has obstructed a correct understanding of ritual behavior. . . . [E]ducated Europeans for the first time began to consider events as inextricable parts of a historical course from which they could never be detached. Not only could the same event never occur twice in its existential singularity: it was not even seriously comparable to any more recent event, since its very essence restricted it to an irreversible past."[99] Moreover, this belief in the irreversibility of the past is coupled with our orientation toward an ever-receding future, a posture exemplified by Gar in *Philadelphia, Here I Come!*, as we have seen. As Dupré further points out, "With the sense of a reversible past has vanished the sense of a meaningful present. It was the ritual's task to preserve both."[100] By returning our focus to ritual throughout the various microrituals of *Faith Healer*—the reiterations of place names, the ritualistic actions of the characters—but particularly here in the repetitious language of this final scene and the imagined, ritualistic murder of Frank Hardy, Friel creates an elastic present space we temporarily occupy along with Frank when he offers himself to his killers and vicariously to us.

In the conclusion of Friel's masterpiece, we have community with his characters, and we experience something like Benjamin's Messianic time, an aesthetically rendered vision of the imminence of Frank's pending sacrifice that revels in the journey itself, not so much the destination.[101] Just as important, we are not cast in the narcissistic position of the contemporary traveler who essentially becomes his own spectacle and worships himself. Instead, we are ineluctably caught up in watching Frank approach his killers, as he steps out in the faith that they will indeed murder him. Our eyes are off ourselves. As Nicholas Grene has said, "The design of the [last] speech is to leave an audience in the theatre unable to resist Frank's mood of awe and elation or the eloquence with which his secular martyrdom is so powerfully expressed."[102] I agree fully with Grene's point about Frank's compelling mood and his verbal eloquence, but it is crucial to stress that his is not a secular martyrdom, but a powerfully spiritual one that borrows from the Judeo-Christian tradition as well as literary and cultural antecedents such as the Cuchulain and Red Hand narratives I have explored above.

Theodor Adorno concludes his *Minima Moralia* with the startling claim (startling because he is writing in the immediate aftermath of the Holocaust) that

> [t]he only philosophy which can be responsibly practiced in face of despair is the attempt to contemplate all things as they would present themselves from the standpoint of redemption. . . . Perspectives must be fashioned that displace and estrange the world, reveal it to be, with its rifts and crevices, as indigent and distorted as it will appear one day in the messianic light.[103]

Written during one of the worst periods of the contemporary Troubles in Northern Ireland, the conclusion of Friel's *Faith Healer* constitutes such an attempt at contemplation from the "standpoint of redemption." The "rifts and crevices" of our "indigent and distorted" world, what Teddy describes in his litany of misery that he and Frank and Grace have experienced during their life together on the road that last night in Ballybeg (*BFP1* 367), what Frank terms "the whole corporeal world—the cobbles, the trees, the sky, those four malign implements—" (ibid.), and, by extension, the ugliness and horror of the Troubles in Northern Ireland, are the distortions revealed in the illuminating light of the play. The messianic light gleams on the other side of Frank's murder.

For these reasons, I disagree with Grene, who argues that Frank's final monologue "offers the spatial closure we look for in the completion of a piece of music. It is also the formal closure of tragedy."[104] In fact, the play's continual openness because of its immanence, achieved through its ritual-like movements, lead us continually back inside its world. It would be difficult to term *Faith Healer* a comedy, but its potentially redemptive conclusion, despite its ostensible closure, points toward openness and healing beyond the individual tragedies of the destroyed lives of Frank, Grace, and Teddy explored in the play. If tragedies move from order to disorder and comedies from disorder to order, *Faith Healer* mimics tragedy's ending but suggests we should expectantly wait for the restoration of order. Finally, if Rene Girard is correct is arguing that "[t]he function of ritual is to 'purify' violence; that is to 'trick' violence into spending itself on victims whose death will provoke no reprisals,"[105] along with its trajectory toward openness, the play offers a different kind of closure than that of tragedy—the suggestion that such a sacrifice of a scapegoat with no reprisal killings afterward may model a way forward in wartorn communities such as those in Northern Ireland. Of course, Friel is not suggesting that some actual, contemporary scapegoat must be sacrificed, but he may be implying that a return to meditating on the actual sacrifice of the ultimate scapegoat, Christ, could begin effecting transformation in Northern Ireland: Catholics and Protestants could celebrate their common spiritual heritage and realize that reprisals never end, but Christ's purifying legacy for believers lives on forever. Again, all of this is not to say or even to imply that Friel endorses or condones Frank's murder.

As Frank walks step by step toward the waiting men, we realize not only that Frank needs this death but also that the farmers need to make it happen, and we need to watch it. This nexus of needs binds us altogether in a community that transcends the page and stage. Drawing on the stage direction, *"he moves very slowly down stage"* and the line of dialogue, "And as I moved across that yard and offered myself to them" (*BFP1* 376), Christopher Murray has convincingly argued that here Frank "addresses the audience with more intimacy than before" in his first monologue and also moves "closer to the audience, in imitation of the movement within the narrative."[106] In this way, Frank Hardy is finally offering himself to us as well. Terry Teachout's comment in his review of the 2006 production of *Faith Healer* at the Booth Theatre on Broadway is pertinent in this regard: "Once again he [Friel] has proved art's power to narrow the fearful gap that separates soul from soul. Like every great writer, he reveals us to one another—and to ourselves."[107] To return to Seamus Deane's insight above that "[t]he violent men who kill the faith healer are intimate with him, for their savage violence and his miraculous gift are no more than obverse versions of one another," we realize from Deane's recognition of the connection between the victim and his killers that they both are conduits for some sort of otherworldly power. This force can be found in the Maenadic frenzy that is about to enter into Frank's killers and his occasional ability to heal that also descends upon him at times. Both are in touch with something beyond themselves that animates and drives their destructive and constructive powers, respectively. Even if we recoil from the destructive power and revel in Frank's healing power, realizing their presence in our world leads us to apprehend how ritual, collective ceremonies, whether the actual or figurative slaughter of a scapegoat or the healing of a person's body, suggest our continued need to return to spirituality through the sacral present offered to us by drama.

Such a spiritual need is a crucial component of community, which continues to be put under intense pressure by a rampant modernity that, for example, promises more community through nearly instantaneous communication but is merely a pale simulacrum of organic community. Beyond the political and even potentially sectarian connotations of this last ritualistic scene lies Friel's critique of modernity.

He represents modernity in *Faith Healer* not only by his rejection of linear time in his embrace of ritual, as we have seen, but also through the hard-edged tools the wedding guests bring back with them to cut and separate Frank's body. These tools, along with the guests' utter skepticism at Frank's ability to heal, despite his healing of Donal's finger, symbolize hard-nosed Western empiricism, whose objective has always been to break down matter into discrete parts. Their view of Frank's body is essentially modern and mechanistic, summed up by Siegfried Giedion, who has noted the tendency in modern biology to perceive "the animate being . . . simply as the sum of its separate parts, assembled like those of a machine."[108] Only in remembering Frank's actions and words as readers and audience-goers can we metaphorically heal him, this imminently-to-be-dismembered character, render him whole, re-membered, as it were. As Susan Sontag has held, "Remembering *is* an ethical act, has ethical value in and of itself. Memory is, achingly, the only relation we can have with the dead."[109]

Friel would speak only three years after the first production of *Faith Healer* of the Field Day Theatre Company's unifying goal—to integrate, not destroy: "I think . . . there is the possibility of a cultural whole available to us—w-h-o-l-e, we're living in the other one [hole]."[110] Late in the process of the play's composition, toward the end of 1978, Friel had mused in his draft notes about this possibility: "To heal—to create order—to *RESTORE*." Then he quickly wondered, "To restore to what was before disorder or to restore to an ideal conception?," speculating further, "And is the disorder an outward sign, a symbol of a . . . perhaps civic and psychic disorder?"[111] Undoubtedly, it was, given the horrific state of sectarianism in Northern Ireland in the late 1970s. The hacked and wounded images of the province's symbols—Cuchulain and the Red Hand—likely also symbolized this "civic and psychic disorder," as we have seen.

Frank and Grace both prize wholeness tremendously—he in his attempts to heal others, and, temporarily, himself, and she in her attempts to forget their dead baby and Frank's vicious murder. In his first monologue, Frank gleefully recalls, "And occasionally it worked—oh, yes, occasionally it *did* work. Oh, yes. And when it did, when I stood before a man and placed my hands on him and watched him become *whole* in my presence, those were nights of exultation, of consummation . . ." (*BFP1* 333; my emphasis). At such times, Frank was so elated not because "I was doing good, giving relief, spreading joy," but "because the questions that undermined my life then became meaningless and because I knew that for those few hours I had become *whole* in myself . . ." (ibid.; my emphasis). At the end of her monologue, Grace attempts to sonically re-member the dismembered Frank, whom she saw ripped apart, by chanting "Kinlochbervie" repeatedly just as she did to signify that site where their dead baby was born and to offer a verbal consolation of wholeness for that lost child: "Aberarder, Kinlochbervie, / Aberayron, Kinlochbervie, / Invergordon, Kinlochbervie . . ." (353). And Frank, in his first monologue, recalls healing Donal's "bent finger" that fateful night and making it "whole" (339). He clearly wants to make himself, Gracie, and Teddy whole, but fails with his death and hers. As Richard Pine writes in his program note for the 2016 Donmar Warehouse production, "The gift of the faith healer is to make whole those who were previously incomplete. That's what Frank Hardy is trying to do to himself, too."[112]

I do not want to suggest his motives are completely pure: he sacrifices himself in part to free himself from the failures of his gift and the maddening questions he keeps asking about it that get more persistent and devastating. In some draft notes, Friel acknowledges, "He goes out at the end to the tractor boys because he can live no longer with questions—with indecision. The questions are never silent; the ambushes more expert, more cunning. The questions send him out."[113] In the final version, Frank voices a variation on these lines that conveys how desperately he wants to escape from questions about his gift: "But they persisted right to the end, those nagging, tormenting, maddening questions that rotted my life. When I refused to confront them, they ambushed me. And when they threatened to submerge me, I silenced them with whiskey" (*BFP1* 334). The pressure he put on himself, and seemingly, that the burden of his gift exerted on him, was tremendous and must have required constant vigilance, leading him to unending exhaustion. Friel admits as much in his draft notes, having Frank convey this wearisome vigilance in terms of a musical instrument quivering with constant anticipation of being played: "I was always a mere instrument; but an instrument quivering in its readiness and exhausted with vigilance—because the moment might come and go in an instant, the gust of wind, the volatile spirit, and the instrument had to be at pitch for benefit to be struck from it."[114] Certainly, Frank desires peace from these questions, this eternal anticipation and vigilance.

But the possibility of cultural and political wholeness Friel spoke of in 1982, above, and that Frank and Grace so desire, is nonetheless adumbrated and offered tantalizingly to us in Frank's sacrifice, which suggests he is integrating himself into a real, spiritual community after a sterile, modernist marriage with its emphasis on materialism, despite his occasional aspirations to transcendence.[115]

In giving himself to his killers, despite his lack of Christian faith, Frank seems to be echoing and enacting Christ's commandment to love our enemies in Luke 6:32–35a: "If you love those who love you, what credit is that to you? Even sinners love those who love them. And if you do good to those who are good to you, what credit is that to you? Even sinners do that. And if you lend to those from whom you expect repayment, what credit is that to you? Even sinners lend to sinners, expecting to be repaid in full. But love your enemies, do good to them, and lend to them without expecting to get anything back" (NIV). Paul Ricoeur argues that this commandment "begins by breaking the rule of reciprocity and requiring the extraordinary. Faithful to the gospel rhetoric of hyperbole, according to this commandment the only gift that is justified is the one given to the enemy, from whom . . . one expects nothing in return."[116] While he is clearly not a believer, Frank's gift of his body to his killers has trappings of Christ's sacrifice. The gift of himself is inherently spiritual, utterly hyperbolic, and even unnecessary; he has plenty of time to leave the premises after being warned by the publican that the farmers will come back and kill him.

And yet, knowing exactly what the men are about to do to him, Frank nonetheless forgives them in advance, recognizing, as Ricoeur so brilliantly argues, that "under the sign of forgiveness, the guilty person is to be considered capable of something other than his offenses and his faults. He is held to be restored to his capacity for acting, and action restored to its capacity for continuing."[117] By giving himself to his murderers in extravagant, unselfish fashion, and forgiving them for their murder of him in advance, Frank Hardy recognizes their common spiritual humanity, frees them from being solely associated with this horrific action, thus giving them the future possibility of acting in positive ways, and finally ensures his own immortality—at least on the stage and the page where he constantly resurrects himself.

Friel's close friend Seamus Heaney specifically recognized this condition of spiritual need in words that echo the most important phrase at the end of Frank Hardy's last monologue: "that even we had ceased to be physical and existed only in spirit, only *in the need* we had for each other" (*BFP1* 376; my emphasis). In his concluding remarks for a discussion of the Field Day Theatre Company's role in Ireland and Northern Ireland in 1983 with Raidio Teilifís Èireann, Heaney articulated "a general malaise . . . a general feeling that is abroad underneath the consumerism and underneath the hectoring and underneath all the codified positions and feelings, even the codified patriotisms, codified everything. Underneath the codes, there is *a sense of need* and it's that *sense of need* that we're trusting."[118]

Friel's masterpiece therefore finally offers this hope to the larger "audience" of Northern Ireland that has shared far too painful a situation over the last few decades. Hope of reconciliation there should spring from the way in which inhabitants of local communities communicate with each other—not in violent action, but in apprehending a common fund of spirituality manifested *in the need we have for each other*, which in turn might lead to radical, hyperbolic acts of forgiveness exemplified by the words of Gordon Wilson, the Christian father of a daughter killed by the Provisional IRA in its Remembrance Day bombing in Enniskillen, Northern Ireland, on November 8, 1987. Astonishingly, hours after the bombing, in which he was also injured, Wilson stated, "I miss my daughter, and we shall miss her but I bear no ill will, I bear no grudge. She was a great wee lassie, she loved her profession [of nurse]. She was a pet and she's dead. She's in heaven, and we'll meet again." He went on to say, "It's part of a greater plan, and God is good. And we shall meet again. I have lost my daughter, and we shall miss her. But I bear no ill will. I bear no grudge. Dirty sort of talk is not going to bring her back to life." He added later, "I shall pray for those people tonight and every night."[119]

"If," as Richard Kearney has argued, "empathy and hospitality toward others are crucial steps in the ethics of remembrance, there is something *more*, something that entails moving beyond narrative imagination to forgiveness, to 'shattering the debt' [to the dead]." That something is pardon, a responsibility placed on us as readers and audience-goers of *Faith Healer*, one we incur after reading and watching Frank offer his body (hospitably, empathically) to his killers. "Such forgiveness demands huge patience," as Kearney points out, "an enduring practice of 'working-through,' mourning, and letting go." And yet, "it is not a forgetful forgiveness. Amnesty can never be based on amnesia." This kind of pardon

> remembers our debt to the dead while at the same time introducing something other, something difficult almost to the point of impossibility, but something all the more important for that reason. One thinks of Brandt kneeling at Warsaw, Havel's apology to the Sudeten Germans, Hume's preparedness to speak with the IRA, Sadat's visit to Jerusalem, Hillesum's refusal to hate her hateful persecutors: all miraculous moments where an ethics of reciprocity is touched by a poetics of pardon. Pardon does not replace justice: both justice and pardon are equally important in the act of remembering past trauma.[120]

In Frank Hardy's act of giving himself to his killers (and in our response to that radical sacrifice), we can appreciate how in the mid- to late-1970s, Friel was continuing to work through—and model for us—the process of remembrance and forgiveness still desperately needed in Northern Ireland, a process he began in *The Freedom of the City* with his persistently speaking, named ghosts of the Troubles.

This need—for each other, for radical, liberating forgiveness— would be movingly demonstrated by the love between the English Yolland and the Irish Maire in Friel's next play, *Translations*, a transnational love that unfortunately lasts only a few brief moments before violent men likely kill Yolland.

7

Interchapter

Friel and the Field Day Theatre Company

The Field Day Theatre Company enabled Friel to offer an exciting, fluid alternative on the stage to the hidebound, binary politics of Northern Ireland by providing a model of communal interrogation and tentative articulation of deep-seated political, religious, and cultural problems that might augur a less divided society in the future. In the process, it allowed him to continue exploring his interrelated concerns of modernity, community, and place through the traveling onstage depictions of local, dynamic communities.

Friel had long sought what he terms the "redemption of the human spirit" through creating community that he argues is the dramatist's function in "The Theatre of Hope and Despair,"[1] which coincided with his search for a community theater group and led him to create the Field Day Theatre Company in 1980 with actor Stephen Rea, who played Skinner in the initial 1973 production of *The Freedom of the City*. "Field Day" incorporates sonic echoes of "Friel" and "Rea" in its title and also connotes something like the festivities of a "day out." Understanding this company and its aims, which cohere with Friel's general philosophy of place, is vital to fully appreciating the rich significance of modernity, community, place, and spirituality in *Translations*, which the next chapter explores. Friel had already committed himself to reaching the collective mind of his audience as he turned fully toward writing drama and away from short fiction in the 1960s, as we saw in the earlier interchapter explaining the reasons for this transition.

Moreover, he had been looking to expand and redefine that audience for some time while still keeping it in the regional context of northwest Ireland. For instance, he remarked in his 1970 interview with John Boyd that "if a new theatre is to be started in the North of Ireland, a new theatre audience has got to be created."[2] D. E. S. Maxwell has pointed out that Friel had pressed the Northern Irish Arts Council repeatedly for a "National Theatre," ideally located outside Belfast, and that "in March 1970 he adjudicated a drama festival presented by the four Derry grammar schools, two Catholic and two Protestant."[3] In his adjudication of this festival, Friel's ideal of an ecumenical theater company based in Londonderry/Derry can be seen in embryo. Finally, Friel formed the theater company he had wanted for some time with Rea, the Belfast-born actor who would star in Field Day's first three plays, all by Friel. Rea had approached Friel with the idea of touring a play because he felt culturally dislocated working in English theater. Rea also commented much later that "you couldn't not be affected by the collapse of society in the North. Everybody was affected and in some sense maimed by it. . . . [A]nd if you were in the business of theatre or writing or acting you had to attempt a principled response."[4] As we have seen in the previous chapters on *The Freedom of the City* and *Faith Healer,* Friel was similarly committed to responding to the conflict in Northern Ireland even as he, like many others, often despaired about its seemingly unremitting violence and intractable nature.

Friel writes in a letter dated November 21, 1979, to Seamus Deane about *Translations,* "This is how Colby and Co. have ended up," and asks for his feedback on the play. He had already selected Stephen Rea to play Owen, as he indicates in this letter, and he states that the two of them "will do it together with Arts Council (N.I.) [Northern Ireland] money, opening in Belfast some time next year. If they get cold feet, we'll go elsewhere."[5] Friel had just finished *Translations* and agreed to form the company as a populist project, touring it across the province and even at the Gate in Dublin during 1980.[6] The play was a wild success, and the company became more

established. Field Day soon came to provide a perfect venue for new
Friel plays. He seemed to have already envisioned something like
Field Day the previous year. There is something uncanny about how
Faith Healer—a drama about a talented faith healer who tours all
over Scotland, Wales, then finally, Ireland—premiered only a year
before Field Day, a company of superbly talented artists dedicated to
touring plays all over the province, burst onto the scene.[7]

Field Day took as its central image the fifth province of Ireland.
Richard Pine notes that Field Day's work was meant to both demonstrate and overcome traditional political polarities on the island:

> [It was intended] both to demonstrate the dualities (indeed polari-
> ties) of life in Northern Ireland and to encourage a closer under-
> standing between the "state of two nations" as Friel put it. The
> "fifth province" was a place beyond these divisions. . . . Friel called
> it "a place for dissenters, traitors to the prevailing mythologies in
> the other four provinces," and elsewhere he said that he and Rea
> "felt there was some tiny little space we might fill that we could
> focus the whole North thing on."[8]

Traditionally, as Pine points out earlier, the four provinces were
known by the Irish word for "fifth," *coicead*, to indicate the presence of a fifth province. Pine sees Field Day as occupying "an experimental field in which the qualities and conditions of being Irish can
be examined and discussed." Moreover, "one vital physical property
which has metaphysical significance is the fact that the point at the
center of the crossroads, the meeting place of the four provinces,
is the *quint-essence*—the fifth place at which the essential secret
or truth is buried."[9] Field Day's attempt to dramatize metaphysical
truths about being Irish fit Friel's general articulation in "The Theatre of Hope and Despair" of the dramatist's ability to redeem the
human spirit.

Indeed, in a 1981 interview, Friel ascribed the siting of the new
theater company in Londonderry/Derry to a "spiritual energy"

that he found in the city's liminal position on the threshold of the Republic:

> I believe in a spiritual energy deriving from Derry which could be a reviving breath throughout the North. I think there is more creative energy here than anywhere else. Derry doesn't look to either Belfast or Dublin, but to itself, that's why I want to work here—piety perhaps. . . . [Derry Catholics] were a dispossessed people living in a state they never subscribed to, with Donegal lying just across the bay. Janus-like they had one head looking to the North and one looking to the South. Now, however, the dispossessed are coming into their own and if this island is to be redefined the essence of redefinition could come from here.[10]

Derry's Catholics, including, by implication, Friel himself, thus had a unique geographic and psychographic condition, poised liminally between Northern Ireland and Ireland and the two attendant, competing identities of each state. Northern Ireland's fertile potential for new identities and reconciliation has been remarked upon by the Northern Irish poet Michael Longley, who cites W. R. Rodgers's "'creative wave of self-consciousness' which can stem from a confluence of cultures."[11]

While Field Day's emphasis on Northernness appealed to Friel's borderless sense of regionalism, its position as a traveling theater fits Friel's notion of arts in flux in "The Theatre of Hope and Despair." In an opening passage from that essay treating the fluidity of the arts in general, Friel writes, "Flux is their only constant." He goes on to essentially outline a model for what would become Field Day when he speaks of the arts searching for a "new concept"; analyzing, exploring, and communicating that concept; and then "moving on; the continuing of the search; the flux. Impermanence is the only constant."[12] Field Day was clearly an attempt by Friel, Rea, and the other leading directors—Heaney, Tom Paulin, David Hammond, and Seamus Deane—to establish a multiyear movement that was intellectually agile, daring, and fluid in their framing of alternative Irish identities, although, as we will see, the group could not escape having a nationalist flavor, in part because of Seamus Deane's eventual unofficial role as its spokesman. In a conversation with Paddy Woodworth in 1982, Rea made clear that there was a "'very passionately felt and expressed ideology,'" but he hastened to add that "he is clearly not talking about a specific political position[,] rather an evolving practice." He finally noted, "'If the impetus fails, if the creativity dies, we won't prolong it.'"[13] Friel's commitment to flux generally and to a literally mobile theater company powerfully suggests how he remained committed to exploring various spaces and charting the change within those spaces, as he does in *Translations*.

During his 1982 interview with Fintan O'Toole, Friel still claimed the theater to be "a very vulgar medium," as he had often in earlier essays and interviews, but he also noted in the very same breath how attractive it was to him.[14] Field Day had been going for three years by then, and it seems that it finally offered Friel a chance to communicate directly with the kind of audience he wanted. For example, he told O'Toole late in that interview that theater audiences outside of Dublin are both more distant from the performances and listen better because the other cities in Ireland, North and South, largely lack a tradition of drama: "These people watch you very carefully. They watch you almost as if we were cattle being paraded around on a fair day. They watch us with that kind of cool assessment. I think they hear things in theatre because they haven't been indoctrinated in the way a metropolitan audience is."[15] By this point in his career, Friel had embraced both Field Day's itinerant nature and its often-provincial audiences whom he believed were both more suited to hearing and seeing his work than metropolitan ones and were more susceptible to his manipulation of them.

Early on in Field Day's history, the directors explored the idea of writing pamphlets to communicate to a wider, not necessarily theatrical audience—and thus to leave lasting documents to complement their ephemerally produced plays. In a letter Friel wrote to Seamus Deane of October 28, 1982, he mentions talking through the pamphlet idea with David Hammond after Deane had left their directors' meeting at Annaghmakerrig. After making the case for

Heaney's poem "An Open Letter" to be the first pamphlet (in the end, it was the second), Friel outlines his and Hammond's plans in terms that illustrate his continuing commitment to local communities: "Pamphlet No. 1 on the street corners and in the coffee-houses as soon as possible." Friel further argues, rather cheekily, that for this broader audience rather than merely an academic one, "these Pamphlets would have the pitch and high-seriousness of the programme notes (i.e. they would be intelligible only to people who hadn't a first in English). The graphics, illustrations (if any), lay-out, paper etc. would be of the very highest standard."[16]

Friel even made a case for intellectual and artistic ferment leading to social, political, and economic change. For example, in his introduction to a pamphlet produced in the late 1980s that gives an overview of both the theater company and its publishing house, he argues that while "it is commonplace to say that the social, political and economic life of Ireland, North and South, is going through an upheaval . . . [w]hat is seldom acknowledged is that the imaginative life of the island is going through a comparable upheaval. Indeed it can be argued that the turmoil of ideas preceded and contributed to the political and social turmoil." As he goes on to claim,

> Field Day is concerned with those ideas, their validity, their potency, their currency, their fluctuations. Seamus Deane, writing about the prevailing idea of what it is that constitutes the Irish reality, says, "Everything, including our politics and our literature, has to be rewritten—i.e. re-read. This will enable new writing, new politics, unblemished by Irishness, but securely Irish." In our theatrical productions, our pamphlets, our publications, and most especially in our new Anthology of Irish writing, we hope to contribute to that enabling process, to make the new writing and the re-reading more accessible to an audience outside the academy and the parliament.[17]

Friel was always interested in the general question of translation, a concern he signals explicitly early in his career at the moment when Private Gar pleads to the Canon in *Philadelphia, Here I Come!*: "[Y]ou could *translate* all this loneliness, this groping, this dreadful bloody buffoonery into Christian terms that will make life bearable for us all. And yet you don't say a word. Why, Canon? Why, arid Canon? Isn't this your job—to translate?" (*BFP1* 88). Friel and the other members of Field Day believed that genuine and beneficent societal change could be introduced and wrought by artists, who could "translate" politics and literature—culture generally—into accessible language for the masses through their traveling plays and writings, including their pamphlets and their stunning but nonetheless criticized *Field Day Anthology of Irish Writing*.[18]

John P. Harrington and Elizabeth Mitchell have observed that "Northern Ireland's charged atmosphere of sectarian division encourages a considerable amount of dramatic political performance within, and about, its borders. . . . Paramilitary violence . . . has been part of larger symbolic performances designed to preserve and consolidate contested political beliefs."[19] As Aidan O'Malley has shown, Field Day recognized that politics in Northern Ireland were essentially performative and, thus, its "theatrical intervention sought to reconfigure the moribund, stereotyped performances through which the political manifested itself in Northern Ireland, and to propose more animated, more inherently problematized, alternatives to these. . . ."[20] As the conflict in Northern Ireland accelerated, Friel realized that drama could offer an important performative intervention, to employ O'Malley's terms, as we have seen in the previous chapters on *Freedom* and *Faith Healer*. The synergy between playwright and actors and, on a wider scale, audience members and actors offered a compelling, energetic alternative to the calcified political binaries available for consumption on the dramatic streets of Northern Ireland.[21]

Early on, Field Day would test Friel's belief that theater could unify audiences. The way in which *Translations* appealed to different audiences in Northern Ireland, Ireland, and England suggests that theater's very essence, its fluidity, depended on audience reaction to particular performances. This effect convinced Friel of the validity of his dramatic theory. Marilynn Richtarik has shown that despite the marked variance in audience interpretations in each of these three polities, each audience cohered around a particularly appealing aspect of the play. She observes that "in the North, the ritual aspect of theatre was uppermost, with the act of performing and attending the play on a level with the dramatist's words themselves. In the Republic, the play was applauded in large part for what was seen as its nationalist and social message. Finally, in London, it was the entertainment value of *Translations* that assured its success." The play's success in Derry, in particular, stemmed from the work of the disparate individuals who came together to stage it in "a co-operative effort among people of many political persuasions."[22]

Translations emphasizes the fluidity of possible interpretations, as O'Malley has noted in his comprehensive study of Field Day: "[T]he play explores these interpretations of the map in such a way that contemporary Irish identities are seen as emerging from a complex, fluid, contingent crisscrossing of these perspectives, rather than out of a secure relationship to a place and to a language."[23] Such a privileging of interpretive possibilities in the text of the play enabled Friel to at least temporarily unify particular audiences in various areas of Northern Ireland, Ireland, and England, as Richtarik has shown. In its dynamic, communal performance and fluid content, *Translations* shows how Friel's belief in flux enabled a productive clash of ideas by 1980 with the founding of Field Day, which imagined an alternative to monolithic notions of identity in the North.

Unfortunately, in its early years, Field Day was seen in some quarters as a "green" or nationalist enterprise, a perception that Friel was eager to dismiss, as was Stephen Rea. Friel wrote Seamus Deane in 1984 that "I'm concerned that the Northern/Protestant/Unionist readers (all one of them) seem to have classified us as hostile/Green Nat./wholly Free State based and oriented. . . . Is there anything we can do abou[t] that?" Then, referencing English-born and Belfast-based critic Edna Longley, by then associated by some nationalist critics with a defense of cultural, if not political, Protestantism in Northern Ireland, Friel states, "I'm not suggesting that we offer a platform to . . . Longley. But there must be someone who recognizes that we are not hostile, indeed that the Free State establishment may well disown us."[24] Friel must have felt by 1984 that word should have gotten out by then about the company's aim to transcend political, cultural, and religious divisions in the North. Field Day also had two directors come onboard from the Protestant community in the province—in addition to cofounder Rea, who had grown up in a Belfast Protestant family—David Hammond and Tom Paulin, another attempt to show its ecumenism. Endeavoring to blunt criticism of the enterprise as nationalist, the directors "agreed to focus on the Protestant idea of liberty in the third set of pamphlets" at the September 1984 board meeting, as Richtarik has noted.[25]

Deane himself, although from a republican, Marxist background in the Bogside community of Londonderry/Derry, advocated for this sort of pluralist understanding of Field Day in his 1984 introduction to Friel's *Selected Plays*, which includes *Translations*. As he writes there, "It was founded to put on plays outside the confines of the established theatre and, through that, to begin to effect a change in the apathetic atmosphere of the North."[26] All these ecumenical, trans-ideological concerns were well meaning, but they cannot be fully squared with Friel's view that Deane and Deane *"alone,"* as he writes him in a letter dated "St. Patrick's Day" of 1989, "gave both cohesion and then voice to the vague and confused political aspirations of F.D. That is never acknowledged by the members. But it is accurate—and it is something that gives me *great* pleasure."[27] Friel had clearly felt this way for some time. He had previously written Deane on July 17, 1982, that "I want to tell you how important your involvement with Field Day is both for F.D. and for me." Moreover, "your line 'It is six characters in search of a story. . . . ' rightly places you as central to the enterprise."[28] And yet, Deane by 1985, "largely because he was more willing than the other directors to discuss the project in abstract terms, had become Field Day's unofficial spokesman," and "[h]is opinions, consequently, were commonly taken to reflect company policy." As Richtarik memorably articulates it, Deane "is an inveterate controversialist," and "although he would doubtless dispute this, the deepest-dyed nationalist on the Field Day board."[29] Deane's tendency to think of the political situation in

Northern Ireland through a rigorously postcolonial lens exacerbated this position, since in such a viewpoint, the "colonized," or Irish Catholics, could never be blamed for any of their problems. Admittedly, the rampant long-term bias against Catholics throughout the island was undoubtedly responsible for a great deal of the poor living conditions, lack of jobs, low-quality housing, etc., but in the postcolonial model, the dichotomy between colonizers and colonized never admits any leakage, and the colonized are never at fault, even for reprisals against unjust politics. The particular problem of Deane's pronounced nationalism was never resolved for Field Day. Almost certainly for other reasons, however, Friel would resign from Field Day by the end of January 1994.

Out of all its idealizing of ecumenism and straddling or even transcending the North's sectarian divide, Field Day's itinerant operation in putting on plays all over the island may have been the most salutary—at least in the abstract—and this practice was not only designed to reach both major communities in Northern Ireland, but also others in the Republic. Rea argued that Field Day's touring throughout the island of Ireland was "an essentially . . . political statement: we were northern but we belonged to the whole country, whatever we were talking about we wanted to address the whole country."[30] And yet, as Martine Pelletier rightly notes,

> From the outset, Field Day's commitment to touring Ireland North and South had rightly been understood as a highly political gesture. Affirming an Ireland culture beyond partition clearly marked Field Day off as a nationalist project in the eyes of many commentators.[31]

Despite Field Day's best efforts, it thus remained perceived as a nationalist endeavor.

The one-night stops of the company may have provided particularly compelling theater through their creation of community, because, as Rea has noted, "On the one-night stands every night's an opening night. You know it's their only bite of the cherry and you want it to be good for them. There is cross-fertilization, but it doesn't happen over tea and buns afterwards, it happens on stage."[32] His comment about "cross-fertilization" suggests that such a process happened onstage during the Field Day tours and also occurred between actors and audiences, delighting Friel, who had always sought to create such heterogeneous communities. Seamus Heaney has remarked about the Field Day plays that their traveling nature actually contributed to their intense impact on audiences: "[T]heatre on tour is specially framed to effect such a transformation. The come-and-go of the encounter does not mean that the effect is fleeting. On the contrary, as Hamlet's fit-up players quickly demonstrate, the occasional nature of their appearance in a place can be just the thing 'to show the very age and body of the time his form and pressure.'"[33]

The Field Day Theatre Company is now generally acknowledged to be the most important theater company in Ireland since the Irish National Theatre was founded at the end of the nineteenth century. Richtarik has noted that *Translations* itself "has become a standard part of the repertoire of the Abbey Theatre in Dublin," and "is now generally regarded as what Michael Sheridan declared it to be two days after it opened: a watershed in Irish theatre."[34] Despite Deane's somewhat more strident nationalism and the moderate nationalism of Friel, Rea, and most of the other intellectuals who came to join the company's board of directors, Field Day early on was easily the most powerful communal artistic contribution to reimagining identity in Northern Ireland during one of its darkest periods with the ongoing Maze hunger strikes. Field Day represents the point in Friel's career where he smuggles Derry and the matter of Northern Ireland back into his drama, not in the dramatic setting but in the traveling settings of his new drama company. In the original production of *Translations*, the fictive village of Ballybeg is inscribed onto the temporary stage of the Guildhall in the actual city of Londonderry/ Derry in a positive revision of the repressive setting of the Guildhall in *The Freedom of the City*. And, as we will see, the short-lived moment of communication, even love, between Maire and Yolland across their linguistic divide augurs qualified hope for all divided societies, including that of Northern Ireland.

8

Translations

Lamenting and Accepting Modernity

> There is no knowing or sensing a place except by being in that
> place, and to be in a place is to be in a position to perceive it.
> —Edward Casey, "How to Get from Space to Place
> in a Fairly Short Stretch of Time"

> John O'Donovan was "aware . . . that ghosts of the old Gaelic
> Order still haunted the landscape he was naming and he wrote
> of those apparitions with understanding and affection."
> —Brian Friel, "Where We Live"

At first glance, *Translations* seems a nearly complete departure from
Faith Healer with its emphasis on history, colonial/native interactions, and lack of a central artistic figure like Frank Hardy. But
when we recall that Friel began *Translations* as a play about Colonel
Colby, the architect of the British Ordnance Survey of Ireland of the
1830s and 1840s, and that Friel was "fascinated" by "the fact that he
had one hand,"[1] we realize that disability haunts these two dramas.
Frank Hardy's soon-to-be severed body parts and Friel's concomitant interest in the myth of the Red Hand of Ulster were undoubtedly
still reverberating in his mind as he turned to a much more public
play. Even though Friel discarded this "Oedipal detail [that] seemed
crucial to me, mesmerized me" after "many deluded months,"[2] the
finished text of *Translations* nevertheless meditates deeply on the
interaction between what Friel came to see as two flawed, even crippled civilizations—the imperial British one and the native Gaelic one

204

in Ireland. To show he rejects nostalgia for Gaelic culture and how he saw it as deeply flawed at the time depicted in *Translations*, he used the language of disability in an interview with Paddy Agnew in 1980 about the representatives of that culture in the play: "[Y]ou have on stage the representatives of a certain community—one is dumb, one is lame and one is alcoholic, a physical maiming which is a public representation of their spiritual deprivation."[3] Just as physical disability signified spiritual deprivation in *Faith Healer*, Friel would again signal such spiritual poverty in *Translations* through portraying disability, certainly a logically inconsistent connection, but nonetheless a powerfully visual rhetorical use of the actors' bodies.

Friel told Stephen Dixon in a little-cited interview of September 1980 that "[t]he play is about the absorption of one culture into another; but I hope it goes a bit deeper than that—about the disquiet between two aesthetics."[4] *Translations* privileges the dying aesthetic of the anti-Western, communal Gaelic culture over the burgeoning, imported British empiricist aesthetic being introduced by the Ordnance Survey. Yet Friel laments the disabled condition of that older culture and suggests two models of rapprochement and accommodation through the embrace of interpenetrating cultures: first, through his portrayal of Yolland, an English member of the surveying team who becomes very sympathetic to the Irish language and culture, but who is likely murdered; and second, through his depiction of the schoolmaster Hugh, who resolves that Irish culture must accommodate itself to certain aspects of modernity—particularly the speaking of English—to survive in the future.

Moreover, this clash between a communal outlook and dehumanizing empiricism in *Translations* strengthens the continuing narrative about the collision of these two philosophies articulated in *The Freedom of the City*, a play that brooded upon the displacements endemic in the city of Londonderry/Derry and within the Guildhall, symbol of unionist domination over Catholics in that then-gerrymandered city. Oddly, Friel wrote a column for *The Irish Press* in the early 1960s titled "Disposing of the Body," in which the narrator of the sketch finally chooses to bury the family's bull terrier "[b]ehind the marble bust of Queen Victoria" in the Guildhall.[5] In an uncanny, heretofore unrecognized act of self-appropriation, nearly twenty years later, *Translations*—a drama that slides toward violence over the disappearance of one of its lead characters, Yolland—was staged in the Guildhall. The conflation of a mysterious burial with the place of imperial power in his adopted city of Londonderry/Derry must have proven irresistible to the playwright as he pondered the continuing resonances of the imperial/colonial conflict in northwestern Ireland/Northern Ireland during the Northern Irish Troubles of the 1970s.

But a political transformation had occurred in the city beginning the year *The Freedom* was first produced and continued through the late 1970s. Christopher Morash notes that "in 1973, electoral reforms gave the city's Catholic population a majority on the City Council, and in 1978—just as Friel was beginning to sift through the ideas that would become *Translations*—they rechristened themselves *Derry* City Council."[6] While the British government still termed the city "Londonderry," as did most local unionists, and there was continued widespread sectarianism and poverty in the city, "local unionist and nationalist politicians had worked out a power-sharing arrangement on the Council, and it was a unionist Lord Mayor, Marlene Jefferson, who helped to make it possible for *Translations* to be staged at the Guildhall."[7] Thus, Kevin Whelan has argued in a program note to the 2011 revival of the play at the Abbey Theatre, "it shows a great dramatist taking the national pulse at a transitional historical moment in Northern Ireland. In that sense, *Translations* can be regarded as a foundational moment in the emergence of the Peace Process."[8] Even more strikingly, Anthony Roche suggests that the range of audience members gathered at the Guildhall for the play's premiere in 1980 were invited to act as performers in the negotiation of the deadlocked political drama of Northern Ireland.

> [They] represented the complete political spectrum of Northern Ireland—from Sinn Fein and the SDLP on the Catholic side through various shades of Unionism on the other. . . . They were

entering and sharing the same space and anticipating by several decades what was to be put in place by the Good Friday Agreement and the power-sharing Executive. The audience . . . were being invited to enter a continuum and a process that was still ongoing and in which they were actively engaged, to face up to the obligation enjoined on the entire community to resolve their deadlocks.[9]

The last part of this chapter thus shifts from a careful exploration of the various linguistic, topological, cultural, and spiritual issues intertwined with place in this drama to a brief consideration of the role *Translations* has played in the cultural and political life of Northern Ireland—particularly, how it offers a model of communication going forward between historically opposed communities.

While *The Freedom of the City* sought to articulate a communal philosophy of imagined residents in a small, impoverished city, *Translations* seeks not only to vocalize an elegy for dying rural culture but also to suggest how that culture might accommodate itself to a worldview that devalues human-inflected landscapes and privileges a numerically inflected philosophy while retaining some of its rich, rural values, including the spiritual and the communal. Friel had already explored the idea of empiricist map-making for exploitative purposes in the West of Ireland through his 1969 farce, *The Mundy Scheme*. At the beginning of Act Three of that play, the stage directions note, "*The old map has been replaced by a new one: and the area blacked in by MOLONEY is now covered in decorative miniature flags.*"[10] In the earlier play, Moloney convinces the fictitious Irish Taoiseach F. X. Ryan that turning the West of Ireland into the world's graveyard would bring in both tourism and great wealth to Ireland. Moloney hilariously reveals to Ryan at the end of Act One his desire to "make the west of Ireland the acknowledged . . . eternal resting place," arguing that "[w]e can supply the very commodity these big cities need—ground, thousands of acres of it—useless ground—crying out for development."[11] From the presentation of this and other scenes, we realize how Friel in this play—which was published around the time he moved to rural Donegal for good and thus affirmed his commitment to rural culture—may be satirizing the contemporary view of rural areas as nonproductive, useless, essentially dead. If *The Mundy Scheme* imagines western Ireland as a future, literal graveyard before Moloney's plan collapses, then *Translations* imagines how that same area's slow cultural death might have been accelerated by both the British Ordnance Survey and some members of the local, Irish agrarian community.

While most criticism of *Translations* has understandably dealt with issues of language, particularly Friel's debt to George Steiner's book *After Babel*, this chapter seeks to understand how such cultural issues are intertwined with the particularities of the local, rural environment.[12] *Translations*, however, continues to be a favorite work of postcolonial theorists working on Irish literature, some of whom have neglected Friel's larger threnody for rural, if flawed, Irish culture and its anti-Western epistemology in their rush to indict the British for their linguistic imperialism in conducting the Ordnance Survey while ignoring the likely killing of Yolland by the violent, proto-republican Donnelly twins, which will expose Ballybeg to English reprisals.[13]

In response to such critics, we should consider that Friel himself, in his preface to historical topographer John O'Donovan's *Ordnance Survey Letters: Donegal*, has expressed both his admiration and contempt for O'Donovan. Yet O'Donovan is one of the inspirations for the play: Friel modeled his character Owen on him. Friel concludes by affirming, "[I]f the Donegal names that he pursued and scrutinized and standardized so earnestly became gradually transmuted over the years, as indeed they must, we can always return to O'Donovan who pinned those names down and gave them a pedigree and endowed them with some permanence. So that for a period of our lives we knew with some certainty where we lived."[14] For a writer who consistently charts the fluidity of his imagined places and who is very cautious about affirming the notion of "home," this admission validates O'Donovan's very real accomplishment and colors our reading of the unease generated by the cultural clash in the play.

The critical tendency to privilege issues of culture, specifically language, in this drama, has led to *Translations* being included in recent editions of *The Norton Anthology of English Literature* under the "Nation and Language" section. Unfortunately, the play is often still read largely in a somewhat reductive, postcolonial context that ignores its environmental and cultural context, which again perpetuates the false divide between culture and nature that this entire study attempts to suture. For example, the headnote to *Translations* in the *Norton Anthology* (which tens of thousands of American college students will likely take as gospel truth) states baldly that it "reimagines the transitional moment when the language of the colonizer is supplanting the language of the colonized."[15] Such a formulation conveniently ignores the historical reality that the English place names of the Ordnance Survey certainly did not supplant the local Irish place names then or, in some cases, ever. Moreover, the reversal of this trajectory toward the language of the colonizer "supplanting the language of the colonized" actually occurs—late in the play when Owen begins translating recently Anglicized place names back into Irish when Captain Lancey threatens reprisals if Yolland is not found (*BFP1*, 439–40). Finally, nothing is mentioned in this headnote about the setting of the play at harvest time, the community's gathering of the hay, or the various communal, rural traditions which are also under siege in the play along with the Irish language. This flattened commentary in the *Norton Anthology* thus neatly divides nature and culture, which Friel instead perceives as always connected.

Ulf Dantanus, who is one of the few Friel commentators to consistently link the playwright's cultural concerns to those of environment, has been a fairly lonely voice in his evocative analysis of the play. Speaking of "Hugh's pomposity" at dismissing William Wordsworth (*BFP1* 417), he nonetheless quickly argues that, "in these few lines," the play suggests "the beginning of the rape of a country's linguistic and cultural heritage."[16] Yet even Dantanus misses the real point of the play—that as Hugh will admit toward the end of the play, some sort of accommodation must be made with modernity, which is represented in the play (along with the French Revolution) by English culture and language: "We must learn those new names. . . . We must learn where we live. We must learn to make them our own.

We must make them our new home" (444). Learning to live in a new language, making it the house of being, as Friel seems to suggest with his evocation of Frank Hardy's ritualistic language at the end of *Faith Healer*, is imperative for the Irish, even as they inflect that language, as Joyce would later and Friel himself has, with their own idiolect and cultural contributions.

In this regard, Friel's statement in his 1972 essay, "Self-Portrait," is crucial for understanding his own sense of having inherited a mixed cultural heritage as a mid- to late-twentieth-century Irish writer. He writes there of "the tortuous task of *surveying* the mixed holding I had inherited" and contrasts that task with that of Irish writers in earlier generations who "learned to speak Irish, took their genetic purity for granted, and soldiered on. . . . We want to know what the word 'native' means, what the word 'foreign' means. . . . [I]f the words have any meaning at all. And persistent considerations like these *erode* old certainties and help clear the building site."[17] The recourse to the language of demolition here uncannily anticipates the central plot device of *Translations* and suggests that Friel's imaginative depiction of the British Ordnance Survey enabled him to survey his own Irishness and discover its mixed nature. Furthermore, the questioning of the terms "native" and "foreign" anticipates how *Translations* would later explore these concepts and show them to be unexpectedly fluid: I am thinking here of the English Yolland's slow conversion to the rural life of Ballybeg and of Hugh's gradual realization that he must learn to live with and in the English language. Finally, the use of "erode" in his last sentence anticipates Yolland's comment late in the play that "[s]omething is being eroded" (*BFP1* 420), suggesting Friel's belief that the "old certainties" he referred to in 1972, such as an imagined Gaelic purity, need to be questioned, even as he privileges certain values in that culture such as community.

Just as *The Freedom of the City* did, this play reflects Friel's nationalist sympathies, but he critiques violent republicanism as well as violent British imperialism, showing his relative even-handedness. He primarily wants to depict the attenuation of local, rural culture because of modernity's arrival in the form of English surveyors in

Ballybeg and the internal pressure of a burgeoning Irish nationalist resistance. Rather than being imbued with a whiff of rural nostalgia, *Translations* articulates Friel's alarm at the loss of local community both in early-nineteenth-century Ireland and worldwide in the present day. This drama inveighs against the advent of the machine in rural culture, which Friel views as evicting laborers, and it also rejects the concurrent Enlightenment emphasis on empiricism and the individual, both of which destroy communal identity as well.

Reading *Translations* through the lens of a robust environmental and intellectual theory frees it from the often-unbalanced early reviews of the sort Richtarik has surveyed in her now-classic book on the Field Day Theatre Company, as well as from the critical tendency to emphasize the linguistic imperialism of the British (save Yolland), which neglects Friel's portrayal of a dying holistic cultural and physical environment.[18] For example, an obsessive focus on the decline of the Irish language in the play relegates its discussion to an Irish and British context, when actually this linguistic displacement is part of a larger attenuation in rural Irish culture and epistemology specifically and in global rural culture generally brought about by modernization. Linguistically oriented criticism of *Translations* tends to argue that it sanctions Irish cultural nationalism and critiques English imperialism, but Friel's play actually implies that both ideologies have been complicit in ushering in pernicious aspects of modernism that have, in their turn, slowly killed rural Irish farming communities and the antimodern, communal worldview these villages espouse. The universality of Friel's drama becomes clear only when the linguistic, cultural, and epistemological tragedies that occur in *Translations* are recognized as Friel's lament for a larger cross-cultural decline in communal ways of perceiving reality.

The large body of criticism on this drama has not addressed these issues sufficiently, and until now, no criticism has explored the play's crucial moment of reconciliation between Yolland and Maire as part of Friel's organic, environmental philosophy. Their linguistic divide is overcome by their joint recitation of local place names in Irish. After Yolland's disappearance, Maire articulates some of his local

English place names as a litany of lament for him. Through this recitation, Friel implies that the common values of a shared transnational
rural culture can perhaps overcome linguistic and political divisions.
Translations thus offers heavily qualified hope for reconciliation in
all societies fraught with violence, as for example, in Northern Ireland, the site of its premiere. It implies the potential of cultural and
political reconciliation between the English and the Irish and also, by
extension, between their descendants, Protestants and Catholics in
Northern Ireland, through the English character Yolland's and Irish
character Maire's shared recognition of the importance of local community across national boundaries. Friel's localized dramatic theory
of place as articulated in *Translations* registers a lament for the passing of a particularized, viable local Irish culture and also urges a
return to its values such as community and personal communication—indeed, the values of local culture generally—as the antidote
to many years of tribal conflict on the island of Ireland, while grudgingly urging an accommodation of sorts with modernity. His most
famous drama thus both warns against the dangers of unchecked
modernism and briefly embraces a hope for province-wide and transnational reconciliation still possible through an emphasis on local
culture and its attendant unifying communal values that remain viable in the twenty-first century.

   Translations is set in 1833, at another historical crossroads for
Ireland, during the British Ordnance Survey, which began in the
northern counties and published its first maps (at a scale of six inches
to one mile) that same year. Friel has been taken to task severely for
fictionalizing events and conditions from this historical period, but
he has never claimed to be a historian. Just as *Freedom* differs in plot
and many details from the actual events of Bloody Sunday, *Translations* departs from many of the actual conditions of the famous
Ordnance Survey. I do not wish to pursue here the famous contro-
versy that arose over some of the liberties Friel took with the facts
of the survey.[19] But I affirm with Friel that there is a truth—sometimes moral, sometimes emotional, sometimes intellectual—that

transcends history, though it may be rooted in it, and it carries more weight than any historical fact. All of us know this truth instinctively and we turn to great literature to discover whatever it may say about ourselves as human beings. For Brian Friel in *Translations* this truth is, as Richtarik argues, "a version of the past which, though ultimately tragic, captures for a brief moment a vision of how two opposed groups could learn to appreciate each other. This possibility of mutual respect is undermined by violent men on both sides. It is in this sense that *Translations* may best be taken to be what Seamus Deane has called it: 'a parable of events in the present day.'"[20] As we have seen, *The Freedom of the City* also envisions such a moment before its protagonists are shot down violently.

More important, *Translations* rises above being a mere critique of nationalism by portraying the clash of an industrialized society with a rural one. Friel contrasts the contemplative English character Yolland—who embraces the cultural and linguistic life of the parish—with the energy and busyness of Captain Lancey and with Yolland's own father, both of whom are ideological children of the French Revolution. Rather than celebrating the new Enlightenment and Romantic emphasis on the individual, *Translations* sanctions an older, communal worldview that provides a somewhat satisfying vocational, emotional, spiritual, and intellectual life for each member of the townland, even its "adopted" members such as Yolland—even though this worldview and its sustaining culture are already dying, compromised from within as well as without. But as Friel shows, the pernicious power of the Ordnance Survey will hasten its death. This intensely local agrarian society is grounded in a shared sense of community located in the typical Irish townland or *clachan* of Ballybeg, as we will see. Maire's rejection of this worldview and desperate attempt to modernize, however, implies that all community members are not happy there. While recognizing the grinding financial poverty often found in rural Irish culture, Friel has always argued with a remarkable degree of consistency that this communal way of life is threatened by encroaching modernity—from both within and without. This communitarian way of life is supplanted by an ideological and spiritual poverty that purports to elevate the individual but instead strips him of his place in the community and often increases his dependence on dehumanizing, mechanized forms of labor.

For Friel, the intense concentration on the townland of Ballybeg, which he had already depicted in earlier dramas, was heightened in *Translations* through his clear adoption of Patrick Kavanagh's theory of parochialism. This embrace of a liberating parochialism helps us understand Friel's artistic statement from 1970: "I would like to write a play that would capture the peculiar spiritual, and indeed material, flux that this country is in at the moment. This has got to be done, for me anyway, and I think it has got to be done *at a local, parochial level*, and hopefully this will have meaning for other people in other countries."[21] *Translations* became the play about spiritual and material flux set in a parochial milieu that Friel had longed to write. It enacts a double lament, grieving both the loss of a centuries-old way of life in Irish agricultural communities occurring in the early 1800s and, implicitly, the rapid urbanization of Ireland in the late twentieth century when he wrote the play.[22]

Alan Peacock misapprehends the epistemological implications of Friel's penchant for parochialism when he argues that the vast array of ideas in *Translations* is merely grounded in the realistic parochial qualities of the community: "[T]he parochial qualities, the focus on a single, small community and the attention paid to representing the life of that community in all its 'momentous daily trivia,' keep the highly developed idea-content of the play firmly rooted in recognizable experience."[23] Instead, Friel suggests that the antimodern worldview of the parish stems from its rural culture; this environment is not simply a recognizable place in which to root his interrogation of Western intellectual history "in recognizable experience."

Friel senses correctly that an application of industrial principles to a particular culture dooms that culture's harmony with the local economy. Friel noted in a letter to me after the first edition of the current study was published that he admired the work of writer and environmentalist Wendell Berry. As Berry argues, even describing native culture quantitatively is a competitive gesture since its relationship with the immediate economy is intrinsically harmonious:

> To presume to describe land, work, people, and community by information, by quantities, seems invariably to throw them into competition with one another. Work is then understood to exploit the land, the people to exploit their work, the community to exploit its people. And then instead of land, work, people, and community, we have the industrial categories of resources, labor, management, consumers, and government. We have exchanged harmony for an interminable fuss, and the work of culture for the timed and harried labor of an industrial economy.[24]

The pending disharmony in *Translations* echoes that situation which Berry warns is created by an application of quantified description to local agricultural communities. The surveyors' insistence on quantification and measurement as the primary constituents of reality, for instance, will likely influence the parish's inhabitants to begin to conceive of themselves as workers and consumers instead of as an organic, caring community. Two contrasting versions of perceiving reality collide in the play with the older, more abstract view suffering grievously. Not just geographic but also ideological and spiritual deracination is sure to follow.

Friel suggests this pending loss of a premodern worldview when Yolland recognizes, in response to Owen's question, "What's happening?" in Act Two, Scene One, "I'm not sure. But I'm concerned about my part in it. It's an eviction of sorts. . . . Something is being eroded" (*BFP1* 419–20). The connotations of erosion here are inherently agricultural and ideological. As we have seen, an "eviction" of a different type figures prominently in Friel's *The Freedom of the City*, when the three central poverty-stricken characters are "evicted" from the Guildhall. As we will see later, Rose and Agnes in *Dancing at Lughnasa* are also effectively evicted from their home by the opening of the new knitwear factory. Here, Friel makes clear that the English soldiers and the modernity associated with most of them—save

Yolland—threatens the agricultural lifestyle and premodern epistemology of the local Irish characters.

Friel wrote a diary entry when creating the play that suggests
how fully he recognizes this looming, wrenching epistemological
change: "In Ballybeg, at the point when the play begins, the cultural
climate is a dying climate—no longer quickened by its past, about
to be plunged overnight in an alien future."[25] If that something that
"is being eroded" is not a contrived, culturally pure form of Irishness, as most commentators now seem to realize, an Irish identity is
nevertheless disappearing. This waning Irish identity is grounded in
the local agricultural community that speaks vernacular Irish and is
relatively economically self-sufficient and interdependent, precisely
because of its agrarian lifestyle.

Friel purposely set *Translations* during August, the traditional
harvest season in Ireland, which both suggests the movement of the
community to traditional agricultural rhythms and implies the wind
of cultural change in this liminal season. The setting for the entire
play is also explicitly agricultural: the opening stage directions mention that *"the hedge-school is held in a disused barn or hay-shed or
byre"* (BFP1 383). Yet when Claire Gleitman correctly observes that
these stage directions "are littered with adjectives that hint at the
obsolete nature of the hedge-school world . . . and those items with
the potential for usefulness (the cart-wheel, the farming tools, the
churn) are 'broken and forgotten,'"[26] she effectively chooses to ignore
other, crucial aspects of the viability of the farming economy in the
play, such as the rich hay crop, although as we will see, the specter
of the potato famine lurks on the horizon. The mechanical surveying
of Lancey, Yolland, and their helpers is being conducted against the
backdrop of the manual hay harvest while Manus's pupils learn their
lessons in the hay-shed. Early in Act One, Maire tells Jimmy, it is
"the best harvest in living memory, they say" (388). Soon after this,
Jimmy, Doalty, and Manus discuss ancient and local agricultural
soil conditions. Jimmy reads out a Latin sentence to Manus, who
translates it as "'Land that is black and rich beneath the pressure of
the plough. . . . '" Doalty wants a chance to finish the sentence, but

Jimmy does it instead: "'And with *cui putre*—with crumbly soil—is in the main best for corn.' There you are!" He goes on to tell Doalty, "Black soil for corn. *That's* what you should have in that upper field of yours—corn, not spuds" (392). Doalty rejects Jimmy's advice, but Jimmy's translation continues the theme of the soil's fertility that has been introduced with Maire's comment about the hay harvest being the best ever.

While Jimmy's sentence is from Book Two of Virgil's *Georgics*, Hugh has set the headline sentence for the day from Book Three of Tacitus's *Agricola*: "It's easier to stamp out learning than to recall it" (*BFP1* 393). This statement resonates with the theme of the loss of Irish place names in the community (and eventually the Irish language itself), but its source is even more important thematically. Agricola, Tacitus's father-in-law, was the first governor of Roman Britain and *The Agricola* contains the first detailed account of the British Isles. The irony is probably lost on Hugh's students, but they are translating an ancient imperial document while contemporary imperial representatives translate their local place names into English. Additionally, their translations strengthen the earlier hints of the local farming economy's self-sufficiency. Besides being the proper name of the first Roman governor of Britain, *agricola* means "farmer." Book Twelve contains a vivid description of the good soil common to the islands: "The soil will produce good crops, except olives, vines, and other plants which usually grow in warmer lands. They are slow to ripen, though they shoot up quickly—both facts being due to the same cause, the extreme moistness of the soil and atmosphere."[27] This leitmotif of rich, fertile soil runs throughout the play and the characters draw both physical and spiritual sustenance from it.

Friel's conception of community is firmly based on the intensely local concept of the townland. The setting for most of his plays is "Ballybeg," the Anglicized compound of two Irish words—*baile* and *beag*. The etymological history of *Baile* is unknown, but it translates into something like "townland." *Beag*, of course, means "small." Literally, then, *Ballybeg* means "small townland," suggesting something akin to the *clachan* type of settlement common in Donegal for hundreds of years, which Friel has specifically identified even into the last century.[28] Ballybeg as it is portrayed in *Translations* resembles a specific village cluster identified as a *clachan*, widespread in Ireland in the years before the Famine and defined by cultural anthropologist E. Esytn Evans as "a formless cluster of small farm houses. . . . Lacking such village attributes as church and public-house, it comprised the homes of a constantly changing number of related families . . . and it . . . expand[ed] and decay[ed] with no conceived plan."[29] While not identified specifically in the text as a *clachan*, Ballybeg accords closely with Evans's description: it has no organized layout, and no church or public houses are mentioned in the play. Furthermore, the villagers have an organic conception of Ballybeg that displays its formal dynamism. Evans notes that the dissolution of the *clachan* "was mostly the work of landlords and required no Enclosure Acts: otherwise it would surely have attracted more attention from economic historians."[30] Although this process did not happen in Donegal, Friel's peasants naturally fear the advent of something like enclosure because it had already occurred during the previous century in the more Anglicized areas of the country.[31] In *Translations*, the threat of razing and enclosure after Yolland's disappearance signifies the destruction and literal division of a typical Irish farming townland bound by communal ties, which works together and even regards reality differently from the modern world.[32] Indeed, the entire parish's existence as a communal village runs counter to the Western tendency toward atomic individualism epitomized by mechanical perception, while Ballybeg's formlessness bespeaks a rural Irish resistance to linear modernity.

Kevin Whelan has articulated the central features of the townland, one of which is the way in which "rural people knew the country by heart through the filaments which bound the townland network to the landscape."[33] The agrarian community of the townland was intensely communal. Whelan notes that "[t]he neighborhood group who cooperated in various tasks—haymaking, saving the harvest, turfcutting, sharing tools and manpower—were townland based. Four to ten families created the '*meitheal*' or '*comhar na gcomharsan'* group within the townlands." There was "mutual celebration and grief at events in the family cycle. Thus, it was traditional for all work to cease in a townland where a neighbor died."[34] Many such examples of the *meitheal*, or communal agricultural work group, exist in Friel's plays but it is perhaps most abundantly seen in *Translations*. For instance, when Hugh first enters, he is drunk and says, "[W]e were celebrating the baptism of Nellie Ruadh's baby" (*BFP1* 397). Outside the schoolhouse, other members of the *meitheal* work communally: the Donnelly twins are reckoned to be "at the turf" (398), and Maire mentions her urge to go to America "as soon as the harvest's all saved" (400).

Friel leaves the exact farming techniques of his prefamine rural community unclear, but the farming practices of his fictional villagers recall the old rundale system, once practiced widely in Ireland and which survived in County Donegal, the setting of *Translations*, well into the twentieth century. His suggestion of the rundale system reinforces his emphasis on community. Evans points out its salient features:

> Intensive use was made of a selected stretch of land, the infield, which might be on a well-drained hillside, an esker, or an old beach or a coastal or river terrace. Because crops were restricted to those sown in spring, and thanks to a ready supply of animal manure partly contributed by wintering livestock, the infield could be kept in more or less permanent cultivation and could, therefore, be worked with a light plough and simple gear . . . it was sometimes pulled by the horse's tail. The plots were very small, however, and spade cultivation was more efficient. . . . Rundale was much simpler and more flexible than the three field system, requiring less equipment and less organization. It was egalitarian, and could operate without the benefit of a landlord.[35]

The most intriguing characteristics of the rundale system in the context of Friel's play are the simple equipment employed, its egalitarianism, and its lack of organization. Friel's Irish characters may or may not employ the specific rundale techniques described by

Evans—there is no clear evidence that they are—but they unques-
tionably distrust mechanized labor, hierarchy, and linearity. As we
have seen in the passages I quote above, they also band together as
a *meitheal* in order to bring in the harvest expeditiously, suggesting
further their rejection of the sort of hyperindividualism associated
with modernity. All of these aspects link it clearly to their premodern
or antimodern worldview. Indeed, a typical rundale community like
the kind extensively documented in Gweedore, Donegal, featured
joint land ownership by groups of tenants of up to twenty or more,
whose plots were only separated by strips of untilled land, together
comprising a communal townland.[36]

Evans points out that some features of rundale communities are
essentially premodern, even pre-Celtic, and recalls his reaction on
first seeing one: "When I first encountered a rundale community in
Donegal I had a strong feeling that I was witnessing the final degraded
phrase of a complex of very ancient practices. I wrote then that I was
'tempted to regard the open-field system as a survival from pre-Celtic
times. Improbably as it seems, there is now . . . some field evidence
to support this wild surmise.'"[37] Recognizing the agricultural practices in *Translations* as a remnant from the pre-Celtic era enables
us to refute simplistic notions that the play enacts a Celtic nostalgia
when it actually laments the eventual passing of a much older society
with communal values. Since at the time Friel wrote *Translations*,
"half of Scotland's 19 million acres" was "owned by 608 land owners, and 10 per cent by 18" land owners, and because in England
"the top 1 per cent of the population own nearly two thirds of the
land,"[38] many British readers or audience members would have been
surprised to read or hear of such communal land ownership patterns
in the 1830s, much less suspect that, in attenuated forms, they survived well into the twentieth century in parts of Ireland.

Despite its general viability as part of such communal systems,
Irish farming was gradually made tenuous by its increasing reliance
on the potato as the major food crop starting in the eighteenth century. Along with the bumper hay crop and rich local soil conditions,
Friel's characters mention the potato crop several times, a crop which

by the time of the play had replaced corn as the staple of the Irish diet. Shortly after the passage from Virgil is discussed, Bridget mentions that her husband Sean told her about "the sweet smell" of the potatoes near where the soldiers "are making the maps" (*BFP1* 394). She is unconsciously displaying her anti-English prejudice by linking the soldiers with the alleged potato blight, and Maire reminds her angrily that the potatoes have never failed in Baile Beag.[39] Bridget's irrational fear nonetheless evokes the loss of the staple of the Irish food supply that would come only a few years later.

The specter of the Irish potato blight in *Translations* has been little examined, but it suggests the fragility of the agricultural environment upon which Friel's community depends. While there are a variety of agricultural activities ongoing in the parish—hay harvesting, salmon netting, turfcutting—all could be lost if the townland is razed. Indeed, Lancey threatens to "shoot all livestock in Ballybeg" (*BFP1* 439) as the first act of destruction if Yolland is not found in twenty-four hours. If, as Joseph Roach has argued about Beckett's *Waiting for Godot*, that drama is in part an analeptic meditation upon the lingering cultural and political repercussions of the potato famine for the Irish at mid-twentieth century, perhaps Friel's *Translations* is the proleptic dramatic bookend to Beckett's play, with the anticipated emptying-out of its rural Donegal landscape.[40]

The second reprisal threatened by the soldiers is the implementation of evictions and clearances after forty-eight hours (*BFP1* 439). The English soldiers conduct themselves according to clock time, which markedly contrasts the natural seasonal and diurnal rhythms by which the parish's inhabitants live their lives. The impending decline of self-sufficient local agriculture could thus be hastened by direct English intervention. Its decline—paradoxically, in the midst of the normally bountiful harvest season—is signified by its first "reaping" of the season, the murder of Yolland, the only English character who truly appreciates the looming loss of a centuries-old way of life in the parish.

While the local inhabitants' agrarian lifestyle is directly endangered by the English soldiers' promised reprisals for Yolland's disappearance, their worldview is more obliquely threatened by the precise quantitative measuring these same soldiers carry out in their surveying of the townland, which accords with a colonialist mindset that valued counting and measurement as part of control over the colonies. In his reply to historian J. H. Andrews's critique of some of the historical liberties he took, Friel notes that one of his original inspirations for the play was his realization that "directly across the River Foyle from where I live in Muff is a place called Magilligan and it was at Magilligan that the first trigonometrical base for the ordnance survey was set up in 1828."[41] The observation leaps out at us because of its precision, and it shows how carefully Friel has studied his local landscape and its history as part of his rejection of instrumental "perception." A quarter-century later, in *The Home Place*, he would again critique such a philosophy with his portrayal of Dr. Richard Gore's eugenicist philosophy and his use of the craniometer to measure locals' heads and determine their intelligence. A passage from that play spoken by Gore demonstrates how Friel has consistently articulated his belief that imperial control depended on numerical mastery: "Are they saying to us—these physical features . . . : Crack our code and we will reveal to you how a man thinks. . . . If we could break into that vault, David, we wouldn't control just an empire. We would rule the entire universe" (*HP* 36).[42] Arjun Appadurai has convincingly argued that, although utilitarian in aim, for the colonial imagination "numbers gradually became more importantly part of the illusion of bureaucratic control and a key to a colonial imaginary in which countable abstractions, of people and resources at every imaginable level and for every conceivable purpose, created the sense of a controllable indigenous reality."[43] Specifically in Britain, by the end of the eighteenth century, only a few decades before the events portrayed in *Translations*, Appadurai shows that "number, like landscape, heritage, and the people, had become part of the language of the British political imagination . . . and the idea had become firmly implanted that a powerful state could not survive without making enumeration a central technique of social control."[44]

Such control was, of course, anathema to traditional Irish society, which had always imagined unity through spirituality despite marginalization, as Proinsias MacCana has shown.[45]

And of course, map making, which the British sappers and surveyors are engaged in during the course of Friel's play, was "a crucial aspect of the modern imperial enterprise," as Zygmunt Bauman, Gerry Smyth, Benedict Anderson, Tim Robinson, and other commentators have pointed out.[46] Bauman has convincingly held that "[t]he elusive goal of the modern space war was the subordination of social space to one and only one, officially approved and state-sponsored map." And, as he points out, "The space structure to emerge at the end of that space war was to be one perfectly legible for the state power and its agents, while remaining . . . resistant to all 'grass-roots' interpretive initiatives which could yet saturate fragments of space with meanings unknown and illegible to the powers-that-be, and so make such fragments invulnerable to control from above."[47] More specifically for our purposes in understanding Friel's depictions of the Ordnance Survey in *Translations*, Smyth holds that Ireland's native tradition of *dinnseanchas* or local place lore (an example of Bauman's "'grass-roots' interpretative initiatives") was gradually diminished through repeated British incursions, military and otherwise, into the country: "The (disputed) meanings of the spaces and places of Gaelic Ireland, much of the time encapsulated within their (disputed) names, were slowly displaced by a different set of concerns which shifted the Irish cultural and political imagination from one spatial paradigm (tribal and caste-based) to another (feudal and colonial)."[48]

Benedict Anderson's observations about European maps and the mindset behind them also illuminate Friel's desire to depict "the disquiet between two aesthetics" in the passage cited at the beginning of this chapter through his play's portrayal of colonial map-making. Anderson notes that, "Like censuses, European-style maps worked on the basis of a totalizing classification, and led their bureaucratic producers and consumers towards policies with revolutionary consequences."[49] Anderson's formulation of the emergence of the "map-as-logo" illuminates the ramifications for community in Friel's play once the Ordnance Survey is carried out:

> Its origins were reasonably innocent—the practice of the imperial states of coloring their colonies on maps with an imperial dye. . . . Dyed this way, each colony appeared like a detachable piece of a jigsaw puzzle. As this "jigsaw" effect became normal, each "piece" could be wholly detached from its geographic context. In its final form all explanatory glosses could be summarily removed: lines of longitude and latitude, place names, signs for rivers, seas, and mountains, *neighbors*. Pure sign, no longer compass to the world.[50]

Thus communities such as Friel's Ballybeg of 1833 could be represented and emptied out of their significance. Familiar faces, glances, gestures, talk—all become abstractions. Dislocation and deracination become the default position in this model. If, as cartographer and folklorist Tim Robinson has argued, "we, personally, cumulatively, communally, create and recreate landscapes—a landscape being not just the terrain but also the human perspectives on it, the land plus its overburden of meanings,"[51] then the process of constructing the "map-as-logo" empties out such a landscape of all its communally and cumulatively created meaning and essentially makes it a cipher.

We should acknowledge that in actuality such a process did not immediately occur: Richtarik has shown that "[l]ocal inhabitants would not have found this process particularly dislocating because the Survey placenames . . . never really caught on. There was no index of townland names until 1862, so the post office simply ignored the changes, as did almost everyone else."[52] But Richtarik neglects the effect that the Ordnance Survey must have had on inhabitants' psyches even if they did not employ the survey's place names in their daily discourse. As we also know, Friel is most concerned with fiction and the possibilities of imagination, not fact, and *Translations* attempts to show through the conflation of the imagination and a factual event what consequences the trajectory of Western empiricism, particularly as practiced by the English, has had for the Irish landscape and local Irish communities over time.

Robinson, again, is helpful on this issue, pointing out how such surveys have continued to be carried out, further disrupting oral and nongeometric conceptions of place. He reports, for instance, that in the Connemara area of western Ireland, on top of the nearby hill Iorras Beag, a recent Ordnance Survey built "a little concrete pillar . . . with a socket on its top in which a radar-like instrument could be firmly and indubitably fixed for measuring the distance to identical pillars on neighboring hills and offshore islands. This highly accurate triangulation was a first step towards the production of a new range of maps, which are being derived by photogrammetry, i.e. by computer analysis of stereoscopic pairs of aerial photographs."[53] Such a sterile map, of course, becomes the official one even if the older place lore lives on in the folk memory of locals, at least for a time. He continues, "I pile on the technological agony only to heighten the contrast I want to draw, the contradiction between true place, with all its dimensions of subjectivity, of memory and the forgotten, and 'location' as established in terms of latitude and longitude or of a six-figure map reference or some other objective, uniform schema."[54] Robinson appreciates and lauds the new technology ("[h]igh-tech cartography is a wonderful procedure") even as he laments it ("[a] concrete stub demeans it [the mountain top], in a way that the traditional hilltop cairn does not, that stone memory-bank of all the people who have clambered up to that height").[55] Like Robinson, Friel appreciates some of the changes that modernity has at times foisted upon us even as he recoils from their excesses. His suggestion in *Translations* that the imagination should continue to color and inflect the Irish landscape, while coexisting with a more objective, empirical system of topography, does not seem unreasonable. In fact, the play seems to advocate some form of accommodation with these representatives of modernity and empiricism, as we shall see, even as it displays a great unease with them.

In this sense, *Translations* opens up a conversation about technology that, as Mark William Roche has argued, literature is "uniquely qualified" to articulate because it helps us "imagine the spatial and temporal, including long-range, effects of our actions." It can do this, he holds, "by uncovering already contemporary consequences that are not immediately recognized or by portraying future consequences, which require more radical vision and for which literature is an ideal medium."[56] Precisely because it deals with the realm of the possible through its portrayal of an only somewhat historically imagined landscape, *Translations'* value lies not in a misguided attempt to offer a snapshot of 1833 rural Donegal. Rather it offers a glimpse of the future in which local culture has been nearly continually subjected to a series of environmental, political, and cultural attacks both from within and without, with devastating consequences for the Irish language, land, and local community.[57]

Terry Eagleton's argument in *Heathcliff and the Great Hunger*, about the emergence of modernism and nationalism on the peripheries of colonized countries, partially underpins my argument. Eagleton, through his reading of Perry Anderson's essay "Modernity and Revolution," argues that "[m]odernism springs from the estranging impact of modernizing forces on a still deeply traditionalist order, in a politically unstable context which opens up social hope as well as spiritual anxiety. Traditional culture provides modernism with an adversary, but also lends it some of the terms in which to inflect itself."[58] As we will see, the representatives of traditional culture, the Donnelly twins, not only function as the adversary of modernity in Friel's play but also introduce an element of modernism into the community, as reprisals in the form of clearances of the village are threatened by Captain Lancey unless Yolland is found.

In fact, Eagleton goes on to postulate, "modernism, then as now, can thrive more vigorously on the colonial or neo-colonial margins than at the metropolitan centre. In an increasingly unified world, where all times and places seem indifferently interchangeable, the 'no-time' and 'no-place' of the disregarded colony, with its fractured history and marginalized space, can become suddenly symbolic of a condition of disinheritance which now seems universal."[59] Eagleton applies his argument to the Irish artistic modernism of Yeats, Joyce, and Beckett in the early to mid-twentieth century, but certainly Friel's *Translations* exemplifies such a condition of disinheritance in geographic and cultural ways that anticipate this later Irish literary modernism.

In another formulation that complements Eagleton's but explores the philosophical and technological underpinnings of Irish modernism, Joe Cleary rejects understanding the emergence of Irish modernism as merely a movement in which "the modern [is] invariably disseminated outwards from a given centre—England, France, Europe or America—to the retarded margins."[60] Noting that members of the failed 1798 Rising in Ireland (an event mentioned in Friel's play) exported their republican ideals to Scotland, England, the United States, and Australia, Cleary instead argues for a more nuanced account of modernism in Ireland in which peripheries "at certain pivotal moments in their histories, at least . . . can function as sites of 'alternative enlightenment' where ideas of the modern are intellectually tested, creatively extended, radicalized and transformed, and indeed transferred eventually to the metropolitan centre."[61] We might then ask, does Friel's fictionalized account of the British Ordnance Survey in Ireland imagine such a moment of alternative enlightenment? Maire's English-speaking and love of English things and culture will be exported with her and perhaps prevent in her future family the spread of a virulent anti-Englishness. More interestingly, Friel's play itself attempts, through its original productions by the Field Day Theatre Company, to dramatize how he became the type of writer who made the English language his own and used it to demonstrate pernicious aspects of modernity, such as the exaltation of the individual at the expense of organic community. By extension, he hints how Irish culture has finally thrived in its adopted home of the English language, even as it nonetheless continues to express the "whiff of unease" with English that he attributes to John O'Donovan's attitude about the Ordnance Survey.[62]

Cleary further shows that such an alternative account of modernity as he has postulated with the 1798 republicans' emigration accords with a process through which the colonized were dislocated far sooner than those in imperial cities were. This theory shows how "the peripheries and their peoples . . . first endured, and with least shelter or state protection, a massive assault on their inherited traditions—the melting of all that had appeared culturally solid in the smelter of imperial conquest and assimilation. Their traumatic experience of cultural convulsion and dislocation only became the substance of everyday life in metropolitan places much later."[63] Such an experience is indeed what Friel's younger characters who remain in Ballybeg will endure, as the play makes clear. His fascination with the principle of flux that I explored in the introduction to this study stems from his realization that the Irish experienced such "cultural convulsion and dislocation" earlier than many of their English counterparts, although he takes pains to show how such a process continued to occur in later stages, such as through industrialism's impact on Ballybeg in *Dancing at Lughnasa*, for example.

Just as Friel rejects in *The Freedom of the City* the empiricist philosophy held by significant British characters as warping their perspective, he similarly critiques the tools and representatives of the Ordnance Survey in *Translations* for the distorting effects on perception they create. Patrick Duffy terms the Ordnance Survey "[a] classic example of an empiricist phase in landscape history . . . [because it] attempted to assemble an enormous range of geological, historical and economic data to match the topographical detail of the six-inch map survey which was being undertaken."[64] The iron theodolite symbolizes such an empiricist approach to landscape in *Translations*. The surveyors use it daily and store it in Maire's family byre "at night sometimes if it's raining," presumably to prevent it from rusting (*BFP1* 390).

Besides showing the uneasy juxtaposition between a symbol of the local Irish agricultural community (the byre) and a symbol of English industrialism (the theodolite), Friel clearly depicts the perniciousness of measuring and quantifying through instrumentation. This way of measuring became a key feature of the materialist philosophy that was consolidated with Galileo's distinction between primary and secondary qualities, which held full sway over much

of Western culture at this time. Galileo posited that primary qualities can be measured or quantified through machines such as micro-
scopes and telescopes, while secondary qualities really only reside in
the perception of the viewer. Galileo's distinctions, however, can be
traced back much further in Western philosophy to the fourteenth-
century thinker William of Occam's doctrine of nominalism, which
denied that universals have a real existence. As intellectual historian
Richard Weaver has pointed out, "The practical result of nominalist
philosophy is to banish the reality which is perceived by the intellect
and to posit as reality that which is perceived by the senses. With this
change in the affirmation of what is real, the whole orientation of
culture takes a turn, and we are on the road to modern empiricism."[65]

The surveyors' monocular use of the theodolite and their related
empiricist worldview contrast the broader perspective of the parish
held by the villagers, who see the area every day by the naked eye and
"measure" with their bodies as all human beings did until mechanical measurements were often forced upon them. As Zygmunt Bauman has pointed out, "Throughout their history and until the quite
recent advent of modernity humans measured the world with their
bodies—feet, handfuls or elbows; with their products—baskets or
pots; with their activities—dividing, for instance, their fields into
'Morgen,' that is into plots which could be ploughed up by a man
working from dawn to dusk."[66] Doalty's moving of the surveying
poles planted after each measurement is just as easily understood as
a gesture against mechanical "perception" as it is a protest against
the Anglicizing of Irish place names. He recounts seeing "the Red
Coats . . . dragging them aul chains and peeping through that big
machine they lug about everywhere with them—you know the name
of it, Manus?" (*BFP1* 390). Displaying the country man's instinctive
distrust of the foreign, he delights in their having to disassemble the
machine after his constant movement of the poles (ibid.), and Friel
thus situates him as a primary protester against perception through
instrumentation.[67] By contrast, Friel repeatedly associates the English
soldiers with mechanical measurement, demonstrating the truth of
Helen Lojek's claim that "[t]heir measuring mentality . . . represents

a clearly partial understanding of landscape."[68] For instance, he later portrays them systematically searching for the vanished Yolland with mechanical devices—the bayonets fixed to their guns—instead of using their naked eyes. Doalty tells the pupils in Act Two that the soldiers are "[p]rodding *every inch* of the ground in front of them with their bayonets and scattering animals and hens in all directions!" (434; my emphasis). The unit of measurement, "every inch," is here linked to the soldiers' disruptions.[69]

The bayonets, like the theodolites, symbolize the advent of an empiricist philosophy that Friel was at pains to critique in a diary entry from this period:

> The victims in this situation are the transitional generation. The old can retreat into and find immunity in the past. The young acquire some facility with the new cultural implements. The in-between ages become lost, wandering around in a strange land. Strays.[70]

The "cultural implements" Friel mentions surely include the theodolite and the bayonet as well. Even if the young become proficient in their use of such devices, they are simultaneously jettisoning their former mode of ocular and tactile perception and its attendant epistemology—a devastating loss. Such a use of tools as substitutes for and indeed replacements for traditional perception accords with the modern worldview of the self as something to be regulated and improved by constant activity and discipline.

Yolland senses the vast metaphysical difference between the end-in-itself worldview espoused by the rural villagers and that instrumental worldview held by his own urbanized father, a faithful colonial servant, in a conversation he has with Owen in Act Two, Scene One, and also by Lancey. He compares Lancey's obsession with order to his own father's similar obsession:

> Lancey's so like my father. I was watching him last night. He met every group of sappers as they reported in. He checked the field kitchens. He examined the horses. He inspected every single

report—even examining the texture of the paper and commenting on the neatness of the handwriting. The perfect colonial servant: not only must the job be done—it must be done with excellence. (*BFP1* 415)

The order of Friel's sentence structure here echoes the neatness and precision with which Lancey's and Yolland's fathers conduct their jobs. Both men orient themselves toward linearity and activity. Yolland goes on to note the penchant his father and Lancey both have for being constantly in motion, which should remind us of Gar O'Donnell's similarly modernist condition in *Philadelphia, Here I Come!* He notes, "Father has that drive, too; that dedication; that indefatigable energy. He builds roads—hopping from one end of the Empire to the other. Can't sit still for five minutes" (ibid.).[71]

Philosopher Charles Taylor has suggested that such activity during the Enlightenment stemmed from "the growing ideal of a human agent who is able to remake himself by methodical and disciplined action. What this calls for is the ability to take an instrumental stance to one's given properties, desires, inclinations, tendencies, habits of thought and feeling, so that they can be *worked on*, doing away with some and strengthening others, until one meets the desired specifications."[72] Human beings, especially those representatives of Empire, who embraced this "instrumental stance" of bodily control in turn often looked outward to colonial holdings, where they might similarly institute control and create a similar philosophy among their subjects, as the implementers of the Ordnance Survey are implicitly trying to do. As Taylor observes about the process by which "first-person experience" was transformed "into an objectified, impersonal mode," he notes that "[t]he point of the whole operation is to gain a kind of control,"[73] a telling remark that, by extension, suggests the driving motivation of the Ordnance Survey as part of England's imperializing ethos.

Another evocation of modernity later in this passage occurs with yet another reference to the French Revolution, a contextual signal that we have seen invoked repeatedly in *Philadelphia, Here I Come!*

to denote Gar's embrace of modernity and once in *The Freedom of the City* to suggest the republican view of Friel's imagined Guildhall victims as overthrowing the ancien régime of unionist rule in Derry. Yolland tells Owen that his father was born the day the Bastille fell in France and that he believes this seeming coincidence characterizes his father's optimistic embrace of the Enlightenment's overemphasis on man's potential:

> Born in 1789—the very day the Bastille fell. I've often thought maybe that gave his whole life its character. Do you think it could? He inherited a new world the day he was born—The Year One. Ancient time was at an end. The world had cast off its old skin. There were no longer any frontiers to man's potential. Possibilities were endless and exciting. (*BFP1* 416)

His father's approval of Enlightenment thinking is emphasized by Yolland's remark later in the same conversation that his family had lived three miles from William Wordsworth several years ago (417). He thus implicitly links his father's penchant for self-improving individualism with Wordsworth's. Both men are ideological children of the Bastille and their worldview is ineradicably grounded in the French Revolution's liberationist aims and its implicit exaltation of the individual at the expense of community.

The lure of this modern worldview was strong even for the traditionalist Irish schoolmaster Hugh early in his life. Late in the play, he fondly recalls going off to fight in the 1798 Irish rebellion with Jimmy. Hugh saw that time as a new philosophical beginning, much as Yolland's father views the post–French Revolution era as a time of great potential for the individual: "The road to Sligo. A spring morning. 1798. Going into battle. Do you remember, James? Two young gallants with pikes across their shoulders and the *Aeneid* in their pockets. Everything seemed to find definition that spring—a congruence, a miraculous matching of hope and past and present and possibility. Striding across the fresh, green land. The rhythms of perception heightened. The whole enterprise of consciousness accelerated" (*BFP1* 445). Such rhetoric chimes with Stephen Toulmin's claim that the "idea of 'starting again with a clean slate' has been as recurrent a preoccupation of modern European thinkers as the quest for certainty itself. The belief that any new construction is truly *rational* only if it demolishes all that was there before and starts from scratch, has played a particular part in the intellectual and political history of France. . . . The most spectacular illustration of this is the French Revolution."[74] But despite their temporary enthrallment to this rationalist worldview that seeks to jettison all tradition as encumbering, Hugh and Jimmy grew homesick after marching 23 miles and returned to their local parish. Hugh says their return was because they missed the older philosophical and cultural order which they were part of in the parish: "Our *pietas*, James, was for older, quieter things" (445–46). Declan Kiberd accurately points out that this account "suggests not so much a fear of the English enemy as a timidity in the face of revolutionary French modernity, a collective decision by the Irish to keep the modern world at bay. Now modernity has caught up with them in the shape of the survey, implemented by a Yolland who scarcely believes in it and by a collaborator who has strong reservations."[75]

Yolland, though associated with the Ordnance Survey, is a sympathetic character who manages to blend his native English upbringing and his adopted affinity for Irishness because of his own parochial background and interest in the local. As the energetic, mechanical Captain Lancey's helper in the survey, Yolland seems associated with the arrival of modernity to Donegal, but in the course of surveying and mapping, he evinces a distinct love for local Irish culture and consciousness. These cultures interpenetrate each other in his character. Eventually Yolland's penchant for premodern culture and consciousness emerges more fully.

Translations features a moment that suggests a hope beyond competing ideologies, analogous to that in *The Freedom of the City*, which comes in the relationship between Yolland and Maire encapsulated in a scene of "pure theatre" that Claudia W. Harris terms "the very *raison d'^etre* of the play."[76] Their courtship illustrates the

skillful way in which Friel emphasizes the local while, at the same
time, universalizing it out of merely an Irish context. Their delight
with each other's culture tentatively suggests a model for easing
political relations on a larger scale, such as in contemporary Northern Ireland.

For example, in Act Two, Scene Two, Yolland tells Maire where
he is from in response to her delivery of the one line of English that
she knows: "In Norfolk we besport ourselves around the maypoll"
(*BFP1* 428). Yolland exclaims, "Good God, do you? That's where
my mother comes from—Norfolk. Norwich actually. Not exactly
Norwich town but a small village called Little Walsingham close
beside it. But in our own village of Winfarthing we have a maypole
too and every year on the first of May . . . —" (ibid.). Maire misunderstands his excitement at discovering their joint origins in small
towns and turns away from him; he woos her back by first saying
her name, then her full name, then a local Irish place name: "Maire.
Maire Chatach. Bun na hAbhann?" (ibid.). As she gradually turns
and listens, a linguistic courtship ensues based on localities Yolland
has mapped and learned how to pronounce:

Druim Dubh?
(*Maire stops. She is listening. Yolland is encouraged.*)
Poll na gCaorach. Lis Maol.
(*Maire turns towards him.*)
Lis na nGall.
Maire: Lis na nGradh.
(*They are now facing each other and begin moving—almost
    imperceptibly—towards one another.*)
Maire: Carraig an Phoill.
Yolland: Carraig na Ri. Loch na nEan.
Maire: Loch an Iubhair. Machaire Buidhe.
Yolland: Machaire Mor. Cnoc na Mona.
Maire: Cnoc na nGabhar.
Yolland: Mullach.
Maire: Port.

Yolland: Tor.
Maire: Lag. (*BFP1* 429)

This dialogue becomes a sort of call and response: Maire starts with the name of a local rock outcropping, "Carraig an Phoill," and Yolland answers with another rocky place—"Carraig na Ri"—then names a local lake. She names another lake, then a "machair," or sandy place found behind dunes; he names another machair, then a "cnoc" or hill. She names another hill and then they each name monosyllabic place names. Their answering litany of local place names assures Maire of his sincerity and effort to learn the Irish language and locale around Ballybeg. The resonance of his mini-litany of English place names that precedes and spurs this longer litany of Irish place names has made them both now realize the intricate way in which they each are connected to similar townlands by a series of associations with larger towns or places. Their nationalities fade away in this joint linguistic/geographic discovery, and they share a kiss at the end of this scene. The irony is strong: he is one of the agents for eradicating Irish place names locally, and she has earlier told Hugh she wants to learn only English now since it is the language of progress. But both feel the pull and tug of local landscapes on their hearts and reach a linguistic and emotional closeness through this recitation. In reaching out to this stranger and becoming linguistically and physically intimate with him, Maire rejects the retreat into rural Irish culture that Hugh's son Manus wants her to pursue with him shortly before this scene, as we will see later.

However fleeting it may seem, this crucial moment of reconciliation helps us understand how Friel perceives communication's potential ability to solve entrenched cultural and political problems between the Irish and the English (as represented in the text of the play) and between Northern Irish Protestants and Catholics (as suggested by the play's original production in the politically and culturally liminal city of Londonderry/Derry). As Friel told Fintan O'Toole in an interview conducted in 1982, communication holds the key to the peace process in Northern Ireland: "I think that is how the political problem of this island is going to be solved. . . . [B]y the recognition of what language means for us on this island." He mused about the difference between the type of English he would speak and that spoken by former Ulster Unionist Member of Parliament Enoch Powell, stating, "Because we are . . . talking about accommodation or marrying of two cultures here, which are ostensibly speaking the same language but which in fact aren't."[77] Although it registers this difference between cultures and languages articulated by Friel here, *Translations* imagines that the specific kind of linguistic interchange and relationship between Yolland and Maire, despite their misunderstanding, previews the general type of communication that has been ongoing between Northern Catholics and Protestants for some years now and that bore fruit in the breakthrough Good Friday Agreement in 1998, the language of which is slippery and also prone to productive misunderstanding, as I have argued elsewhere.[78] And yet, the miscommunication among the other representatives of English and Irish culture later in the play shows the disasters that can result from such mistakes, including Yolland's disappearance.

Friel's consistent emphasis on and hope for cultural communication here makes Elizabeth Butler Cullingford's and Nicholas Grene's assessments of this scene, short-lived as it is, seem overly harsh. For instance, Cullingford points out the misunderstanding at the end of their joint place-name litany and argues that Maire abstracts Englishness:

> The famous scene in which they communicate their love through the recitation of Irish place names ends in misunderstanding: Yolland insists that he will never leave, while Maire begs him to "take me away." . . . [T]o her the names of English villages—Winfarthing, Barton Bendish, Saxingham Nethergate—represent the exotic Other. Even after Yolland's death she persists in her desire to speak English, though in Brooklyn rather than Barton Bendish.[79]

Grene is not any more sanguine, arguing that the scene's brevity signals its impossibility then and now:

[A]s a means of communication it can only have its fragile moment before it is destroyed by the violent forces of history. The pathos of the scene lies in its very brevity, the sense of its ultimate impossibility. Within the colonial context the dream of intermarriage is like the attempt at interpretation, a hopeless hope. . . . [T]he tragedy of *Translations* speaks to something like a postcolonial orthodoxy in which the colonial connection is seen retrospectively as a "doom," vitiating everything and everyone, colonizer and colonized alike.[80]

Grene's response resonates with the events in Northern Ireland that were occurring during the first week of the performances of *Translations*. Christopher Morash observes that was the same week that "talks with republican prisoners collapsed; within a month, some of the same prisoners would begin a hunger strike in which ten would die. That same week, 900 people lost their jobs in Derry, as a DuPont chemical plant and a shirt factory closed, adding to the 13,000 job losses in the Province over the previous nine months."[81]

But I believe the litany of Irish place names that Yolland and Maire recite succeeds even though it begins in and is grounded in misinterpretation and despite the brevity of this scene. I also agree with Aidan O'Malley that Maire's proclamation, "I want to live with you—anywhere—anywhere at all—always—always—" (*BFP1* 430), a statement that establishes her as a contemporary Ruth figure, which is closely followed by "Yolland's almost immediate disappearance after the love scene[,] shows how 'always' is at the mercy of historical, social, and political factors. In this categorical manner, Friel resists presenting the love scene as a fully consummated, ideal translation."[82] Their imagination in this crucial scene springs from their love for each other, which in turn temporarily transforms the contested space of the play. In a strikingly relevant passage from his introduction to *The Poetics of Space*, Gaston Bachelard, invoking and quickly rejecting the language of the surveyor that colors the British empiricist philosophy in *Translations*, argues that "[s]pace that has been seized upon by the imagination cannot remain indifferent space subject to the measures and estimates of the surveyor.

It has been lived in, not in its positivity, but with all the partiality of the imagination. Particularly, it nearly always exercises an attraction. For it concentrates being within limits that protect."[83] Thus, although Yolland himself is almost surely murdered, Maire's love for him lives on; moreover, this central space of Friel's play, which has been lovingly if imperfectly "translated" and rendered as a specific place by their joint recitation, itself lingers and lives on in our minds. Yolland and Maire's created place thus models through its intimacy, trust, and even its misunderstanding the type of dialogue needed for communication and reconciliation in Northern Ireland, where the inhabitants are often still divided despite speaking an ostensibly common language.

After Yolland's disappearance in Act Three, Maire mourns him by reiterating his earlier litany of English place names to Owen and tracing them on an imaginary map she draws with her finger. She concludes, "I have it all in my head now: Winfarthing—Barton Bendish—Saxingham Nethergate—Little Walsingham—Norwich—Norfolk. Strange sounds, aren't they? But nice sounds like Jimmy Jack reciting his Homer" (*BFP1* 437–38).

Maire continues, commenting that "I didn't get a chance to do my geography last night. The master'll be angry with me" (*BFP1* 438), but in fact, her courtship with Yolland yields the most important revelation of the play. The geography and cartography she explores with Yolland on the strand to learn the town names that widen out from his hometown becomes the most important lesson she could learn. She has expanded her mind to incorporate another locale that, despite its strange English names, oddly resembles hers. She and Yolland have now twice enacted the reverse of Friel's geographic trajectory common to most of his dramas—the gradual narrowing from factual nation to factual region to real town to fictive townland. Their contour maps instead broaden out from the tiniest real townland to the actual countries of Ireland and England, suggesting an expansiveness springing from the parochial that serves to culturally connect two often-opposed countries. This is the crucial point at which Friel's conception of potential reconciliation coheres with his essentially agrarian outlook: the two moments of intimacy (one depicted, one only iterated by Maire) between the English Yolland and Irish Maire are created by their articulation of each other's intimacy with their local landscape. For Friel, moments of cultural reconciliation spring from and are grounded in the local. This philosophy departs from the sometimes vacuous globalizing impetus behind some contemporary reconciliation movements that are not attentive to local details and conditions.

Unfortunately, some critics have misread their exchange. For example, in Declan Kiberd's discussion of *Translations* in *Inventing Ireland*, he delineates the real problems associated with the imperialist aspect of the English Ordnance Survey, but then he claims this moment signifies Yolland's imperialist attempt to force an English landscape upon Maire:

> The iterative image of such imperial designs in this play is Lieutenant Yolland's attempt to draw a map of his native Norfolk for his Irish lover on the wet sands of Baile Beag. The hopeless stupidity of the attempt to impose a foreign grid on Irish reality is manifest in the fact that Yolland's model is etched in shifting sands. His attempt to draw Norfolk on the Donegal seashore is a fair image of what his own government is trying to do in the Ordnance Survey. Such a map, however romantic in this particular context, is the usual occupier's response to what he perceives as uncharted wilderness.[84]

Kiberd mischaracterizes this written "mapping" process since he reads it by itself, out of the context of linguistic and geographic exchange set up by the previous oral "mapping" of the parish that Yolland and Maire enact. This cultural exchange significantly overcomes the difficulties of translation in each mapping exercise and suggests the growth of a bond between the two characters that, had not Yolland been murdered, could have overcome any future linguistic ambiguity between them, whether written or oral. Any sensitive reading of this scene, moreover, should recognize the realistic emotional epiphany shared by these two characters that signifies their growing relationship.

Once again, however, this moment disappears like a will-o'-the-wisp: the hope symbolized by Yolland and Maire's joint recitation of Irish townlands fades and we realize that he has been harvested in this new season of reaping and death. For later in Act Three, Owen enacts a terrifying translation into Irish of Captain Lancey's litany in English of local places where he threatens evictions if Yolland is not found. Whereas the first recitation of place names between Yolland and Maire took place in Irish only and in the private space of the schoolroom, this alternating litany of translations from English into Irish occurs in the now-public space of the schoolroom in front of the assembled pupils. The peaceful, even intimate potential of the earlier private moment in Irish is shattered by the threat of outright violence in a public moment in which English becomes the "official" language of coercion.

Lancey, who exemplifies what Charles Taylor calls "the punctual self," the typical figure of modernity who is nearly clinically disengaged from emotion and pursues objectivity at all costs,[85] links his threatened reprisals to mechanical clock-time, directly contrasting the language of the translating Owen, who retranslates his objectivist, mechanized language back into the diurnal, natural rhythms of the village. The shocked Owen cannot believe Lancey's change in demeanor and can barely translate the disturbing details, finally doing so in a seemingly wooden but actually deeply emotional manner that contrasts Lancey's cold, stripped-down language of disengagement (*BFP1* 439–40). This passage concludes ominously:

> Lancey: If by then the lieutenant hasn't been found, we will proceed until a complete clearance is made of this entire section.
> Owen: If Yolland hasn't been got by then, they will ravish the whole parish. (440)

Whereas Owen's translations of Lancey's words earlier in the play tend to soft-peddle the changes being made to the local Irish place names, here he pulls no punches, having realized the full threat facing the village. He has given Lancey a complete map of the parish through his work as translator and now that map can be used with devastating consequences for the villagers. In what is presumably one of his last acts as translator—for he will either be fired or quit in disgust if the clearances are carried out—he realizes his treachery.

In response to Hugh's injunction, "We must learn where we live" (*BFP1* 444), however, Owen calmly but strongly says, "I know where I live" (445). He leaves to go see Dan Doalty, who has persistently moved the surveying poles and who has just vowed to fight the English after Lancey's pronouncement: "I've damned little to defend but he'll not put me out without a fight. And there'll be others who think the same as me" (441). The implication is that the translator Owen—continually pulled between two cultures—has, in a moment of crisis, decided to fight the English along with Doalty. Cultural reconciliation now becomes a mere dream for these characters. Widespread local reprisals against the British will surely follow the threatened evictions. Violence thus begets violence, and the chain of events that began with Yolland's death (likely at the hands of the Donnelly twins) will continue ad infinitum.

As Friel was working on the play, Seamus Deane suggested to him that a British soldier disappear, and Friel took his advice. Friel hilariously thanks Deane in a 1980 letter for the suggestion, even jokingly promising him a small amount of the proceeds of Field Day's touring production of the play: "Remember—we talked about it. . . . You suggested a Brit. soldier disappearing. Idea used. 1% of all Cork, Tralee, Carrickmore and Newry royalties will be forwarded."[86] Deane and Friel were extremely close in this period of their careers, brought together both by their love for Derry and Irish culture, and finally their work together for Field Day. Moreover, Deane had just written the introduction for an edition of Friel's *Selected Stories*. While Deane was no republican, his nationalism was harder-edged than Friel's, inflected in part by his childhood years in the republican Bogside of Derry with its widespread poverty and distrust of

British rule. He likely meant to lend *Translations* a contemporary resonance from the Troubles with this idea of the British soldier Yolland disappearing.

Here again Friel's relative political and cultural evenhandedness emerges since the Donnelly twins, never pictured but always whispered about, represent the violent local Irish response to the survey and now to the threatened evictions—a pre-republican movement. Richtarik argues that "the implication is that he has been abducted and killed by the mysterious 'Donnelly twins,' delinquent hedge scholars."[87] Nicholas Grene goes so far as to call them the "proto-Provo Donnelly twins, who haunt the edges of the action and are responsible for the (presumed) death of Yolland."[88] The twins are figures who contribute to the destruction of the local townland by likely killing Yolland, a hybrid character who values the premodern view of that community.[89] Friel seems to suggest that the twins and, by extension, violent nationalist or republican movements simply exacerbate violent responses from the English and sometimes even cause these responses. They are forerunners of republicans who end up ruining the very communities they set out to defend, thus making them unwittingly in league with the British surveyors who would destroy Ballybeg's agrarian, communal identity. Thus, Friel's unsympathetic portrayal of the Donnellys becomes a contemporary critique of the Irish Republican Army, whose activities during the contemporary Troubles often resulted in the death and destruction of the very members of the Catholic community they purported to defend. Hence, we can see Friel—in his portrayal of the Donnelly twins' actions and the presumed consequences—anticipating the historical formation of the violent strand of nationalism that he had already depicted as making martyrs of the three civil rights protesters in *The Freedom of the City*. Across these two plays, he seeks to expose the rhetorical vacuity of this nationalism from its imagined, embryonic beginnings to its frightfully imagined, but no less real, contemporary application to the current Troubles.[90]

Yolland's disappearance may anticipate both the future victims of IRA violence and the looming disappearance of the Irish language in the play. If we believe that the Donnelly twins, the "proto-Provos," killed him and now do not reveal his body, then he may function symbolically as one of the so-called disappeared, an anticipation of a long line of IRA victims whose burial spot has never been revealed to their grieving families.[91] Yolland's interest in preserving the *dinnseanchas* or placelore of the local terrain therefore becomes eerily wiped out in his own disappearance. His whereabouts become a sort of reverse *dinnseanchas*, an empty narrative signifying nothing, authored by furious representatives who purport to defend local culture, including the decline of the Irish language.

The implication that Yolland is "sacrificed" for espousing a certain worldview accords with similarly destroyed Friel characters past and future. He is finally sacrificed, like Friel's other antimodern characters, including Frank Hardy in *Faith Healer* and Rose and Agnes in *Dancing at Lughnasa*. The Donnelly twins' exclusivist outlook refuses to recognize Yolland's potential cultural hybridity, which he is already putting into practice. Yolland finds himself perfectly at home in Ballybeg, whose inhabitants display a communal consciousness at ease with itself and implicitly antimodern in its refusal to equate epistemology solely with the qualitative measurements symbolized by the surveying of the English soldiers.

Through his reading of J. H. Andrews's *A Paper Landscape*, an acknowledged inspiration for Friel's play, Scott Boltwood has shown that Friel modeled Yolland upon Lieutenant Thomas Aiskew Larcom, who competed with Colonel T. F. Colby, the director of the Ordnance Survey. He finds that according to Andrews, Colby was prejudiced "'against the Irish . . . ' [but that] Larcom emerges as Colby's foil: a well-known admirer of Irish culture, for nearly twenty years he advocated greater Irish influence in the Survey," and himself "reviewed each recommended toponym from every Survey team and decided the name each site would have on the final Ordnance map."[92] He even "studied the Irish language under the tutelage of John O'Donovan, the model for Friel's Owen," and "appointed a series of 'toponymic field workers' to perform local research, which included both the consultation of local documents" and a record of names as spoken by local Irish-speakers.[93] Thus, although Yolland has been critiqued by several critics as overly romantic or even delusional,[94] Friel likely sanctions his attitude and behavior (despite his naiveté) as representing a sympathetic historical English figure who vigorously sought to make the Ordnance Survey as attentive to local Irish idiolects as possible.

Yolland's contemplative temperament differs from the very busyness and energy that characterizes his father. He tells Owen of experiencing "a curious sensation" upon his arrival in "Ballybeg," then quickly corrects his pronunciation of the village to its Irish, "*Baile Beag*," indicating his own allegiance to the worldview held by the villagers (*BFP1* 416). Owen does not follow him, asking him if he means he had stepped "[b]ack into ancient time?" Yolland's reply conveys his acute appreciation of the local consciousness: "It wasn't an awareness of *direction* being changed but of experience being of a totally different order. I had moved into a consciousness that wasn't striving nor agitated, but at its ease and with its own conviction and assurance" (ibid.). As Edward Casey argues, we cannot know a place except by being in that place because, contra Kant, "Knowledge of place is not . . . subsequent to perception . . . but is an ingredient in perception itself."[95] The different order of experience Yolland perceives by living in the parish and being receptive to its organic rhythms represents a much older one than that held by his father or even by Wordsworth. He has encountered a culture that did not pledge allegiance to the modernist worldview then (and now) dominant in the Western world. This worldview views human experience in an atomistic fashion, emphasizing quantitative rather than qualitative aspects of our experience.

Along with privileging Yolland's transformation into a hybrid character, able to appreciate both the English and Irish languages and culture, Friel also sanctions Hugh's change into such a character. For most of the play, Hugh tends to idealize the past in a reflexive, mechanical way, but he finally becomes the play's voice of qualified hope. No commentator has realized that Hugh's veneration for classical learning is the rhetorical analogue to the empiricist attitude of the

English surveyors (except for Yolland) who wield literal machines in their work. His repetitive trotting-out of rote passages from the classics shows him to be largely incapable of realizing how such works might enable him to live a richer, fuller life in the present until the end of the play. In a little-noticed passage from his autobiographical essay "Self-Portrait," Friel mentions being "slightly resentful" at his own schoolmasters, whose attitude toward the classics uncannily anticipates that of Hugh for most of the play. He terms them "those men who taught me the literature of Rome and Greece and England and Ireland as if they were *pieces of intricate machinery*, created for no reason and designed for no purpose. . . . [F]or years we *tinkered with them, pulling them apart, putting them together again*, translating, scanning, conjugating, never once suspecting that these texts were the testimony of sad, happy, assured, confused people like ourselves."[96] Note the recourse here to the rhetoric and imagery of the machine and the implied distant attitude toward the past engendered in the students by this sort of teaching. Similarly, Friel's Hugh clearly loves Latin and Greek but cannot see its relevance to more fruitful living until the conclusion of the play.

As the play ends, Hugh resolves to learn the new English place names for the parish, indicating his desire to become more open to this aspect of modernity: "We must learn these new names. . . . We must learn where we live. We must learn to make them our own. We must make them our new home" (*BFP1* 444). Shortly after this statement, in response to Owen's resonant remark, "I know where I live," Hugh responds, "James thinks he knows too. I look at James and three thoughts occur to me: A—that it is not the literal past, the 'facts' of history, that shape us, but images of the past embodied in language." Further, he affirms, "B—we must never cease renewing those images; because once we do, we fossilize" (445). In an interview from 1980, the same year that *Translations* was first produced, Friel himself cites this speech, then says, "That is, we must make these English language words distinctive and unique to us."[97] Shortly afterward, in the same interview, he echoes this language very closely, saying, "We must continually look at ourselves, recognize and identify ourselves. We must make English identifiably our own language."[98] For the grandson of two sets of Irish-speaking grandparents to make such a statement may be surprising, but Friel clearly recognized not only the need for the Irish to make English their own language and stamp it with their own idiom, rhythms, and culture but also to "continually" do so as an ongoing act of self- and national examination.

In his 1983 Field Day pamphlet *A New Look at the Language Question*, one of the group's directors, Tom Paulin, argues for the recognition and promotion of Irish English in terms that amplify and clarify Hugh's position in the play and, by extension, Friel's as well. Opening by suggesting that "the history of a language is often a story of possession and dispossession, territorial struggle and the establishment of imposition of a culture,"[99] Paulin articulates the peculiar situation of Irish English, wherein "the English language in Ireland, like English in America, became so naturalized that it appeared to be indigenous." And yet, since "the Irish language was not completely suppressed or rejected . . . it became central to the new national consciousness which formed in the late nineteenth century."[100] Irish also became the national language of the new Free State, later the Republic of Ireland, and still features on school syllabi in the Republic and in Catholic-run schools in Northern Ireland, but not in state schools in the North. Its institutional persistence, along with its living presence in Gaeltacht areas, help illuminate Friel's insistence in maintaining and renewing Irish English, which preserves remnants of Irish and features dialect and other "non-standard" English words. Continuing in memorable phrases that echo the situation in *Translations*, Paulin laments, "Many words are homeless. They live in the careless richness of speech, but they rarely appear in print. When they do, many readers are unable to understand them." While there are now several dictionaries of Hiberno-English, obviating Paulin's complaint at the time of their absence, it is nonetheless largely true that, as he states, Irish English is "impoverished as a literary medium," and "like some strange creature of the open air, it exists simply as *Geist* or spirit."[101] *Translations* attempts to appreciate and enrich Irish

English as a literary medium, not simply mourn the Irish language's decline and English's rise. It thus privileges a hybrid language, a linguistic strategy that mediates between Irish and English.

Neil Corcoran reads Hugh's closing speeches as recommending "cultural survival" through "an act of subtlety, stealth and subversion, an act of reclamation in which retrospect may create the conditions of a fulfilling future."[102] Boltwood critiques Hugh's language here negatively, however, perceiving him as the play's "most compelling example of the voluntary abandonment of Irish culture for classical."[103] Boltwood argues that Hugh's 23-mile march during the 1798 Rising, on which he and Jimmy Jack carried the *Aeneid*, along with his composition of poetry in Latin "after the style of Ovid" (*BFP1* 417) and his ignorance of the then-contemporary Gaelic poetry revival in England, shows that "Hugh has developed an interest in an academic and artificial poetic tradition to the exclusion of the surviving Irish one."[104] But Corcoran correctly argues that Hugh's retrospective retelling of this incident from 1798 at the end of the play in a "mock-heroic" mode "is the pre-condition of Hugh's wisdom."[105]

Now able to satirize himself, Hugh is likely to also be more skeptical of his previous allegiances and receptive to forming new ones. In this regard, his insistence in accommodating himself to modernity at play's end bespeaks his new uneasiness with locking himself into a classical past and his interest not only in learning English ways but also, perhaps, in investigating and contributing to the burgeoning reinvigoration of Irish cultural traditions. As evidence of his new unease with the Classics we should look to his final speech, in which he attempts to recite the passage from Virgil's *Aeneid* in which that author relates Juno's plans for Carthage while predicting its downfall at the hands of "a race springing from Trojan blood." (*BFP1* 447). The usual reading of these lines links not only the Romans to this emerging "race," but also the British, with the Irish playing the role of the modern-day Carthaginians.[106] Hugh cannot remember the exact words, eventually stammering "such was—such was the course—such was the course ordained—ordained by fate . . . What the hell's wrong with me? Sure I know it backwards. I'll begin again" (ibid.). It is certainly plausible to read Hugh's forgetting and stammering here as evidence of his entrapment in the ancient classical past, but such a reading runs counter to the thrust of all his subsequent speeches late in the play. Instead, it seems more likely that he is unconsciously taking his own earlier advice—"To remember everything is a form of madness" (ibid.)—and has already made room in his mind for more modern acts of translation and accommodation.

In case there are any lingering doubts that Friel rejects a sheer idealization, even idolatry of Irish rural culture in *Translations*, we might briefly consider the case of Manus, Hugh's other son, a character in full cultural retreat who, as we saw in the introduction to this study, is anticipated by the narrow-minded Manus in *The Gentle Island*. In *Translations*, unlike Owen, who finally leaves the survey and resolves to fight the British, Manus vows to withdraw totally from Ballybeg and immerse himself in local culture in a more distant spot, on the island of Inis Meadhon. He has been asked to go there "and start a hedge-school," noting excitedly that "[t]hey're giving me a free house, free turf, and free milk; a rood of standing corn; twelve drills of potatoes; and—. . . . A salary of 42 pounds a year!" (*BFP1* 423). Friel questions the viability of such schools and the potato crop and indicates that Manus's retreat is likely doomed, whereas he suggests instead that hybridized characters such as Hugh and Yolland model the sort of culturally nimble citizens needed in Ireland, Northern Ireland, and indeed England. In this sense, the fragile, heterogeneous communities they are attempting to form accord with those Friel had earlier depicted in *The Freedom of the City*, among his three main characters trapped in the Derry Guildhall, and in *Faith Healer*, among Grace, Teddy, and Frank and between Frank and his killers.

Even more important in this context, *Translations* inscribes and privileges a powerful spirituality in the relationship between Maire and Yolland, members of opposite "tribes." Patrick Grant has pointed out that despite Friel's own background growing up as a Catholic and nationalist, which allows him to "depict with special authority" the local Ballybeg community, "the play's spiritual centre lies beyond the confinements of the endogamous, ethnic, prejudiced, and escapist aspects of Ballybeg." Instead of simply privileging Ballybeg's culture and faith, "Friel's art points out rather to the silent mystery of our personal privacies, from which we are called to the liberating transgressions of love and communication, the true spiritual centre."[107] The love between Maire and Yolland, who speak powerfully of their attraction to and care for each other despite knowing only a few words of the other's language, transcends linguistic communication. Their love privileges Friel's conviction that spirituality lies beyond words and is ineffable but nonetheless real.[108] In recognition of his contribution to promoting tolerance and reconciliation in Ireland with scenes such as this in his landmark drama, Friel won the 1985 Christopher Ewart-Biggs Memorial Prize of 5,000 pounds.

The excitement created through Field Day's plays, in particular the first production of *Translations*, was palpable. Longtime theatergoer and drama professor John Devitt told Nicholas Grene over twenty-five years after seeing it that "there was no way of missing one of their productions: nobody in their right mind would miss them. I remember the excitement of the first production of *Translations* was colossal."[109] The play continues to inspire rave reviews, suggesting its staying power in the dramatic canon because of its appeal to that desire in us to form community that is anchored yet inclusive. In 2007, the *Wall Street Journal*'s drama critic Terry Teachout made a revealing remark about the Garry Hynes production that ran at the Manhattan Theatre Club in late 2006 through the spring of 2007: "The cast of 'Translations' is beyond praise—they act as though they'd grown up together—and I came away feeling that I had seen not a production but the play itself, stripped of all exterior trappings and reduced to its purest essence."[110]

Friel would undoubtedly be pleased with such a description since Teachout indicates the actors formed a real, organic community onstage, which is a crucial performative maneuver for this play that portrays the closeness of a tight-knit local community and yet suggests the necessity for that community's opening itself to sympathetic outsiders and vice versa. If theatergoers and readers of this drama also form such temporary, spiritual communities and yet at the same time experience, albeit vicariously, the cultural shocks and dislocations that Friel's rural villagers do with the British Ordnance Survey of 1833–46, his accomplishment is tremendous indeed.

9

Dancing at Lughnasa

Placing and Recreating Memory

The unease at the profound cultural changes being ushered in by the Ordnance Survey, signaled by Yolland's language of erosion, which permeates the Ballybeg of 1833 in *Translations*, also colors the atmosphere of 1936 Ballybeg in *Dancing at Lughnasa*. As older Michael tells us toward the end of his opening monologue: "[E]ven though I was only a child of seven at the time I know *I had a sense of unease*, some awareness of a widening breach between what seemed to be and what was, of things changing too quickly before my eyes, of becoming what they ought not to be" (*DL* 2; my emphasis). Whereas the harvest themes of reaping and sacrifice are more implicit in *Philadelphia, Here I Come!*, *Faith Healer*, and *Translations*, the Lughnasa Festival and Father Jack's memories of the Ryangan harvest both explicitly suggest that this is a society in transition, about to be propelled full force into the twentieth century along with other rural societies around the world. Fittingly, there are more images of sacrifice in this drama than in any other: the imminent death of Father Jack, the emigration of Rose and Agnes, the goats slaughtered by both the Lughnasa and Ryangan celebrants, and the killing of Rose's rooster. These sacrifices all signal the decline of local culture even as some of them, like the Lughnasa and Ryangan harvest festivals, express the viability of pagan remnants in such cultures.

Once again, just as in *Translations* when the bountiful hay harvest seems to signal fertility and plenty but is undercut by the threatened evictions and loss of the sympathetic Yolland, in *Lughnasa*

251

the hay and corn harvest promises abundance. But we are given a starving family, three of whose members will soon disappear: Father Jack dies within twelve months of the events of the play, and two of Michael's spinster aunts, Rose and Agnes, sacrifice themselves for the family and emigrate to London. Friel signified the importance of harvest for the play when he listed (among others) two possible titles for it in his working notebook of May and July 1989: "The Harvest Dance" and "Harvest."[1] The agents of the "eviction" in this case are indirectly the Roman Catholic Church and the pernicious aspects of machine culture, particularly the new knitwear factory that will soon open nearby. Hopefully, the local Catholic priest will not countenance Rose's probable rape by Danny Bradley. And yet he probably will so shame Rose, the victim, that she will become a local pariah, especially if she becomes pregnant and has a child out of wedlock. Once Rose and Agnes learn their hand-knitted goods will be made unnecessary to the local economy by the new knitting factory, they leave, both to save the family the shame of embarrassment because of Rose's likely sexual assault and possible pregnancy and in the hope that the reduced family with two less mouths to feed will not starve to death. *Lughnasa* thus ironizes the harvest season for the Mundy family through depicting these grim human "reapings" in the midst of this fertile season.

Dancing at Lughnasa is the most emplaced of all Friel's dramas. He gives us a series of widening circles of emplacement, beginning with the bodies of the five sisters, the seemingly living cottage where they dwell, the back hills where the Festival of Lughnasa fires burn brightly at night, and finally the dusty village of Ryanga, Africa, from whence Father Jack has returned. Friel invites us to ponder the profound resonances of place for these ensouled bodies, this cottage, and these two marginalized locations in order to understand the wrenching cultural and sexual dislocations this soon-to-be dismembered family is experiencing and also to glimpse the possibility of spiritual wholeness offered briefly to them. I use the term "dismembered" purposely here to evoke our memories of the proleptic conclusion of *Faith Healer*, when Frank Hardy's limbs are about to be severed from his body, as well as of the crippled Gaelic culture in *Translations*. Here, Friel shows us again that the local, rural culture is already divided unhealthily by the Catholic Church and that creeping modernization and industrialization will create the fatal, "widening breach" of which Michael speaks above. In Friel's view, the Church during its devotional revolution and the rapid rise of industrialization in Ireland were both factors that sought to divorce soul from body with devastating consequences for the health of the self and the wider community.

This chapter draws on theories of the body and place articulated by several writers and scholars, including the neoagrarian Wendell Berry, especially his articulation of how technology can devalue the body and of how our bodies are divorced from the earth; philosopher Gaston Bachelard, who articulated a theory of "topoanalysis" or "the systematic psychological study of the sites of our intimate lives";[2] and Edward Casey and his recent phenomenological theories of place, particularly his insistence on the role of the lived body and the way in which place gathers the animate and inanimate. I use these concepts to show how modernity's severing of nature and culture, body and soul, body and earth has estranged us from ourselves and each other. Seemingly, it is only in the dancing of the sisters that the beginning of the process of restoring these broken connections can be glimpsed as they embrace their neglected bodies; but even in the most famous of those dances, they are rendered as grotesque, isolated from each other, symbols finally of a rural culture turning in and feeding upon itself. It is finally only in the last monologue, through Michael's memory, a necessary illusion for him as an adult and, apparently, for us, that that dance is rendered golden, revivifying, whole. But in fact it is a dance of five maenads, "shrieking strangers" (*DL* 2), who are close to ripping the family apart and dismembering it. Our reading of the play depends on our balancing of both this concluding golden memory of the sisters' dancing with the bleak, anarchic ugliness of the actual dance itself: somewhere on this knife's edge of hope and despair lies the play's rich emplacement of a vanishing culture of rural life in Ireland.

Berry's prophetic 1977 essay, "The Body and the Earth," employs precisely the language of dismemberment concerning culture that I have used above to show the rifts in our contemporary culture, fissures that certainly were present in 1930s Ireland but have widened considerably since then. He articulates "the concept of the disintegral life of our time" as a "dismembered cathedral, the various concerns of culture no longer existing in reference to each other or within the discipline of any understanding of their unity."[3] The spiritual fracturing to which he alludes seems particularly appropriate to the concerns of Friel's play: he has stressed the play's depiction of paganism as necessary for our daily living. As a later portion of this chapter will show, the play seems to endorse such a transnational paganism with sites in remote areas of Donegal and Ryanga, Africa. I am more concerned now with exploring the ramifications for Friel's familial community through Berry's articulation of a complementary image of Western culture: "a dismembered household."[4] Such an image resonates both for the wider culture of *Lughnasa* and for the Mundy household itself, because both are rapidly disintegrating even as the power of the Irish state and the Catholic Church in Ireland were quickly being consolidated.

Part of the appeal of Friel's five fictional women (fictions modeled on his own mother and her four sisters) stems from their fully embodied presence in the play. After the disembodied presences of the spectral Lily, Michael, and Skinner in *The Freedom of the City* and of the ghostly Frank and Grace in *Faith Healer*, we are likely relieved to meet such embodied characters. But then we are rapidly dismayed as we realize how their culture and Church have separated them from their bodies. Whole in appearance, they are nonetheless deeply divided from their natural dwelling, the place of their bodies, by their immersion in both a rapidly anglicizing Irish state and an increasingly ascetic Irish Catholicism, ushered in by the Devotional Revolution of the late nineteenth and early twentieth centuries.

Edward Casey argues that we must recognize how the body is crucial to emplacement, noting that "lived bodies belong to places and help to constitute them. . . . By the same token, however, places belong to lived bodies and depend on them. . . . The lived body is the material condition of possibility for the place-world while itself being a member of that same world."[5] Recall how the imposed surveying of the literal and cultural landscape of 1833 Donegal is momentarily held at bay by the joint recitation of place names performed by Maire and Yolland, symbolizing their transnational interest in local idiolect and place. The Mundy sisters' major dance in *Lughnasa* functions similarly to emplace and momentarily preserve the pagan remnants of their disappearing culture, which is under assault from both the lingering influence of British empiricism and the consolidating power of the Irish Catholic Church. As they return to their bodies in this and other dances in the play, seemingly paradoxically, they enact and perform a positive concept of place that anchors them in their fleshly place of the body and the material dwelling of their Donegal cottage. This double inhabitation enables them to briefly become vicarious performers in the Lughnasa rites being celebrated in the back hills outside Donegal and, by extension, in any pagan rituals in the world, such as those embraced by their beloved brother Jack in Ryanga.

Casey notes, "Places . . . gather experiences and histories, even languages and thoughts." But he does not use "gather" in the sense of "merely amassing"; instead, he believes that places gather in significant ways. Places

> hold . . . *together* in a particular configuration: hence our sense of an ordered arrangement of things in a place even when those things are radically disparate and quite conflictual. The arrangement allows for certain things—people, ideas, and so forth—to overlap with, and sometimes to occlude, others as they recede or come forward together. Second, the hold is a holding *in* and a holding *out*. It retains the occupants of a place within its boundaries. . . . But, equally, a place holds out, beckoning to its inhabitants and, assembling them, making them manifest. . . . It can move place-holders toward the margins of its own presentation while, nevertheless, holding them within its own ambiance. Third, the holding at issue in the gathering of place reflects the layout of the local landscape, its continuous contour, even as the outlines and

inlines of the things held in that place are respected. . . . Fourth, intrinsic to the holding operation of place is *keeping*. What is kept in place primarily are experiencing bodies regarded as privileged residents rather than as orchestrating forces. . . . And last, places also keep such unbodylike entities as thoughts and memories.[6]

This long passage affords us a series of key insights into the gathering function of place in Friel's *Dancing at Lughnasa* that structure the argument of this chapter.

The first of these, "a holding together in a particular configuration" of "radically disparate" things, reveals how Friel uses the place of the stage to bring together the group of five very different sisters as well as how he employs the wider place of Ballybeg and the back hills to gather and present to us the conflict between the official Irish state religion of Catholicism and the marginal, lingering manifestations of Irish paganism. Friel's representations of Catholicism, commingled with paganism in the dance of the Mundy sisters, the images of wheat onstage, the bilberries picked by Rose and Agnes, and the pagan practices in the "back hills" above Ballybeg, combine to produce a startling effect on the reader or audience. In short, Friel's dramatic aim with these pagan images recalls what Weldon Thornton has brilliantly argued is John Millington Synge's intent in *Riders to the Sea*: "[I]n spite of the almost inescapable inclination to see the Christianity-paganism issue in either-or terms, the play does not present it so simply. It suggests that the Christian view is not so much rejected as subsumed into something larger."[7] As Thornton finally posits, Synge did not "intend to vindicate or to undercut either a Christian or a pagan view of reality, or even to show the necessary opposition of the two. His purpose was rather to present as faithfully as he could the world-view he found on the islands, and to challenge us to empathize with a perspective that eludes our ordinary categorizations."[8] Friel similarly evokes the pagan worldview that may have been fading in the Donegal of the 1930s but was still prevalent among many inhabitants of that county and indeed throughout many parts of Ireland.

But in doing so, he is not merely trying to present Irish paganism as manifested specifically through the harvest festival of Lughnasa but to assert its necessity in our lives, much as he shows the function of Irish mythology in *Faith Healer*.

Friel has admitted that *"Dancing at Lughnasa* is about the necessity for paganism."[9] The various images associated with the Festival of Lughnasa in the play work seamlessly to show that necessity and its persistence through specific sites of emplacement. While audience attention naturally focuses on the sisters' wild dance in Act One and Michael's memory of that dance, Friel also memorably evokes the marginalized dancing round the Lughnasa fires in the "back hills" above Ballybeg. Rose has already told Kate about the bonfires that are lit "beside a spring well" and the dancing that takes place round this bonfire (*DL* 16). These images seem wholly consistent with Máire MacNeill's description of Lughnasa festivals in her classic work, *The Festival of Lughnasa*, excerpts from which were published in the program accompanying the play's first production, as several commentators have pointed out. MacNeill documents a number of Lughnasa festivals that were still taking place in Ireland at the time of her survey of Lughnasa customs and beliefs in 1942. As she notes, "The essence of the festival was that it celebrated the beginning of the harvest of the main subsistence crops: corn, in earlier times and, in later times, potatoes. Its most distinctive manifestation was an assembly at a traditional site, always a remarkable natural feature, either a height (often the top of a mountain) or a water-side: a lake, river, or well. In many instances the sites have both features, e.g., a spring on a height, a lake near a mountain-top."[10] Certainly, the harvest motif runs throughout Friel's play; a 2000 production at the Abbey Theatre even featured a set draped in sheaves of wheat.[11] The Lughnasa fires above Friel's Ballybeg are also placed on a height and located at a spring, displaying both dominant features MacNeill describes as typical of these festivals. As we will see later in my analysis of a common stage set for Friel's play, the element of a gigantic wheat field, continuous with the fourth wall of the Mundy cottage, has given rise to criticism of so-called "golden" productions of *Lughnasa* that perceive it as overly nostalgic, although that set designer did not intend this perception.

The central scene of the play involves the five Mundy sisters dancing in a frenzied fashion that recalls some of the anarchic energies and release associated with the Festival of Lughnasa. Katharine Worth, a theater critic who attended the Abbey Theatre's production of *Lughnasa* on October 15, 1990, concludes her essay on storytelling in Friel emphasizing the positive emotion engendered in the London audience that night:

> [R]unning strongly against the currents of irony and anxiety was another, more powerful impression of immense inner resilience and vitality. A rare warmth of feeling spread through the theatre, a response to the humour and bravery of the sisters, their gift for enlarging their pinched lives with joyful excitement: a few Wild Woodbines could do it, or a child's kite. The dance to the old Irish music may have been only a shadow of a folk rite, but it came over as something thrilling and necessary. The audience rejoiced, with sporadic ripples of applause, when decorous Kate threw away restraint and joined the bacchanal, dancing by herself, "totally concentrated, totally private." We should all have liked to join in when Stephen Dillane's debonair Gerry took his Chris (and then, touchingly, Agnes) dancing a foxtrot round the garden to beguiling thirties tunes from the old radio. Foot-tapping began in the auditorium and currents of sympathy flowed toward the scapegrace.[12]

This study has often tried to show how Friel desires audience involvement—how he wants them to form a community among themselves and with the actors onstage, an engagement that is surely suggested by the "currents of sympathy" that "flowed" in Worth's account.

What then is the problem with such an admittedly moving narrative of Lughnasa's effect on its London audience on that October night in 1990? First, we might ponder whether the sisters' dance is really "thrilling and necessary" and part of the "joyful excitement" they attempt to create in their lives. I argue instead that they perform this famous dance to finally mourn their marginalization as women and the disappearing pagan, rural culture around them. Friel achieves this remarkable performance through his portrayal of the conflation between an enabling technology (the radio) and the ancient Irish tradition of keening.

Worth does not mention in her account any visual representations of the radio in the play, but it precipitates their dancing, connects them to both the pagan past and technological present, and becomes sacralized by the sisters. Maggie wants to call it "Lugh after the old Celtic God of the Harvest," but the sisters end up calling the radio "Marconi" because "that was the name emblazoned on the set" and Kate "said it would be sinful to christen an inanimate object with any kind of name, not to talk of a pagan god" (*DL* 1). But the anarchic, grotesque face of "Marconi," surrounded by waving golden wheat, occupies the top half of the Abbey Theatre's 2000 production brochure and program, visually suggesting how the radio quickly became emplaced in the sisters' cottage to inspire their own Lughnasa dance. Understanding the place of the radio in the sisters' home and how it periodically inspires their dancing enables a richer understanding of that movement itself.

Friel privileges technological innovations that can bring humans closer into community with each other if properly controlled, but the sisters often cannot control the radio's operation as it spontaneously bursts into life at times and then just as quickly goes silent because of poor reception. F. C. McGrath offers the best previous analysis of the vacillating and strange role of the radio in the play. He likens Marconi to Henry Adams's dynamo in *The Education of Henry Adams* in its unseen and mysterious energy. McGrath finally suggests that the radio "both induces the nostalgia with its music and, because it is also associated with the process of modernization represented by the knitting factory that costs Agnes and Rose their income, announces the end of the era for which the nostalgia is produced. Thus it represents simultaneously the Dionysian subversion of conventional values and the nostalgia for the era of those values with all their contradictions."[13] Yet despite the insightfulness of this argument concerning Marconi's role, a fuller understanding of the radio in the play can be gained by appreciating how its oscillating power leads the sisters to singularize, even sacralize it as they obsessively react to its intense demands on them.

Rudolf Arnheim's essay "Disciplining the Gramophone, Radio, Telephone, and Television," published in *Sapere* magazine while he was living in fascist Italy in December 1937, the year after the setting of Friel's play, illuminates both the peril and promise of such technology. Arnheim argues toward the beginning of his essay that these then-new media are "for the concentration and elevation of the mind, reserved for rare and precious hours. For this reason, their use should remain more limited than, say, that of eye-glasses or zippers."[14] He clearly distinguishes here and elsewhere between the only occasional necessity for entertainment provided by these devices and the everyday need for the practical function of eyeglasses and zippers.

This passage from Arnheim reveals his fear of the exceptional power of the radio, among other electronic media, and indeed, in *Dancing at Lughnasa*, there is a great power ascribed to Marconi, even to the point where it seems sacralized. Igor Kopytoff has convincingly argued that the Western "conceptual polarity of individualized persons and commoditized things is recent and, culturally speaking, exceptional."[15] He notes how people have often been commoditized in the past, with his prime example being slavery, and goes on to show how things have their own cultural biographies, which illuminate their use: "[W]hat is significant about the adoption of alien objects—as of alien ideas—is not the fact that they are adopted, but the way they are culturally redefined and put to use."[16] As we have seen, the sisters' desire to call the radio "Lugh" "because it arrived as August was about to begin" and, with it, the Festival of Lughnasa (*DL* 1). Thus, the sisters are already attempting to enfold this technology into the lingering Lughnasa festival and its rituals; indeed, their listening to the radio becomes a new ritual for them, so taken are they with it. In fact, the second sentence of Michael's opening monologue in the play begins with his memory of the radio and its power over him and the sisters: "We got our first wireless set that summer—well, a sort of set; and it obsessed us" (ibid.). To use the language of Kopytoff again (himself drawing on Emile Durkheim), if "societies need to set apart a certain portion of their environment, marking it as 'sacred,' singularization is one means to this end. Culture ensures that some things remain unambiguously singular[;] it resists the commoditization of others; and it sometimes resingularizes what has been commoditized."[17] Because Friel's five sisters have gradually made their own household a sacred sphere, which is especially evident, as we will see, when they absent themselves (except for Rose) from the Lughnasa festivities, it is natural that they "resingularize" the radio, which they imagine has particular sacral powers, not the least of which is its ability to inspire their occasional dancing that summer.[18]

A significant indication of Marconi's sacral power over the sisters is revealed by their devoted, concentrated listening to it, which recalls the way in which Friel's Gar religiously devotes himself to the cinema in *Philadelphia, Here I Come!*. Part of their devotion and concentration stems from the radio's poor reception: for example, early in Act One, Rose switches on the set and gets a "three-second blast of 'The British Grenadiers,'" then it goes out (*DL* 4). Christina Hunt Mahony has observed that in Ireland, "Early radio listening required concentration, as poor reception was a fact of life."[19] In *Lughnasa*, the sisters' resingularization of Marconi occurs partially because of its intermittent reception, the way in which it occasionally bursts into life; when it does come on, the sisters generally drop everything they are doing and listen intently and often then dance. Mahony notes that "[l]istening to the radio in the early years was not 'the thing you do while doing something else,' as an American marketing expert recently described it. Early listeners focused all their attention on radio listening, unlike today's listeners, who hear radio . . . as background noise that only occasionally impinges in a lasting or meaningful sense."[20] Arnheim similarly argues in his essay that in order to fully appreciate the power of radio, "you must not listen distractedly as you perform other actions."[21]

Along with offering their concentration and devotion to Marconi during the brief moments that it bursts into sound, Friel's sisters quickly slip into the habit of listening to it in a ritualized way. "Long after radio's introduction, radio listening," as Mahony points out, "also continued to be something of a ritualized practice."[22] Friel, as we have seen periodically through this study, often privileges ritual, most supremely, perhaps, in *Faith Healer*, but he also can critique its use, as he does in portraying the deaths of his three main characters in *The Freedom of the City*. In *Lughnasa*, the ritualized practice of listening intently to the radio often occasions the lasting ritual that Michael reimagines in the conclusion of the play—the nearly wordless dancing of the sisters that casts them and us into a trance.

When Chris turns on Marconi and begins ironing again halfway through Act One, we are told that "*[t]he music, at first scarcely audible, is Irish dance music—'The Mason's Apron,' played by a ceili band. Very fast; very heavy beat; a raucous sound. At first we are aware of the beat only. Then, as the volume increases slowly, we hear the melody*" (DL 21). Friel recalled in 1999 that he used *ceili* music in both *Philadelphia, Here I Come!* and *Dancing at Lughnasa* to give the characters "a new language." As he noted, when he employed the *ceili* music, "words offer neither an adequate means of expression nor a valve for emotional release."[23] The radio unleashes anarchic energies in this scene, just as Friel suggests, and in so doing, all the conventions of the family's life are exploded—but so are some of the conventions of the Catholic Church, as we will see. In this sense, Marconi signifies the necessity for paganism that Friel has affirmed using in the play: "I think there's a need for the pagan in life. . . . I think of it as disrupting civility. If too much obeisance is offered to manners, then in some way we lose or suppress the grumbling and dangerous beast that's underneath the ground."[24] Unfortunately, as both Patrick Lonergan and Patrick Burke have shown, the Abbey Theatre's director Patrick Mason and sound director David Nowlan so intensified the music driving the dance that it was heard as celebratory in seminal productions of the play.[25]

After Marconi comes on, *"[f]or about ten seconds—until the sound has established itself—the women continue with their tasks"* (*DL* 21) until Maggie turns around and prepares herself to dance.[26] As Maggie starts, *"her features become animated by a look of defiance, of aggression; a crude mask of happiness"* (ibid.). Maggie's expression here echoes the look of the radio's disturbing "face," as portrayed on the play's promotional poster and program, and the *"crude, cruel, grinning face, primitively drawn, garishly painted"* that Michael has drawn on each of his kites (70). She then absorbs the rhythm and covers her face with flour by pulling her flour-covered "hands down her cheeks and patterns her face with an instant mask" (21). If her features have previously become "a crude mask of happiness," now a mask made out of flour covers that one (ibid.). As she "dons" this second mask, which seemingly enables her to free herself of the restraining convention associated with this house, she simultaneously shrieks and starts to move, inviting her sisters to join her: *"[S]he opens her mouth and emits a wild raucous 'Yaaaah'— and immediately begins to dance, arms, legs, hair, long bootlaces flying. And as she dances she lilts—sings—shouts and calls, 'Come on and join me! Come on! Come on!' For about ten seconds she dances alone—a white-faced, frantic dervish. Her sisters watch her"* (ibid.). Finally, Rose, then Agnes, then Chris, and last of all Kate begin dancing. Kate's entry into the dancing echoes Maggie's: she *"suddenly leaps to her feet, flings her head back, and emits a loud 'Yaaaah'!"* (22). Kate dances alone and silently, while the rest of the sisters dance together and *"shout—call—sing—to each other"* (ibid.). Kate likely does not want to admit her dependence on them (she likes their reliance on her); also, having rejected Lughnasa as a pagan festival, she refuses to admit it has any power over her.

Reading this crucial scene not as a moment of joy, as Katharine Worth reports above that the London audience did in October 1990, but as mournful enables us to properly see it as a lament for the other lives the sisters could have had. Many interpretations of this dance unfortunately focus on its celebratory aspect: one recent commentator, for example, notes that "the circle dance of women is ritually significant as a celebration of life," and while admitting that it is "raucous, even grotesque," claims the "women's faces are radiant" and that this is a moment of "ecstatic release."[27] Terry John Bates, choreographer of the 1990 premiere and 1999 revival of the play, supports my reading of this dance, noting, "It's total frustration. It's not a celebration at all. It's pure frustration. It's just like, you know, what the hell am I doing?"[28] Richard Allen Cave has suggested that the "manic quality" of the sisters' dance here "brings it all close to a caricature of the contained orderliness of traditional Irish dance," concluding that "[t]his is little short of frenzy. More is involved here than merely joy in dancing."[29] And Bernadette Sweeney, without going into detail, correctly argues that "the dance of the sisters is intended as a literal representation of their frustrations, as they dance that 'crude caricature' of themselves."[30]

Instead of caricaturing the traditional Irish dance, however, the Irish cultural practice that this dance much more closely resembles is that of the keen, although it does not share the keen's public dimension. Anthony Roche has shown that J. M. Synge's 1907 prose work, *The Aran Islands*, influenced Friel in writing *Dancing at Lughnasa* more even than Synge's plays. Roche equates the type of ecstatic dancing by the Mundy sisters and the screaming as Kate joins their dance with the keening Synge recalls the women of the Aran Islands performing in his prose classic. Roche's citation of Synge, however, has even more bearing on the Mundy sisters' dance than he imagines:

> While the grave was being opened the women sat down among the flat tombstones . . . and began the wild keen, or crying for the dead. Each old woman, as she took her turn in the leading recitative, seemed possessed for the moment with a wild ecstasy of grief, swaying to and fro, and bending her forehead to the stone before her, while she called out to the dead with a perpetually recurring chant of sobs.[31]

While Roche posits the ecstasy of the dancing Mundy sisters as an analog to the swaying of the Aran women, a close reading of

Friel's passage reveals even more interesting connections with Synge's account. Particularly noteworthy is the emphasis on the *order* of the ritual in both Synge and Friel. Synge's women take turns "in the leading recitative," while Friel's female characters do likewise in beginning what becomes a communal dance of grief set to Irish dance music over the radio.

Far from being joyful, the sisters perform this dance of mourning for all the men they could have had in their lives. Kevin Whelan has noted that "[b]ecause the *caoineadh* [Irish for "keen"] was pre-eminently a woman's genre, it could code gendered rhetorics of resistance within the mourning formalities," further observing that "[i]t could also give a direct voice to marital strife and conflicts between kin groups, precisely because the wake brought the two families together physically, and because the shock of death exposed or released raw emotional states."[32] In *Lughnasa*, the dancing women perform a sort of modified version of a keen with such "rhetorics of resistance," also voicing their unhappiness with each other (they often fight over their household roles) through the "raw emotional states" that they release. In this sense, Edward Casey's notion of the ability of place to *gather* that I cite above is instructive since "a place holds out, beckoning to its inhabitants and, assembling them, making them manifest."[33] The sisters' recognition and claim of their emplaced bodies thus enables the space of their cottage kitchen to become a place: a neutral space is encultured by their brief reclamation of pre-Famine Irish cultural practices and they assemble and are gathered by these places and presented to us.

Friel's five sisters' privately rendered and silent group litany of these men's names recalls the litany of her sons that Maurya verbalizes at the end of *Riders to the Sea*. Yet Maurya mourns publicly and is content, while Maggie and her sisters mourn silently and are still dissatisfied that they are each alone. My reading of this aspect of the scene thus accords with Patrick Lonergan's suggestion that because of the uncertainties in the play, such as "Friel's unwillingness to present or speculate about the inner life of Agnes and Rose," we must "fill in the gaps in Friel's narrative for ourselves."[34]

Maggie's dance is prompted by Kate's account of meeting Maggie's childhood friend Bernie O'Donnell in town that afternoon. Maggie then recalls a previous Lughnasa dance (Kate has just told them they are not going to the annual Lughnasa dance in Ballybeg) she went to when she was 16 with Bernie. This dance "was this time of year, the beginning of August" (*DL* 20), and it soon becomes clear that its memory evokes Maggie's lingering affection for Brian McGuinness, who actually went to the dance that night with Bernie, while Maggie went with a fellow named Tim Carlin. Maggie emphasizes the dance contest that Bernie and Brian rightfully should have won, but the subtext of her narrative implies Maggie's continuing loneliness. She recalls that that was the last time she saw Brian; he left for Australia after that. Terry John Bates, the choreographer for two productions of the play, makes her loss clear, stating that Maggie dances because of this recognition: "It's awful really because she knows she'll never get married. And that's the awful moment. It's just suddenly that [she realizes that] the one boy she really likes lives in Australia."[35] Likewise, Derbhle Crotty, who played the role of Maggie, points out "[t]he moment in *Lughnasa* where Maggie declines to make peace with her terrible disappointment and instead abandons herself to a dance of savage longing."[36] Maggie's dancing then, both attempts to recapture that last moment of potential happiness with Brian symbolized by that long-ago Lughnasa dance and to make up for not going to the current Lughnasa dance and possibly meeting a man there.

Finally, Maggie's dancing—all the sisters' dancing, in fact— laments the lack of men in their lives. Rose's relationship with Danny Bradley will never materialize into something significant; the same holds true for Agnes's vague hopes of being with Gerry Evans, the father of Chris's son Michael. Chris, too, knows Gerry will never stick around for long; Kate is interested in the local merchant Austin Morgan but will find out shortly he is engaged. This knowledge leads to their near-keening, and its piercing quality and their close dancing finally emphasize their female unity and their utter lack of intimate connection with men.[37] Because of their longing for men past and present, the four sisters who dance together thus cling to each other tightly as if they are each other's long-sought-for male mates. This joint embrace makes the dance *"grotesque"* (21), which, combined with the overly loud music and beat, create a scene reminiscent of an out-of-control calliope in a carnival—a typical child's nightmare.

The entire ritual also signifies the sisters' recognition of their outcast status in a Catholic society that valued women in direct proportion to their relationships with men. As Cathy Leeney noted in the program for the Abbey Theatre's production of the play in 2000, the lives of single women in Ireland of the 1930s "differed radically from those of their married sisters, far more than the lives of single men from those of husbands. . . . Pope Pius XI warned of women without children 'being considered outcasts, slaves to the lusts of men.' To invent a life for oneself as a single woman was a challenge requiring imagination and ingenuity in the face of huge social and economic pressures."[38] The Mundy sisters' imaginative invention of their lives marks them as courageous and intellectually nimble, so much so that they can even be considered as artists of a kind as they seek to make their quotidian lives exciting and significant. As Edward Casey has argued, "[T]he possibilizing activity of imagination in art opens up an experiential domain that would not otherwise have been available either to the artist or to the spectator. This domain is one in which *everything appears as purely possible.*"[39] In this sense, the sisters' creativity in imagining the possible reveals them as characters whose mental life is far superior to, say, Friel's Gar in *Philadelphia, Here I Come!*, whose imagination has already been foreclosed upon and shaped by Hollywood cinema with the result that even his supposedly free inner life is simply a series of mimetic recreations of stereotypical plots from American cinema.

Additionally, their dance may subconsciously reject British empiricism and rationalism, continuing the critique of that often pernicious mindset that Friel objects to in all of the previous plays analyzed in this study. If we read their dancing as, in part, a diminished relic of keening, and realize the subversive quality of that practice, we apprehend Friel's privileging of their dancing as a protest against the coercive aspects of British imperialism. As Kevin Whelan has articulated, Irish keening's "theatrical performance of emotion" signified to the imperial British mind a "Celtic inconsistency, the lack of the fully formed, regulated, rational personality of civil Anglo-Saxon society."[40] Because the keen stood out as a "barbaric mark of primitivism" to the imperializing project of Ireland, which gained vigor and speed as the nineteenth century progressed, British authorities determined to stamp it out and produce a "newly disciplined Irish body [that] could then participate in the formation of a new ethnic subject—rational, self-interested and above all consistent."[41] Such a body would then be sufficiently displaced from Irish culture and able to be controlled.

One of Maggie's initial movements, where she *"patterns her face in an instant mask"* by putting flour on it in the dance passage cited above, adroitly suggests how she briefly puts on a type of literal but also figurative white-face, briefly becoming "white." She thus frees herself temporarily from the lingering British imperial concept of the "native Irish" as black primitives, while paradoxically linking herself to the black Ryangan villagers in the two Ugandan harvest festivals Father Jack describes to them in the play's second act. Jack tells his sisters that the villagers' "ritual dance" gradually "grows naturally into a secular celebration" in which the community begins celebrating: "We light fires round the periphery of the circle; and *we paint our faces with coloured powders*; and we sing local songs; and we drink palm wine" (*DL* 48; my emphasis). *Lughnasa*'s choreographer, Bates, recognizes this general connection between the two ritual dances when he remarks that the sisters' dance "sort of echoes Africa and Father Jack. There are little moments where it's all picked up from Africa."[42] The sisters, led by Maggie, finally dance not just because they are frustrated but also so that they are recognized as human beings, although their official religious culture and the British imperial mindset refuse them this acknowledgement. Crucially, although they are linked to the Ryangan villagers through their ritualistic dancing and through Maggie's white-masking, they are finally disconnected from their native culture in profound ways: while the Ryangans are actually celebrating a fruitful harvest and relaxing for hours on end, the Mundy sisters' dance parodies all notions of fertility. Moreover, the Ryangans dance securely within their culture, while the Mundy sisters feel largely locked out of the local remnants of pagan culture and official Catholic Irish culture because of their usual distance from their own bodies, urged upon them by the then-dominant strain of Jansenism in the Catholic Church, among other factors.[43]

Although Frantz Fanon's 1967 classic, *Black Skin, White Masks*, analyzes black consciousness, one of his concluding statements perfectly captures the marginalized Mundy sisters' desire they try to express through their dance: "As soon as I *desire* I am asking to be considered. I am not merely here-and-now, sealed into thingness. I am for somewhere else and for something else. . . . He who is reluctant to recognize me opposes me. In a savage struggle I am willing to accept convulsions of death, invincible dissolution, but also the possibility of the impossible."[44] As we will see in the conclusion to this study, as part of my analysis of Molly Sweeney's tarantella in that later play, Molly dances that frenzied dance of death for precisely such a recognition that our so-called normal society usually only reluctantly gives to the blind. Here, Friel's Mundy sisters assert their presence, but even more important for the ending of this play, they affirm their futurity as well through their dervish-like dancing. Every time we read this scene in Friel's play or watch this moment onstage, they beckon to us, asking to be heard, seen, and understood—to be recognized.

Because I believe that Michael finally becomes a figure of the artist in his final speech that refigures the sisters' original, constricting dance into one of potential, thus recognizing them and their harsh lives, I disagree with Catriona Clutterbuck, who argues that "Michael as narrator unwittingly colludes with *Dancing at Lughnasa*'s overt target of critique—the forces of imperialism which work through the constriction of the power exercisable in the domestic zone."[45] In fact, the entire play renders these women real and gives them voices in a cultural context where they were slowly being rendered voiceless, bodiless.

In order to rebel against one of those oppressing discourses, that of the Catholic Church in Ireland, Chris joins the sisters' dance by first tossing Jack's surplice that she has been folding over her head. She is now a woman wearing a priestly vestment—a heretical subversion in the eyes of the Church. Her increasingly pagan dance with the other sisters heightens the sense of revolution. She seems to temporarily overthrow the Catholic disposition of the household, and Kate, the keeper of that order, "*cries out in remonstration, 'Oh, Christina—!' But her protest is drowned*" (*DL* 21). To further emphasize the overturning of this Catholic order, Friel's stage directions point out the nightmarish aspect of all the sisters' dancing and its Dionysiac quality: "*With this too loud music, this pounding beat, this shouting—calling—singing, this parodic reel, there is a sense of order being consciously subverted, of the women consciously and crudely caricaturing themselves, indeed of near-hysteria being induced*" (22). Now the earlier order of the dance, when sister by sister each stepped out in turn, is itself rendered chaotic. The music from the radio abruptly stops in "mid-phrase" and the sisters stop one by one, embarrassed, ashamed, even defiant (ibid.), probably because they realize they have effectively brought the Lughnasa dance into their house and admitted their lack of men.

In the chatter that follows, Maggie admits the orgasmic power of their dance while Chris rejects the control of the Catholic Church over their bodies. First, Maggie drags on a cigarette (suggesting that the dance was a sexual release valve) and only half-jokingly declares, "Wonderful Wild Woodbines. Next best thing to a wonderful, wild man" (*DL* 23), reminding us of each sister's lack of a husband with this comment. Then, Kate asks, "Please take that surplice off, Christina" (ibid.). But Chris is busy trying to fix the radio that Maggie had originally wanted to call "Lugh" after the pagan god for whom the harvest festival was named. She wonders if a valve has blown and Kate asks, "Have you no sense of propriety?" Chris's reply is ostensibly about the radio but surely is meant to be double-edged: "If you ask me we should throw it out" (ibid.). She thus cunningly refers to the surplice and the Catholic Church, suggesting they be discarded. Father Jack anticipates her subversive stance since he has effectively excommunicated himself from the Church by his embrace of paganism and cast off all trappings of the Church.

As they dance, the sisters, inspired by the music transmitted by the radio, likely imagine their potential lives if their past relationships with men had led to marriage. The sisters' rich, individual reveries that Friel chooses not to show us accord with French radio pioneer Paul Deharme's conviction in 1928 that "today's minds have a need for imagination and lyrical transformation that cannot be satisfied by any conventional or even recent art forms, except for a radiophonic art. . . . It seems to me that the waves of the wireless, remote and mysterious like the sources of our thought, can and should feed our imagination with the new inspiration that it deserves."[46] Friel shows in the scenes of radio listening and dancing in *Lughnasa* that this oral technology can inspire vivid imaginings on the part of his main characters and even on the part of his reading and viewing audience.

Intriguingly for the sisters' brief rebellion against Catholicism in their joint dance, the Catholic hierarchy in Ireland promoted radio use to consolidate and promulgate the faith in the years leading up to the events portrayed in *Lughnasa*, although church leaders could not have imagined the reverence and devotion that Marconi would inspire on the part of Friel's sisters, much less their resulting frenzied dancing. Declan Kiberd has pointed out that the proliferation of radios in Ireland had occurred in 1932 "so that loyal Catholics could tune into the Eucharistic Congress celebrations broadcast from Dublin."[47] And indeed, as Kiberd observes, "What was broadcast from national transmitters in the great capital cities was what a people's lords and masters wishes it to hear."[48] The sisters' sacralizing of the radio and the singularity and power expressed in their often subsequent dancing, then, is all the more astonishing as they shape their listening of broadcasts from the metropole to their emotional needs, which enables them to "perform" in their local harvest festival.

Their dancing thus signifies not only their subversiveness—unconscious or not—of the British imperializing project but also their willing rejection of the increasingly controlling Catholic Church in Ireland. Whelan has argued that after the Devotional Revolution took hold of the Irish Catholic Church in the years after the Famine, the church not only opposed the *caoineadh* or keen since "it was women's work and rooted in a vernacular culture of expression and structure of feeling," but also it "turned against the robust tradition of dance, because it could be free, intoxicating, spontaneous and sexual." He observes further that "[d]ance belonged to the participants without mediator or masters. The church moved to domesticate its wilder energies and to control the time and places of performance," especially after the Famine.[49] Because of these fears of the unbridled emotion and coded sexuality of unregulated Irish dancing, particularly dances in Donegal (the setting of *Lughnasa*) and Connemara, the Catholic clergy introduced the "Dance Hall Act of 1935," the year before the major events of Friel's play, in order to ensure the "moral hygiene" of their parishioners through supervised dances. The resulting lack of intimacy and contact in the emerging Irish dance style that was increasingly promoted by church and state was "purposely asexual" and was part of an Irish dance evolution "from passion to pallor, from erotic to neurotic."[50] Because the Dance Hall Act of 1935 was so "draconian," it was "practically impossible to hold dances without the sanction of the trinity of clergy, police and judiciary,"[51] making the Mundy sisters' frenzied dancing all the more revolutionary in its rejection of organized Irish Catholicism and British empiricism. They briefly take control of their own bodies even as they surrender them to the manic energies that arise in response to the *ceili* music.

These manic energies clearly hearken back to pagan, Dionysian revels. David Krause's statement about modern Irish drama's comic purpose perfectly captures the Dionysian spirit of the sisters' dancing:

It is perhaps the main . . . comic purpose of modern Irish drama, and probably of all compensatory laughter, to undo the burden of

Apollonian renunciation and retrieve the mythic sense of a denied
or lost Dionysian freedom and joy.[52]

Having renounced relationships with the opposite sex for so long
and, consequently, their own bodies, the Mundy sisters' dancing
gropes clumsily toward that promised Dionysian freedom and joy
they wish could be theirs forever. But their stoic determination to get
there seems to impede that freedom and joy's full entrance even into
this manic dance.

The frenzied, broken quality of the sisters' dance also signals
their despair and rejection of the by-then-inexorable historical con-
solidation of power by the Church in the South and its strong influence over the embryonic Irish government under Eamon de Valera.
Catholicism in the South in 1936 was ascendant, even triumphal,
in the wake of de Valera's growing emphasis on the Catholic nature
of the new state. In a St. Patrick's Day broadcast in 1935, de Valera
remarked that Ireland "remains a Catholic nation."[53] Oliver Rafferty
points out that "[t]he [1932 Eucharistic] [C]ongress was an occasion for [C]atholic triumphalism on both sides of the border. Many
[C]atholic streets in towns throughout the north were bedecked
with bunting, and mini-altars were erected at which people gathered
nightly for the recitation of the rosary and other prayers."[54] This
event also marked the moment at which the Catholic hierarchy in
the South finally warmed up to de Valera: they permitted the first
president of the Free State, William T. Cosgrave, and de Valera "to
bear the papal legate's canopy" during the congress.[55] The Irish state
became increasingly identified with the Church; this identification
finally culminated in the 1937 Irish constitution de Valera wrote.
Roy Foster has noted that de Valera's constitution assumed that "the
nature and identity of the Irish polity was Catholic, reflected in five
articles defining 'rights.' These were much influenced by papal encyc-
licals and current Catholic social teaching. Divorce was prohibited;
the idea of working mothers denounced; the Roman Catholic Church
granted a 'special position . . . as the guardian of the faith professed
by the great majority of the citizens.'"[56] On the local level, parish

priests continued to display a great deal of control over their parishioners, just as the local Ballybeg priest does in Friel's play.

The reach of the Catholic Church at this time is epitomized by Kate, who functions as the female head of household in the absence of an adult male (the sisters' father or their brother Jack) and who, despite her brief dancing in this famous scene, often promotes the erasure of the female body. As a Catholic schoolteacher, she also represents the Church and tries to cast the family as complete adherents to the faith. Her concern for their respectable image as Catholic spinsters makes her prevent the sisters from attending the harvest dance in town. As she argues, "Dancing at our time of day? That's for young people with no duties and no responsibilities and nothing in their heads but pleasure. . . . Do you want the whole countryside to be laughing at us?—women of our years?—mature women *dancing*? What's come over you all?" (*DL* 13). Chris especially is bitterly critical of Kate to others, telling the father of her child, Gerry Evans, on his return, that she is helping with "the usual—housework—looking after his lordship" (29), a statement that effectively masculinizes the nearly asexual Kate. As a schoolteacher in the local Catholic school who consistently elevates the mind over the body, propriety over fun, Kate's distance from her own body leads her to try to render the entire household body-less.

Kate, for instance, becomes alarmed at Gerry Evans's return that summer so she attempts to regulate Chris's interaction with him and prevent another pregnancy. When he first comes back, Kate tells Chris tenderly that he can spend "the night if he wants to. (*Firm again*) But in the outside loft. And alone" (*DL* 26). Understandably, Kate wants to protect her sister both from another birth that the family cannot financially support and from getting her heart broken again, but her role as enforcer for the mores of the Catholic Church gradually turns some of the other sisters against her—especially Chris and Agnes, who later calls her "such a damned righteous bitch!" (34).

Although she is rendered sexless, even stereotypically male through such behavior, Kate also tries to call upon the masculinized authority of the Catholic Church in the form of their brother Jack to cinch her case in essentially banning the sisters from going to the Lughnasa dance. She states that "[a]nd this is Father Jack's home—we must never forget that—ever. No, no, we're going to no harvest dance" (*DL* 13). Kate's reclaims the home as Father Jack's to almost literally make their family a sort of micro-parish with him in charge.

The sisters' dancing that subverts Kate's attempt to keep the family utterly Catholic also unites them in a sort of provisional community that reinscribes and reimagines the festivals taking place locally. While Lughnasa dances traditionally took place on a community-wide basis, often around an outside bonfire, the Mundy sisters' dance domesticates this tradition: they end up dancing only with each other—around their own turf fire—to the music of the resingularized and thus sacral radio named Marconi.

In this famous dance and in the many other brief dances that occur, often spontaneously, we see the Mundy sisters and other characters such as the peripatetic Gerry Evans employing their bodies in exceptionally ritualistic ways that enable them to reenter place consistently. Of course, all their quotidian activities, such as ironing, preparing food, feeding the chickens, and so on bring them into place repeatedly. As Casey notes, "My body continually *takes me into place*. It is at once agent and vehicle, articulator and witness of being-in-place."[57] But these more specialized and ritualistic dance movements inscribe the spaces in which they occur—inside the sisters' cottage when they dance together, outside by the lane when Gerry and Chris, then later Gerry and Agnes, dance—with a sacred quality, implying that their bodies have marked the interior of the house and its yard, making them sites of memory that can be accessed in the future, as indeed older Michael does in the future when he concludes the play with his dreamy, mesmeric monologue. Casey observes that "[p]ersons who live in places—who inhabit or re-inhabit them—come to share features with the local landscape; but equally so, they make a difference to, perhaps indelibly mark, the land in which they dwell."[58] Thus, the sisters are marked with certain aspects of the local Donegal topography even as they mark it and inflect it themselves in distinctive, ceremonial, ritualistic maneuvers. If the local landscape and culture of *Translations* are rapidly becoming "unmarked" or eroded through the metaphysical violence of the Ordnance Survey and the threatened, real violence of evictions after Yolland's disappearance, the local Donegal landscape and the interior of the Mundy cottage in *Lughnasa* is constantly being reinscribed with ceremonial movements, particularly dancing, that render it numinous, sacralized, memorable. Every time someone in the play's present or future walks back over these sites—literally or, as older Michael does, figuratively in his mind—they reenter them and experience their power. Such reenterings lead us out of our busy lives and into different rhythms than the ones that we move to on a daily basis.

Because of their sacralizing of the radio, the sisters become briefly attuned to their emplaced bodies even as they lament their lack of husbands, but they and Michael also sacralize the next circle of place in the play, the cottage, which becomes a vehicle for older Michael's memories whenever he remembers it. Siegfried Giedion has suggested that architecture takes on a life of its own and can linger long after its surroundings disappear: "[O]nce it appears it constitutes an organism itself, with its own character and its own continuing life. Its value cannot be stated in the sociological or economic terms by which we explain its origin, and its influence may continue after its original environment has altered or disappeared. Architecture can reach out beyond the period of its birth, beyond the social class that called it into being, beyond the style to which it belongs."[59] Giedion takes as an example of the continuing life of specific architecture the "undulating church façade" invented by a "Roman baroque architect" in the late seventeenth century that was used "in the great dwelling complexes of the eighteenth and early nineteenth centuries,"[60] but I am more interested in understanding his statement figuratively and applying it to the way in which the Mundy cottage lingers in Michael's mind and in our mind by virtue of its vernacular architecture.[61]

Vernacular architecture, which the Mundy house exemplifies, draws on and is consistent with its native environment; thus, the cottage affirms its inhabitants' emplacedness in this rural culture and their essential continuity with the immediate environment. As T. J. Corringe has pointed out, "The vernacular tradition responded to local climate conditions, and also embodied a deep knowledge of, and respect for, its materials: it understood the difference between beech, oak and pine, the capacities and limitations of granite or limestone, of slate or marl, and it adapted design accordingly."[62] Friel's opening stage directions suggest just how well the cottage is sited to take advantage of the natural environment. For example, "*There is a sycamore tree off right. One of its branches reaches over part of the house.*" This tree would shade the house in summer and provide a type of exterior insulation in the winter. Inside, there is "*a large iron range, large turf box beside it, table and chairs, dresser, oil lamp, buckets with water at the back door, etc., etc.*" (*DL* n.p.). The sisters use local fuel and almost certainly well water along with providing their meat and egg needs from their chickens. This, in short, is a largely self-sufficient household that in both design and function harmonizes well with its local environment as most examples of vernacular living do, even though the family is clearly on the edge of poverty. Its very simplicity, connection to the natural world, and uncluttered nature appeals to contemporary audiences weary of our materialistic society and the resultant clutter most of us accrue. Moreover, although I do not have the space to develop this point, the radiant simplicity of the cottage architecture reinforces Friel's own precise, chiseled, evocative words.

As Gaston Bachelard has suggested in his marvelous topoanalysis of the house in *The Poetics of Space*, "[W]e 'write a room,' 'read a room,' or 'read a house,'" and if the writer succeeds at his "first poetic overture, the reader who is 'reading a room' leaves off reading and starts to think of some place in his own past. . . . The values of intimacy are so absorbing that the reader has ceased to read your room: he sees his own again."[63] Friel, who always seeks to evoke community onstage and create communities among audience and actors, effects this process in his poetically rendered play that evokes the authentic place of that cottage, in part thanks to Joe Vanek's creative set.

In his *Places of the Soul,* architect Christopher Day argues that "[m]ost people . . . don't normally look at our surroundings. We breathe them in . . . [and] the experience only touches our hearts when it becomes an ambience we can breathe."[64] Despite the tendency for audiences, as we have seen, to misread Friel's stage set as "golden," or nostalgic, its arrangement and spacing recreates the atmosphere of an Irish cottage kitchen that we can breathe in. And its authenticity keeps it from becoming the stereotypical Irish kitchen of many earlier plays and invites us gently inside to partake of the life of the house. Set designer Joe Vanek, who envisioned the set for the 1990 premiere and the 1999 revival of *Lughnasa,* constructed a set that invites the audience in while simultaneously anchoring us in this environment and letting it seemingly hover in front of our eyes, giving it an ethereal, even spiritual presence. As Vanek recalls:

> We quickly reduced the basics of the house as described in the text to a single, diagonal wall that contained all the necessary physical elements; a stove, a press, and a door to the rest of the house. As we developed the floorplan of the kitchen and its arrangement of furniture, the walls and the windows gradually vanished and the main flagstone floor floated free as three open sides anchored by the fourth main wall with its gigantic angled beam and massive sill. The overall framing of the set developed simultaneously, from a harsh, angled granite walled box in a wash of naturalistic greens and browns of the mountainside to a more neutral, simply textured white box, hazed with a wash of amber pollen or dust.[65]

The set thus enables us to gaze deeply into the cottage and figuratively into the hearts and minds of its inhabitants. The set's exterior framing, rendered in white, the color of innocence and hope, cradles the objects and subjects of the play much like a house itself does, particularly a house from our childhood. As Bachelard argues, "[T]he house thrusts aside contingencies, its councils of continuity are unceasing. Without it, man would be a dispersed being. . . . Before he is 'cast into the world,' . . . man is laid in the cradle of the house. . . . Life begins well, it begins enclosed, protected, all warm in the bosom of the house."[66]

The cradling quality of Vanek's house in his set, as well as the similarly warm quality Michael ascribes to his life in the house in the script, echo what Caitríona Clear has pointed out about the family structure that children experienced in Ireland from approximately 1870 through the early decades of the twentieth century. Such children "grew up with several never-married aunts and uncles, and late-marrying or single elder siblings. . . . [T]hese relatives took an intense interest in the younger generation. . . . The presence of so many elders forged a strong family culture."[67] And yet despite the cradling effect that Clear describes, Bachelard suggests, and Vanek's set enacts with its massive flagstones, beam, and sill, the simultaneous openness, the porosity, of the set helps us to realize how fragile this house and its occupants are—that the slightest disturbance can bring it all crashing down round their heads, as indeed happens in the play. The "amber pollen or dust" suggests that we will see a series of moments preserved in amber for all time, but they are not meant to be static because the play's title implies that this action is somehow ongoing, immemorial, each time we read the play or see it.

Bachelard observes that after we leave our original childhood home, "when memories of other places we have lived in come back to us, we travel to the land of Motionless Childhood, motionless the way all Immemorial things are. We live fixations, fixations of happiness."[68] As we will see later in my analysis of Michael's concluding monologue about his aunts' dance, that "memory" too, which proves to be a recreation, a necessary fiction, is such a moving fixation of happiness.

Vanek's rendering of the wheat field, a symbol that accrues multivalent meanings in the play according to him, has unfortunately led to a widespread misreading of the play as a sentimental exercise in nostalgia, as Patrick Lonergan has argued. Lonergan notes that "Catherine Byrne, who played Chris in the play's 1990 premiere and Agnes in its 1999 'Friel Festival' revival, states that [director] Patrick

Mason's *Lughnasa* was intended to be seen as a 'golden production.' 'There's a bleak side to Brian's plays but he doesn't always like that highlighted,' she explains. 'But,' Byrne adds, 'there's another production of *Dancing at Lughnasa* we haven't seen yet. We haven't seen how dark it is.' Mason's *Lughnasa* was 'all golden corn and poppies, beautiful lighting; the women were colour-coordinated.'"[69]

But Vanek at least did not intend to evoke such a monovalent, joyous meaning with his set. As he notes:

> That we wanted a field of wheat to figure in some respect was an early decision, although there was no mention of one in the script. . . . After various experiments with angles . . . we conceived the field as the rear wall of the house itself, rising in an improbable but dramatic wedge. Through the wheat we chose to carve a path, cutting diagonally and opening out into the scrubby garden, now reduced to little more than an undulating arm of dried grass and dusty topsoil. Visitors to the house would be viewed approaching.[70]

When I saw the 2000 production of *Lughnasa* at the Abbey with this same stage set, my vision was certainly drawn to the wheatfield, and it evoked a feeling of warmth in me that numerous audience members have remarked upon. But in retrospect, I can see that wheat field functioning much differently, suggesting with its overwhelming light and promise of a good harvest how the Mundys are surrounded with such literal and figurative promise but, ironically, remain infertile in three crucial respects: literally (the sisters are slowly starving to death), biologically (Chris is the only sister with a child), and politically (the marginalized sisters will not figure prominently in the new Irish state then being consolidated). Crucially, Vanek's set enables them to peer out into this world of promise, but they are outcasts at the feast, increasingly so as the play proceeds. Their only real "reaping" will consist of a few bilberries, a rooster, Father Jack's death, and the voluntary emigration of Rose and Agnes to London.

The place of the path that Vanek depicts in this wheat field has usually been ignored in criticism of his stage set, but he saw it as crucial for the action and meaning of the play. Early in rehearsals, he and others realized that the path's openness could "damage the effects immeasurably," so it was "sealed with wheat and the path became suspended behind the house with plain doorway openings set into the walls on either side of the stage. The tree was to vanish also. This starker and more suggestive world clearly could not support the huge naturalism as depicted, especially on the fringe of the set."[71] In effect, Vanek's path *sealed off the house* from the double image of beckoning fertility—the abandoned garden and the wheat field, troped as a golden land of promise, making a "starker and more suggestive world" and, one might add, a darker one.

Vanek has pointed out further that the wheat field was meant to evoke different feelings at various times in the play: "The field of wheat with its path served as several visual metaphors which changed subtly with the intensity of the russet-hued, softly focused break-up gobos that Trevor Dawson used to light it. At times it seemed like the smouldering Lughnasa fires that are referred to in the script; whilst at the end of Act One, to the accompaniment of distant jungle drums, it resembles an expanse of veld, baking in the sun."[72] Clearly, the wheat field of the production symbolized promise; exclusion; the anarchic, fiery paganism of the Lughnasa festival; and African paganism as well. But audiences, conditioned in part by what they believed to be celebratory music that led them to misperceive the sisters' mournful dancing, saw it as nostalgic and warm. Properly understood, however, Vanek's stage set registers the desperation and longing of the main characters on the precipice of a massive series of changes.

Since places gather "experiences and histories, even languages and thoughts," as Casey has observed, "even when I recall people and things and circumstances in an ordinary place, I have the sense that these various recollecta have been kept securely in place, harbored there, as it were."[73] As we have seen, Vanek's stage set, through its sealed-off path and golden wheat field, evokes the two outer circles of sacred place in the play that are gathered centripetally, as it were, into the sisters' bodies and the intimate, sacred place of their cottage: the back hills outside Ballybeg and Ryanga, Africa, both sites of ritualistic, pagan practice. Father Jack's presence and their frenzied dance during those moments in the kitchen introduce these places into their intimate world, allowing their bodies and the cradle-space of the cottage to be interpenetrated by their primal force and energy. In remarks strikingly relevant to Friel's play, Wendell Berry argues in "The Body and the Earth" that a resilient culture "must somehow involve within itself a ceremonious generosity toward the wilderness of natural force and instinct. The farm must yield a place to the forest . . . as a sacred grove . . . a place for people to go, free of work and presumption, to let themselves alone."[74] As we have seen, since the sisters are forbidden by Kate from dancing in town at the presumably buttoned-down harvest dance and also from dancing in the back hills at the anarchic Lughnasa fire dance, they bring the whirling energy of those celebrations into their cottage through the power of Marconi that they inflect with their repressed desires. And Father Jack's lingering affection for the Ryangan rituals that he has now absorbed enables that African community to flourish for a time within their Ballybeg kitchen.

Significantly, Máire MacNeill shows that, in Donegal, the dominant Lughnasa festival took place on an elevated site, which differed from other Lughnasa festivals in its lack of assimilation into local Christian festivals. These assemblies "show no signs of having been taken over by Christianity. The country-people did not think of them as having any religious significance and accepted them simply as traditional occasions for festive outings."[75] Friel's Lughnasa festivals of the back hills above Ballybeg do have innocuous trappings, such as the typical bilberries that Rose and Agnes gather, but their dominant feature resembles the Mundy sisters' dance—the subversion of social, even sexual order. Thus, Friel accentuates the lack of connection with Christianity displayed in these traditional pagan assemblies located in isolated hilltops common in Ulster (MacNeill's map shows eight of these in 1942 Donegal). In drawing on these utterly pagan Donegal assemblies, Friel implies the lingering presence of a much older order in his region of Ireland than that imposed by the local manifestation of the Catholic Church. As he noted in an interview with John Lahr,

"I think there is a value in religion. . . . I think whether we want to call it religion or the acknowledgement of mystery or a salute to the otherness, it can be enriching. But in Ireland we have perverted that enriching process and made it into some kind of disabling process."[76]

He acknowledges spiritual mystery through the introduction of a character named Sweeney, a local boy who has been burned in one of the fires.[77] Sweeney's name obviously evokes the legend of the mythic Irish Sweeney who was sentenced to a life in the trees of Ireland for murdering a local holy man. Sweeney was known for his great leaping ability (he did not actually fly, as is sometimes thought), and Friel's character Sweeney seemingly has attempted a great leap over the traditional Lughnasa fire. MacNeill explains that leaps at the site of the fires were a commonplace of Lughnasa festivals, perhaps suggestive of the "fourteenth-century poem [which] tells of Lugh as a marvellous leaper."[78] She goes on to speculate that Lugh's mythic arrival in Ireland may have been incorporated into an even older, more primitive tradition associated with the pre-Celtic peoples of Ireland: "They [the leaps] may have belonged originally to a more primitive cosmology than the religion of the incoming Celts and been adapted here by the Celtic invaders who imagined their hero as arriving suddenly from the Otherworld overseas."[79] MacNeill's speculation indicates how myths have survived and flourished through thousands of years in Ireland and been adapted by different groups of people. Friel's subtle incorporation of the leaping motif through the name of the Sweeney boy evokes this adaptation process and hints at his belief that myths and religions can be unifying—or that they still can impart meaning to our lives (as we saw in *Faith Healer*)—if incorporated into the life of the local community appropriately. This mythical motif of leaping implies the truth of Declan Kiberd's comment that the play "manages . . . to suggest that something good is being lost, and even more tantalizingly, that the society depicted had within its reach the sources of its own renewal."[80]

These dramatic representations of this ancient Celtic festival and Uncle Jack's adopted Ugandan religion suggest a Donegal in the 1930s where pagan practices and more traditional Catholic ones coexisted uneasily. As Oliver Rafferty has noted, Ulster Catholicism was historically different from that practiced within the Pale and the major outlying towns such as Galway in the early seventeenth century: "In Ulster[,] Catholicism had failed in its civilizing influence, and Christianity was but precariously integrated into a distinct Celtic understanding of life in both its spiritual and its material dimensions."[81] *Dancing at Lughnasa* recognizes the lingering way in which Christianity remained sublimated into a Celtic worldview in conservative cultural pockets such as Donegal into the early twentieth century. As the Gaelic order faded, many Celtic customs were adapted to Christianity, but in parts of the province of Ulster where the plantations were least effective, such as Donegal, a number of Celtic traditions lingered, such as the Festival of Lughnasa.

Kate's exchange with Rose early in the play demonstrates this persistence of pagan ways in Friel's imagined 1936 Ballybeg. Rose is a regular attendee at Mass and wears a miraculous medal (*DL* 6), but she is also fascinated by the Lughnasa rituals in the back hills above Ballybeg. The fluidity with which characters such as Rose and Father Jack move between Celtic and Catholic Christian worldviews represents the Frielian model of religion generally in which characters oscillate between worldviews. Something like this dynamic process is needed, Friel suggests, for religion generally to become once more an enriching process in our lives.

When the fate of the local Sweeney boy is raised in the family, Rose alone appreciates the cyclical, mythic nature of the Lughnasa ritual that led to his burning whereas states Kate flatly that he was critically burned because of "[s]ome silly prank up in the hills." Rose muses, "(*Quietly, resolutely*) It was last Sunday week, the first night of the Festival of Lughnasa; and they were doing what they do every year up there in the back hills" (*DL* 16). An outraged Kate tries to interrupt Rose's account, but Rose serenely continues: "First they light a bonfire beside a spring well. Then they dance around it. Then they drive their cattle through the flames to banish the devil out of them" (ibid.). Kate again interrupts but Rose concludes by saying, "And this year there was an extra big crowd of boys and girls. And they were off their heads with drink. And young Sweeney's trousers caught fire and he went up like a torch. That's what happened" (ibid.). Kate demands, "Who filled your head with that nonsense?" and Rose simply answers, "They do it every Lughnasa. I'm telling you. That's what happened" (ibid.). Kate answers with an astonishing amount of invective: "And they're savages! I know those people from the back hills! I've taught them! Savages—that's what they are! And what pagan practices they have are no concerns of ours—none whatever! It's a sorry day to hear talk like that in a Christian home, a Catholic home! (17). Her anger is probably atypical of the local attitude toward the Lughnasa festival since even the priest seems more exercised by Jack's paganism than the pagan practices taking place in the hills above town. Rose's fascination with these local pagan practices easily accommodates her Catholic faith. She is a "simple-minded" character in the play, but somehow her simplicity makes her more receptive to and thoughtful about these ancient practices than Kate, with her obviously superior intellect. Because of this receptivity, however, Rose likely falls prey to the sexual advances of Danny Bradley, who is associated with the sexual anarchy of Lughnasa. Bradley's probable rape of Rose, along with the Sweeney boy's burned body, together signify the darker aspects of paganism in the play and the former of these leads directly to Rose and Agnes's emigration from the house and that rural culture.

Although their time together is never portrayed in the play (Frank McGuinness's film script depicts Bradley rocking Rose back and forth violently in a small boat on a mountain lake to frighten her),[82] Friel provides us with a series of clues that suggest Rose has been sexually assaulted by Bradley. Until recently, no one has suggested that such an incident occurred, but Martin W. Walsh has stated (without supplying any evidence) that "[p]erhaps she [Rose] loses her virginity to Danny Bradley, quite possibly by rape; perhaps she escapes his drunken lust, as the film would have it."[83] The first clue Friel offers to Rose's possible rape comes with the compelling analogy he introduces between the more innocuous Gerry Evans and the more sinister Bradley. Both are married (we find out about Evans's family in Wales toward the end of the play from a note another Michael Evans sends to the Donegal Michael in the 1950s from Wales); both cheat on their wives with another: Gerry with Chris Mundy and Danny with Rose Mundy. Friel intended Evans to be represented as a prowling fox, while Danny Bradley is symbolically linked to the fox that kills the sisters' rooster. Catherine Byrne, one of Friel's favorite actresses, told Tony Coult in 2000 that "when Gerry Evans arrives at the house for the first time—Brian said it should be like a fox coming to the henhouse door."[84]

Not long after Rose returns from her liaison with Danny Bradley, and shortly before the sisters prepare to eat their meager supper outside, she enters the garden *"dressed as in Act I"* (*DL* 67), signifying she has turned inward again after her time with Bradley. This stage direction is significant because it shows that Rose has changed out of her blue cardigan and good dress that she wore to meet Bradley and is now wearing *"the drab, wrap-around overalls/aprons of the time"* that she and Maggie and Agnes usually wear (n.p.). Rose is also portrayed in these opening stage directions as wearing *"wellingtons even though the day is warm"* (n.p.). Rose has redonned her usual "costume," withdrawing back into herself and is now again wearing her protective "shell" after she had displayed a radical curiosity in going to meet Bradley.

As she enters the garden, she carries the dead rooster that *"is stained with blood,"* but she *"is calm, almost matter-of-fact"* (*DL* 67), connoting the shock she continues to feel after this probable sexual assault. Her manner here is portrayed in very similar language as it is on her return from meeting Bradley several pages earlier: *"All of these movements . . . are done not dreamily, abstractedly, but calmly, naturally"* (59). Rose flatly tells them, "My rooster's dead," and says in reply to Agnes's remonstrations that "Maggie warned me the fox was about. (*To all*) That's the end of my pet rooster. The fox must have got him. You were right, Maggie" (ibid.). She refuses Agnes's offer of another one (the rooster was white, implying her innocence and virginity), which implies what she has lost (her virginity) is irreplaceable. Finally, when Maggie says, "We can hardly expect him to lay for us now," we realize that Rose herself has been irreversibly damaged (68).

Along with her change in clothes, her desensitized manner, and her association with the blood-stained, white rooster, Rose is associated with a red poppy and with red bilberry juice, two symbols that suggest she has been deflowered. She is described as having "*a red poppy that she plucked casually along the road*" (*DL* 56) and as eating Agnes's berries after this and then wiping her "*stained fingers*" on "*her skirt*" (57). This blood imagery connotes that she has lost her virginity and she wipes her stained fingers on her skirt as a blazon of that loss.

After she is interrogated by an outraged Kate, Rose tells them a story replete with ominous sexual connotations. She acknowledges meeting Danny and riding in "his father's blue boat" on Lough Anna, and concluding, "then the two of us went up through the back hills. He showed me what was left of the Lughnasa fires" (*DL* 59). In his reading of the influence of Synge's *In the Shadow of the Glen* on *Dancing at Lughnasa*, Roche—without explicitly arguing Rose is sexually assaulted—has observed that "the world of order and security which Kate is struggling to maintain is contrasted with all those outside forces which threaten social and sexual anarchy. The locale which comes to represent these forces in the play is inscribed by the phrase, 'the back hills.' It is to the 'back hills' that . . . Danny Bradley proposes taking her; it is also in the 'back hills' that the Lughnasa festival is celebrated."[85] The back hills thus signify anarchy and a general abandonment. After telling her sisters that he "calls me his Rosebud, Aggie," Rose says that he walked her home and then states emphatically to Kate, "And that's all I'm going to tell you. (*To all*) That's all any of you are going to hear" (ibid.). Clearly, the gap in Rose's narrative implies her shame and inability to relate what else happened to her in the back hills—almost surely Bradley's sexual assault of her, probably his rape of her. Kate is sufficiently upset by what Rose has said that she exclaims (implicitly invoking the Virgin Mary's sexual innocence), "Mother of God, will we ever be able to lift our heads ever again . . . ?" (ibid.).

This incident precipitates the family's doom, in part through the emigration of Rose and Agnes soon afterward. If Rose has had sex and Kate finds out, she will be very harsh with her, and Agnes, as always, wants to protect her. Worse, if Rose becomes pregnant and tells Agnes, this could be another reason they leave: Kate may not allow Rose in the house, and the village priest would certainly condemn the Mundys for having two illegitimate children. While the Mundy sisters briefly reconnect to their bodies in their earlier Dionysiac dance that mourns their marginalized status in an oppressive society, Rose has been forcefully connected to her own body in a pernicious way by Danny Bradley; her probable rape will likely result in her future distancing of herself from her body. Friel thus juxtaposes two potentially fruitful women—Chris and Rose—against the other sisters who are barren, while all of them are essentially locked out of the rich agricultural harvest and Lughnasa festival. Literally and spiritually starving, these women can only look on at the feast and are even fed on by the foxes—Gerry Evans and Danny Bradley— who repeatedly enter their lives to target them.

Whereas Friel grounded his theory of the need humans evince for each other through a shared spirituality in *Faith Healer*, he shows this necessity as well in *Dancing at Lughnasa*, but in a much more ominous way. The decline of the rural community so laden with potential for spiritual renewal at the end of *Faith Healer* is much starker in *Dancing at Lughnasa*. Friel conveys this decline through the motif of leaping, symbolized by the Sweeney boy who is burned during the Lughnasa celebrations in the back hills.

One final implication of leaping in the play remains to be examined—the leap into the unknown all the characters are about to make. As Michael tells us at the end of Act One, "Some of Aunt Kate's forebodings weren't all that inaccurate. Indeed some of them were fulfilled before the Festival of Lughnasa was over" (*DL* 41). The significance of harvest time as a liminal season thus signals the changes about to take place in the Mundy family. In his insightful analysis of the clash between Apollonian and Dionysian forces in the play, F. C. McGrath shrewdly observes that "the regenerative power of the Dionysian is somehow dependent on its destructiveness: the harvest is secured only by means of a sacrificial offering; death and dismemberment are a ritual prelude to renewal."[86] Unfortunately, McGrath does not consider the future "sacrifice" of Father Jack's pending death or the present sacrifice that Rose and Agnes make in leaving the family: he simply invokes "Father Jack's mutilated lepers dancing to appease the Great Goddess Obi" as a past example of dismemberment and sacrifice.[87] Michael further relates that Jack's return home was not because of mental instability but because of the Church's growing wariness about his paganism; observes that Kate would lose her job in the next month; and states that Rose and Agnes would soon leave.

Rose and Agnes leave for a variety of reasons, not the least of which is that they have become redundant. Their hand-knit gloves are no longer needed now that a new, machinized knitwear factory has come to Donegal Town. Older Michael muses that "[t]he Industrial Revolution had finally caught up with Ballybeg" (59). Jim MacLaughlin remarks that the real-life analogues of workers like Agnes and Rose who sewed in the so-called informal sector in early-twentieth-century Donegal "constituted a very important element in the total cash incomes of poor families."[88] Although Vera McLaughlin urges Agnes and Rose to apply for jobs at the new factory, Michael tells us, "They didn't apply, even though they had no other means of making a living, and they never discussed their situation with their sisters. Perhaps Agnes made the decision for both of them because she knew Rose wouldn't have got work there anyway. Or perhaps, as Kate believed, because Agnes was just too notionate to work in a factory. Or perhaps the two of them just wanted . . . away" (ibid.).

Despite these two sisters' financial contributions, the family is already desperate for food. Maggie valiantly tries to jazz up their traditional menu toward the end of the play by offering the usual tea and "Eggs Ballybeg; in other words scrambled and served on lightly toasted caraway-seed bread. Followed—for those so inclined—by one magnificent Wild Woodbine" (*DL* 58). There are only three eggs for eight of them that night and the offer of a cigarette seems not

so much an after-dinner treat, but a very real attempt to stave off
the inevitable hunger pangs associated with too little food. Starva-
tion is the specter haunting this fragile community of sisters, their
brother Jack, and the young Michael. The bilberry picking of Rose
and Agnes is therefore not just the remnant of a lingering pagan tradition but also a necessary addition to the sisters' meager diet, and
Rose's rooster becomes a welcome short-term supply of meat.

Their hunger suggests Friel's poignant critique of agrarianism's
continuing failure in Ireland, at least in part because of the introduction of mechanized labor. There were major advances in Irish
agriculture during the period 1870–1922, particularly the gradual
changeover of land ownership from landlords to tenants, but as farm
holdings increased, small farms declined and farming became more
commercialized.[89] In addition to Father Jack's pending death the
following year, the bitter harvest of this fictional 1936 community
of sisters is the emigration of Rose and Agnes to London to avert
their being a financial burden on the remaining sisters and perhaps
to escape the shame of Rose's probable rape by Danny Bradley and
possible pregnancy. If the potato blight and Great Famine are uncannily prefigured in *Translations*, the legacy of the Famine lingers in
Dancing at Lughnasa. Post-independence Ireland was ravaged by
the civil war and characterized by "abysmally low" agricultural pro-
ductivity, according to Roy Foster.[90] Foster points out that by the
1930s, "The fundamental reality behind the image of rural Ireland
remained that of an emigrating population."[91] He further notes that
the relative population growth of this period "was counteracted by
the rate of emigration: 6 per 1,000 of the total population through
1926–46, with single people, especially women, predominating, and
a pronounced rural-urban drift."[92] Rose and Agnes Mundy thus represent these emigrating, single Irishwomen of the period, forced off
the land by a declining agricultural economy mired in monocropping
techniques and further debilitated by the gradual mechanization of
traditional industry. This is where Friel's affection for rural culture
receives its harshest criticism—from Friel himself. Aware of over-
dependence on this lifestyle—at least in the forms in which it was

practiced in 1930s Ireland—he is lamenting its passing in the form of a dramatic threnody for a community near and dear to him, the Mundy sisters, who were based on his own mother and her sisters.

Michael's final monologue illustrates Friel's conception about the fulfillment of the dramatist's words in "The Theatre of Hope and Despair," which have been epitomized previously by Frank Hardy's enchantment of us as he walks to his death at the end of *Faith Healer*. The "public spell" that Friel wants to cast in his plays is fully realized here, and he invokes a highly aestheticized theory of language in order for the audience to access the spiritual world inhabited by the fictional Mundys. Michael's striving to articulate his memory of his aunts' and mother's dance is more easily understood by Friel's further explanation of the way in which the text of any play should manifest itself:

> [T]hese written words aren't fully empowered until an actor liberates and fulfills them, [and] when that happens . . . then that theatrical language acquires its own special joy and delight; because what is written to be sung is now being sung.[93]

In such a moment, he conceives of language as having complete semantic fulfillment—and, by implication, the Mundy sisters and Father Jack attaining somatic and spiritual wholeness through Michael's final words that body them forth for us. His words acquire a special resonance here when viewed in light of Friel's theory of theatrical language. Michael's most important memory of that time—the dance shared by his mother and her sisters—typically for Friel has an imaginative rather than factual truth to it. As Michael recalls late in the play, "[W]hat fascinates me about that memory is that it owes nothing to fact. In that memory atmosphere is more real than incident and everything is simultaneously actual and illusory" (*DL* 71).

Michael's memories are grounded in "a mirage of sound—a dream music that is both heard and imagined; that seems to be both itself and its own echo; a sound so alluring and so mesmeric that the afternoon is bewitched, maybe haunted, by it" (*DL* 71). In his narrative recreation, his aunts and mother are dancing "more to the mood of the music than to its beat" (ibid.). The final four sentences of Michael's last monologue themselves exemplify the incantatory art of the playwright Friel enjoys deploying. Each sentence begins with the present participle "Dancing," which is coupled three times with "as if," establishing an eternal semantic condition in which the past becomes constantly rendered present in an analogous way to the repetitions in Frank Hardy's last monologue in *Faith Healer*:

> Dancing with eyes half closed because to open them would break the spell. Dancing as if language had surrendered to movement—as if this ritual, this wordless ceremony, was now the way to speak, to whisper private and sacred things, to be in touch with some otherness. Dancing as if the very heart of life and all its hopes might be found in those assuaging notes and those hushed rhythms and in those silent and hypnotic movements. Dancing as if language no longer existed because words were no longer necessary. (*DL* 71)

As Friel remarks above, "what is written to be sung is now being sung." The words dance, on the page and in the mouth of the actor playing Michael. Friel's words "are now fulfilling themselves completely." Their poetic, incantatory power evokes that lost world more richly than more realistic prose ever could. Every time we pick up the script of this play or see it performed, we are reentering that lost world of the Mundys, before Rose and Agnes's emigration, before Gerry's departure for the Spanish Civil War, and before Jack's death.[94]

Michael's freedom in reconceiving and recasting the Mundy sisters' dance reveals how Friel privileges expansion and freedom in the play's conclusion through affirming these qualities in his monologue and contrasting them with the various restricting discourses we have seen the sisters rebel against in their dance. In *Imagining*, Edward Casey argues in remarks directly relevant to Friel's conclusion that "[i]magination multiplies mentation and is its freest form of movement. It is mind in its polymorphic profusion. It is also mind in the process of self-completion, and as such includes an element of self-enchantment."[95] In this memorable, mesmerizing passage, Friel portrays just such a glimpse of an imagining "mind in its polymorphic profusion," whirling round and round, spinning out images of women dancing around that long-ago cottage kitchen. Michael Mundy's mother's and aunts' gift him incantatory, imaginative language, one that even finally enchants him himself. Poor in material things, their courage despite terrible conditions in the 1930s and their use of language to transform their daily lives remains a powerful example of words' ability to change our perception. So this now-grown man paints a picture of the past that is misleading, even mendacious, but finally freeing, a fantastic act of recreation.

But Friel does not let us fully forget that earlier dance: he reintroduces it and the grinning radio Marconi through the hovering kites that fly at the end of the play as Michael performs his incantatory rhetorical magic. In the past of the play, Michael shows his kites to Father Jack, who personifies pagan African culture. We are told, "On each kite is painted a crude, cruel, grinning face, primitively drawn, garishly painted" (*DL* 70). These kite faces recall both the image of Marconi on the 2000 flyer and program for the play at the Abbey Theatre as well as the sisters' faces during their famous dance. Recall Maggie wears "a crude mask of happiness" before she patterns her face with flour (21). As Michael delivers his final monologue, the tableau of his assembled mother, aunts, and uncle are portrayed as "*sway[ing] very slightly from side to side—even the grinning kites. The movement is so minimal that we cannot be quite certain if it is happening or if we imagine it*" (71). This frozen "dance" signifies the stultifying lives that each character will continue to lead in the future, except perhaps Michael. The freedom of the kites, soaring over what is at times a boring life, beckons young Michael just as that long-ago dance did for his mother and aunts. After Father Jack dies and Rose and Agnes leave, Michael admits that "the heart seemed to go out of the house" (70). The house, as we have seen, is something akin to a living organism throughout the play.

But older Michael's final monologue seems to deliberately mislead us about the family's happiness: we know that Rose and Agnes will leave less than a month after the events portrayed in August 1936 (*DL* 41, 60) and that Father Jack will die less than a year later, appropriately, for he is another type of harvest victim, "*on the very eve of the following La Lughnasa*" (60–61). How and why is Michael's mesmerizing concluding soliloquy so deceptive? Casey has articulated the process of how traumatic body memory can be recalled pleasurably, an insight that finally helps us resolve the contradiction between Michael's golden "memory" of his aunts' famous dance and its ugly reality that hovers over his final words in the form of those swaying bodies and grinning kites. Casey observes that "[t]he phenomenon of 'afterglow' refers to the process in which some quite traumatic body memories—which may have been devastating at the moment of origin—will come in the course of time to seem acceptable and even pleasurable to remember."[96] How can this be? Casey notes that our innately human capacity to transform such traumas into recollections enables these memories to "have attained an autonomy sufficient for me to take independent pleasure in reactivating them in . . . these comparatively innocent forms," finally holding that we eventually domesticate such memories through ruminating upon them, then reminiscing about them to ourselves or others. Thus we recreate them:

> When memories, even very painful ones, have become remote from their own point of origin, they often acquire a domesticated quality that encourages our ruminating over them—instead of simply replaying or radically repressing them (i.e., the two most likely ways of treating the memories of recent traumatic events). When we reminisce about them as well (e.g., by narrating them to ourselves or to others), we enter into a ruminescent state; and in turning them over in our minds this way, we tame them yet further—to the point where they become our own *re*-creation.[97]

Michael's final narration, enacted in the radically luminous place of his mind that dwells imaginatively on those sacred places from the past in Donegal, exemplifies this process of rumination, then reminiscence, then additional rumination, thus leading him to literally recreate the memory of the famous dance scene as a pleasurable narrative that he relates as an artist. Unlike Friel's Frank Hardy, whose dwelling on his violent end so unsettles him that he must resort to reciting litanies of the geopathologies of his past to steady him and enable his healing narrative flow, Michael mesmerizes us and believably recreates his aunts' dance as peaceful and stabilizing when in actuality it was anarchic and fragmented. He recreates this memory in order to enchant and heal himself as well and to gather us into community with him even as we remember the bitter, isolated deaths of Rose and Agnes in London, the loneliness of Michael as a child, the confused mentality of Father Jack and then his death, the general marginalization of the Mundy family—all symbolized by their and the kites' swaying movement while Michael chants his lovely, revivifying language to us.

Michael Mundy's final monologue also creates (as does the entire play) a rich receptivity to the flow of everyday life and human beings around us, recognizing the worth of his mother, aunts, and Father Jack, even of the quotidian household objects around them, preparing us for true wisdom. Norman Wirzba has argued that "[i]nsofar as we desire to understand the world . . . we must be prepared to commit ourselves to the world in all its incomparable uniqueness and particularity. . . . Unqualified affirmation presupposes that we allow the world of things and bodies to become fully present to us, to let their demands be felt by us, and that we not distort or block . . . the stream of reality that continually surrounds us. We must also learn to respect the integrity of things by giving them the space to be themselves."[98] Such a receptivity will allow us to open ourselves to love, "for it is in terms of love that the true marks of knowing can emerge: openness, affection, resilience, patience, humility, vulnerability, kindness, intimacy, responsibility, and perhaps most important, repentance."[99] Although it has become commonplace to accept Friel's own argument that his 1960s plays such as *Philadelphia, Here I Come!* were focused on love, the relative rigidity of this category has ensured that relatively little attention has been paid to this theme in his later work. *Dancing at Lughnasa* supremely meditates upon love—for a particular place and time, for singularized, sacralized objects, for family, for ritual, of words, music, and dance—all in the face of despair.

As the play's conclusion so movingly shows, it does not matter for Michael or, by extension, for us if the Mundy sisters' place of 1936 Donegal has literally vanished. It rises up in front of us, teeming with its pleasures and its pains, beckoning to us: "Enter me," it seems to say. And when we do, we enter back into our true selves, reconnecting with our occluded souls and with communities past and present. As Gaston Bachelard has noted about how we daydream about our childhood home(s), "we are never real historians, but always near poets, and our emotion perhaps nothing but an expression of a poetry that was lost."[100] Michael has become, along with Frank Hardy, one of Friel's two most imaginative artist figures through his poetic recreation and loving reimagining of this compelling, frenetic dance through which the sisters briefly reconnect soul to body while mourning their marginalized place in patriarchal, Irish Catholic society.

10

Home and Beyond

Molly Sweeney, The Home Place, and Hedda Gabler (after Ibsen)

> The idea of the "state of rest," of immobility, makes sense only in a world that stays still or could be taken for such; in a place with solid walls, fixed roads and signposts steady enough to have time to rust. One cannot "stay put" in moving sands. Neither can one stay put in this late-modern or postmodern world of ours—a world with reference points set on wheels and known for their vexing habit of vanishing from view before the instruction they offer has been read out in full, pondered and acted upon.
>
> —Zygmunt Bauman, *Globalization: The Human Consequences*

If, as Edward Casey argues in his *Getting Back into Place*, "the modern era . . . brought with it the suppression of place as a central category of human experience,"[1] then Brian Friel's drama seeks to return place to its centrality in our lives. Throughout his long career, he reclaimed a formerly marginal philosophical category by showing how place exerts a consistent call upon us and how we in turn inflect particular places with our desires. Yet criticism on Friel's rich

This chapter includes material reprinted from "Home, Exile, and Unease in Brian Friel's Globalized Drama since 1990: *Molly Sweeney, The Home Place*, and *Hedda Gabler* (after Ibsen)," *Modern Drama* 56, no. 2 (2013): 206–31. Reprinted with permission from University of Toronto Press (https://utpjournals.press), DOI: 10.3138/md.2012-0514, Copyright © 2013 University of Toronto.

theory of place usually has not kept pace with its dynamism and evolution. For example, Helen Lojek argues for a mostly geographical
and postcolonial reading in her thoughtful survey of Friel and place,
holding that his "twenty full-length stage plays map Ireland's divided
self."[2] But such a formulation neglects the trajectory in later Friel,
anticipated in the earlier plays such as *The Enemy Within* and *Philadelphia, Here I Come!*, toward mapping the divided terrain of the
self and attempting to articulate how such selves might nevertheless
cohere in liminal, hybrid spaces often characterized by imaginative
cultural acts despite the continuing pressures exerted by pernicious
aspects of modernity and the accelerating pace of globalization.

Friel's divided characters are often exiles who leave their home
place, and understanding his theory about the artist's relationship to
exile illuminates this dramatic escapism, which is compounded by
many of his characters' simultaneous desire to return home. While
many commentators have pointed out that Friel's Ballybeg, or Baile
Beag in Irish, means "small town[land]," only Ulf Dantanus has also
pointed out that *baile* means "home" as well.[3] Friel has consistently
made clear that home as dwelling in a single, physical, stationary
place is a nearly unattainable concept for himself and his characters.
For example, when Fintan O' Toole asked him in 1982 to define the
concept of home, he quickly responded that "once I would achieve
it and once it would be acquired then I'd be off again."[4] Clearly, by
the early 1980s, home became a mobile concept for Friel, perhaps
temporarily achievable, but which then leads to another search. That
search has driven this study, which has attempted to articulate how
Friel settles the question of the dialectical relationship between home
and exile through his explorations of place. While his characters are
jolted by the unease inherent to a particular period, they often finally
settle into an "ease" with a place—even a place of the mind—in the
midst of modernizing pressures such as technological advances.

Friel's consistent interest in exploring the effects of technology on
well-emplaced selves—ranging from the apprehension expressed by
Gar's father at his son riding in the jet plane in *Philadelphia, Here
I Come!* through the piercing bullets fired at the protesters in *The*

Freedom of the City and the dislocating effects on local Irish culture introduced by English instrumentation in *Translations*, but also the unifying use of the radio in *Dancing at Lughnasa*—suggests its vacillating power to destroy and bring together community. But for the most part, his major plays chart how a too-rapid introduction of technological "innovations" can crush human communication and culture. Citing Michael Benedikt, Zygmunt Bauman has shown how true community at the local level is destroyed by the growing scale and speed of technology: "The kind of unity made possible in small communities by the near-simultaneity and near-zero cost of natural voice communications, posters and leaflets, collapses at the larger scale. Social cohesion . . . depends crucially on early, and strict, education in—and memory of—culture. Social flexibility, conversely, depends on forgetting and cheap communication."[5] Consistently in Friel's work, however, intimacy in the context of remembered culture hallmarks his communities, even when, and sometimes especially when, violence is committed against its members, such as the pending murder of Frank Hardy by the farmers at the end of *Faith Healer*. In such plays and others, "he grasps moments when the source culture from which the Irish were evicted still lurks in the background, and [he] attempts to salvage something of that culture that could still sustain the emptied-out present."[6]

As we have seen, eviction and exile drive Friel's drama, but he instantiates temporary sites of sacredness over against that trajectory. Thus, within the generalized locale of his major plays, Friel establishes sacred places where ritual can flourish and "sustain the emptied-out present," suggesting how such places transcend time itself and catch us up into dynamic community. As Louis Dupré argues, "The higher we ascend to the pure experience of time" through ritual, "the more freely we leap back and forth across the tightly cemented continuance of spatio-temporality."[7] Such rituals occur at the heart of major plays in this study: Gar's "filming" of his last night in Ballybeg in *Philadelphia, Here I Come!*, the ritualistic procession of the three protestors toward their sure death at the end of *The Freedom of the City*, Frank Hardy's slow walk into the intimate immensity of the "stage" of his murder at the end of *Faith Healer*, Maire and Yolland's recitation of place names in Irish to each other in *Translations*, and the double ritual of the Mundy sisters' grotesque dance of grief and its later, golden remembrance by the adult Michael in *Dancing at Lughnasa*. These moments are always transitory in Friel's work, but in showing the possibility for their existence, he maintains the hope of radiant, timeless community, paradoxically in the midst of rapid change.

This study has privileged the category of place as dynamic and populated over against space as inert and depopulated—particularly as phenomenologist Edward Casey has defined place. Place enfolds related issues of time, memory, and history into its bumpy and contested contours. When I discuss spatial movement in performances of the Friel dramas under consideration, I understand such performative movement as part of the ongoing event that is place—whether onstage or in real life. Casey has convincingly claimed that "a place is more an *event* than *thing* to be assimilated to known categories," and further, that "[a]s an event, it is unique, idiolocal. Its peculiarity calls not for assumption into the already known . . . but for the imaginative constitution of terms respecting its idiolocality."[8] Furthermore, conceiving of place as an event assumes that place is populated with living beings—humans, flora, and fauna. Friel's sense of place as an event thus privileges place and its natural rhythms over those more rapid dislocations that his rural characters and their real-life counterparts experienced with the beginnings and subsequent progressive stages of modernism in Ireland.

His long-standing emphasis on place has proven prophetic: much recent Irish drama criticism is centrally concerned with the vexed problem of place, especially given the accelerating pressures put on the concept and the actuality of place since the early 1990s and Ireland's rapid economic ascent, which has turned out to be short-lived. For instance, Martine Pelletier suggests that Friel's *Dancing at Lughnasa* (1990), Donal O'Kelly's *Asylum! Asylum!* (1994), Elizabeth Kuti's *Treehouses* (2000), Emile-Jean Dumay and Dermot Bolger's *Depart et Arriveé* (2004), and Friel's *The Home Place* (2005) all "show characters striving to find a place they could call home in the full sense of the word."[9] Patrick Lonergan has given us the fullest and best analysis so far of globalization's impact on contemporary Irish theatre that deals with issues of place. Lonergan has shown how, beginning around 1990, the date of *Dancing at Lughnasa*'s publication and production, Irish theater began to become more globalized just as the Irish state did. Moreover, he explains how *Lughnasa* was not fully accepted and lauded in Ireland until it had toured Broadway and garnered great acclaim there.[10]

Friel's veritable obsession with place as an unstable, haunting category consistently occupied him throughout his career. In this regard, his oeuvre seems to anticipate what Paul Ricoeur has observed in *Memory, History, Forgetting*:

> Placing and displacing oneself are primordial activities that make place something to be sought out. And it would be frightening not ever to find it. We ourselves would be devastated. The feeling of uneasiness—*Unheimlichkeit*—joined to the feeling of not being in one's place, of not feeling at home, haunts us and this would be the realm of emptiness. But there is a question of place because space is not yet filled, not saturated. In truth, it is always possible, often urgent, to displace oneself, with the risk of becoming that passerby, that wanderer, that *flaneur*, that vagabond, stray dog that our fragmented contemporary culture both sets in motion and paralyzes.[11]

The dialectic between rootedness in a particular place and exile, an active and necessary search shot through with uneasiness as Ricoeur suggests, is at the heart of Friel's major plays, from the first stage play he allowed to remain in print, *The Enemy Within*, to his version of Ibsen's *Hedda Gabler* (2008). But how do Friel's characters actively engage with place as an event, especially given the pressures that globalization has put on place?

Three of Friel's post-*Lughnasa* plays demonstrate how his theory of place has evolved since 1990, and this chapter thoroughly assesses these three plays in this context. The conclusion of *Molly Sweeney* (1994) suggests how the title character has come to be at ease, if not "home," in the vigorous imaginative world of the mind even though her husband Frank is never satisfied with staying in one place for long and has recently moved to Ethiopia, while Friel's last original play, *The Home Place* (2005), and his last work, his adaptation of Ibsen's *Hedda Gabler*, also probe the problem of place in a globalizing context. In *The Home Place*, Friel again (as he did in *Translations*) critiques a technological innovation that promises seemingly great insight into human beings but is reductive (Dr. Richard Gore's craniometer). He also meditates upon the possibility of a stable home in both that play and in his version of *Hedda Gabler*, whose restless heroine performs another Frielian frenzy that leads to her death. In all three of these plays, written during the rapid globalization of Ireland, Friel affirms the creation of dynamic, often heterogeneous communities that transcend the borders of time, space, and sex through the workings of the imagination.

These later plays also consider seriously spiritual issues, including paganism, as we have seen in *Dancing at Lughnasa*. Famously, Friel did not let the Field Day Theatre Company produce *Lughnasa*, where he articulated our need for paganism. Did Friel feel Field Day—dedicated to overcoming sectarianism in Northern Ireland— was unequipped to handle the paganism he privileged in *Lughnasa*? No one seems to have addressed this question in the considerable literature on Field Day, but it is worth asking. Regardless, Friel's later dramas make clear his lasting interest in how ineffable but deep issues of spirituality drive the human condition, as we will see in my analyses of *Molly Sweeney* and *Hedda Gabler*.

Partly because of the great commercial success of *Lughnasa*, later dramas by Friel have not yet received sufficient critical attention, and when they have, they sometimes have been misunderstood in crucial ways. For instance, George O'Brien has argued that Friel's late plays beginning with *Wonderful Tennessee* (1993) display a "heightened sense of place and of theatrical space, most readily evident in Ballybeg's altered standing. Previously, Ballybeg was a site of community. The late plays are largely post-communal, however, making Ballybeg much more liminal." Now, he argues, "Ballybeg is as much a condition as a location . . . a name which instead of designating a place signifies a framework within which outcomes fall through, and the ground upon which Friel's late plays almost, but not quite, articulate a theatre of stasis."[12] I agree with O'Brien that a later play such as *Molly Sweeney*, for example, is "largely post-communal" in a traditional sense of that phrase, but I believe that Friel is redefining the concept of community in such a play by showing how even the condition of solitude, so despised by our supposedly ultra-connected world, can be enabling given an embrace of the active imagination, which can create conversations between the living and the dead and thus populate the mind with a rich community. Molly Sweeney herself enters such a spiritual community in her final monologue in coming to be at ease, if not home, in the vigorous imaginative world of her mind. Even though critics tend to read the conclusion of her final monologue negatively, she, like Friel in his own move from Northern Ireland into the Republic of Ireland and in his consistent examinations of divided selves and nations, affirms "my borderline country . . . where I live now" (*BFP2* 509). Molly's homecoming to herself enables her to rest contentedly in a condition that would drive most people mad who privilege ratiocination above all else.

Molly's satisfaction at having learned to dwell in fluidity on the border between fact and fiction enables Friel, through her, to reject static notions of place and traditional boundaries while similarly rejecting mental illness and utter flux. Dwelling in between these states is a delicate balance she has learned over a long process. And while *The Home Place* suggests a negative, relative stasis in its final portrayal of Christopher Gore, it offers life and movement in the character of Margaret and her relationships, along with the local singers who seem to be briefly liberated from their poverty while singing Thomas Moore's music. Finally, in his reimagining of Ibsen's *Hedda*, Friel upholds the life of the imagination through the emplaced artistic and spiritual collaboration between Thea Elvsted and George Tesman that will enable them to recreate Eilert Loevborg's destroyed manuscript, even as its antiheroine turns in upon herself and performs a frantic dance of death, representing the collapse of the worst aspects of frenetic modernity, which he found rampant in contemporary Ireland.

Instead of O'Brien's conception of Friel's late drama as a condition of near-stasis, I endorse Seamus Heaney's description of Friel's "late style" as one full of movement and life that creates community: Heaney terms it "that final stage of freedom and mastery when technique is second nature, knowledge of life seems to brim over and there is an uncanny sureness . . . a readiness to take risks and trust that the audience will follow," noting that these late dramas "have an uncanny fluidity and airiness about them, at once total play and the truth in earnest."[13] Late Friel has pitched his perennial emphasis on flux to such a level that we, too, in our own fluidity, can enter into the dancing rhythms of these moving plays and into community with these richly drawn characters. In that movement lies not a stationary home, but something like an ease in the dance itself that Friel privileges and into which he invites us as well.

At the end of *Molly Sweeney*, the title character lies in hospital recovering from the severe diminution of her vision after her surgeon, Mr. Rice, has supposedly healed her at her husband Frank's insistence. Molly's surname, "Sweeney," recalls other desperate leapers in Friel's plays, ranging from Gar's Aunt Lizzie Sweeney in *Philadelphia* to the burned Sweeney boy in *Lughnasa*. Here, Friel uses this name to signify how Frank leaps at the chance to "cure" Molly and how the surgery's effects upon her threaten to overwhelm her. Molly's poetic dream-language in the last several pages of the play recalls Michael Mundy's concluding monologue that mesmerizes himself and us in *Dancing at Lughnasa*, but her sheer dependence upon words—not any of the five senses—shows her to have gone beyond Michael in becoming a word-mage. Although she can see almost nothing—she tells us at the beginning of her last monologue that "I certainly wouldn't see the shadow of Frank's hand in front of my face"—she has retreated inward to a fantastic world that briefly makes us believe she can actually see (*BFP2* 507). Then we realize that we are misperceiving the entire situation. She has no real desire or need to actually visually see anymore and Friel favors her dream-scape she weaves for us. In the middle of this monologue, she gives an extremely detailed description of Dan McGrew's wife Lou, who "appeared in a crazy green cloche hat and deep purple gloves up to here (elbow) and eyeshadow half-way down her cheek and a shock-ing black woolen dress that scarcely covered her bum!" (ibid.). What has such language to do with any notion of place, however?

Molly, who had previously been so attached to her home and village that she could negotiate them by sight—so much so that her "home place" was her only comfort zone—now could be anywhere because she is completely at home in language. She only briefly recalls her original home during this last monologue, noting, "They light an odd fire in the house, too, to keep it aired for Frank" (*BFP2* 507). With Frank gone to Africa and with Mr. Rice having left as well, Molly is forced to turn inward and create her new home around her in the sterile hospital through words. She does this through the description of Lou McGrew I have just cited, but also through "see-ing" the ghost of her long-dead mother, who "comes in occasion-ally; in her pale blue headscarf and muddy wellingtons" (508). She muses about her mother, who had been institutionalized in this same hospital for so long it became a sort of home to her, "She spent so much time here herself, I suppose she has an affection for the place" (ibid.). Molly comes to know her mother much more fully after her mother's death than she ever did when she was alive: "But when she sits uneasily on the edge of my bed, as if she were waiting to be summoned, her face always frozen in that nervous half-smile, I think I know her better than I ever knew her and I begin to love her all over again" (ibid.). Just as Michael Mundy in *Lughnasa* has only fully come to know and love his mother and maiden aunts decades after their death, Molly Sweeney has only apprehended the depths of her love for her mother and father (whose ghost also visits) years later. And just as in *Lughnasa*, knowledge and love here are inter-twined and indivisible, but only available in seemingly impossible, cross-generational "conversations" with the dead summoned up by the artist-figure's fertile imagination.

Molly concludes her monologue with a resonant, evocative meditation on place that she immediately qualifies:

> I think I see nothing at all now. But I'm not absolutely sure of that.
> Anyhow my borderline country is where I live now. I'm at home
> there. Well . . . at ease there. It certainly doesn't worry me any more
> that what I think I see may be fantasy or indeed what I take to be
> imagined may very well be real—what's Frank's term—external
> reality. Real—imagined—fact—fiction—fantasy—reality—there
> it seems to be. And it seems to be all right. And why should I ques-
> tion any of it any more? (*BFP2* 509)

Later Friel dramas revel in such ambiguity, as a number of critics
have shown. For instance, drawing on William Demastes's *Theatre
of Chaos*, José Lanters has lucidly analyzed Friel's growing penchant
for indeterminacy. Although she does not explore this condition in
Molly Sweeney, which seems an ideal play for her theory, she recapit-
ulates some of Molly's final words in refusing to distinguish between
real and unreal: "For Friel, art itself, and theatre in particular, is the
closest one can get to that mystery [of possibility] without 'touching'
and thereby destroying it, because theatre, with its actors performing a fictional drama, is created where two paradoxical worlds meet:
being and non-being, fiction and reality."[14] More specifically, Molly's
embrace of that "borderline country" is quintessentially Frielian.

Friel was always personally skeptical of notions of home, and
he even stated repeatedly, "There is no home . . . no hearth . . . I
acknowledge no community."[15] Indeed, his plays show great distrust
of home—from Gar's vacillation between Ballybeg and Philadelphia
to the Mundy sisters' estrangement from official Catholic and unofficial, vernacular Irish culture in *Philadelphia, Here I Come!* and
Lughnasa, respectively. And Molly herself quickly recalls her statement that "I'm at home there," amending it to "at ease there." Given
the fact that her mother in the passage cited above "sits uneasily" on
the edge of Molly's bed when she "visits," and given Friel's consistent

evocation of characters who are *uneasy* within their own culture, Molly's affirmation that she is "at ease" in her "borderline" country has the force of revelation. No longer striving to be "sighted," she sees more clearly than ever through her imagining, dreaming mind.

Realizing her embrace of this populated, imaginative world helps us to reject one line of criticism on the play that argues, "Trusting the men in her life, as so many women do, Molly relinquishes her pleasure, her independence, her unique mastery of her surroundings. She trusts and ceases to exist."[16] Seamus Heaney seems to repeat this misreading of Molly's final condition in his note for the play's production at the Gate Theatre in Dublin in 2011 when he holds that "once Frank sweeps in on Mr. Rice with his request that he perform the operation, and once Mr. Rice allows himself to risk it, her final fatal descent to the mental hospital has started."[17] Claudia Harris's essay on the play features many insights into the various conditions of Friel's female characters, but her monocular pursuit of gender issues leads her to misread its conclusion. Instead of her insistence on Molly's loss of independence because of her trust in men, Friel shows that it is precisely because Molly does not need the men in her life anymore that she can have such imaginative freedom. Heaney tentatively recognizes Molly's imaginative release in her very last lines when he suggests that she "is once again a seer: she knows the presences who come and go at her bedside are fantasies—and yet it is not as clear-cut as that." He continues: "In the final words of the play there are a couple of lines which lay the action to rest, for the audience as well as for Molly: 'Real—imagined—fact—fiction—fantasy—reality—there it seems to be. And it seems to be alright.'"[18]

Occupying this positively but potentially painful liminal position appeals finally to Molly as wordsmith—creator of her own new reality—as well as to her creator Friel. Reading Friel's approval of drama as ritual through the theories of liminality developed by Victor Turner, Richard Pine has argued that when the state of liminality is reached as the "artist, shaman or diviner" occupies the threshold position, he is at his most vulnerable, and the experience is most painful. To conduct the tribe, or even one's incomplete self, from one side of the membrane to the other, demands that the artist become membrane himself, establish the threshold, or medium, by which each world can address the other. The *sacerdos liminalis* is therefore a polyglot, able to translate both worlds, but a citizen in neither.[19]

Although Pine refuses to believe that Molly becomes such a placeless citizen dwelling in liminality,[20] there is considerable evidence that Friel privileges her as a *sacerdos liminalis* who both carries herself and the audience away by her fantastic language. For example, in his diary entries on the evolution of *Molly Sweeney*, he approvingly quotes Carl Jung: "The unexpected and the incredible belong in this world. Only then is life whole. For me the world has from the beginning been infinite and ungraspable."[21] As further evidence of Friel's approval of her condition in the conclusion, Catherine Byrne, the actress who played Molly in the original 1994 production at the Gate Theatre in Dublin, then later that year at the Almeida in London, and after that, in New York, recalls that Friel "wanted hope at the end of *Molly Sweeney*."[22] One critic writing on Byrne's performance suggested in his review for the *New York Times* that she conveys Molly's hope at the end of the play with the concluding image: "On her face, when you last see it, flicker the beginnings of a smile."[23] John C. Kerrigan, whose "Swimming in Words" is otherwise a sensitive appreciation of how the play's "contiguous, overlapping nature" of monologues "enacts a sort of spiritual communion of words that extends outside the bounds of physical presence," thus misapprehends the thrust of its conclusion when he observes, "Despite Molly's tragic end, the play offers the theatergoer the consolation of being carried away by its language."[24] Molly, too, has this wonderful spiritual consolation and therein lies the hope of the play.

The production history of *Molly Sweeney*, which largely accords with Friel's stage directions for a relatively static set, emphasizes the text's privileging of the event of place through actors' monologues; that is, the dynamism of place is created through the shifting iterations of overlapping and sometimes competing versions of Molly's journey from blind to sighted then back to a shadowy world. This dynamism, however, has rarely been recognized by theater reviewers, who have focused largely on the way in which Friel's monologues and staging emphasize the characters' isolation from each other and presumed general stasis. For instance, Karen DeVinney observed how in the premiere production at the Gate Theatre in Dublin during 1994, directed by Friel himself, "when each actor spoke, he or she stood while the others sat on their plain, straight-backed chairs. Each character occupied a personal space of memory that did not overlap with the others." She argues that such staging reinforces the Frielian monologue's insistence on isolation by "making physical for the audience their emotional and, indeed, experiential isolation from each other."[25] Similarly, when the production transferred to London's Almeida Theatre that November, other reviewers noted how its staging produced spatial isolation among the three characters. For instance, Marvin Carlson pointed out how "each had his/her own spotlighted chair against a colored cyclorama with a single suspended window and a small fallen column for scenic background. Molly rarely moved from her chair."[26] This isolation amongst the characters has too often been read as symptomatic of Molly's retreat into passive solipsism, when instead she gains a rich, dynamic mental community in the play's conclusion and a community with the observing audience as well through her newly reclaimed agency. Christopher Murray recognizes her new power when he observes, "Though about to die Molly is mistress of her own world and can admit and exclude those she will."[27]

Out of all the productions of the play so far, the 2011 revival of *Molly Sweeney* at the Gate Theatre, which I saw, has most emphasized the joint consolation and hope for both audience and Molly through its staging. The stark white stage, variously suggestive of Mr. Rice's clinical operating room and the later mental institution where Molly lives, was adorned only with six to eight chairs scattered around. For each monologue, the speaking actor would occupy a chair, while the other two actors would stand up with their backs to the audience. In her review of this production, Sara Keating argued that "Director Patrick Mason attempts to bring movement to the play by having the characters walk slowly between the angled chairs of Paul Keogan's clinical waiting-room setting, but the characters seem limited rather than liberated by the deliberate choreography."[28] But Keating does not realize that each of the three characters' world-view (save for Molly's in the play's conclusion) *is* meant to be limited in certain ways. Such staging created a visual inscription of two audiences—the first, more intimate one of speaking, seated actor with the other two standing, listening actors, and the second, wider one with speaking actor and audience. Mr. Rice and Frank both vie for our attention through their clinical and flamboyant verbal performances, respectively; Mr. Rice even self-consciously sees himself as an artist when he somewhat grudgingly adopts his surgeon friend Bloomstein's insistence that "we're not mechanics. We're artists. We perform" (*BFP2* 488). And when he recalls the seventy-five-minute operation he conducted on Molly, he speaks of it reverently as a miraculous performance: "The darkness miraculously lifted, and I performed—I watched myself do it—I performed so assuredly and with skill, so elegantly, so efficiently, so economically" (489).

Given this production's emphasis on contrasts of white and dark throughout, the words of Friel must largely suffice to create the lived, dynamic place of Molly's evolving mind. Keating helpfully observes that "when Molly is not delivering her lines, she stands for the most part upstage, hand against the wall in a bluish half-light. This is a provocative, stilled image that suggests that Molly is testing the limits of her space." Undoubtedly, this point is true, but when Keating then goes on to conclude that "although by the end of the play she has no interest in pushing the real boundaries of her disability anymore, and has retreated entirely into a fantasy world instead; as if to reflect this, she sits unmoving centre-stage in the final scene," she fails to realize that Molly finally does not see her lack of vision as a "disability" anymore but revels in how it helps her create the new fantasy world she hopefully occupies and imbues with movement through her mind.[29]

Unlike the Almeida production that featured a spotlight on each character's chair, which could imply an equality among the viewpoints expressed by each character, the 2011 Gate production featured a single, dangling light bulb above each character's head, but this light bulb only came on when Molly spoke, thereby privileging her narration as more truthful than the stories told by Mr. Rice and Frank. This visual (and literal) illumination finally allowed this production to show how Molly becomes the real performer in the final scene through the verbal tapestry she weaves in her incantatory last narrative about dwelling in the "borderline country" where she is "at ease." In so doing, she breaks down the metaphorical fourth wall of theater and invites the audience directly into the play to experience both her terror and delight. And as Anthony Roche has articulated about the way in which the spare stage set of the play baffles the audience and enables Molly's agency, "By removing traditional visual properties from the setting, the playwright plunges the audience into the dark and hence into the same position as Molly Sweeney. She is no longer the most disabled but the most enabled of the three characters, positioned to relate directly to the audience and bring them to participate in the world she inhabits."[30]

Friel must privilege her position in this medial zone because her imagination is given full rein, not constrained by the pressures of family, history, or time, yet nonetheless enacts a kind of virtual, imaginative community. Her condition at the end of this remarkable play instead suggests the truth of William James's claim in *The Principles of Psychology* that "the mind is at every stage a theater of simultaneous possibilities."[31] If the place of the stage itself was the height of possibility at the end of Friel's best play, *Faith Healer*, fifteen years later in *Molly Sweeney*, he affirmed the place where his lead character is at ease—and where he himself is—the theater of the mind, a place that the condition of exile can productively create and populate with its own richly imagined characters. As David Richards observed in his review of the original 1994 production, "Isn't this borderline world also that of the poet, the artist, the playwright? If Molly Sweeney is Mr. Friel's most vivid heroine to date, it is, I suspect, because in describing her special vision, he is also delineating his own."[32] In this enlivening and dynamic sense, *Molly Sweeney* affirms the truth of Edward Casey's contention that memory

> not only registers modes of participation between animate and inanimate things, minds and bodies, selves and others, persons and places; it also contributes its own re-enlivening capacities to the festival of cosmic participation. Its very porousness, its open-endedness and ongoingness, its ability to bond deeply across remotenesses of time and space, its own virtual dimension—all of these help to make memory a powerful participatory force in the world. Or more exactly: *as* the world.[33]

Molly Sweeney's particular type of memory, colored by her intense imagining that was precipitated by her blindness, enables her to make the new spiritual world she inhabits so resonantly and powerfully in the play's conclusion.

Given the final imaginative community Friel privileges through memory's "ongoingness" in the conclusion of *Molly Sweeney*, it may seem odd, then, that he would entitle his 2005 drama *The Home Place*. The use of the definite article coupled with both the words Friel habitually flees from in interviews, "home" and "place," connoting an actual, physical site, suggest already a Frielian irony. Does he really believe in the validity of such a phrase? Despite its setting during harvest time, in *"late August"* 1878 (*HP* 11, 8), at The Lodge in Ballybeg, where "most of the action takes place on the unkempt lawn" (8), *The Home Place*, through its negative depiction of Dr. Richard Gore, who is "from the home place in Kent" (39), and much more sympathetic portrayal of his cousin, Christopher Gore, ironizes any stable sense of home and suggests instead that "home" may be best signified through the fleeting music sung by Clement's choir. Once again, "a whiff of unease" (25) is in the air, in this case, because of agrarian unrest in 1878 County Donegal. Yet this drama is no exercise in nostalgia: as Lonergan has shown, *The Home Place* may enact a conversation with issues of place in contemporary, globalizing Ireland, especially given its performance seven months after the Irish government's 2004 referendum that redefined Irish citizenship, stripping it from Irish immigrants whose children were born in the country after June 2004.[34]

The 2017 Irish Repertory Theatre's New York production of *The Home Place* directed by Charlotte Moore led Terry Teachout to conclude that "to see it is to come away certain that 'The Home Place' is one of Mr. Friel's half-dozen masterpieces."[35] It is hard to disagree with Teachout's assessment: *The Home Place* is classic Friel in its brilliantly realized depictions of what it means to be human, and thus a spiritual being, and what constitutes home in a divided society. Its rejection of empirical modernity's excesses and affirmation of emplaced community life links it to other Friel masterpieces such as *Translations*, whose depiction of an earlier divided community in the context of an imperial measuring endeavor must have inspired it in part.

A series of characters in the play are shown to be estranged from their original homes: Margaret and Christopher Gore, in particular, epitomize the way in which they have recreated a life for themselves at The Lodge that members of their original communities cannot understand. When the local girl Sally wonderingly asks Margaret, "Do you never go home now at all, Maggie?" (*HP* 13), we realize that Margaret has made her life at The Lodge her home since she arrived there at the age of fourteen. Her attitude toward the violent Con, who is courting Sally, epitomizes her disconnection from the local community outside The Lodge. She terms Con a "wastrel" and accuses him of "trespassing" on Lodge land early in the play, finally threatening to send Sally "back down below herding your one cow" when Sally exclaims, "You'd do anything to be one of the toffs, Maggie, wouldn't you?" (16).

Margaret's relationship with David, son of Christopher Gore, patriarch of The Lodge, ostensibly recalls that of the Irish character Maire who desperately wants to learn English and the English character Yolland who values local Irish culture in *Translations* because Margaret has embraced the Englishness of this home and its grounds and David, the local life of Ballybeg. Margaret knows that Christopher also loves her, and her realistic hybridity and that of Christopher consigns them to a liminal zone outside the world of the local agrarian Irish agitators and the racist mindset of the English Richard Gore, who sees all Irish as primitives. Margaret does not want to return to the life of the village and Christopher does not really want to return to his "home place," Kent, even though he is a bit homesick for it at one point. They value The Lodge's liminality, metaphorically halfway between the Irish Ballybeg and the English Kent, just as Molly Sweeney comes to be at ease in her psychological borderland.

Christopher fears that there is a list of local landlords who will be killed shortly, and he poignantly tells Margaret after relating the story of Lord Lifford's murder, probably by men allied with the burgeoning Irish Land League movement of the 1870s and 1880s, "I love this place so much, Margaret. This is the only home I've ever known" (*HP* 18). As he goes on to muse, "The truth is I *hated* being shipped over to the home place every damned summer," but then he admits that after relating his childhood memories of Kent the previous night at supper, "all those memories of Kent—they almost made me homesick" (19). Late in the play, he comments to Margaret in language very similar to the description of County Kent in Friel's *Making History*,

> I can't tell you how beautiful the home place is at this time of year. And how tranquil. And how—replete. The orchards; and the deer park; and the lines of bee-hives in the pampered walled garden; and the great placid fields of wheat and oats and barley. A golden and beneficent land. Days without blemish. Every young man's memory, isn't it?—or fiction?—or whatever. Your father hasn't a monopoly on romance and easy sentiment. I'm an exile from both that memory and this fact now, amn't I? (62–63).

As he acknowledges by the end of the play, he is effectively locked out of that landscape and house and is close to being exiled from his current home place in Donegal.

The stage set used in the Dublin and London premieres emphasized that pending exile for Christopher Gore and his landlord class.
For example, Charlotte Loveridge pointed out in her 2005 review of
the play at London's Comedy Theatre after its transfer from Dublin's
Gate Theatre earlier that year,

> The set is stunningly beautiful, portraying a parlour room on the
> periphery of an immense framed opening onto the outside land.
> This seems a visual reflection of England's presence in Ireland—
> a partial and adequate colonization. Slightly asymmetrical paral-
> lel tree trunks dominate the background. They are the "doomed"
> trees whose fate comes to represent Christopher's class.[36]

That stage set emphasized the doom of Christopher Gore's English
landlord class represented by the incomplete fusion of the domestic
English parlor and the imported English trees outside.

More intriguingly, the lush landscape of Christopher's home
place in Donegal effectively competed with his evocative memory
of Kent through the different set used in the American tour. In his
review, Matthew A. Everett praised Frank Hallinan Flood's set for
the 2007 production of *The Home Place* at the Tyrone Guthrie Theater in Minneapolis, noting that audiences often applaud Flood's set
when the play opens

> because it's gorgeous. The façade of a stone house, cracked open so
> the audience can see inside without obstruction, surrounded quite
> literally by a small forest of different types of trees. It's lush, just
> like a photograph out of a book. An added bonus is that some real
> trees are mixed in with some fabricated ones, so if you sit close
> enough, you can actually smell the set—the scent of the outdoors,
> lingering indoors.[37]

Such a lovely intrusion of the natural world that threatens to overwhelm the domesticated Planter world of The Lodge is warranted
from Friel's set directions: "*A crescent of trees encloses the entire*

house and lawn; it seems to press in on them. This meniscus is most dense down stage left" (*HP* 8). The crack in the house's façade and the pressing trees could suggest how the local natives will take back over eventually from their landlords on the eve of the Irish Land League's pending Land Wars beginning in 1878, the time of the play. More interestingly, Friel may have been implying how unruly nature always will creep back into man's settlements—be they English, Irish, or of any nationality.

If Margaret and Christopher occupy a space of hybridity, betwixt and between Irish cultural life and English cultural life, characters like Richard Gore and Con and Johnny MacLoone symbolize reductive conceptions of home that are based upon false notions of purity. Such a reductive notion of place is anticipated by Molly Sweeney, who finally rejects a concept of home privileged by the sighted in favor of an imagined verbal world. In *The Home Place*, Friel again critiques the representatives of an empiricist philosophy, as he did in *The Freedom of the City* and *Translations*. The imperialistic English Richard Gore sees all the local Irish, such as the servant Sally, as "a primeval people really" (*HP* 31), and his anthropometric work with the craniometer allows him distance from them, enabling him to treat them as specimens, not fellow human beings. In his review of the Irish Repertory Theatre's 2017 production of the play, Teachout points out that Richard Gore is "a heartless anthropologist who has come to Ballybeg to measure the skulls of the natives, conducting himself very like Henry Higgins in 'Pygmalion,'" observing further, "Small wonder that his mere presence incites them to violence: He is the living symbol of the cold modernity that will soon lay waste to the village life that Christopher treasures."[38] Friel clearly rejects Richard Gore's reading of personality through face and bodily form, and he further exposes this pseudo-science by including an excerpt of Professor A. C. Haddon's "research" published in his *Studies in Irish Craniology: The Aran Islands, Co. Galway* as an appendix in the Gallery Press edition of his play (*HP* 76–79).[39]

Con and Johnny MacLoone, who represent local Irish culture, represent the ideological counterparts of Richard Gore and his helper Perkins because they too physically insist on notions of purity as categories into which humans can be slotted, regardless of their complexity. Richard Gore is portrayed as taking *"the measurement efficiently and brusquely"* of Christopher's tenant Maisie in Act Two (*HP* 50) and as rapping *"Tommy's head sharply with his knuckles"* while measuring him (54), while the watching Con and Johnny finally threaten physical violence if the anthropologist and Perkins do not leave. Con quietly asks Christopher to have his cousin stop the measurement of Tommy and, when a bewildered Christopher tries to laugh it off, tells him ominously, "We have no quarrel with you, Mr. Gore. But I'm not going to say this again. Tell your cousin to pack his things and leave. Himself and his assistant" (ibid.). Con then orders Mary, Maisie, and Tommy home. When Perkins tries to throw Con out, Johnny displays a cudgel, and Christopher's language makes clear that Con and Johnny are akin to later Irish republicans by stating, "I understood you came here as a volunteer. I now suspect you are here to make a political gesture." (56). The use of "volunteer," often used in the twentieth century to designate a member of the Irish Republican Army, marks Con and Johnny as successors to earlier Friel characters such as the violent Donnelly twins in *Translations* and the republican predecessors of those who perceive Friel's characters trapped in the Derry Guildhall as martyrs in *The Freedom of the City*. In all three cases, these violent characters react strongly against representatives who engage in empirical judgments and represent the British Empire in some way or another. When Con informs Christopher that three men are waiting below to help them if need be, Christopher orders Richard and Perkins to leave, and Richard asks, "Are you betraying me, Christopher?," repeating a loaded word that occurs in various forms throughout the play and that is used by characters who preach purity of affiliation (58).

Christopher's admission about Clement O'Donnell that "we don't share a language" (*HP* 67) recalls the linguistic difficulties of *Translations* and implies that the cultural opening he and Margaret have made and shared for a time between English and Irish communities is closing; he is consigned to a condition of "no home, no country, a life of isolation and resentment. . . . The doomed nexus of those who believe themselves the possessors and those who believe they're dispossessed" (68). While Friel clearly privileges Molly Sweeney's placelessness as a condition of the artist dwelling in liminality, he sympathizes with Christopher Gore's stateless condition, which to some degree he shared as a writer born in the United Kingdom (Country Tyrone, Northern Ireland), but who lived in the Republic of Ireland (County Donegal) beginning in the late 1960s. In this regard, Charles Spencer noted in his review for the *Daily Telegraph* of the 2005 London production that Tom Courtenay, who played Christopher Gore, conveyed a lovable haplessness with which the playwright sympathizes: "His cracked voice and ineffectual hand gestures beautifully conjure up a particularly lovable kind of English eccentricity and Friel's evident sympathy for the character, who by the end painfully realizes he has no real home in either England or Ireland, proves deeply moving."[40] Unlike Molly Sweeney, however, who successfully occupies her "borderline country" at the conclusion of that play, this landlord can no longer stay in a liminal, mediating place between two cultures—English and Irish.

Christopher's commitment to carrying out the thinning of trees on his property at the end of the play sadly implies that he is regressing into the language of the original English Planters, whose records he finds and quotes from. His chilling statement that "first thing is to identify the specimens. They'll be distinctive. And they'll need most space. Any tree that encroaches on their territory will have to go" recalls his cousin Richard's remarks about the locals earlier in the play (*HP* 70). When David accidentally splashes the whitewash they are using to mark the trees that they will cut down on his father's chest and the record of the trees' planting too (73), we realize that Christopher Gore and the entire way of life he represents has been marked for felling too—that he and the Planters' culture will die. The imminent felling of trees, this man, and a particular culture are, appropriately for a writer often called "the Irish Chekhov," eerily reminiscent of the end of *The Cherry Orchard*, where the thudding axes of the woodsmen outside symbolize not just the felling of the beloved orchard but the collapse of a centuries-old way of life for the Russian aristocracy. As contemporary Ireland continues to experience immigration that irreversibly changes its landscape and population, Friel's lament for the pending death of Christopher Gore and qualified sympathy for Planter culture in the Ireland of the 1870s and 1880s in the face of both British and Irish representatives of racism suggest how contemporary proponents of an imagined Irish racial purity irrevocably damage the possibility of flourishing, heterogeneous communities.[41]

If dancing becomes the ideal condition in which to dwell at the end of *Dancing at Lughnasa* and if that condition is represented through Molly's dreamscape at the end of *Molly Sweeney*, it is finally music, specifically Thomas Moore's music, that becomes a place of ease nonetheless shot through with some tension, as we will see, for Clement O'Donnell and his singers in *The Home Place*, if not their real home. Such a temporary, performative space, however, is rendered both politicized and transcendent because of Moore's romanticism. When Margaret vows to go home to her father, Clement, after telling Christopher she loves David, we see her movement out of the liminal zone of the Lodge and the hyphenated identity that it represents and back toward local Irish culture. Anna McMullan has convincingly argued that Margaret is "caught between legacies: that of the Lodge, already a choice of the son over the father, and that of her own father, who though himself in decline through alcohol abuse, is the guardian in turn of the musical legacy of Thomas Moore. Indeed, it is perhaps through the claiming or reclaiming of occluded legacies that *The Home Place* poses the question of home."[42]

Friel was particularly alert to how Moore's songs were intertwined with questions of home in Ireland. He wrote perceptively about Moore's *Melodies* in the context of introducing John O'Donovan's letters that the topographer wrote during the 1835 Ordnance Survey of Donegal, arguing that "the tenth and final edition of Tom Moore's *Irish Melodies* appeared in 1834, the year before O'Donovan immersed himself in the place-names of Donegal and because both men were engaged in similar pursuits: Moore had done with his songs what O'Donovan was doing with his place-names." Moreover, Friel approvingly cites Seamus Deane's contention in the *Field Day Anthology of Irish Writing* that "'Moore was the most outstanding figure in the long process of transformation that had begun in the eighteenth century and was to be carried on into the twentieth— the transformation of one culture into the idiom of another while attempting to preserve in the old idiom as much as possible of the old culture.'"[43] Based on this reading of Moore, Friel also sees the character of Moore in *The Home Place* as an agent of transformation who might "preserve in the old idiom as much as possible of the old culture," a qualified endorsement of Moore's ability to translate into English well-loved Irish phrases and melodies, temporarily anchoring those in Ireland caught between their linguistic past and their linguistic future—much as he posits O'Donovan "pinned those names down and gave them a pedigree and endowed them with some permanence."[44] As Csilla Bertha has argued in a sensitive essay focusing on memory and music in *The Home Place*, "Friel's play makes audiences aware of the impossibility of going back to any pure, authentic source culture as Moore's poems and songs themselves grew out of both Irish and English traditions." Thus, "despite all the irony Moore's songs and the play's choir director are imbued in, Moore's oeuvre does hold a mirror up to the Irish caught between those traditions."[45] There is undoubtedly linguistic and cultural loss here, as is also depicted in *Translations*, but also "some permanence" for Friel in these two cultural moments he was pondering in the early to mid-2000s: the 1834 publication of the tenth edition of Moore's *Melodies* and the local Donegal residents' singing and rehabilitation of those melodies in the context of the Land League in 1878.

Clement's comment that "the music liberates them briefly from their poverty, Mr. Richard. . . . When they sing they fashion their own ethereal opulence and become a little heavenly themselves" (*HP* 40) suggests his belief in how music can free us from material conditions and establish a temporary place of refuge in the imagination. Even though he admits that Thomas Moore was "a romantic man and given to easy sentiment, as I am myself," he claims that "he has our true measure, Mr. Richard. He divines us accurately. He reproduces features of our history and our character" (42). Clement gently tells Richard Gore here that music, not metrics, is the measure of the man, hinting that art gives us truer insight into the real character of human beings than any scientific instrumentalism ever can.[46] At the same time, what Simon Kress terms Moore's "sentimental nationalism" also registers the political presence of the local Catholic Irish culture in the play and the injustices that have been committed against them by many of the local landlords, if not by the Gores. Kress is particularly convincing when he argues that song's presence in "Irish cultural discourse" in general displays "a profoundly generative ambivalence, which allows a poem or song to sound in two registers—the universal and the local—that in turn sound off each other, infusing one with the sentimental charge of political injustice, and providing the other with an aura of transcendence."[47]

Because of this series of movements—the (qualified) liberating quality of Moore's music for its singers, Christopher Gore's reclamation of his dying Planter heritage, Margaret's trajectory back toward local Irish culture—I would argue against George O'Brien's claim above that Friel's late plays come very close to "articulat[ing] a theatre of stasis." Instead, they tentatively suggest models of gradual movement away from staid conceptions of space and into the more figurative, imaginative place of the mind, whether it be in the imagined, hopeful future for Catholics in Northern Ireland, in Gore's negative, increasing identification with his Planter past, or in Margaret's hope of rejoining her local community.[48]

In conclusion, I would like to explore Friel's 2008 translation of Ibsen's *Hedda Gabler* to show how he continues to probe issues of place and displacement, rootedness and alienation, affirmative and negative spirituality, particularly through the character of Hedda herself. Hedda symbolizes both a pernicious aspect of modernism and a destructive paganism because of her association with control and brisk efficiency, and with fire and Dionysian rites—especially the evolution of the tarantula myth—respectively. In his adaptation of Ibsen's classic, Friel seeks to create an atmosphere of unease in what

Fintan O'Toole has called his "complete rethinking of the text." O'Toole argues that Friel's substitution of a new line for Aunt Juliana at the very beginning of the play—"I was afraid of that," instead of Ibsen's "Why, I don't believe they're up yet"—functions "as a simple and subtle harbinger of unease, a sign that all is not right."[49] In this sense, Friel's *Hedda Gabler* opens in a similar fashion to his *Dancing at Lughnasa* when the young Michael Mundy voices his fear in his opening monologue that "even though I was only a child of seven at the time I know *I had a sense of unease*, some awareness of a widening breach between what seemed to be and what was, of things changing too quickly before my eyes, of becoming what they ought not to be" (*DL* 2; my emphasis). The multiple circles of place in *Lughnasa* centripetally enfold those characters and temporarily emplace them into their bodies and into a series of concrete yet dynamic spaces such as the cottage, the back hills, and even Ryanga, Africa. But in Friel's *Hedda*, Hedda herself seeks to become the embodied "place" around which the other characters circle, only to see her controlling actions spiral out of control centrifugally and wreak havoc on all the characters before they (especially George and Thea) move toward each other and create a place of spiritual community as soul mates in lovingly reconstructing the dead Eilert Loevborg's manuscript.

Friel was likely also drawn to Hedda's near-constant efficiency, restlessness, and control as reflective of the increasingly alienated and individualistic Victorian (and by extension, modern) age, just as he was to Gar's near-constant mental and physical activity to portray modernity's penchant for speed in *Philadelphia, Here I Come!* and Lancey's and Yolland's father's bureaucratic efficiency in *Translations* to depict British imperialism. Friel signals such restlessness throughout *Hedda*: in his perspicacious review of the play, O'Toole, for example, points out that Aunt Juliana defends Hedda's having unpacked her own trunks rather than letting the servant Bertha do it by archly observing, "'She's a very efficient young woman.'"[50] Hedda's frustrated attempts at control are perhaps epitomized by a passage early in Act One after Aunt Juliana has just told Hedda and George that she will come to see them every day: Hedda *"paces the room in scarcely controlled fury, her arms raised above her head, her fists clenched"* (HG 23). She is angry at what she sees as Juliana's interference in their lives and, even more, at something she can control even less—her pregnancy. Most important, Hedda's selfishness and rejection of community—including that of her husband and her unborn child—exemplify that condition of the solipsistic self that is exiled from community, including spiritual community, that Friel always takes pains to critique. Such a condition symbolizes modernity's emphasis on what Seamus Deane calls "the cult of the individual" that leads not to "personal fulfillment," but makes a "virtue of alienation and a fetish of integrity."[51]

Moreover, Hedda's association with fire throughout the play suggests both her power to inspire and destroy those around her: while at first she inspires her husband, George, and his competition, the scholar Eilert Loevborg, she is finally the figure of the demonic in the play that finally unleashes death on Loevborg and on herself. Repeatedly, Friel portrays Hedda as having a personality that smolders beneath a seemingly cool and unruffled surface. J. R. Northam has shown how, as Ibsen progressed through drafts of the play, he gradually associated Hedda with the stove to complement her past threat when she was schoolmates with Thea to burn her hair and her future act of burning Eilert's manuscript.[52] Northam argues that the scene where Hedda burns the manuscript "brings together all the earlier references, verbal and visual, to fire, burning of hair, all the hints of violent, dangerous reaction to emotional frustration, hatred of her unborn child."[53] In *Dancing at Lughnasa*, Friel deploys images of fire in multivalent ways to suggest "the malaise of the island as a spiritual disease"—the anarchic, even destructive qualities of the Lughnasa fire that burns young Sweeney; the heat of the sun, which director Patrick Mason has termed "unusually Mediterranean for Donegal"; the heat associated with the radio Marconi; and the turf fire inside the Mundy cottage, which provides light, heat, and the power to cook food for the family.[54] In his version of *Hedda Gabler*, Friel again portrays spiritual malaise through fire imagery, but now he associates it with a particular strand of European modernism more generally. If, as Toril Moi has argued, *Hedda Gabler* exposes the vacuity of idealist aesthetics in Hedda's rejection of the "idealist opposition between female sacrifice and male heroism," the play also shows how "the everyday has turned poisonous, and idealism has become an incomprehensible anachronism."[55] Taking Northam's understanding of Hedda's association with heat and inspiration together with Moi's apprehension of late Ibsen's caution about the everyday as a site of transcendence, we see how Hedda's fiery frustration with the quotidian makes her a figure of veneration for the men in the play who see her as a site of exotic excitement even as she attempts to control them and everyone around her.

Furthermore, if we follow James McFarlane in seeing Hedda as a "pagan priestess" officiating at a Dionysian rite,[56] then we perceive how she is also officiating at the shrine of the destructive side of paganism that is incompatible with quotidian, routinized modernism. In this sense, Friel's portrayal of paganism as destructive in *Hedda Gabler* opposes his position in *Lughnasa* where he sought to demonstrate the positive aspect of paganism in daily life as a necessary resource that beneficially disrupts civility and organized religion.

Our understanding of Hedda Gabler as a priestess figure presiding over a contemporary series of Bacchanalian rites—with the potential power and agency of Molly Sweeney in her liminal position—is heightened when we realize how closely Ibsen and thus Friel might be linking Hedda to the mythology of the tarantula. This mythology is first evoked in Ibsen's portrayal of Nora's tarantella in *A Doll House*, later in Molly Sweeney's wild dancing, and now in Hedda's manic piano playing. John Crompton has suggested in *The Life of the Spider* that "Bacchanalian rites flourished" near Taranto, Italy, where there were many tarantulas. Apparently, "the priestesses of the rites dressed, and acted, much as the victims of the bite of the tarantula. Then the authorities decided to stamp out these orgies, which were merely an excuse for a sexual debauch," but the priestesses invented the story of the necessity for dancing out the poison of the tarantulas in order to maintain the rites.[57] Even more interesting is the mating habit of the tarantula, which hunts a mate in "the heat of August" and after breeding with a male, generally kills and eats him.[58] Hedda thus functions as both priestess and preying spider in her desire to see Eilert Loevborg covered in vine leaves (an image from the Dionysian revels) and then in her metaphorical devouring of him through her urging him on to suicide during this harvest season (the play is set in early September). As in so many of Friel's plays set during harvest season (such as *Philadelphia, Here I Come!*, *Faith Healer*, *Translations*, and *Dancing at Lughnasa*), this harvest season too will feature victims reaped, cut down, in the prime of their lives—both Eilert and Hedda.

Friel may have also been led to *Hedda Gabler* by the title character's frantic playing of the piano in the conclusion, which recalls Molly Sweeney's manic dancing shortly before she has her eye surgery. Molly's words at the party the evening before her operation suggest the similar situation that Hedda finds herself in at the end of Ibsen's play when her husband, George, and her friend Thea resolve to work together to reconstruct the dead Eilert Loevborg's destroyed manuscript, which will leave her alone, *placeless*, and exposed to the affections of Judge Brack. Molly muses, "I wondered—I wondered would I ever be as close to them [Frank and Mr. Rice] as I was now. . . . And then I knew, suddenly I knew why I was so desolate. It was the dread of exile, of being sent away. It was the desolation of homesickness" (*BFP2* 473). Molly, of course, has this fear long before her concluding affirmation of being "at ease" in a verbal world of delight. Because she is so fearful of not being as close to Frank and Rice as before, of being exiled from her deep knowledge of them, Molly screams, "'Now watch me! Just you watch me!' And in a rage of anger and defiance I danced a wild and furious dance round and round that room; then out to the hall; then round the kitchen; then back to the room again and round it a third time. Mad and wild and frenzied. But so adroit, so efficient. No timidity, no hesitations, no falterings. . . . Weaving . . . with absolute confidence" (ibid.). We mourn with Molly here as she dances the death of her old self, but we rejoice with her later as a new self emerges from the ashes of that failed operation.

But Hedda is a character we love to hate, and as she plays her manic music toward the end of Friel's translation, we are not caught up in her frenetic energy as we are with Molly (or even with the mourning Mundy sisters in *Lughnasa*), but recoil from her, whereas we emotionally move toward George and Thea and the emplaced community they are gradually forming. George has earlier thrust himself into an exaggerated, comic activity when Hedda tells him that she burned Eilert's manuscript to protect George's reputation and that she is pregnant: now we are told that these bits of information "*collide in his head and detonate. Now he is suddenly released—propelled—hurled into exaggerated manic activity*" (HG 89–90). George's "buffoonery" (90) stems from his great happiness at what he perceives as Hedda's generosity in burning the manuscript (Eilert's symbolic "child") and having his real child, but her reaction to his manic energy is telling: "*During all this extravaganza Hedda sits absolutely still, rigid, upright, her eyes closed tight, her face a mask*" (ibid.). George trots out one potential baby name after another and speculates about a series of potential activities for their child, such as horse-riding and piano playing (90–91). After these extended imaginative riffs, Hedda is still portrayed as "*(still rigid, eyes closed tight, body erect)*," and she now moans, "Oh God . . . dear God . . . oh dear God." (91). She is realizing that her role in the household will soon change—that she will be mere "mother" rather than "Hedda" or "the General's daughter." And worse—that this new role may lock her into it and that she may never escape it. No more pistol shooting, no more manipulating other people's lives.[59] Just maternal domesticity. Every bit of her rebels against this looming role in which she will have a marked loss of agency. Her closing manic piano playing signals her fear that she will become prey to Judge Brack's advances and signifies her jealousy as George and Thea increasingly spend time together reconstructing Eilert's manuscript, with these latter two forming a deep, ensouled relationship she has never had with George.

Early in the play, Thea unburdens herself to Hedda about this relationship, noting, "We wrote that book together; six hours a day for eighteen months. 'Collaborators'—that was his name for us. And during that eighteen months I discovered that our deliverance was more than just a liberation. It had within it an approval, maybe even a *benediction* on what we were doing together: Thea and Eilert, collaborators." (*HG* 33; my emphasis). In the play's conclusion, Hedda clearly links Thea's new collaborative work with George to her earlier work with Eilert, taunting her with that memory, but then finally despairingly asking, "So I'm of no use to you two soul-mates?" (101), repeating Thea's earlier spiritual language—"benediction"—to describe her collaboration with Eilert.

Friel clearly privileges Hedda's spirituality in her plangent question to Thea and George cited above where she terms them "soul-mates" in Friel's version. Other well-known translations do not describe them spiritually at all: Rolf Fjelde's popular translation for Signet simply calls them "the two of you," while Jens Arup's translation for the Oxford World's Classics edition is even more banal—"you two." Rick Davis and Brian Johnston's translation for the Norton critical edition of Ibsen's *Selected Plays* is the same as Arup's translation: "you two."[60] Friel clearly registers not only Hedda's quotidian predicament—"What will I do alone here every evening?"—but also what he perceives as her spiritual dilemma.[61] Hedda correctly senses that Thea and George are united spiritually in deep and sustaining ways that she never has been with George as his wife.

Toril Moi's reading of the tarantella Ibsen's Nora dances in his earlier play *A Doll House* offers crucial insights into Hedda's similar wild piano playing shortly before she kills herself—including how Friel captures Hedda's longing to be recognized as an ensouled figure of agency. Drawing on Stanley Cavell's study *Contesting Tears: The Hollywood Melodrama of the Unknown Woman*, Moi perceives Ibsen's Nora, in an interpretation relevant to understanding Hedda's manic piano playing and suicide, as "a reaction to the fear of the 'extreme states of voicelessness' that can overcome us once we start wondering whether we can ever manage to make others recognize and acknowledge our humanity." We have seen such a reaction before in Friel—notably in the Mundy sisters' repeated dancing in *Dancing at Lughnasa* as they try to express their humanity even as it is being denied all around them by forces outside of their control. Just as Nora "has to try to assert her existence by finding a voice, by launching into what Cavell elsewhere calls her 'cogito performance,' an aria-like expression of her soul intended to proclaim, declaim, declare her existence," so too must Hedda, and thus we can read her wild piano playing as that "aria-like expression of her soul," an anguished cry at her soul-exclusion from Thea and George in their imagined future.[62] As Moi posits, Cavell's argument suggests how the "melodramatic obsession with states of terror, of suffocation, of forced expression, expresses fear of human isolation, of being reduced to a thing, of death."[63] This is exactly Hedda's fear, and in response, associating herself again and finally with "a thing"—her father's revolvers—she "reduces" herself to death. Thus she preserves her (by then greatly limited) agency till the end to spare herself from being prey to Judge Brack's advances, after he suggestively says "nothing would pleasure me more" than to "entertain" Hedda while Thea and George work (*HG* 101).[64] We quickly recognize Hedda's sense of the melodramatic when we read or view the play; but more often than not, there may be a tendency to dismiss her real sadness and wistfulness at being excluded from Thea's friendship and companionship with her husband in the conclusion because of her posturing throughout.

Much like Nora in *A Doll House*, who is often reduced by the men around her—especially her husband, Torvald—to mere embodiment, so is Hedda, but in both cases, these compelling female characters are much more than sheerly objectified bodies, a view that is essentially pornographic. Rather, they are embodied souls. Moi's reading of Nora crucially captures this spiritual aspect of her over against the romantic fantasy of soul commingling with bodily contact and, at the other extreme, the postmodern rejection of any soul-talk as "a merely metaphysical construct."[65] I follow Moi in appropriating Wittgenstein's argument—for Nora, and by extension, for Ibsen's and Friel's Hedda—that "the human body is the best picture of the soul."[66] Just because we do not actually see Hedda playing this manic dance tune (unlike the fully visible dancing of Nora's tarantella) should not lessen its sense of soul-anguish, as she physically pounds the piano keys and speaks to the others behind the curtains that shield her from their inquiring gazes. The percussive taps of the keys anticipate the pending percussion of the pistol with which she shoots herself. Hedda's authentic soul-music rings out loudly at the end of Friel's play—more richly than it does in any previous translations of this scene—and he clearly laments her demise and the others' refusal to recognize her as an embodied, ensouled fellow human being. At the same time, he witheringly suggests how Hedda represents a restless, inward-turning modernity that finally rejects spiritual possibilities—just as the other major characters do for her—in favor of a shriveled, individualistic agency she affirms in destroying herself.[67]

As George and Thea try to decipher Eilert's handwriting in his notes, "*Hedda begins playing a wild, near-manic dance on the piano*" (*HG* 101).[68] Always attempting to alleviate boredom, Hedda typifies how Ibsen's "last plays investigate the various ways in which a human life can become frozen, static, immobile, meaningless."[69] Often concerned to depict meaningful life as in flux, Friel rejects Hedda's final frenzy as the dying throes of a life of frustrated stasis and privileges instead the natural, communal rhythms of everyday life epitomized by George and Thea's growing relationship with each other. Hedda's restlessness—perhaps symbolizing contemporary Ireland's frenetic pace for Friel—has now turned in upon itself, and she finally shoots herself with the brisk efficiency she has always displayed. She believes she has enacted the unique, beautiful death that she urged upon the suicidal Eilert, who shoots himself in the stomach in Ibsen's play and in the groin in Friel's version (98), yet her failed effort to purify, through her manic piano playing, the poison of modernist narcissism and of jealousy from her veins renders her victim of her own created mythology, suggesting that rather than a singular artistic act, her suicide functions as a mimetic, passive enactment of a discredited myth. In this sense, Friel's critique of Hedda's frenzied, violent, modernist individualism brings his career full circle as it accords with his rejection of the Christian monk Columba's previously held and similarly excessive and bellicose individualism in *The*

Enemy Within. Each play enacts its critique in the context of early and late globalization, respectively.

Because he was consistently interested in questions of literal and figurative fertility, Friel likely was drawn to both Hedda's pregnancy and to the question of artistic fertility often raised in the play and associated negatively with Hedda as a symbolic pagan priestess/spider and destructive inspirer. Thus, he almost certainly affirms the play's movement away from her solitary, manipulative destructiveness toward a much more positive, communal model of inspiration. The question of Hedda's pregnancy is implied strongly in Ibsen's script but made explicit in Friel's when Hedda finally confesses to George that she will give birth in four months (*HG* 89). By killing herself, she also kills their unborn child: as George says to Brack in the conclusion, "She has killed herself, Judge Brack, and handsome young Joachim or maybe exquisite young Rena, Judge Brack" (103). Hedda's desire to destroy figurative and literal children, such as Eilert's manuscript—which is referred to by Thea as the "child" she mentally conceived with Eilert (81) and which Hedda burns at the end of Act Three—and her unborn child through her own suicide, indicates her will to live selfishly only in the present (Eilert's manuscript dealt with aspects of the future), and by extension, suggests the culmination of the pernicious and still-dominant strand of modernity that worships itself and its own processes. Unlike Friel's Mundy sisters, who often unconsciously distance themselves from their bodies because of their oppressive culture, Hedda's pregnancy renders her so closely emplaced to her own body, which she cannot control, that she desires to kill herself.

But hope for the future can be found in George and Thea's devotion to the other "child" of the play, Eilert's manuscript, which they will carefully, lovingly, painstakingly reconstruct, drawing them into community with each other and with art, in the process creating a new, localized place for themselves. Friel himself has referred to his plays as "children" and thus was likely drawn to this characterization of Loevborg's manuscript as a child. In this regard, Elgy Gillespie notes that when *Faith Healer* was poorly received, "You feel, as Friel says, as you do about a sickly child, for a panned play," to which Friel then responds, "But as [Tyrone] Guthrie said, a playwright only survives as a body of work. Now the thing is this one. Your children grow up and leave home after their run; the newborn babe-in-arms is the one you concentrate all your love upon."[70]

Moreover, through the act of remembering Eilert's book, George and Thea are creating difference within their microcommunity, a version of the Frielian heterogeneous community found in his earlier plays, such as *The Freedom of the City* and *Dancing at Lughnasa*. Casey argues that "in remembering, we do not repeat the past as different each time. We regain the past as different each time. Or more exactly, we regain it as different in its very sameness. . . . [I]t is precisely memory's thick autonomy that makes this possible. In and through the dense operations of autonomous remembering, I recall the same past differently on successive occasions: now as I recapture it in reminiscence, now in body memory, now commemoratively, now even in recognition."[71] By collectively remembering and then recreating Eilert's manuscript, George and Thea create a rich textual site of memory and reconstruction, imaginatively helping to "birth" this "child." This hybrid community in formation—part human and part text—constitutes yet another richly imagined Frielian family that transcends time and space even as its members enact a dynamic sense of place.

Moreover, this imagined and imaginative dyad strongly indicates how Friel continued to see artistic collaboration—and art in general—as inherently spiritual toward the end of his life. Ibsen's spirituality has often been downplayed in favor of reading him as representing a theater of verisimilitude, but the symbolic always remains strong in his drama (think of, perhaps most famously, the wild duck in the play of that name), which often shades into the spiritual. Arthur Miller expressed his admiration for Ibsen's spiritual drama: "In this slow unfolding was wonder, even god." Moreover, Miller muses, "He and the Greeks were related . . . through their powerful integrative impulse which, at least in theory, could make possible a total picture of a human being—character sprang from action, and like a spiritual

CAT scan the drama could conceivably offer up a human being seen from within and without at the same time."[72]

The language of "benediction" and "soul-mates" Friel uses to describe George and Thea's collaboration in working to recreate Eilert's manuscript, cited above, anticipates and accords with the remarks he made at the dedication of the newly redesigned Lyric Theatre in Belfast in 2011. Offering what he called "secular prayers," Friel consistently emphasized the theater as a spiritual space and artistic collaboration as spiritual. For instance, he offered this prayer: "I pray that this may be a sacred place because what will happen here—when it's at its truest—really has to do with the unworldly and the spirit. I pray that this will be a place that is impatient of what is conventional."[73] A significant part of his unconventionality was his consistent embrace of human beings and the actors who represent them as spiritual—not mere bodies processing before us onstage. Rejecting both the overly spiritualized concept of the self as transcendently spiritual and bodiless by the Romantics and the modernist or even postmodernist concept of the self as sheerly embodied, Friel saw us as embodied souls and the theater as the sacred space where we meet, mingle, and form community. In his closing remarks at the Lyric Theatre, he resonantly affirms his vision of the theater and of the necessity of its work to remind us of our values in rediscovering our ensouled natures:

> And finally a heartfelt prayer for all the creative people who will work here in the coming decades and donate their lives to that strange and almost sacred pursuit we call theatre—because donating their lives is what they do. I pray that they will find their reward in putting us in touch again with our heedless souls, of lifting the veil again on those neglected values that we need to embrace if we are to be fully human. I solemnly pray that they will indeed find great, great reward in that unique venture.[74]

Gone is the language Friel employed in such essays from the 1960s surveyed in the interchapter of this study on his turn from short

fiction to drama where he termed the theater audience a "mob."
Instead, he lauds "all the creative people" associated with dramatic
productions as gifting their lives to us and leading us back into touch
"with our heedless souls," recovering our "neglected values" as audience members. We clearly need such creative types, but equally, so do
they need us to form community.

Among other philosophical and spiritual thinkers, Wittgenstein,
particularly his notion of a realm of the unsayable beyond speech,
was helpful to Friel's formulation of a theatrical metaphysics. We
know Friel read Wittgenstein periodically; in writing *Give Me Your
Answer, Do!* (1996), he records reading the philosopher's *Tractatus
Logico-Philosophicus*. In a diary entry of April 17, 1995, written
while researching that play, he muses on the Wittgensteinian notion
that "in imposing the self-discipline of saying only what can be said
and thus enjoining silence in the realm of metaphysics, genuine metaphysical impulses are released. The unsayable is not said but it is
nevertheless manifest." Moreover, "the very act of taking care to
say only what can be said 'shows' another silent realm beyond language (and logic) and so beyond description."[75] Late Friel, as we have
seen starting with the concluding scene of *Dancing at Lughnasa*,
ironically attempts to use words to convey the impression of silence
and, by extension, spirituality. Music, dance, and other media that
expresses the movement of ensouled bodies may also substitute for
language. He pointed out, for example, that in both *Philadelphia,
Here I Come!* and *Dancing at Lughnasa*, *ceili* music was used in crucial scenes in each play "because at that specific point emotion has
staggered into inarticulacy beyond the boundaries of language. . . .
Because it [music] is wordless it can hit straight and unmediated into
the vein of deep emotion."[76] "Deep emotion" works as a synonym
here for spirituality, a spirituality unmediated by church or priest or
even others.

Friel has remarked upon a Russian folktale about an imaginary
town called Kitzeh in terms that suggest his belief in theater as a
spiritual place. The town could enclose itself within a mist when
invaders came and shrink and disappear, but even when it vanished,

its church bell kept ringing and was audible to all. The point of the tale as Friel applies it to the theater seems to be that theater enables the survival of the sacred:

> For me the true gift of theatre, the real benediction of all art, is the ringing bell which reverberates quietly and persistently in the head long after the curtain has come down and the audience has gone home.[77]

The "sacred song" of the theater not only brings us clarity, but also carries us into a spiritual community, even if only for the duration of a play's performance. In his major plays, including his version of *Hedda Gabler*—epitomized by her violent piano playing—he registers the agonized longing of the human soul to be recognized by others and to enter into our memories and thus to enact some sort of kinship with us as readers and audience-goers.

He clearly privileged audience as part of a spiritual community perhaps best captured and epitomized by live performance onstage. These "neglected values" he moots in his secular prayers for the Lyric, as this study has attempted to explore and document, include our dwelling in the dynamic flux of place wherein we form radiant, living, spiritual communities with others on- and offstage and care for each other. In his role that he described in thinking about his time observing Tyrone Guthrie's embryonic theater in Minneapolis during 1963 as having "a dedication and a nobility and a selflessness that one associates only with a theoretical priesthood," he exemplified how the theater and its rituals practiced in the living, imaginative communities that form before our eyes and that we too enter into might sustain us and our souls.[78] He thus saw himself as an humble acolyte to private mysteries that he then publicly transmitted through words, actions, and music to audiences that he wanted to transform into a community, even a temporary one lasting for the duration of one play's performance.

In his seventy-ninth year, Brian Friel's version of Ibsen's *Hedda Gabler* powerfully affirmed the place of spiritual, imaginative art at the heart of his work. He seemed to suggest here that there is still a future, albeit uncertain, in reimagining ourselves in community with those gone before us, like the fictional character Eilert Loevborg and his creator, Ibsen, and with those as yet unborn.

If "place is no empty substratum to which cultural predicates come to be attached" but, instead, "an already plenary presence permeated with culturally constituted institutions and practices,"[79] then Friel's places amply demonstrate the ongoing life of culture in them even as that culture is assaulted from without by modernity or from within by modernizing or reactionary forces. In recovering and retrieving forgotten places, including past and present physical sites in Derry and Donegal, and the more intimate places of the body, mind, spirit, and stage, Friel has shown how place gathers and remembers its former and current inhabitants, and readers and audience members alike, into heterogeneous but empathetic communities. His emphasis on occluded or forgotten characters remained consistent throughout his career: a procession of apostates, deracinated selves, homosexuals, disabled men, outcast women, children, single mothers and impoverished women, and the aged file through his drama and beckon us to hear their stories. The remarks he made about the characters in Tom Kilroy's novel *The Big Chapel* in 2009 are apposite to understanding the centrality of such characters to Friel's own work as well: "As in all his angular plays, the people in this novel have their home—a term they wouldn't be fully at ease with—at the margins. They are not of the centre, of the consensus. But they are not a marginalized people: the margins are their centre."[80] Through his consistent portrayals of characters uneasily inhabiting the margins of past and current cultures, Friel brings these characters and their real-life analogues out of the shadows and onto center stage and into real and imagined community with us.

Repeatedly, he depicts such characters moving toward each other in space, creating a place through their embrace of each other in community, from Gar's filmic projection of his home place even as he is about to enter his future Irish American community in *Philadelphia, Here I Come!*; to the protestors' temporary community in the Derry Guildhall in *The Freedom of the City* and Frank Hardy's slow movement toward his killers in *Faith Healer*; to Maire and Yolland's literal and linguistic embraces and Hugh's gradual opening of himself to modernity even as he vows to humanize it and speak an Irish-English idiom in *Translations*; through the adult Michael's intimate verbal reimagining of the Mundy sisters' dancing in *Dancing at Lughnasa*. More recently, he depicts Molly Sweeney's communion with the living and the dead; Margaret's movement away from community in the Big House and back toward the community she shares with the town below in *The Home Place*; and the new "family" of George, Thea, and the manuscript in his adaptation of *Hedda Gabler*.

For Friel, who always felt displaced and somewhat homeless, first living as a minority Catholic in Counties Tyrone and Londonderry/Derry, then later on the Inishowen Peninsula in Donegal as an exile from Northern Ireland, he finally learned to make his home not just with his family of his wife and five children, but also in his words. As Adorno remarked, "For a man who no longer has a homeland, writing becomes a place to live."[81] And live Friel did—and still does—in his remarkable works of short fiction and drama that span more than five decades.

Every time we read one of his dramas and encounter these characters enacting place, every time we attend one of his plays and form a temporary community with the actors portraying such characters, we too engage with place through our creative interactions. Brian Friel's dramas enact Matei Calinescu's multilayered theory of rereading by their haunting of us, just as "we, active rereaders . . . are haunting the texts. We revisit them to understand why they attract us or to enjoy the surprise of rediscovering them, of re-experiencing their ability to come alive and renew themselves."[82] Through such mental, somatic, and spiritual activity, we find ourselves, like these characters and works, emplaced into culture, even sometimes "at ease" there, if not at home.

NOTES

WORKS CITED

INDEX

Notes

Preface and Acknowledgments for the Second Edition

1. Boltwood, *Brian Friel: Readers' Guides to Essential Criticism*, 144.

2. O'Toole, "*Collected Plays* by Brian Friel Review: 29 Survivors of Their Maker's Culls," n.p.

3. All quotations from Flaherty, Carswell, and McGreevy, "Meryl Streep on Brian Friel: 'Tender Dramatist Lovely Man,'" n.p.

4. See Nightingale, "Brian Friel, Irish Playwright of Poetic Beauty, Dies at 86," and Brantley, "Recalling an Artist's Eloquent Loneliness," n.p.

5. Teachout, "Remembering Brian Friel (1929–2015): A Poet of the Particular," n.p.

6. Murray's study has an unusually cursory treatment of one of Friel's masterpieces, *Translations*, at a little less than two pages. Perhaps he feels that it has been overanalyzed? For my review of the considerable strengths but also the shortcomings of Murray's book on Friel, see "*The Theatre of Brian Friel: Tradition and Modernity.*"

Introduction

1. Smyth, *Space and the Irish Cultural Imagination*, 22.

2. Cronin, "Lived and Learned Landscapes: Literary Geographies and the Irish Topographical Tradition," 107.

3. Friel, "In Interview with Fintan O'Toole (1982)," 110.

4. Deane, "Brian Friel: The Double Stage," 166.

5. But see Helen Lojek's 2004 essay, "Brian Friel's Sense of Place," for a helpful general discussion of the importance of Friel's imaginative place for his work. She terms his fictive small town of Ballybeg "an imaginary Donegal town with a significance in Irish literature comparable to the significance of William Faulkner's Yoknapatawpha in American literature" (177). Moreover, Lojek's chapter on Friel's *Translations* in *The Spaces of Irish Drama* constitutes a sterling exploration of how

that landmark drama probes "the spaces of Ireland—how they are known, how they are described, how they are controlled, who belongs in them and who does not" (35).

6. Quoted in Wallace and Armbruster, "Introduction: Why Go Beyond Nature Writing, and Where To?," 7.

7. Casey, "How to Get from Space to Place in a Fairly Short Stretch of Time," 33, 33–34.

8. Friel, "Self-Portrait (1972)," 45.

9. O'Brien, *Brian Friel*, 29.

10. McGrath, *Brian Friel's (Post) Colonial Drama*, 2.

11. Ibid., 2.

12. Although the original manuscript of this book was finished before Lojek's *The Spaces of Irish Drama* appeared in 2011, I recognized then that her book represents a pioneering effort to rehabilitate and employ theories of dramatic space as inflected by "cultural and historical realities" inhering in place and "the immediate reality of staging that shapes audience reactions" (1).

13. See my essay, "Brian Friel's Short Fiction: Place, Community, and Modernity," for an analysis of the seminal stories "Kelly's Hall," "The Diviner," "The Saucer of Larks," "Foundry House," "Among the Ruins," "The Potato Gatherers," and "Everything Neat and Tidy" using the theories of place developed here.

14. Crawley, "Brian Friel: Seven Key Plays," n.p.

15. Leavy, "Brian Friel One Year On: A Critical Overview," n.p.

16. O' Toole, "Tracing a Rocky Path from the Past," n.p.

17. Burke, "Friel and Performance History," 120, 121–27.

18. Anonymous, "Living Lines: Friel's Finest Dramas," n.p.

19. Kiberd, *Inventing Ireland*, 615.

20. Bertha, "Brian Friel as Postcolonial Playwright," 158.

21. Appadurai, *Modernity at Large*, 29.

22. Dupré, "Ritual: The Divine Play of Time," 206.

23. Cleary, "Introduction: Ireland and Modernity," 7.

24. Chaudhuri, *Staging Place*, xii.

25. O'Toole, *Lie of the Land: Irish Identities*, 67.

26. Chaudhuri, *Staging Place*, 4.

27. Casey, "How to Get from Space to Place," 26.

28. Cave, "Friel's Dramaturgy: The Visual Dimension," 132.

29. O' Toole, "Tracing a Rocky Path from the Past," n.p. Richards, "Brian Friel: Seizing the Moment of Flux," 254.

30. Friel, Linehan, Leonard, and Keane, "Future of Irish Drama," 14.

31. Friel, "Theatre of Hope and Despair (1967)," 16.

32. Ibid., 16.

33. de Valera, "Undeserted Village Ireland," 747–50.

34. Friel, "Theatre of Hope and Despair," 19.

35. Keating, "Delving Deep into Divided Donegal Landscape," n.p.

36. Friel, "In Interview with Laurence Finnegan (1986)," 131.

37. Barr, *Rooms with a View*, 2.

38. Friel, "Theatre of Hope and Despair (1967)," 24; my emphasis.

39. Maxwell, *Brian Friel*, 110.

40. O'Brien, *Brian Friel*, 124.

41. Quoted in Worthen, *Modern Drama and the Rhetoric of Theater*, 3.

42. Toulmin, *Cosmopolis: The Hidden Agenda of Modernity*, 192.

43. Ibid., 207.

44. Friel, "In Interview with Paddy Agnew (1980)," 87.

45. Friel, "Extracts from a Sporadic Diary (1976–78): *Aristocrats*," 63.

46. Kimmer, "'Like Walking through Madame Tussaud's,'" 201.

47. Ibid., 203.

48. For explorations of this Russian dimension of his drama, see Friel's own introduction to *A Month in the Country*, "Ivan Turgenev (1818–1883)," 9–11; Pine's "Friel's Irish Russia"; Tracy's "Russian Connection: Friel and Chekhov"; York's "Friel's Russia"; Csikai's "Brian Friel's Adaptations of Chekhov"; and Pelletier's "From Moscow to Ballybeg: Brian Friel's Richly Metabiotic Relationship with Anton Chekhov."

49. Friel, "Seven Notes for a Festival Programme (1999)," 179.

50. O' Toole, "Celebrating the Life and Genius of Brian," n.p.

51. Appadurai, *Modernity at Large*, 185.

52. Friel, "Extracts from a Sporadic Diary (1979): *Translations*," 77.

53. "Brian Friel's First Book," 3. Quoted in Delaney, *Brian Friel in Conversation*, 249.

54. Anthony Roche, *Contemporary Irish Drama from Beckett to McGuinness*, 105.

55. Grene, *Politics of Irish Drama*, 211, 212.

56. Ibid., 212.

57. Corbett, *Brian Friel: Decoding the Language of the Tribe*, 84.

58. Maxwell, *Brian Friel*, 97.

59. Friel, *Gentle Island*, 65–66.

60. Ibid., 26, 22.

61. Lojek, "Brian Friel's Gentle Island of Lamentation," 55.

62. Friel, *Gentle Island*, 54.

63. Ibid.

64. José Lanters, "Queer Creatures, Queer Place: Otherness and Normativity in Irish Drama from Synge to Friel." And yet as she points out, "material goods from around the world have not changed the prevailing inward-looking mindset" (64).

65. Friel, *Gentle Island*, 41.

66. Quoted in Lojek, "Brian Friel's Gentle Island of Lamentation," 49.

67. Ibid., 52; 51–52.

68. Roche, *Contemporary Irish Drama*, 2nd ed., 80.

69. Zapf, "State of Ecocriticism and the Function of Literature as Cultural Ecology," 51.

70. Ibid., 52.

71. Wallace and Armbruster, "Introduction: Why Go Beyond Nature Writing, and Where To?", 7.

72. Friel, "Plays Peasant and Unpeasant," 52.

73. Deane, "Introduction" to *Diviner*, 12–13.

74. Taylor, *Sources of the Self*, 35.

75. Ibid., 35.

76. Ibid., 36.

76. Quoted in Dupré, "Ritual: The Divine Play of Time," 206.

77. Zapf, "State of Ecocriticism," 53.

78. Toulmin, *Cosmopolis: The Hidden Agenda of Modernity*, 179.

79. Ibid., 184.

80. Ibid., 186–92.

81. Nicholas Daly, *Literature, Technology, and Modernity, 1860–2000*, 2.

82. Ibid., 3

83. Enda Duffy, *Speed Handbook: Velocity, Pleasure, Modernism*, 6.

84. Pine, *Diviner*, 84.

1. Interchapter: The Enemy Within: *Self and Spirituality in Exile*

1. Boltwood, "'An Emperor or Something': Brian Friel's Columba, Migrancy, and Postcolonial Theory," 58.

2. Ibid.

3. Friel, "In Interview with Peter Lennon (1964)," 2.

4. Elmer Andrews, *Art of Brian Friel*, 82.

5. Ibid., 84. Andrews wrongly emphasizes individuality, even an atomistic, Enlightenment view of individuality, not community, at the end of the play in recalling Grillaan's advice to Columba to begin over and over to gain sanctity: "Grillaan indicates a concept of the subject as continuously in the process of construction. He reminds us of Brecht: 'The continuity of the ego is a myth. A man is an atom that perpetually breaks up and forms anew'" (84).

6. See *EW* 20 and 30, for his localized laments for his family farm and his wider lament for Donegal, respectively.

7. Boltwood, "'An Emperor or Something,'" 53.

8. Friel, "In Interview with Peter Lennon (1964)," 2.

9. Ibid., 2.

10. Anthony Roche, *Brian Friel: Theatre and Politics*, 30.

11. Ibid., citing Kilroy, "The Early Plays," 9; Anthony Roche, *Brian Friel: Theatre and Politics*, 31.

12. For the best and most thorough treatment of this topic, see the suggestively titled, masterly study by Marianne Elliott, *When God Took Sides: Religion and Identity in Ireland—Unfinished History*.

13. Kilroy, "Early Plays," 10.

2. Mediascape, Harvest, Crash: *Philadelphia, Here I Come!* and Gar O'Donnell's Modernity

1. Deane, "Introduction" to *Brian Friel: Plays 1*, 14.

2. See Friel, *Selected Stories*, 49–57, and my discussion of this story in "Brian Friel's Short Fiction: Place, Modernity, and Community," 318–19.

3. Weaver, *Ideas Have Consequences*, 79.

4. Ibid., 79–80.

5. Ibid., 81.

6. Deane, "Introduction" to *Brian Friel: Plays 1*, 14.

7. Ibid., 14.

8. Thompson, "Edmund Burke's *Reflections on the Revolution in France* and the Subject of Eurocentrism," 245.

9. Kilroy, "Early Plays," 11.

10. Appadurai, *Modernity at Large*, 33.

11. Ibid., 35.

12. Ibid., 36.

13. McLoone, "Inventions and Re-imaginings: Some Thoughts on Identity and Broadcasting in Ireland," 10.

14. Ferriter, *Transformation of Ireland*, 553. See ibid., 465, for the figure of 412,000.

15. Fallon, *An Age of Innocence: Irish Culture, 1930–1960*, 257.

16. Brown, *Ireland: A Social and Cultural History, 1922–2002*, 229–30.

17. Fallon, *An Age of Innocence*, 260.

18. Friel, "In Interview with Des Hickey and Gus Smith (1972)," 47.

19. Benjamin, "Work of Art in the Age of Mechanical Reproduction," 236.

20. Murray, *Twentieth-Century Irish Drama*, 169.

21. McLoone, "Inventions and Re-imaginings," 24, 25.

22. Berry, "Regional Motive," 67.

23. Friel, "In Interview with Graham Morrison (1965)," 14.

24. Brown, *Ireland: A Social and Cultural History*, 141.

25. Ferriter, *Transformation of Ireland*, 429.

26. Weaver, *Ideas Have Consequences*, 101.

27. Ibid., 111.

28. Gibbons, "Projecting the Nation: Cinema and Culture," 210.

29. Fallon, *An Age of Innocence*, argues that Browne's resignation led to a renascence of "anti-clericalism [that] began to show itself both publicly and privately," partly because the hierarchy was so reactionary in its stance against a state medicine scheme and partly because the public hated the spectacle of a decent man who was brought down by the church, politicians, and wealthy doctors (265). The people's outrage, often published in letters to various newspapers like *The Irish Times*, led to a quiet revolution in which "the power and authority of the Catholic hierarchy began to decline, until it reached its present nadir" (266).

30. Whelan, "Cultural Effects of the Famine," 140.

31. Gibbons, "Projecting the Nation: Cinema and Culture," 211.

32. Through most of the 1950s, however, Catholicism in Ireland flourished, as Ferriter, *Transformation of Ireland*, has shown: the decade "witnessed the cult of Marianism and all its attendant sodalities, shrines and worship, as well as a fascination with Lourdes and Fatima, religious devotion that extended well beyond the traditional parochial structures. Devotion to the rosary became the cornerstone of many Catholic families' daily prayer, while according to the *Irish Catholic* the formula for peace in time of Cold War and communism was a pair of rosary beads lying on the table of every house in Ireland" (517).

33. Friel, "In Interview with Peter Lennon (1964)," 2.

34. Friel, "After *Philadelphia*," 49. Friel makes this statement in the context of his commitment to living on the island of Ireland during the Troubles, but it suggests his implicit privileging of a particular place.

35. Friel, "In Interview with Peter Lennon (1964)," 2.

36. Public Gar tells Kate when she leaves, "Be sure to call the first one after me," suggesting that she will have many children (*BFP1* 79). Gar himself desperately wants children, seeing himself as the father of fourteen twice (45, 80).

37. Mary E. Daly, "'Oh, Kathleen Ni Houlihan,'" 116.

38. See Friel, *Selected Stories*, 118–26.

39. Davidson, "Mirror for Artists," 34.

40. Ibid.

41. Thornton, *Antimodernism of Joyce's Portrait*, 27.

42. Baumer, *Modern European Thought*, 261.

43. Nicholas Daly, *Literature, Technology, and Modernity*, 114.

44. Ibid., 37.

45. Friel, *Philadelphia, Here I Come!*, motion picture.

46. Friel, "In Interview with Graham Morrison (1965)," 14.

47. Enda Duffy, *Speed Handbook*, 9.

48. For another example of the fear of flying in Friel, see the passage in *Molly Sweeney* about Roger Bloomstein's crash: "[T]he engine stopped suddenly, and for a couple of seconds the plane seemed to sit suspended in the sky, golden and glittering in the setting sun, and then plummeted into the sea just south of Martha's Vineyard" (*BFP2* 504).

49. See my discussion of this moment in "Brian Friel's Short Fiction," 319–22.

50. See Franklin Baumer, *Modern European Thought: Continuity and Change in Ideas, 1600–1950*, 20: "Becoming has superseded being as the major category in European thinking between the times of Francis Bacon and Henri Bergson (and down to the present)."

51. Ibid., 403.

52. Steiner, *Grammars of Creation*, 263.

53. Ibid.

54. Friel, "Self-Portrait (1972)," 39.

55. See Friel, *Selected Stories*, 109: "The past did have meaning. It was neither reality nor dreams, neither today's patchy oaks nor the great woods of his boyhood. It was simply continuance, life repeating itself and surviving."

56. Kiberd, *After Ireland*, 121.

57. Friel, "1ˢᵗ Notes on *Philadelphia*."

58. Deane, *Strange Country*, 166.

59. Ibid.

60. Anthony Roche, *Contemporary Irish Drama from Beckett to McGuinness*, 98.

61. Ibid., 102; Roche's emphases.

62. Benjamin, "Work of Art," 224.

63. Whelan, "Cultural Effects of the Famine," 152.

3. Interchapter: Why Friel Left Short Fiction for Drama

1. Friel, "In Interview with Graham Morrison (1965)," 4.

2. Ling, "Faber and Irish Literature," 566. Contrary to Ling's hyperbolic assertion, Friel's decision to leave short fiction was made at least by 1968, if not before, so faulting Gallery's admirable decision (reached in accord with Friel himself) to publish by 1979 what Friel and Peter Fallon, Gallery's editor, felt were Friel's ten best short stories as *Selected Stories* (with an introduction by Seamus Deane) is specious. Moreover, O'Brien Press brought out the same edition of stories, calling them *The Diviner: Brian Friel's Best Stories*, by 1983 to ensure that the stories reached the wider audience that they deserved. Finally, Michael O'Brien, editor

of O'Brien Press, did actually approach Frank Pike at Faber in a July 5, 1982, letter, asking Faber to copublish the then-forthcoming volume of short stories with O'Brien. Pike replied in a letter of August 17, 1982, suggesting that the press had economic and logistical commitments until July of 1983, that O'Brien Press would control the main market for such stories—Ireland—and that if Faber ever wanted to publish the stories, it would likely want to negotiate about publishing there. The stories have never been published by Faber, and the surprised tone in Pike's letter implies that the press had never seriously considered doing so. Gallery Press brought out a subsequent edition of *Selected Stories* (without the Deane introduction) in 1994, which was reprinted in 2005, followed by a revised, enlarged edition with three additional stories in 2017. Those three extra, previously published stories ("Mr Sing My Heart's Delight," "A Man's World," and "My Father and the Sergeant") were published by Gallery in 2010 as *A Man's World* in a limited edition illustrated by Basil Blackshaw. But again, the major fault with Ling's reading is that Friel had decided by 1968, if not earlier, not to write any more short fiction, making her speculation about Faber's inability or disinclination to publish the short fiction moot. I discuss this publishing history of Friel's short stories fully in my essay "Brian Friel's Short Fiction: Place, Community, and Modernity."

3. Anthony Roche, *Contemporary Irish Drama from Beckett to McGuinness*, articulates the most thoughtful version of this narrative, citing Pine, *Brian Friel and Ireland's Drama*, 56, on what Roche terms the "limitations of the *New Yorker* format" (74), but noting as more disabling the "shadow . . . cast by the formidable cultural presences in the 1950s of Sean O'Faolain and Frank O'Connor" that Friel himself has pointed out, and concluding by affirming George O'Brien's account in *Brian Friel*, 6, that Friel's short stories display "little sense of development" (quoted in Roche, 74). I should point out that John Wilson Foster, *Forces and Themes in Ulster Fiction*, was the first critic to articulate Friel's sense of writing in a formulaic vein too close to that of his exemplars O'Faolain, O'Connor, and others, arguing, "many of Friel's short stories feature "a character's initiation into the reality behind illusion. . . . [while] allow[ing] his characters to retain an altered illusion to make life bearable for them. The whole process is rather formulaic" (64). Foster goes on to wonder "whether he is doing much more than playing deftly with an emotional and structural formula learned from O'Connor, O'Faolain, McLaverty, and Kiely" (65). Friel himself said in Friel, "Interview with Fintan O'Toole (1982)," that his stories were imitative of O'Faolain and O'Connor and he needed to break free from that: "I know now why I stopped writing short stories. It was at the point when I recognized how difficult they were. It would have meant a whole reappraisal. I mean, I was very much under the influence, as everyone at the time was, of [Sean] O'Faolain and [Frank] O'Connor, particularly. O'Connor dominated our lives. I suppose they [Friel's short stories] really were some kind of imitation of O'Connor's

work. I'm just guessing at it, but I think at some point round about that period, the recognition of the difficulty of the thing, you know, that maybe there was the need for the discovery of a voice and that I was just echoing somebody else" (109).

4. Russell, "Seamus Heaney's Creative Work for BBC Northern Ireland Radio, 1968–71," 141. See also my chapter on the subject, "Recording Bigotry and Creating a New Province: Heaney and BBC Northern Ireland Radio, 1967–1973," for an extended argument about it in *Seamus Heaney's Regions*, 66–100.

5. Heaney, "Regional Forecast," 10.

6. Cathcart, *The Most Contrary Region*, 181.

7. Rattigan, *Theatre of Sound*, 1.

8. Ibid., 119.

9. Ibid.

10. The quotation here is from P. M. Lewis's remarks concerning the survey he conducted through the *Radio Times* in 1986 that asked listeners their reasons for tuning into radio plays: "Those who wrote to me repeatedly stressed that they looked to plays for relief and entertainment. . . . 'Problem plays' are likely to include the portrayal of strong emotions which in some listeners stir unwelcome echoes" (quoted in ibid., 107).

11. Friel, "In Interview with Eavan Boland (1973)," 59.

12. Pine, *Diviner*, 97.

13. Ibid., 99. Interestingly, Friel himself has claimed in "Interview with Brian Friel: Lewis Funke, 1968," 3, "I think what the radio plays did for me was show me I could write dialogue."

14. Pine, *Diviner*, 99.

15. Boltwood, "'More Real for Northern Irish Catholics Than Anybody Else,'" 5–6.

16. Rattigan, *Theatre of Sound*, 13.

17. Dantanus, *Brian Friel*, 53. Dantanus is quoting Jonathan Raban's "Icon or Symbol," 81.

18. Dantanus, *Brian Friel*, 76.

19. Ibid., 76.

20. Matthews, "Brian Friel, The BBC, and Ronald Mason," 482. For a compelling assessment of how influential Mason was to Friel's short radio drama career and also for the claim that Mason was "equally influential, if not more so," than Tyrone Guthrie "on the young schoolteacher's vocation to write for the stage" (471), see Matthews.

21. O'Brien, "Meet Brian Friel: The *Irish Press* Columns," 39.

22. Ibid., 32.

23. Boltwood, *Brian Friel, Ireland, and the North*, 12.

24. Ibid., 13, 14.

25. Ibid., 16.

26. Ibid., 36, 38.

27. O'Toole, "Celebrating the Life and Genius of Brian," n.p.

28. Friel, "Theatre of Hope and Despair (1967)," 16.

29. Maxwell, *Brian Friel*, 110.

30. Deane, "Introduction" to *Selected Stories: Brian Friel*, 10.

31. Ibid.

32. Friel, "In Interview with Graham Morrison (1965)," 4.

33. Frank O'Connor, *Lonely Voice*, 19, 21.

34. Interestingly, in "Interview with Des Hickey and Gus Smith (1972)," Friel claimed, "I abandoned short-story writing before I grew tired of it and now that I am becoming disenchanted with the theatre the chances are that I will go back to writing stories" (49). Such a statement seems another rhetorical flourish designed to disguise his great affection for theater even as the process of writing plays would often prove maddening to him.

35. Elmer Andrews, *Art of Brian Friel*, 45.

36. Boltwood, *Brian Friel, Ireland, and the North*, 12. See Boltwood's article, "'Mildly Eccentric,'" for an illuminating reading of some of the seventy-six columns Friel wrote for the *Irish Times* from September 1957 to May 1962, which "occupy a shifting, often overlapping space between journalism and fiction." Together, Boltwood argues these "mixed-genre pieces" alter our understanding of the early Friel's career in "several ways: first . . . by pushing back the date of Friel's emergence as a professional writer by more than two years, by altering our understanding of his work for the *Irish Press* from April 1962 to August 1963, and by changing our view of the stories that were published by the *New Yorker* from 1959 to 1965" (306).

37. McGrath, *Brian Friel's (Post) Colonial Drama*, 97.

38. Quoted in Anthony Roche, *Brian Friel: Theatre and Politics*, 8.

39. Friel, "In Interview with Desmond Rushe (1970)," 32.

40. See Elmer Andrews, *Art of Brian Friel*, 45–46, for an interesting reading of heterogeneity generally in Friel's drama, concluding with his contention that "in the light of Bakhtinian theory, Friel's commitment to drama may thus be seen as reflecting his deliberate embracement of diversity, heterogeneity, and 'difference'" (46).

41. Friel, "Self-Portrait (1972)," 41.

42. Ibid., 42.

43. Ibid., 42. Friel, "In Interview with Peter Lennon (1964)," 1, says that his training for the priesthood at Maynooth was "an awful experience, it nearly drove me cracked. It is one thing I want to forget."

44. Friel, "Giant of Monaghan," 94. Quoted in Anthony Roche, *Brian Friel: Theatre and Politics*, 38.

45. Quoted in Anthony Roche, *Brian Friel: Theatre and Politics*, 38.

46. Ibid.

47. Deane, "Brian Friel: The Double Stage," 168.

48. Friel, "Theatre of Hope and Despair (1967)," 21–22.

49. Ibid., 24.

50. Friel, "In Interview with Graham Morrison (1965)," 5–6.

51. Friel, "Theatre of Hope and Despair (1967)," 19.

52. Friel, "In Interview with Desmond Rushe (1970)," 33.

53. Dowling, "Staging Friel," 188.

54. Friel, "In Interview with Desmond Rushe (1970)," 30.

55. Ibid., 32.

56. Ibid.

57. Bennett, *Theatre Audiences*, 150.

58. Kennedy, *Spectator and the Spectacle*, 14. He is quoting Blau, *Eye of Prey*, 171.

59. See his remarks on the subject in Friel, "Seven Notes for a Festival Programme (1999)," 178.

60. Quoted in Freshwater, *Theatre and Audience*, 7.

61. I write about this temporary community in my chapter on *The Freedom of the City* in this study.

62. Blau, *Audience*, 25.

63. Barr, *Rooms with a View*, 16.

64. Friel, "Seven Notes for a Festival Programme (1999)," 174.

65. Friel, "Plays Peasant and Unpeasant (1972)," 52.

66. Ibid., 54.

67. Kennedy, *Spectator and the Spectacle*, 171.

68. Ibid., 172.

69. Friel, "In Interview with Laurence Finnegan (1986)," 125–26.

70. Friel, "Seven Notes for a Festival Programme (1999)," 177.

71. O'Toole, "Celebrating the Life and Genius of Brian," n.p.

4. Raising and Remembering the Dead of the Troubles:
The Imagined Ghostly Community of *The Freedom of the City*

1. McGrath, *Brian Friel's (Post) Colonial Drama*, 1.

2. Friel, "Brian Friel."

3. Friel, "After *Philadelphia*," 49.

4. In a 1982 BBC Northern Ireland Radio interview, Friel discussed the way in which "the Northern situation" influences the lives of the Catholic minority there and how it influences his own work: "Well, of course, the Northern situation

is basic to everything, I think, that one does here. And if you are, as I was, a member of what is known as the Northern minority, I think you're conditioned, almost from birth. Of course, it's bound to filter into and pigment everything you write. Now I've tackled it only once, directly, in a play called *The Freedom of the City*, a play that I'm not particularly happy with now. But I still think that it's true of all the Northern writers, if it's not handled directly, it certainly informs everything they write, and it informs all their attitudes" (Friel, "Brian Friel").

5. Harrington and Mitchell, "Introduction," 1.

6. See Friel's perception of Derry as a large town in "The Green Years," 18: "[M]uch as we boast of our city status, we're not really a city at all. We haven't the drive nor the vitality nor the impermanence nor the anonymity of a city. And if it goes to that, the texture of city life doesn't appeal to us. We are villagers at heart, or at best inhabitants of a market town. We have our industries, but they haven't made us industrial. We have a port that sees ships from every nation, but we scarcely know what the word cosmopolitan means. We are concerned about the individual, and if we don't know him personally at least we know his brother or his wife's aunt, or a cousin of his father's uncle."

7. Deane, "Introduction" to *Brian Friel: Plays 1*, 12.

8. Rotman, "Automedial Ghosts," 119.

9. Rayner, *Ghosts: Death's Double and the Phenomena of Theatre*, 57, 61.

10. Elmer Andrews, "Fifth Province," 35.

11. Friel, "Plays Peasant and Unpeasant," 52.

12. Dantanus, *Brian Friel: A Study*, 43–44.

13. Fulton, "Hegemonic Discourses in Brian Friel's *The Freedom of the City*," 75.

14. Cohen and Fukui, "Introduction" to *Humanizing the City?*, 5.

15. Branford and Geddes, *Coming Polity*, 158; quoted in Corringe, *A Theology of the Built Environment*, 139.

16. Pine, *Diviner*, 67.

17. Elliott, *Catholics of Ulster*, 411.

18. See ibid., 407–16, for a clear account of O'Neill's modernization program in Northern Ireland that genuinely tried to help Catholics achieve parity with Protestants.

19. Ibid., 415–16.

20. Ibid., 417.

21. Ibid., 481.

22. Cave, "Friel's Dramaturgy: The Visual Dimension," 136.

23. Ibid., 136–37.

24. Anthony Roche, *Brian Friel: Theatre and Politics*, 116–17.

25. Elliott, *Catholics of Ulster*, 412.

26. See Anthony Roche, *Brian Friel: Theatre and Politics*, for a compelling argument about how Michael, Lily, and Skinner transform the mayor's parlor, beginning with the fact that "its three central characters were marchers," seeking "to establish a foundational space by walking" (118). All three gradually walk around the parlor, taking possession of it and transforming "the space from the foreign to the familiar," particularly Skinner, who makes it "a temporary home for this man of no fixed abode and no known antecedents" (119).

27. Corringe, *Theology of the Built Environment*, 210–11.

28. Friel, *"The Freedom of the City* (1973): Manuscripts."

29. Ulick O'Connor, *Brian Friel: Crisis and Commitment*, 10.

30. Parker, "Forms of Redress," 272. Parker notes on 295n2 that during one demonstration, a member of this group "seized control of the Guildhall council chamber and declared himself Mayor." The action of this man, Finbar Doherty, "clearly anticipates Skinner's antics in Friel's play."

31. Winkler, "Brian Friel's *The Freedom of the City*," 12–13, points out that several plays about the Troubles were produced in the early 1970s, including John Boyd's *The Flats* (1971), Wilson John Haire's *Within Two Shadows* (1972), Haire's *Bloom of the Diamond Stone* (1973), and Patrick Galvin's *Nightfall to Belfast* (1973).

32. Friel, "Brian Friel: Dramatist and Short Story Writer."

33. Anthony Roche, *Brian Friel: Theatre and Politics*, 114–15.

34. Friel, "In Interview with Eavan Boland (1973)," 58.

35. Anthony Roche, *Brian Friel: Theatre and Politics*, 102. Roche states that Friel's notes disprove Boland's claim that *The Freedom of the City* grew out of *John Butt's Bothy* and that the play that *Bothy* became was *Volunteers* (1975).

36. Friel, "In Interview with Eavan Boland (1973)," my emphasis; 58.

37. Please see 46–49 of my essay, "Liberating Fictional Truth of Community in Brian Friel's *The Freedom of the City*," for a full explanation of these weaknesses.

38. Anthony Roche, *Brian Friel: Theatre and Politics*, 115.

39. See Russell, "Liberating Fictional Truth of Community," 46–49.

40. Friel, *"The Freedom of the City*: Program."

41. Sontag, *Regarding the Suffering of Others*, 22.

42. Ibid.

43. See Pringle and Jacobson's *Those Are Real Bullets: Bloody Sunday, Derry, 1972* for examples of Peress's pictures of a water cannon spraying rioters and peaceful protesters with purple dye and Paddy Doherty's being shot from behind, along with Grimaldi's picture of a dying Jack Duddy, face smeared with blood and tended by Father Edward Daly and Charlie Glenn, a Knights of Malta paramedic (photospread between 150 and 151).

44. In the last photograph reproduced in Pringle and Jacobson, *Those Are Real Bullets*, immediately before the picture of Jack Duddy on 151, the caption

notes that Grimaldi "was later trapped in a flat as six bullets were pumped through a window."

45. Benjamin, "Work of Art," 226.

46. See Mullan's *Bloody Sunday: Massacre in Northern Ireland*, photospread between 32–33.

47. Sontag, *Regarding the Pain of Others*, 22–23.

48. Ibid., 24.

49. Parker, "Forms of Redress," 276.

50. Germanou, "An American in Ireland," 261.

51. There is no critical consensus on Dodds's rhetoric in the play. I follow Parker, in his "Forms of Redress," who argues that Dodds's generalizing of the poor everywhere denies "the very particularity of Derry that the play insists upon and which is embodied in Michael, Lily, and Skinner, who are clearly individualized and not simply members of a homogenous caste or class" (281–82). To an American ear, Dodds's condescension toward Northern Irish Catholics recalls the past racist white attitude toward black Americans as fun-loving and sensual, particularly when he argues that "[p]resent-orientated living, for example, may sharpen one's attitude for spontaneity and for excitement, for the appreciation of the sensual, for the indulgence of impulse" (*BFP1* 135).

52. McKenna, *Rupture, Representation, and Identity*, 31.

53. Dantanus, *Brian Friel*, 140.

54. Elmer Andrews suggests the playwright accentuates human potential through these characters but he minimizes the relevance this insistence on human freedom has for the political situation: "In emphasizing this kind of broadly human rather than a strictly political potential, Friel suggests a universal freedom from which no creed or class need feel excluded. (He could hardly have chosen a more 'Orange' name for one of his characters than Lily!) Friel's agitators are redeemed of all doctrinal prejudice, racist nationalism, class oppression and totalitarian ambition. They represent a morality that does not lie in formulated code nor explicit programme, but respect for the rich variousness of life" ("Fifth Province," 34–35).

55. Zapf, "State of Eco-criticism," 52.

56. York, "Friel's Russia," 176.

57. Murray, "Friel and O'Casey Juxtaposed," 18.

58. Brown, "'Have We a Context?,'" 191.

59. Dantanus, *Brian Friel*, 138.

60. Elmer Andrews, *Art of Brian Friel*, 133.

61. Winkler, "Brian Friel's *The Freedom*," 19, 29.

62. Csicsila, "'Isn't It the Stupidest Thing?'" 22.

63. Fulton, "Hegemonic Discourses in Brian Friel's *Freedom of the City*," 74, 69.

64. Friel, "Plays Peasant and Unpeasant (1972)," 56.

65. Boltwood, "Brian Friel: Staging the Struggle with Nationalism," 309.

66. Deane, "Introduction" to *Brian Friel: Plays 1*, 12.

67. Ibid.

68. Donoghue, *Speaking of Beauty*, 109.

69. Ibid., 114.

70. McGrath, *Brian Friel's (Post)Colonial Drama*, 121.

71. Schrank, "Politics, Language, Metatheatre," 141, 142.

72. See Parker, "Forms of Redress," passim.

73. Derrida, *Specters of Marx*, xviii–xix.

74. Watkin, *On Mourning*, 201.

75. Ibid., 205.

76. Watt, "Friel and the Northern Ireland 'Troubles' Play," 36, intriguingly suggests that these bodies function "much like placards or other explanatory signs in Brecht's theatre."

77. Myerhoff, "Death in Due Time," 151, 152.

78. Murray, *The Theatre of Brian Friel*, insightfully observes that "three out of the four conclusions Friel's Judge offers stem from the [*Widgery*] *Report*, although appearing more outrageous because the points are summarized somewhat in the style of 'translation' Friel was later to provide Owen with in *Translations*" (50). See Murray's helpful discussion of these conclusions on 50–51.

79. Ibid., 60.

80. Friel, "In Interview with Desmond Rushe (1970)," 32.

81. Davis, "*Etát Présent*: Hauntology, Spectres, and Phantoms," 373.

82. Ibid.

83. Ibid., 379.

84. Rayner, *Ghosts*, 72.

85. Ibid., 55.

86. Ibid., 56.

87. Anthony Roche, *Brian Friel: Theatre and Politics*, 118.

88. Friel came to feel that the play was written too close to the events of Bloody Sunday. In a 1982 interview, he admitted, "I think one of the problems with that play was that the experience of Bloody Sunday wasn't adequately distilled in me. I wrote it out of some kind of heat and some kind of passion that I would want to have quieted a bit before I did it" ("In Interview with Fintan O'Toole [1982]," 110). And in a 1986 interview, he explicitly compared *Freedom* to *Translations*, saying, "*The Freedom of the City* was a more reckless play and a much more ill-considered play because it was written out of the kind of anger at the Bloody Sunday events in Derry. I don't say I regret it but I certainly wouldn't do it now" ("In Interview with Laurence Finnegan [1986]," 125).

89. Deane, "Introduction" to *Brian Friel: Plays 1*, 17–18.

90. Dantanus, *Brian Friel*, 34.

91. Boltwood, "Brian Friel: Staging the Struggle with Nationalism," 318.

92. Elmer Andrews, *Art of Brian Friel*, 36.

93. This cyclical, reductive nationalist view of Irish history plays into British attempts to restrain what they see as a rebellious population. For example, Fulton, "Hegemonic Discourses in Brian Friel's *The Freedom of the City*," argues that the nationalist discourse in the play "has become incorporated into the hegemonic view of Northern Ireland as a society inevitably based on division and war, a view that may be used to legitimate coercive state control" (75).

94. "Families 'Need to Know' Soldiers' Names," n.p.

95. Friel, "Self-Portrait (1972)," 37.

96. Maley, "Dwelling in Dissonance," 70.

97. Mark William Roche, *Why Literature Matters in the 21st Century*, 245.

98. Ricoeur, *Memory, History, Forgetting*, 85.

99. O'Clery, "Bloody Sunday Victims Can 'Rest in Peace,'" n.p. For the complete report from Lord Saville's inquiry, see "Report of the Bloody Sunday Inquiry."

100. O'Clery, "Bloody Sunday Victims," n.p.

101. Mumford, *City in History*, 655–56; quoted in Gorringe, *Theology of the Built Environment*, 148.

102. Kearney, "Memory in Irish Culture," 149. I am grateful to my former student Makenzie Fitzgerald for leading me to this passage from Kearney, which she used in a conference paper on Elizabeth Bowen.

103. Virginie Roche-Tiengo, "The Voices of the Dead and the Silence of the Living in Brian Friel's Drama," 202, citing Artaud, *The Theatre and Its Double*, 32.

104. Ibid., 202–3.

105. Ibid., 203.

6. *Faith Healer*: Woundedness, Homecoming, and Wholeness

1. Friel, "In Interview with Fintan O'Toole (1982)," 106.

2. Kurdi, "An Interview with Richard Pine," 311.

3. Friel, "*Faith Healer*: original notes (May 19, 1975)."

4. Friel, "*Faith Healer*: original notes (July 19, 1975)."

5. Friel, "Broadway? Who Cares!," 124.

6. Boltwood, *Brian Friel, Ireland, and the North*, 126, argues that Seamus Deane, in his introduction to *Brian Friel: Plays 1*, "articulates the common assumption that '*Faith Healer* has no political background' whatsoever," a statement that accurately conveys the thrust of most readings of the play, but finally misleads,

given Deane's position later in that same paragraph when he states, "the return to home and death out of exile, often inspected by Friel before . . . reinstitutes the social and political dimension which had been otherwise so subdued" (Deane, "Introduction" to *BFP1*, 19, 20).

7. Friel, "Friel's Sense of Conflict," 196.

8. Friel, "In Interview with Fintan O'Toole (1982)," 115.

9. Chaudhuri, *Staging Place*, 55.

10. Ibid., 57–58.

11. McGuinness, "*Faith Healer*: All the Dead Voices," 61.

12. Deane, "Brian Friel: The Name of the Game," 110–11.

13. Walter Benjamin, "Theses on the Philosophy of History," 263.

14. Adorno, *Minima Moralia*, 222.

15. Tracy, "Brian Friel's Rituals of Memory," 398–99.

16. Ibid., 405.

17. Welch, "Sacrament and Significance," 109.

18. Dupré, "Ritual, the Divine Play of Time," 210.

19. Elmer Andrews, *Art of Brian Friel*, 161.

20. Grene, "Five Ways of Looking at *Faith Healer*," 62.

21. Ibid., 64.

22. Heaney, "For Liberation: Brian Friel and the Use of Memory," 240.

23. Benjamin, "Work of Art," 223–24.

24. Cave, "Questing for Ritual and Ceremony," 183.

25. Friel, "Self-Portrait," 37.

26. Davis, "Etát Present," 379.

27. Grene, *Politics of Irish Drama*, 265.

28. Tracy, "Brian Friel's Rituals of Memory," 405.

29. Dantanus, *Brian Friel*, 178.

30. Pine, *Diviner*, 56.

31. Grene, "Friel and Transparency," 136, 137.

32. Rayner, *Ghosts*, xii.

33. Kearney, "Language Play," 83.

34. Turner, *From Ritual to Theatre*, 45. I formulated the following analysis of liminality and ritual in *Faith Healer* on my own, although I was later pleased to find that Richard Pine employs Turner's theories to briefly argue that Friel is "almost inevitably fulfilling a liminal, shamanistic role as he sets about his task of divining the elements of ritual and translating them into drama" in plays such as *Faith Healer* and others (*Diviner*, 69).

35. Turner, *From Ritual to Theatre*, 47–48.

36. Ibid., 48.

37. Friel, "*Faith Healer*: original notes (Oct. 17, 1975)."

38. See Wyse, "Traumatizing Romanticism in Brian Friel's *Faith Healer*," 448–63, for an interesting analysis of how Frank functions as the archetype of the Romantic artist. Gleitman, "Three Characters in Search of a Play," agrees with Wyse, but adds that "in this regard Frank is not qualitatively different from, but merely a magnified version of, those around him, all of whom long to refashion the people whom they love or desire in such a way as to satisfy their own needs" (99).

39. Turner, *Dramas, Fields, and Metaphors*, 232.

40. Ibid.

41. Turner, *Ritual Process*, 95.

42. Turner, *Dramas, Fields, and Metaphors*, 232; my emphasis.

43. Strain, "'Renouncing Change,'" one of the few commentators on the play to attend to this passage, thus wrongly reads it as a moment in which Frank and Teddy "exchange acknowledgments—one frees Teddy from guilt [supposedly of loving Grace more than a friend], the other assures Frank that Grace will not be alone" (75).

44. George O'Brien is a rare critical exception in pointing out the emotional need of characters in the play. He notes in his *Brian Friel*, 100, that "Grace is another Crystal [from Friel's earlier play, *Crystal and Fox*] in her thankless but crucial role as an embodiment of emotional need," observing further that "*Faith Healer* also recalls another Friel play, *Living Quarters*, with its emphasis on being trapped in recollection and emotional deprivation." Unfortunately, O'Brien does not realize the temporary emotional healing that Frank creates that night in the pub, and further, wrongly sees the crucial phrase at the end of the play, "the need we had for each other," as a manifestation of Grace's emotional need for Frank (99–100), when it clearly signifies Frank and his killers' spiritual need for each other, and by extension, society's need for a revived spirituality.

45. Heaney, "For Liberation," 237.

46. Friel, "Theatre of Hope and Despair (1967)," 23; my emphases.

47. See Niel, "Disability as Motif and Meaning in Friel's Drama," 215–16, for a brief discussion of disability in *Faith Healer* that does not analyze McGarvey's disability but those of the disabled whom Frank meets and attempts to heal in the past and Frank's own "disability."

48. Nietzsche, *Birth of Tragedy*, 52.

49. Ibid.

50. Ibid.

51. Kiberd, "Brian Friel's *Faith Healer*," 224.

52. Lady Augusta Gregory, *Cuchulain of Muirthemne*, 252.

53. Friel cites "the mythology of the Red Branch" but stresses the myth's individual, not cultural value: "[You can] find out what the relevance of that is to yourself but not to your Irishness—just to yourself. . . . I'm not asking whether

it's relevant or instructive or informative for your Irishness. I'm just saying that it might tell you something about yourself" ("In Interview with Laurence Finnegan [1986]," 132).

54. John Wilson Foster, "Brightest Candle of the Gael," 8.

55. Ibid., 11.

56. Welch, *The Cold of May Day Monday*, 241.

57. Niel, "Disability as Motif and Meaning in Friel's Drama," 216.

58. Boltwood, *Brian Friel, Ireland, and the North*, 130, argues that "[w]ith Frank's multiple associations to the working class of the Republic . . . and Grace's to the professional aristocracy of the North, the couple embodies not so much the contentious marriage of the two Irelands as their mutual failure. . . . Ultimately, Friel cannot imagine them living together on the island or socially legitimating their 'mixed' marriage through progeny."

59. See McAuley, "Cuchullain and an RPG-7," 55–61, especially 55–56, for a discussion of how Cuchullain has been mobilized as a symbol of Ulster Protestant identity, particularly by such "historians" as Ian Adamson.

60. John Wilson Foster, "Brightest Candle of the Gael," 13.

61. Boltwood, *Brian Friel, Ireland, and the North*, passim.

62. See Peter Taylor's *Loyalists*, 152–55, for a discussion of the activities of this group that was feared even within the Protestant loyalist community. The savagery of the Shankill Butchers is epitomized for Taylor by the murder of the Catholic Francis Crossan on November 25, 1975, when Lenny Murphy, the psychopathic leader of the gang, slashed Crossan's throat "until the head was almost severed from the trunk" (154). Friel may have recalled this frenzied near-decapitation when he was writing of Frank Hardy's imminent murder, and it may have inspired his portrayal of the farming implements (the Shankill Butchers used a meat cleaver and butcher's knives).

63. O'Neill, "Ancient Red Hand Symbol of Ulster," n.p.

64. Deane, "Introduction" to *Brian Friel: Plays 1*, 20.

65. Heaney, *Opened Ground*, 63, 113. Although I arrived at this reading of the play through Heaney on my own, I was pleased to find Anthony Roche quotes the same crucial line from Heaney's "Punishment" in his *Contemporary Irish Drama*, 127.

66. Dupré, "Ritual: The Divine Play of Time," 209.

67. Cooper, "The Gospels of Frank," 240–41.

68. Strain, "'Renouncing Change,'" 78, 71. Strain overreaches in her reading of the final scene and in her analysis of Grace's name as signifying how grace "remains always already present and accessible through free will" (70). "Grace" and "Frank" must be two of the most ironically named characters in literary history: "Grace" offers herself freely to Frank but is always rejected; Frank lies repeatedly

and is not open as his name might suggest. Finally, Strain rather conveniently leaves out the fact that Grace kills herself after Frank's murder, which contravenes her point.

69. John Wilson Foster, "Brightest Candle of the Gael," 3.

70. Grene, "Friel and Transparency," 137.

71. Ibid., 143.

72. Friel, "*Faith Healer*: original notes (May 29, 1975)."

73. Anthony Roche, *Contemporary Irish Drama*, 115.

74. Ibid., 108.

75. Rayner, *Ghosts*, 112.

76. Kennedy, *Spectator and the Spectacle*, 214.

77. Kilroy, "Theatrical Text and Literary Text," 101.

78. Elmer Andrews, "Fifth Province," 47. Andrews reads *Faith Healer* as "continually contradicting and deconstructing itself" (46), finally arguing that "this is, in Roland Barthes' terms, a 'writerly' as opposed to a 'readerly' text, one which forces each member of the audience into an active, productive role rather than that of a mere passive consumer" (47). But Andrews does not acknowledge how the play forms a community within the audience, and only offers two roles for them—the first affirmative, the second pejorative, in the process neglecting the possibility of an actively listening, enchanted audience.

79. Friel, "Philadelphia, Here the Author Comes," 45.

80. Anderson, *Imagined Communities*, 6.

81. Anthony Roche, *Brian Friel: Theatre and Politics*, 155. See 155–58 for a very helpful explanation of how Friel developed various drafts of what would become *Faith Healer* as we know it, including how the intervention of the actor Niall Tóibín (who suggested Friel add a scene from the stage manager's perspective) and producer Oscar Lewenstein (who suggested he write a fourth and final monologue in which Frank Hardy returns in order to land a well-known actor for the part) changed the play for the better.

82. Friel, *Bannermen*, 14.

83. Friel was nervous about this conclusion being recognized as sharing the ritualistic movement of the protestors out of the Guild Hall in Derry City, who were called by soldiers on a loud speaker and then shot by the British Army at the end of *The Freedom of the City*, warning himself in a draft note, "[careful that his going out to the lads hasn't echoes of *Freedom*/loud hailer]" (Friel, "*Faith Healer*: original notes [May 22, 1975]). For a different reading than mine that emphasizes the "luxurious and meticulously precise" language Frank employs in this scene to rewrite and reject "the scene of squalor," see Gleitman, "Three Characters in Search of a Play," 106.

84. Bachelard, *Poetics of Space*, 201.

85. Ibid.

86. Grene, "*Faith Healer* in New York and Dublin," 143.

87. Friel, "In Interview with Victoria Radin (1981)," 94.

88. Friel, "*Faith Healer* Comes to New York," 518. Friel reflects at one point that Mason "was so impressive today, in high good form, on top of his craft; perhaps because of a flattering piece about him in today's *Times*. He keeps reaching for innovation and development. His Irish accent no longer annoys me or maybe it is being erased. And he works with impish glee, attempting new things, fresh intonations, different positions" (517). Friel sensed that Kaye's breakdown was hurting her marriage to Mason, but he never showed it, and Friel consistently praises Mason's performance, along with that of Flanders, "who was frequently brilliant": "Mason grew with each performance. If he was going through a domestic crisis— and he must have been—he revealed nothing to us. That icy, polite English carapace was always in place, intact." In a classic understatement, Friel concludes, "We opened and ran for about three weeks. A very difficult time" (518).

89. O'Toole, "Modern Ireland in 100 Artworks," n.p.; O'Toole, "The 'Eerie Afterlife' of Donal McCann," n.p.

90. Toíbín, "Colm Toíbín on a Time of Theatrical Miracles for Brian Friel," n.p.

91. Grene, "Brian Friel and the Sovereignty of Language," 43–44.

92. Brantley, "Recalling an Artist's Eloquent Loneliness," A18.

93. *New York Times* theater critic Charles Isherwood made much the same point, noting, "It moved me immensely. But I also felt it to be an artistic failure. Strange as it may sound, it was simultaneously unsuccessful on a technical level and beautiful to behold. Now Ms. Jones is probably incapable of incompetence at this juncture of her career, and certainly her work in 'Faith Healer' evinced the same integrity that has marked all the performances I've seen her give. But it also seemed to contain a distracting element of unease, a touch of strain. In the role of the slavishly loving wife of the itinerant faith healer of the title (Ralph Fiennes), Ms. Jones's emotional intensity sometimes overwhelmed the considered eloquence of Mr. Friel's words. It seemed to me that Ms. Jones was bringing an almost destructive force of interpretive feeling to bear on a delicate text. Put simply, she was trying too hard." Fascinatingly and compellingly, though, Isherwood felt Jones's struggle with the character illuminates *Faith Healer*'s argument about the difficulties and failures in creating art: "'Faith Healer' is on one level an allegory of the struggle of the artist to live with the mystery of his own creative power. So paradoxically the valiant inward battle I detected in Ms. Jones's intense but overdetermined performance, far from detracting from the effectiveness of the production, was a moving illumination of this layer of the play's meaning" ("Cherry Jones's 'Faith Healer' Performance Illuminates an Artist's Struggle," n.p.). Moreover, Jones was

criticized for her accent, which did not seem to some audience members and critics to be sufficiently English or Irish. Jones pointed out in an interview that "I would have loved to have gone and hung out in her part of Northern Ireland, but Mr. Friel made it clear that he did not want a tremendously specific dialect. He feels that this is a universal play, and if you make it too specific it becomes a smaller experience. So as long as I have this vaguely Anglo-Irish accent, that's okay" (Cherry Jones, "Keeping the Faith"). In the end, Friel actually flew over to coach Jones on both her accent and performance and was never satisfied with either as he later told me in a letter after I informed him that Jones and I had had the same creative drama teacher, Mrs. Ruby Krider, during our childhood years in Paris, Tennessee. Irish actress Rosaleen Linehan confirmed this penchant of Friel's for not insisting on a Donegal or Northern Irish accent (and there are many of these), noting, "Friel himself is always saying, 'God, would they ever stop those dreadful Northern accents! Don't play it with a Donegal accent!'" (quoted in Coult, *About Friel*, 150).

94. I write extensively about that production in my essay "Deprovincializing Brian Friel's Drama in America, 2009 and 2014," 109–15.

95. Friel, *Bannermen*, 14.

96. Kearney, "Language Play," 85.

97. Kilroy, "Theatrical Text and Literary Text," 101.

98. Cooper, "The Gospels of Frank," 243.

99. Dupré, "Ritual: The Divine Play of Time," 205–6.

100. Ibid., 207.

101. Benjamin, "Theses on the Philosophy of History," 264, observes that for the Jews waiting for their Messiah, "every second of time was the strait gate through which the Messiah might enter."

102. Grene, "Brian Friel and the Sovereignty of Language," 44.

103. Adorno, *Minima Moralia*, 247.

104. Grene, "Five Ways of Looking at *Faith Healer*," 63.

105. Girard, *Violence and the Sacred*, 36.

106. Murray, "Friel's 'Emblems of Adversity,'" 88.

107. Teachout, "Great Play, Great Player."

108. Giedion, *Mechanization Takes Command*, 718.

109. Sontag, *Regarding the Pain of Others*, 115.

110. Friel, "In Interview with Fintan O'Toole (1982)," 113.

111. Friel, "*Faith Healer*: original notes (Nov. 8, 1978)."

112. Pine, "Coming Home to the Truth," n.p. In this same program note, Pine expands upon his conception of the importance of wholeness for Friel in the play: "In my opinion, *Faith Healer* is Friel's most important play . . . because he also questioned his own role as an artist, as a conduit of voices, as a magician.

Faith-healing is like playwriting: an attempt at wholeness. It is more compelling than reality, which is why we go to it."

113. Friel, "*Faith Healer*: original notes (Oct. 1975)."

114. Friel, "*Faith Healer*: original notes (Oct. 17, 1975)."

115. Without making a link to *Faith Healer*, Murray, in his introduction to *Brian Friel: Essays, Diaries, Interviews: 1964–1999*, observes that Friel's 1958 radio play, *A Sort of Freedom*, portrays a couple with marriage and fertility problems, concluding, "A sterile marriage is here a metaphor for a sterile materialism" (x).

116. Ricoeur, *Memory, History, Forgetting*, 482.

117. Ibid., 493.

118. Heaney, "Brian Friel and Field Day," 191; my emphases.

119. Wilson, "Gordon Wilson," n.p.

120. Kearney, "Memory in Irish Culture," 150.

7. Interchapter: Friel and the Field Day Theatre Company

1. Friel, "Theatre of Hope and Despair (1967)," 24.

2. Friel, "Brian Friel: Dramatist and Short Story Writer."

3. Maxwell, *Brian Friel*, 28.

4. Quoted in Ciarán Deane, "Brian Friel's *Translations*," 18. I found this quotation in Richtarik, who cites this source in "Brian Friel and Field Day," 360.

5. Friel, "Letter to Seamus Deane," Nov. 21, 1979.

6. Richtarik, *Acting between the Lines*, 10–11.

7. Friel continued to champion a professional theater for Derry—this time using a permanent, dedicated building—well into the late 1990s after he left Field Day. See the correspondence between him and the Derry Theatre Trust in 1998 and 1999 in Friel, "Theatre for Derry."

8. Pine, *Diviner*, 168.

9. Ibid., 25.

10. Friel, "Friel Takes Derry by Storm," 159.

11. Longley, *Tuppenny Stung*, 75.

12. Friel, "Theatre of Hope and Despair (1967)," 16.

13. Woodworth, "Reasons for Having a Field Day," n.p.

14. Friel, "In Interview with Fintan O'Toole (1982)," 111.

15. Ibid., 114.

16. Friel, "Letter to Seamus Deane," Oct. 28, 1982.

17. Friel, "Field Day: An Introduction," n.p.

18. For analyses of the Field Day plays and the pamphlets from 1980–84, see Richtarik, *Acting between the Lines*. For a more comprehensive analysis of

the entire enterprise drawing on both the Field Day Archive and the Friel Papers at the National Library of Ireland, see O'Malley, *Field Day and the Translation of Irish Identities*. Friel was passionately committed to the anthology and hurt by the charge levied by feminist critics that it did not sufficiently represent women's contributions to Irish writing. He may have felt the anthology could capture in its dispassionate and comprehensive prose introductions to various authors and literary works the evolution of Irish writing—what he could not in his dramas. Friel, who often featured strong female characters in his plays, clearly felt the charges against the anthology were unfair and that the attacks on it were exacerbated by the directors' silence. In the end, the anthology has never been as widely praised as it might have been. In fact, somewhat replicating the issue of the overly male makeup of the first three volumes, two subsequent volumes, edited entirely by women and featuring *only* female contributors, have appeared.

19. Harrington and Mitchell, "Introduction," 1. See Tuite, "'Walking in the Steps of Your Forefathers,'" for a fascinating discussion of how theater and politics merge in the public performances put on every year in Derry by the Crimson Players to commemorate "Derry's successful defense during the Jacobite siege of 1688–89" (167) for the unionist Apprentice Boys, members of the Royal Ulster Constabulary, and assembled journalists.

20. O'Malley, *Field Day*, 20.

21. Indeed, in that same Oct. 28, 1982, letter to Deane cited above, Friel excitedly mentions having had a letter from Tom Kilroy that morning and speculates that he could perhaps contribute a pamphlet. Crucially, Kilroy, who would later contribute a play, *Double Cross*, that was staged by the company in 1986, and who would become one of the directors in 1988 (the only one born in the Republic of Ireland), echoed how Friel felt Field Day could transcend identitarian politics in Northern Ireland. Friel cites Kilroy's response in his letter to Deane: "Personally I would love to see Field Day transcending the particulars in the North—clearly rising above the irrelevance of the divisions, projecting into a future where it will all be looked-back-on with mere sadness. And it *is* so irrelevant—Catholic Protestant, Nationalist, Unionist—the *lot*, and I have a feeling many, many people are just waiting for this to be said loudly. So there!"

22. Richtarik, *Acting between the Lines*, 51.

23. O'Malley, *Field Day*, 27–28.

24. Friel, "Letter to Seamus Deane," June 21, 1984. For a measured assessment of Longley's take on Field Day in her 1985 essay "Poetry and Politics in Northern Ireland," see Richtarik, *Acting between the Lines*, 242–43. Richtarik does not feel that Longley proves her contention about Field Day's nationalist ideology, but notes that it was understandable, especially given the nationalist Deane's outsized role as unofficial company spokesman.

25. Richtarik, "Brian Friel and Field Day," 368.

26. Deane, "Introduction" to *Brian Friel: Plays 1*, 20.

27. Friel, "Letter to Seamus Deane," Mar. 17, 1989. I realize this and a few of the other letters from Friel to Deane I cite in this interchapter have been cited in part by my friend, the Irish drama scholar Marilynn Richtarik, "Brian Friel and Field Day," passim. But since I discovered these letters in the Seamus Deane Papers and copied them in 2012 and later directed Richtarik to them, as she acknowledges in her article (371n7), and had long planned to cite them, I am citing them myself without acknowledging their appearance in Richtarik's article beyond this statement. There are other letters and statements from those involved with Field Day I did not copy during that research trip to Emory, and thus I cite those when they appear in Richtarik's thoughtful essay.

28. Friel, "Letter to Seamus Deane," July 17, 1982.

29. Richtarik, *Acting between the Lines*, 243. She succinctly identifies the project's three major areas of tension by 1985: "[B]etween the artistic and the critical impulses within Field Day, between individual directors and the group, and inherent in Field Day's desire to articulate a Northern voice in Irish cultural politics without being regarded as simply a northern nationalist voice" (239).

30. Quoted in Pelletier, "'Creating Ideas to Live By,'" 52. I found this quotation in Richtarik, who cites this source in "Brian Friel and Field Day," 361.

31. Pelletier, "*Translations*, the Field Day Debate, and the Re-Imagining of Irish Identity," 74.

32. Woodworth, "Reasons for Having a Field Day," n.p.

33. Heaney, "Sparks in the Tin Hut," 4.

34. Richtarik, *Acting between the Lines*, 28.

8. *Translations*: Lamenting and Accepting Modernity

1. Friel, "Reply to J. H. Andrews," 118.

2. Ibid.

3. Friel, "In Interview with Paddy Agnew (1980)," 87. I cite Friel's complete quotation in his answer here in the introduction to this study. Almost certainly drawing on Friel's comments in this interview, Whelan, in "Between: The Politics of Culture in 'Translations,'" observes that "*Translations* circles around the awkward question of whether Irish culture is fatally flawed internally, a flaw that renders it vulnerable to outside influence. *Baile Beag*/Ballybeg is a cul-de-sac for young women and the play is full of damaged characters—dumb Sarah, alcoholic Hugh, lame Manus (damaged when his drunken father fell asleep across him), deluded Jimmy Jack."

4. Dixon, "Mapping Cultural Imperialism," 136.

5. Quoted in O'Brien, "Meet Brian Friel: The *Irish Press* Columns, 34.

6. Morash, *History of Irish Theatre, 1601–2000*, 234–35.

7. Ibid., 235. Lonergan, *Theatre and Globalization*, argues that the staging of *Translations* in the Guildhall just a few years after *Freedom* was set there "was not necessarily an attempt to 'occupy' a space associated with Unionism, but perhaps could be seen as an assertion of the equality of the nationalist and unionist communities in Northern Ireland, or as a symbol of the possibility of reconciliation between both sides in the conflict" (34).

8. Whelan, "Between: The Politics of Culture in 'Translations.'"

9. Anthony Roche, *Brian Friel: Theatre and Politics*, 151.

10. Friel, *Mundy Scheme*, 257.

11. Ibid., 204.

12. See Richtarik, *Acting between the Lines*, 33–34, for a helpful discussion of Steiner's influence on the play.

13. See, for example, Liz Cullingford's influential essay "British Romans and Irish Carthaginians," where she argues that the Irish characters such as Maire and Hugh's use of Latin in reference to the English surveyors in several critical moments links the British representatives in 1833 to those of imperial Rome, while conveniently leaving out the Donnelly twins' role and Maire's desire to learn English, for example (231–32).

14. Friel, "Where We Live," ix.

15. "Brian Friel," 2475.

16. Dantanus, *Brian Friel*, 187.

17. Friel, "Self-Portrait," 45; my emphases.

18. Richtarik shows in *Acting between the Lines* that reviews of performances in Northern Ireland tended to be remarkably ecumenical: they generally praised what they perceived correctly as the balanced portraits of both British and Irish characters, while Irish reviewers tended to focus on the linguistic issues "in unambiguous political terms" (51–54; 55), specifically on the imperial linguistic project of the English surveyors in translating place names from Irish into English as part of the 1833 British Ordnance Survey. But even the Northern Irish reviewers generally neglected the larger epistemological and cultural issues raised by the advent of modernity in Friel's fictive village of Ballybeg.

19. See, for example, Richtarik, ibid., who cites an inaccuracy about the National Schools being compulsory at this time and especially "glaring misrepresentations of the British officers," notably that "Yolland's courtship of Maire is implausible, though more from the standpoint of class than of race" (43). Richtarik further notes the facts that British survey soldiers would not have had bayonets and generally enjoyed good public relations and that "the official policy of the Survey from 1830 on was to adopt the variant spelling that came closest to the original Irish form of the name" (44). Hewitt, "Ordnance Survey in Ireland: A

Bloody Military Operation?," points out that "[b]y the late 1830s, when over two thousand Ordnance Surveyors were present in Ireland, the number of Irish employees outnumbered the British mapmakers by four to one. . . . The 'Topographical Branch' was staffed by some of Ireland's most accomplished linguists, most of whom conceived their researches to promote Irish cultural heritage in the face of 'the collective folly and stupid intellect of the Empire,' as one of those scholars put it" (n.p.). Friel and the historian J. H. Andrews, whose *A Paper Landscape* partially inspired the play, exchanged a series of statements about the discrepancies. See Friel, Andrews, and Kevin Barry's forum discussion, "*Translations* and *A Paper Landscape*"; Andrews's "Notes for a Future Edition of Brian Friel's *Translations*"; and Friel's "Making a Reply to the Criticisms of *Translations* by J. H. Andrews" and "Where We Live." Interestingly, the program for the 1998 production of *Translations* at Belfast's Lyric Theatre offers five pages of extracts from documents ranging from William Carleton's *Hedge School* and P. J. Dowling's *Hedge Schools of Ireland* to histories of Ireland and Colby's *Ordnance Survey of Ireland* (1835), presumably part of that company's effort to show how the play is historically grounded ("Brian Friel's *Translations*," Program).

20. Richtarik, *Acting between the Lines*, 49.

21. Friel, Linehan, Leonard, and Keane, "Future of Irish Drama," 14.

22. See Friel's lament of the increasing emphasis on prosperity in the Ireland of the early 1970s in "Interview with Desmond Rushe (1970)": "I think the emphasis is on having at least one car and preferably two. One has only to go into any of the posh Dublin hotels and one can see the new Ireland sprawled around in the lounges. This development is terrifying" (27).

23. Peacock, "Translating the Past," 121.

24. Berry, "People, Land, and Community," 73.

25. Friel, "Extracts from a Sporadic Diary (1979): *Translations*," 75.

26. Gleitman, "'I'll See You Yesterday,'" 31.

27. Tacitus, *Agricola*, 63.

28. Friel tried out an opening narrative for Frank Hardy at one point in "*Faith Healer*: original notes (May 29, 1975)," in which he indicates awareness of this type of settlement: "When I was a boy, I lived in a *clachan* or tiny group of houses that clung together on the west coast of Donegal."

29. Evans, *Personality of Ireland*, 60.

30. Ibid., 55.

31. Evans notes that "[t]he larger 'English' openfields of the Leinster lowlands were enclosed for the most part in the eighteenth century in the course of the agrarian revolution" (ibid., 57).

32. Friel's critique of precise measurement and land division here and elsewhere in the play suggests the hitherto-unrecognized influence of an Irish literary

work that also laments the passing of rural culture and fears the beginning of enclosure, Oliver Goldsmith's "The Deserted Village." Goldsmith's poem deplores the rural depopulation of the village of Auburn because of the destruction of English cottages by the wealthy to improve their vistas, and, more significantly for our discussion of Friel's purposes here, because of the private enclosure of formerly public lands. Goldsmith's Auburn looks startlingly like Friel's Ballybeg could with the advent of enclosure and industrialism. His poem even laments the passing of an astonishingly learned schoolmaster who, like Hugh in Friel's play, ruled his little school strictly. See Goldsmith, "Deserted Village," 1255.

33. Whelan, "Bases for Regionalism," 7.

34. Ibid.

35. Evans, *Personality of Ireland*, 60.

36. See Evans's "Appendix," where he comments extensively on the rundale system in Gweedore by focusing on Lord George Hill's 1845 pamphlet, *Facts from Gweedore* (ibid., 89–110).

37. Ibid., 61–62.

38. Gorringe, *Theology of the Built Environment*, 51, quoting the Royal Commission on the Distribution of Income and Wealth, which was released in 1979. I am aware of the periodic attempts to revive communal land ownership practices in mainland Britain; for a helpful brief history of such attempts from the Middle Ages through the early to mid-twentieth century, see ibid., 67–68.

39. After Lancey has threatened to shoot all the animals, Bridget runs to the hedge-school and sniffs the air in panic, claiming, "The sweet smell! Smell it! It's the sweet smell! Jesus, it's the potato blight" (*BFP1* 441). Doalty tells her, "It's the army tents burning, Bridget," and she calms down.

40. Roach, "'All the Dead Voices': The Landscape of Famine in *Waiting for Godot.*"

41. Friel, "Making a Reply to the Criticism of *Translations* by J. H. Andrews (1983)," 117.

42. Friel's appendix to that play, an extract from *Studies in Irish Craniology: The Aran Islands, Co. Galway* by Professor A. C. Haddon, disturbingly demonstrates this imperial ideology as (mal)practiced upon the Irish.

43. Appadurai, *Modernity at Large*, 117.

44. Ibid.

45. See MacCana, "Early Irish Ideology and the Concept of Unity," where he argues for a spiritual unity to early Irish society, not a coherence based upon historical facts or central control.

46. Smyth, *Space and the Irish Cultural Imagination*, 42.

47. Bauman, *Globalization: The Human Consequences*, 31. Bauman's chapter on this issue, "Space Wars: A Career Report," 27–54, is required reading for

anyone seeking to understand how the battle to control public and private spaces has progressed or, more precisely, regressed over our history.

48. Smyth, *Space and the Irish Cultural Imagination*, 49. See 54–56 for Smyth's discussion of Friel's play. At the same time, it must be said that the *dinnseanchas* themselves have considerable variety in their dates of composition and are part of a pseudohistorical Irish tradition. Hamon, "Landscape, *Senchas*, and the Medieval Irish Mind," 35, notes that this placelore features both harmony and plurality: "harmony because the collection is a complete whole with far-reaching influences which give an inclusive description of Irish landscape; and plurality because the origin of the separate entities, which have sometimes local, sometimes antiquarian, sometimes political purposes, were re-appropriated by the compiler while still frequently retaining their open-ended approach to multiple origins."

49. Anderson, *Imagined Communities*, 173.

50. Ibid., 175.

51. Robinson, *Setting Foot on the Shores of Connemara*, 162.

52. Richtarik, *Acting between the Lines*, 45.

53. Robinson, *Setting Foot*, 163.

54. Ibid.

55. Ibid., 163, 164.

56. Mark William Roche, *Why Literature Matters in the 21st Century*, 239.

57. See Lysaght, "Contrasting Natures: The Issue of Names," for a thoughtful and comprehensive survey of the way in which the decline of Gaelic has led to a gradual dissociation from nature, even in *Gaeltacht* areas. As evidence of this trajectory, Lysaght cites the botanist Michael Viney, who pointed out in 1986 that although "Irish names for natural things linger on" in his area of Connacht, "I doubt very much if many of these names are being passed on to the children: they hold Irish in such contempt . . . the intimacy with nature that the 'old people' knew has, indeed, been overtaken by 'a sort of silence'" (442).

58. Eagleton, *Heathcliff and the Great Hunger*, 297.

59. Ibid., 298.

60. Cleary, "Introduction: Ireland and Modernity," 5.

61. Ibid., 6.

62. See Friel, "Where We Live," ix, where he notes that "for all his briskness and energy and dedication, every now and then a whiff of unease arises from these letters. Perhaps because—even though he never publicly acknowledged this—he was taking part in a major military operation. Perhaps because the work he was doing with his sapper companions occasionally created a distance between himself and the people who provided the information for his name-book."

63. Cleary, "Introduction: Ireland and Modernity," 6–7.

64. Duffy, *Exploring the History and Heritage of Irish Landscapes*, 21.

65. Weaver, *Ideas Have Consequences*, 3.

66. Bauman, *Globalization: The Human Consequences*, 27.

67. The only other commentator besides myself that has written at any length about the significance of Doalty's moving of the surveying poles is Mays, "A Nation Once Again?," 134, who offers a political, not perceptual reading of Doalty's actions: "[I]f the surveyor's pole is part of the *materiel* of a more efficient control of the country, that weapon is double-edged: turned back upon itself, it confuses and confounds, subverts through misdirection, that very effort at total control."

68. Lojek, *Spaces of Irish Drama*, 25.

69. I am aware that along with Richtarik (see n. 19 above), J. H. Andrews has pointed out that sappers did not carry bayonets: "Before soldiers went on Survey duty they had to hand in their bayonets. Confronted with crime or civil disturbance, what Captain Lancy would really have done is withdraw and leave everything to the local constabulary" (quoted in Friel, "Making a Reply to the Criticisms of *Translations* by J. H. Andrews [1983]," 184). Friel's point nonetheless remains that instruments like theodolites and bayonets symbolize the advent of mechanical "culture," if one can call it that, with devastating consequences for Ballybeg's inhabitants.

70. Friel, "Extracts from a Sporadic Diary (1979): *Translations*," 75.

71. But even Lancey cannot fully articulate the abstraction of a two-dimensional map taken out of the context of local culture. See Lojek, *Spaces of Irish Drama*, 32–33, for an insightful discussion of Lancey's attempt to explain the mapping process to the locals. She argues that when he trails off in the passage concluding with "a scaled drawing on paper of—of—of—" (*BFP1* 406), that his stuttering here "signals the difficulty of summing up precisely what it is that a map does. The inarticulate *ofs* are finally more profound and thought-provoking than the subsequent smooth assemblage of technolanguage focused on hydrographic and topographic information" (33).

72. Charles Taylor, *Sources of the Self*, 159–60.

73. Ibid., 163.

74. Toulmin, *Cosmopolis: The Hidden Agenda of Modernity*, 175.

75. Kiberd, *Inventing Ireland*, 621.

76. Harris, "Engendered Space," 72n3. See the majority of this endnote for a survey of contemporary reviews of this scene. Harris argues that "pure theatre is achieved finally in the performance not in the writing. . . . Moments such as these are very nearly indestructible" (44).

77. Friel, "In Interview with Fintan O'Toole (1982)," 115.

78. See my discussion of the poetic language of the Agreement with specific reference to the poets Michael Longley's and Seamus Heaney's comments on it in my *Poetry and Peace*, 308–9.

79. Cullingford, "Gender, Sexuality, and Englishness," 169.

80. Grene, *Politics of Irish Drama*, 43.

81. Morash, *History of Irish Theatre: 1601–2000*, 234.

82. O'Malley, *Field Day and the Translation of Irish Identities*, 40.

83. Bachelard, Introduction to *Poetics of Space*, xxxvi.

84. Kiberd, *Inventing Ireland*, 620.

85. Charles Taylor, *Sources of the Self*, 161.

86. Friel, "Letter to Seamus Deane," Oct. 3, 1980.

87. Richtarik, *Acting between the Lines*, 31.

88. Grene, *Politics of Irish Drama*, 45.

89. Cullingford, "Gender, Sexuality, and Englishness," 170, also suggests that the Donnelly twins are forerunners of the modern IRA and intriguingly argues that Yolland's abduction "replicates the 1977 disappearance of the SAS undercover operative Captain Robert Nairac," whose romanticism and supposed love of Irish culture leads her to link Nairac to Yolland. But Nairac was actively involved in trying to penetrate the IRA and could only be construed as contributing to "'peace in Ireland,'" as Cullingford cites one of Nairac's sisters as saying, by "the British, whose press portrayed Nairac as a gallant idealist murdered by the IRA." Suggesting that Friel's gentle Yolland, clearly a romantic but one devoted to learning local Irish culture and language, is analogous to Nairac, a member of the elite special forces British military unit, elides their vocational differences and neglects Yolland's pursuit of Irish culture and of Maire out of curiosity and love.

90. For the most compelling analysis of the contemporary sectarian resonances of *Translations*, see Anthony Roche's discussion of it in *Brian Friel: Theatre and Politics*, 148–50, as a reflection on the consequences engendered by the introduction of the British policy of internment beginning in 1971. In brief, even though the disastrous policy, which led directly to an upsurge in IRA recruiting, was quickly abandoned, "The violence of reprisal and counter-reprisal had now developed its own momentum" (149).

91. For an excellent synopsis about "The Disappeared" and official and unofficial lists of their victims, see Melaugh and McKenna's "Violence—Details of 'the Disappeared.'"

92. Boltwood, *Brian Friel, Ireland, and the North*, 160.

93. Ibid.

94. For example, the usually thoughtful Gleitman, "'I'll See You Yesterday,'" argues, "In Friel's play, Romantic Ireland is granted fitful life in the form of the doddering Hugh and Jimmy Jack. Yolland falls for them as does the audience, but his dewy-eyed myopia alerts us to what we might otherwise overlook: these loveable linguists can barely clothe or sustain themselves, and at least one of them is clearly a drunk" (32–33). Besides misapprehending the character of Hugh, who is

clearly committed by play's end to accommodating himself to the new place names of the survey and to modernity generally, such a comment diminishes Friel's great sympathy for Yolland and that character's clear commitment to local Irish culture in one stroke.

95. Casey, "How to Get from Space to Place," 18.

96. Friel, "Self-Portrait," 40; my emphases.

97. Friel, "In Interview with Paddy Agnew (1980)," 85.

98. Ibid., 87. But see Fionn Bennett, "Translating the Facts of Landscape into the Facts of Language," for a fascinating account of what Irish culture likely lost by following Hugh's position—the glossopoietic language "that constituted a phonetic echo of the astro-meteoro-hydro-geological facts of the place where his community dwelt" (49).

99. Paulin, *A New Look at the Language Question*, 293.

100. Ibid., 295.

101. Ibid., 296. For a cogent analysis of Paulin's pamphlet in the context of Field Day's aims with questions of translation, see Worthen, "Homeless Words," 24–26. Worthen, however, differs from my own position here in seeing "Friel's use of Irish English in *Translations*" as displaying "a more tentative agenda" for it than in Paulin's pamphlet or in his translation of *Antigone*. He posits that "not only is Irish English shown to produce both Irish language and Irish history as an absence, but the radical instability operating between languages seems finally to undermine translation between them and between their competing versions of culture, agency, and identity" (35). Instead of what Worthen claims, *Translations* attempts acts of linguistic preservation with Irish through Irish English. And Maire and Yolland's relationship, which he does not discuss at all, is the best riposte to his second claim about "the radical instability operating between languages."

102. Corcoran, "Penalties of Retrospect," 27.

103. Boltwood, *Brian Friel, Ireland, and the North*, 157.

104. Ibid., 157; see 157–58 for the entire discussion of Hugh in this context.

105. Corcoran, "Penalties of Retrospect," 28.

106. See Saunders, "Classical Antiquity in Brian Friel's *Translations*," 138–41, for an example of this typical reading of Hugh's recitation and for how Saunders believes the British in the play are "very visibly the beneficiaries of the kind of teleological structure of history promoted by the *Aeneid*" (138). But see Welch, *The Cold of May Day Monday*, who offers a surprising and audacious reading of Hugh's peroration, arguing that while we traditionally understand the race "springing from Trojan blood" as Romans, "translated" in the play as the Britons under Yancey who are invading Ballybeg, and the Carthaginians as the Irish, instead, in "Hugh's damaged mind it is the Irish who are the Romans, who will bring about the downfall of the race who appear so favored, the British." Thus, "we are left

thinking, what if it is the case that the Empire will end where it began, in Ireland? The Donnellys will never be reconciled until they achieve what they are determined to achieve. A terrible prospect, but one that delivers deep theatrical excitement of a kind that is not entirely licit" (244).

107. Grant, *Breaking Enmities*, 93.

108. Even a powerfully perceptive critic such as Deane misapprehends this thrust of the play, reductively arguing in his introduction to *Brian Friel: Plays 1* that "most of all," *Translations* "is a play about the final incoherence that has always characterized the relationship between the two countries, the incoherence that comes from sharing a common language which is based upon different presuppositions" (22). But as Bernard O'Donoghue points out in his assessment of the play's many "confused interchanges" between characters, "Something about the linguistic condition of Ireland—in relation to English, Irish, and to some degree the Latin-derived liturgy of the Church—means that uncertainty and confusion of meaning are more accepted than in more wholly monoglot cultures. The condition of Ireland is more ready than most places to conclude, as Hugh does in the play, that 'Confusion is not an ignoble condition'" ("Borders in Brian Friel's *Translations*," 928). Moreover, Maire and Yolland's love is based upon linguistic "incoherence," yet it transcends that confusion through their powerful recitation of Irish town names that effectively maps their clearly articulated love for each other onto the Donegal landscape.

109. Devitt, *Shifting Scenes*, 88–89.

110. Teachout, "Very Best We Have," W7. In this regard, one of Friel's favorite actors, Stephen Rea, approvingly told Thomas Kilroy that Friel's plays are so enjoyable for actors because they have this "sense of people who are well used to living together" (quoted in Kilroy, "Theatrical Text and Literary Text," 92). Contrast this seamless production with the Conall Morrison production at the Abbey Theatre that ran from June 23 to August 13, 2011. I attended the Saturday, July 9 matinee production featuring the brilliant Donal O'Kelly, who stole the show as Jimmy Jack. O'Kelly seemed like a drunker but more articulate version of Beckett's Didi. And yet O'Kelly and the cast played for laughs too much in the first part of the play, leading to an incongruous performance wherein the audience did not seem prepared for the tragedies that occurred after intermission.

9. *Dancing at Lughnasa*: Placing and Recreating Memory

1. Friel, "*Dancing at Lughnasa* (1990): Background Research & Manuscripts."
2. Bachelard, *Poetics of Space*, 8.
3. Berry, "Body and the Earth," 111–12.
4. Ibid., 112.

5. Casey, "How to Get from Space to Place," 24.

6. Ibid., 25.

7. Thornton, *J. M. Synge and the Western Mind*, 115.

8. Ibid.

9. Friel, "In Interview with Mel Gussow," 148.

10. MacNeill, *Festival of Lughnasa*, ix.

11. Even the cover of the playbill from that 2000 performance features grain. It surrounds the sisters' radio, the cover of which looks like a grimacing mask ("Brian Friel's *Dancing at Lughnasa*," Playbill).

12. Worth, "Translations of History," 86.

13. McGrath, *Brian Friel's (Post) Colonial Drama*, 238; 244–45.

14. Arnheim, "Disciplining the Gramophone, Radio, Telephone, and Television," 422.

15. Kopytoff, "Cultural Biography of Things," 64.

16. Ibid., on slavery; 67.

17. Ibid., 73.

18. Because of my reading of the place of the radio in the sisters' household here, I disagree with Sweeney, *Performing the Body in Irish Theatre*, who argues that the radio has "a patriarchal authority over the sisters' behavior, which shifts at points throughout the play as they are released by its music" (118). In fact, the radio's lack of masculine authority is suggested by Chris's comment after the sisters' dance that "Maybe a valve has gone [in the radio]" (*DL* 23); while it enabled them to dance as a release valve, it is almost as if this inanimate object is now exhausted.

19. Mahony, "Memory and Belonging," 12.

20. Ibid.

21. Arnheim, "Disciplining the Gramophone," 424.

22. Mahony, "Memory and Belonging," 12.

23. Friel, "Seven Notes for a Festival Programme (1999)," 177.

24. Quoted in Lahr, "In *Dancing at Lughnasa*," 214.

25. Lonergan, *Theatre and Globalization*, 47–48. After noting that this percussive music "contrasts strongly with Friel's own stage directions," which call for a subversion of order, Lonergan cites Burke, "As if Language No Longer Existed": "Such an emphasis on celebration tended to ignore the text's emphasis on the ugly aspects of the dance" (19). In his essay, "'Dancing on a One-Way Street,'" Lonergan argues that "the darkness implicit in the play was not only ignored but that it may even have been suppressed in favor of a less provocative presentation of the play; it seems also that it emphasized euphoric release where Friel wanted grotesque near-hysteria, and that it made characters such as Kate appear ridiculous rather than sympathetic" (155). One major reason for such a euphoric presentation was that the play was seen as potentially appealing to a wide audience and thus, "rather

than producing the play in a way that would have been of exclusive interest to an Irish audience, the Abbey instead emphasized the qualities of the play likely to make it appealing internationally" (ibid.).

26. Maggie's parodic dance probably has its origin in a passage from Friel's short story "Aunt Maggie, the Strong One." When Aunt Maggie's nephew Bernard (one of Friel's birth certificates has "Bernard O'Friel" on it) comes to visit her in the rest home to convince her to give up smoking, the narrator tells us that "she danced up to him and pirouetted in clumsy burlesque before him" (*Saucer of Larks* 129). This aged Maggie, who had always been vigorous before she left Donegal, hides her decline by this false dance.

27. Gagné, "Three Dances," 124. For a helpful overview of contemporary responses to this dance that largely focuses on its liberating, even joyful qualities, see Harris, "Engendered Space," 45–46.

28. Bates, quoted in Coult, *About Friel*, 197.

29. Cave, "Questing for Ritual and Ceremony," 191.

30. Sweeney, *Performing the Body in Irish Theatre*, 123.

31. Quoted in Anthony Roche, "Friel and Synge," 156.

32. Whelan, "Cultural Effects of the Famine," 141.

33. Casey, "How to Get from Space to Place," 25.

34. Lonergan, *Theatre and Globalization*, 40

35. Bates, quoted in Coult, *About Friel*, 197.

36. Crotty, "Brian Friel: A Dramatic Life," n.p.

37. This same issue is raised in Friel's autobiographical short story, "A Man's World," very likely the source for *Lughnasa* along with "Aunt Maggie, the Strong One." The unnamed boy in the former story "had five maiden aunts [in Donegal] and they doted on me" (*Saucer of Larks* 106). The narrator tells us that his aunts did not know what to say to his father, "since they had no experience of men" (108).

38. Leeney, "Dancing at Lughnasa," n.p. I could not find statistics for single women in Donegal during the 1930s, but Clear, *Social Change and Everyday Life in Ireland, 1850–1922*, 76, notes that "Donegal had one of the highest percentages in the whole country of middle-aged single women in 1911, at 38 per cent."

39. Casey, *Imagining*, 206.

40. Whelan, "Cultural Effects of the Famine," 142.

41. Ibid.

42. Quoted in Coult, *About Friel*, 197.

43. See Wilson and Donnan, *Anthropology of Ireland*, 43–67, for a helpful summary of anthropological studies of Irish attitudes toward the body that were held through most of the twentieth century. They cite Nancy Scheper-Hughes's study of a village in 1970s County Kerry as typical of rigid attitudes toward the body displayed by the rural Irish after the Devotional Revolution took place in

the Irish Catholic Church. Through her extensive use of Thematic Apperception Tests, Scheper-Hughes found that along with strict gender separation in daily life during work and leisure time, "Villagers were careful about the boundaries of their body [*sic*], and were anxious both about activities (such as dancing) that might bring them into physical contact with the opposite sex" (quoted on 47). Wilson and Donnan then cite John Messenger's research into the suppressive role of local, Jansenist-influenced priests on 47–48.

44. Fanon, *Black Skin, White Masks*, 218.

45. Clutterbuck, "*Lughnasa* after *Easter*," 110–11.

46. Deharme, "Proposition for a Radiophonic Art," 406.

47. Kiberd, "*Dancing at Lughnasa*," 155.

48. Ibid., 161.

49. Whelan, "Cultural Effects of the Famine," 142, 143.

50. Ibid., 145.

51. Ibid.

52. Krause, *The Profane Book of Irish Comedy*, 20.

53. Rafferty, *Catholicism in Ulster, 1603–1983*, 234.

54. Ibid.

55. Fitzpatrick, "Ireland since 1870," 265.

56. Roy Foster, *Modern Ireland 1600–1972*, 544.

57. Casey, *Getting Back into Place*, 48.

58. Ibid., 305.

59. Giedion, *Space, Time, and Architecture*, 20.

60. Ibid.

61. For an interesting discussion of modern Irish architecture, see Campbell's "Modern Architecture and National Identity in Ireland." But Campbell's account generally downplays vernacular architecture in favor of major public building projects like the hydroelectric dam on the River Shannon in the late 1920s and Michael Scott's 1939 design for an Irish Pavilion that he brought to the New York World's Fair.

62. Corringe, *Theology of the Built Environment*, 92.

63. Bachelard, *Poetics of Space*, 14.

64. Day, *Places of the Soul*, 10.

65. Quoted in Coult, *About Friel*, 206.

66. Bachelard, *Poetics of Space*, 7.

67. Clear, *Social Change and Everyday Life in Ireland*, 81.

68. Bachelard, *Poetics of Space*, 5–6.

69. Lonergan, *Theatre and Globalization*, 47.

70. Vanek, quoted in Coult, *About Friel*, 206.

71. Ibid., 206–7.

72. Ibid., 207.

73. Casey, "How to Get from Space to Place," 24, 25.

74. Berry, "Body and the Earth," 125.

75. MacNeill, *Festival of Lughnasa*, 140.

76. Lahr, "Brian Friel Celebrates Life's Pagan Joys," 215.

77. The circumstances of Sweeney's burning only emerge later. Kate tells Maggie, "That young Sweeney boy from the back hills—the boy who was anointed—his trousers didn't catch fire, as Rose said. They were doing some devilish thing with a goat—some sort of sacrifice for the Lughnasa Festival; and Sweeney was so drunk he toppled over into the middle of the bonfire" (35). This sacrifice of the goat parallels Jack's discussion of goat sacrifices in Ryanga, further linking pagan practices in Donegal with those in Africa (*DL* 47–48).

78. MacNeill, *Festival of Lughnasa*, 665.

79. Ibid., 666.

80. Kiberd, "*Dancing at Lughnasa*," 159. The brand name of the gramophones that Gerry Evans peddles, "Minerva," evokes the Greek goddess of wisdom represented as an owl, implying that modern advertising continues to draw on our residual substratum of myth.

81. Rafferty, *Catholicism in Ulster*, 13.

82. McGuinness, "Brian Friel's *Dancing at Lughnasa*," 79–80.

83. Walsh, "Ominous Festivals, Ambivalent Nostalgia," 140–41.

84. Quoted in Coult, *About Friel*, 158.

85. Anthony Roche, "Friel and Synge," 156.

86. McGrath, *Brian Friel's (Post) Colonial Drama*, 239.

87. Ibid.

88. MacLaughlin, "Donegal and the New Ireland," 286. MacLaughlin argues that during the late nineteenth century, "In an effort to diversify the local economy and provide employment . . . the Congested Districts Board supplied families in Donegal's poorer districts with sewing machines, which they paid for in installments" (ibid.). But Friel portrays Agnes and Rose as hand-knitting in the 1930s for dramatic effect, suggesting an abrupt transformation from manual labor to mechanized labor.

89. See Clear, *Social Change and Everyday Life in Ireland*, 4–23, for an overview of transformation and continuity during the period 1850–1922.

90. Roy Foster, *Modern Ireland 1600–1972*, 523.

91. Ibid., 538.

92. Ibid., 539.

93. Friel, "Seven Notes for a Festival Programme (1999)," 173.

94. White, *Music and the Irish Literary Imagination*, argues, "If this whole passage also recalls the shattered dream of *Translations*, it does so specifically in

regard to a vanished discourse, a private space, and ultimately, a culture that has disappeared" (221).

95. Casey, *Imagining*, 233.

96. Casey, *Remembering*, 156.

97. Ibid., 156–57.

98. Wirzba, "Placing the Soul," 88–89.

99. Ibid., 89.

100. Bachelard, *Poetics of Space*, 6.

10. Home and Beyond: *Molly Sweeney, The Home Place,* and *Hedda Gabler* (after Ibsen)

1. Casey, *Getting Back into Place*, 312.

2. Lojek, "Brian Friel's Sense of Place," 178.

3. Dantanus, *Brian Friel*, 220n8.

4. Friel, "In Interview with Fintan O'Toole (1982)," 112, 113.

5. Quoted in Bauman, *Globalization: The Human Consequences*, 15–16. Benedikt's remarks appear in his essay, "On Cyberspace and Virtual Reality," 41.

6. Bertha, "Brian Friel as Postcolonial Playwright," 163.

7. Dupré, "Ritual: The Divine Play of Time," 201.

8. Casey, "How to Get from Space to Place," 26.

9. Pelletier, "'New Articulations of Irishness and Otherness' on the Contemporary Irish Stage," 115.

10. Lonergan, *Theatre and Globalization*, 43–54.

11. Ricoeur, *Memory, History, Forgetting*, 149.

12. O'Brien, "Late Plays," 91.

13. Heaney, *Spelling It Out*, n.p.

14. Lanters, "Brian Friel's Uncertainty Principle," 175.

15. Quoted in Pine, *Diviner*, 13.

16. Harris, "Engendered Space," 64.

17. Heaney, "Vision," n.p.

18. Ibid. Another line of criticism treating the significance of Molly's "borderline country" sees her variously as a "subaltern" (Pine, *Diviner*, 298–304) and, more specifically, as an analog for the formerly colonized Ireland, a Cathleen figure through which Friel's play "narrows its focus [from that on *Translations'* on an entire culture] to the colonizer's impact on the life of the individual Irish woman" (Moloney, "Molly Astray," 287 and passim). But the play itself eschews politics perhaps more than any other work by Friel.

19. Pine, *Diviner*, 63.

20. Ibid., 304.

21. Friel, "Extracts from a Sporadic Diary (1992–94): *Molly Sweeney*," 155. But to qualify his use of Jung, I should note that he crossed out this passage six months before the idea for *Molly Sweeney* came to him and even appended "*WONDERFUL TENNESSEE?*" immediately after the Jung passage (ibid.). Kerrigan, "Swimming in Words," 160, quotes a fuller portion of this passage in his fine discussion of the play.

22. Quoted in Coult, *About Friel*, 156.

23. David Richards, "Now Starring in Dublin," n.p.

24. Kerrigan, "Swimming in Words," 160, 161.

25. DeVinney, "Monologue as Dramatic Action in Brian Friel's *Faith Healer* and *Molly Sweeney*," 112.

26. Carlson, "*Molly Sweeney*. By Brian Friel," 424.

27. Murray, "Introduction" to *Brian Friel: Plays 2*, xxii.

28. Keating, "*Molly Sweeney*," n.p.

29. Ibid.

30. Anthony Roche, *Brian Friel: Theatre and Politics*, 194.

31. Quoted in Casey, *Imagining*, 231.

32. David Richards, "Now Starring in Dublin," n.p. In a bizarre turn of events, Friel actually had cataract surgery while conceiving of and drafting *Molly Sweeney*!

33. Casey, *Imagining*, 312–13.

34. Lonergan, *Theatre and Globalization*, 193, 191–96.

35. Teachout, "'The Home Place' Review," n.p.

36. Loveridge, "*The Home Place*," n.p.

37. Everett, "Review—*The Home Place*—Guthrie—5 Stars," n.p.

38. Teachout, "'The Home Place' Review," n.p.

39. See also in this regard Friel's similar rejection of the assigning of physiognomical features to particular families by John O'Donovan, a major historical topographer assigned to the Ordnance Survey in Donegal, the subject of *Translations*, in a preface to O'Donovan's letters Friel wrote in 2000, only a few years before he wrote *The Home Place*. Friel points out that "writing from Glenties on October 16 [1835], he throws discrimination to the winds and engages in wild generalizations—perhaps because he was in great pain from a sprained ankle: 'The ancient families here can be yet distinguished by their forms and features. The O'Donnells are corpulent and heavy, with manly faces and acquiline noses. The O'Boyles are ruddy and stout—pictures of health when well fed. The Mac Devits are tall and stubborn, much degenerated in their peasant state but all have good faces. The Mac Swynes are spirited and tall, but of pale and reagh color. Among them all the O'Boyles and O'Dogherties are by far the finest human animals'" ("Where We Live," ix).

40. Spencer, "Friel Falls Short of the Russian Master," n.p.

41. For a thorough treatment of how this tendency toward a "pure" Irishness has evolved, see John Brannigan's pioneering book *Race in Modern Irish Literature and Culture*.

42. McMullan, "*The Home Place*," 66.

43. Friel, "Where We Live," viii.

44. Ibid., ix.

45. Bertha, "Memory, Art, *Lieux de Mémoire* in Brian Friel's *The Home Place*," 230.

46. Such a position, which Friel clearly privileges, along with his qualified endorsement of Moore as mediating between English and Irish culture in his introduction to O'Donovan's Ordnance Survey letters, together give the lie to George O'Brien's belief that Clement's view of Moore is "one more instance of unity imposed upon division, the division in all instances being Anglo-Irish. Clement's position is the inverse of Richard Gore's. Margaret dismisses Richard as '[j]ust so caught up in his own world' ([*HP*] 13). But so is her father" ("The Late Plays," 99).

47. Kress, "The Music of the Sentimental Nationalist Heart," 131.

48. In his introduction to *Brian Friel: Plays 3*, Christopher Murray offers a more sobering assessment and suggests how the play looks past its late-1870s context to beyond the Belfast Agreement and how Christopher Gore's situation presages the potential decline of the Unionist community. Comparing Gore's dilemma to the opportunity for hope in Chekhov's *Uncle Vanya*, a version of which Friel wrote in 1998, Murray observes, "For Gore there is no 'new life' hereafter, as Sonya promises Vanya, and no 'peace.' The future is balanced on a political knife-edge. Since he is a unionist landlord for whom 'the home place' is forever England, Gore's situation is instructive regarding the future history of conflict in Northern Ireland. Unless people change and maintain a spirit of reconciliation, Gore's collapse is prophetic. . . . The fictional past, staged for the audience as the present, speaks of a future dilemma beyond the Belfast Peace Agreement" (xxiii).

49. O'Toole, "Friel Does More Than Simply Translate Ibsen's Classic Play, He Makes It Better," 6.

50. Ibid.

51. Deane, "Introduction" to *Brian Friel: Plays 1*, 12–13.

52. Northam, *Ibsen's Dramatic Method*, 155.

53. Ibid., 165.

54. Mason, "Eggs de Valera," 42, 41.

55. Moi, *Henrik Ibsen and the Birth of Modernism*, 318.

56. McFarlane, "Introduction" to *The Lady from the Sea, Hedda Gabler, The Master Builder*, 14.

57. Crompton, *Life of the Spider*, 71.

58. Ibid., 84.

59. Emilie Pine, however, argues how Anna Mackmin's direction of the play and Oliver Fenwick's "atmospheric lighting" in the 2008 Abbey Theatre production work to create a negative portrayal of Thea: "The image of Mrs. Elvsted (Andrea Irvine), kneeling center stage holding Loevborg's notes to her chest, under the glow of a golden spotlight . . . underscores the production's clever message; it is not Hedda but Thea, the inveterate social climber and moulder of men, who is the arch manipulator of this claustrophobic play" ("Music of the Tribe," 34). Such an interpretation, however, runs counter to both Ibsen's play and Friel's adaptation of it: both Ibsen and Friel focus on Hedda's manipulation of others, not Thea's, and while Thea's relationship with Eilert as inspirer of his work is proleptically likened to the role she will likely play for George in the conclusion, Friel (and Ibsen) make clear that Thea's work with both men as muse and collaborator is positive.

60. See Ibsen, *Hedda Gabler*, in *A Doll House, The Wild Duck, Hedda Gabler, The Master Builder*, trans. Rolf Fjelde, 303; Ibsen, *Hedda Gabler*, in *Four Major Plays*, trans. Jens Arup, 263; Ibsen, *Hedda Gabler*, in *Ibsen's Selected Plays*, trans. Rick Davis and Brian Johnston, 355.

61. Friel's emphasis on Hedda's fear of future solitary evenings subtly heightens Ibsen's language: "What will I do evenings over here?" (*Hedda Gabler*, trans. Fjelde, 303). Reviews of productions of Friel's *Hedda* have tended to focus on other sorts of dilemmas: Michael Billington, the well-known theater critic for the *Guardian*, claimed in his review of the (London) Old Vic's production in 2012 that "Hedda's tragedy is partly that she realises that, with her aristocratic instincts and distaste for intellectual pursuits, she is an anachronism in a world of growing equality between the sexes: that is her dilemma rather than that she is a female Jekyll and Hyde" ("*Hedda Gabler*—Review," n.p.).

62. Moi, *Henrik Ibsen*, 236, drawing on Cavell's reading of Ingrid Bergman's character launching into her "aria of revenge" in the film *Gaslight* (*Contesting Tears*, 59–60) and quoting his "discussion of the unknown woman's cogito performance as singing, in 'Opera and the Lease of Voice,'" in Cavell, *A Pitch of Philosophy*, 129–69.

63. Moi, *Henrik Ibsen*, 237. Moi quotes Cavell, *Contesting Tears*, 43.

64. Garton, "Middle Plays," articulates Hedda's use of the pistols well for my purposes here except in her last claim about them: "That they are in her possession is perfectly well motivated on a realistic level; they are the one thing the general left to her. They console her for everything she lacks in her present existence. Symbolically, they supply her with her defence against male invasion; with them, she has a strength—and a power to shock—not available to most women. They keep Løvborg at a distance, and deter Brack—though significantly, not for long. The latter takes her pistol from her after she fires at him as he will ultimately take from

her the last vestiges of her self-determination" (122). I disagree that Brack takes Hedda's "last vestiges of her self-determination" since her decision to kill herself preserves her from his future sexual advances that he terms in Friel's version "a most special delectation" (*HG* 102). Garton helpfully captures her much-diminished agency in her act of self-slaughter: "The one act of defiance she can perform is an act of self-destruction, a pitiful parody of the glorious self-assertion of which she had dreamed" ("Middle Plays," 123).

65. Moi, *Henrik Ibsen*, 239; for this full critique of romanticism's denial of the body and postmodernism's denial of the soul, see 238–39.

66. Wittgenstein, *Philosophical Investigations*, 178, quoted in Moi, *Henrik Ibsen*, 238. For her entire argument here on how Nora combines bodily theatricality and internal authenticity centered upon her soul's anguish, see 236–47. Moi's brilliant contention that "Ibsen's double perspective, his awareness of the impossibility of either choosing or not choosing between theatricality and authenticity, stands at the center of Ibsen's modernism" has become one of the seminal insights into his drama (240).

67. Hedda makes her decision to kill herself under the pressure of Judge Brack's blackmail attempt in threatening to reveal she lent Loevborg the pistol with which he killed himself. He speculates upon the great scandal that would result if her role in Loevborg's suicide emerges, and she plaintively mourns, "I'm altogether in your power then?," while he protests he will not "abuse that position." She vehemently states, "But you'd own me!," and then she quickly exclaims, "No, Judge, no! That won't happen!" Suggesting she will revert to her old, titular identity rather than that of simply being George's wife, she vows in response to Brack's comment "People can learn to live with what they can't change, Hedda Tesman": "Hedda Gabler can't, Judge Brack" (*HG* 100). Interestingly, as Leonard Conolly suggests, director Anna Mackmin's decision in the Old Vic production for Brack to "enter the inner room where Hedda lay dead, smear his hands and arms in her blood, and then grin ghoulishly at the audience as he wiped the blood down the glass door of the inner room" makes clearer the Judge's complicity in her suicide, although this horrific addition goes against Friel's simple stage direction: "*Fade to black*" (Conolly, "A Tale of Two *Hedda Gablers*," 13; *HG* 103).

68. Friel crucially changes the usual translation of the description of Hedda's piano playing, subtly likening it to the frenzied dancing of the sisters in *Lughnasa* and the other frenzied actions at climactic moments in many of his plays—and thus bringing it much closer in spirit to Nora's dancing of the tarantella in *A Doll House*. Fjelde, *Hedda Gabler*, translates the phrase as "a wild dance melody" (303), while Arup, *Hedda Gabler*, translates it as "a wild dance tune" (263), and Davis and Johnston, *Hedda Gabler*, "a wild dance melody" (355).

69. Moi, *Henrik Ibsen*, 319.

70. Friel, "The Saturday Interview," 156.

71. Casey, *Remembering*, 286.

72. Miller, "Ibsen and the Drama of Today," 229.

73. Friel, "'Secular Prayers' for the New Lyric Theatre, Belfast," 18.

74. Ibid., 19.

75. Friel, "Extracts from a Sporadic Diary (1995–96): *Give Me Your Answer, Do!*," 167.

76. Friel, "Seven Notes for a Festival Programme (1999)," 177.

77. Ibid., 180.

78. Friel, "Self-Portrait (1972)," 42.

79. Casey, "How to Get from Space to Place," 46.

80. Friel, Foreword to *The Big Chapel*, 1.

81. Adorno, *Minima Moralia*, 87.

82. Calinescu, *Rereading*, xi–xii.

Works Cited

Adorno, Theodor. *Minima Moralia*. London: Verso, 1997.

Anderson, Benedict. *Imagined Communities: Reflections on the Origin and Spread of Nationalism*. Rev. ed. New York: Verso, 1991.

Andrews, Elmer. *The Art of Brian Friel: Neither Reality nor Dreams*. New York: St. Martin's, 1995.

———. "The Fifth Province." In *The Achievement of Brian Friel*, edited by Alan J. Peacock, 29–48.

Andrews, John. "Notes for a Future Edition of Brian Friel's *Translations*." *Irish Review* 13 (1992–93): 93–106.

Appadurai, Arjun. *Modernity at Large: Cultural Dimensions of Globalization*. Minneapolis: University of Minnesota Press, 1996.

Arnheim, Rudolf. "Disciplining the Gramophone, Radio, Telephone, and Television." *Sapere* (Dec. 15, 1937): n.p. Reprint, *Modernism/Modernity* 16, no. 2 (Apr. 2009): 422–26.

Bachelard, Gaston. *The Poetics of Space*, translated by Maria Jolas. 1969. Reprint, Boston: Beacon, 1994.

Barr, Richard. *Rooms with a View: The Stages of Community in the Modern Theater*. Ann Arbor: University of Michigan Press, 1998.

Bauman, Zygmunt. *Globalization: The Human Consequences*. New York: Columbia University Press, 1998.

Baumer, Franklin L. *Modern European Thought: Continuity and Change in Ideas, 1600–1950*. New York: Macmillan, 1977.

Benedikt, Michael. "On Cyberspace and Virtual Reality." In *Man and Information Technology*. ed. unknown. Stockholm: Royal Swedish Academy of Engineering Sciences, 1995.

Benjamin, Walter. *Illuminations*. New York: Schocken, 1969.

———. "Theses on the Philosophy of History." In *Illuminations*, edited by Walter Benjamin, 253–64.

———. "The Work of Art in the Age of Mechanical Reproduction." *Illuminations,* edited by Walter Benjamin, 217–51.

Bennett, Fionn. "Translating the Facts of Landscape into the Facts of Language: Ethnoecological Ruminations on Glossopoiesis in Early Ireland." In *Irish Contemporary Landscapes in Literature and the Arts,* edited by Marie Mianowski, 39–50.

Bennett, Susan. *Theatre Audiences: A Theory of Production and Reception.* New York: Routledge, 1990.

Berry, Wendell. "The Body and the Earth." In Wirzba, *Art of the Commonplace,* 93–134.

———. "People, Land, and Community." *Standing by Words.* San Francisco: North Point Press, 1983, 64–79.

———. "The Regional Motive." *A Continuous Harmony.* Washington, DC: Shoemaker & Hoard, 1972, 61–68.

Bertha, Csilla. "Brian Friel as Postcolonial Playwright." In *The Cambridge Companion to Brian Friel,* edited by Anthony Roche, 154–65.

———. "Memory, Art, *Lieux de Mémoire* in Brian Friel's *The Home Place.*" In *The Theatre of Brian Friel: Tradition and Modernity,* by Christopher Murray, 230–45. London: Bloomsbury, 2014.

Billington, Michael. "*Hedda Gabler*—Review." Directed by Anna Mackmin, Old Vic Theatre, London. *Guardian,* Sept. 13, 2012. https://www.theguardian.com/stage/2012/sep/13/hedda-gabler-review.

Blau, Herbert. *The Audience.* Baltimore: Johns Hopkins University Press, 1990.

———. *The Eye of Prey: Subversions of the Postmodern.* Bloomington: Indiana University Press, 1987.

Bloody Sunday. Dir. Paul Greengrass. Paramount Pictures, 2002.

"The Bloody Sunday Inquiry." http://webarchive.nationalarchives.gov.uk/20101103103930/http:/report.bloody-sunday-inquiry.org/. Accessed June 26, 20009.

Boltwood, Scott. *Brian Friel, Ireland, and the North.* Cambridge: Cambridge University Press, 2007.

———. *Brian Friel: Readers' Guides to Essential Criticism.* New York: Palgrave, 2018.

———. "Brian Friel: Staging the Struggle with Nationalism." *Irish University Review* 32, no. 2 (Autumn/Winter 2002): 303–18.

———. "'An Emperor or Something': Brian Friel's Columba, Migrancy, and Postcolonial Theory." *Irish Studies Review* 10, no. 1 (2002): 51–61.

———. "'Mildly Eccentric': Brian Friel's Writings for the *Irish Times* and the *New Yorker*." *Irish University Review* 44, no. 2 (Autumn/Winter 2014): 305–22.

———. "'More Real for Northern Irish Catholics than Anybody Else': Brian Friel's Earliest Plays." *Irish Theatre International* 2, no. 1 (Aug. 2009): 4–15.

Bradley, Anthony, and Maryann Gialanella Valiulis, eds. *Gender and Sexuality in Modern Ireland*. Amherst: University of Massachusetts Press, 1997.

Branford, Victor, and Paul Geddes. *The Coming Polity: A Study in Reconstruction*. London: Williams & Norgate, 1917.

Brantley, Ben. "Recalling an Artist's Eloquent Loneliness." *New York Times*, Oct. 3, 2015. A18.

Brannigan, John. *Race in Modern Irish Literature and Culture*. Edinburgh: Edinburgh University Press, 2010.

Brewster, Scott, and Michael Parker, eds. *Irish Literature since 1990: Diverse Voices*. Manchester: Manchester University Press, 2006.

"Brian Friel." In *The Norton Anthology of English Literature*, edited by Stephen Greenblatt, 2475–76. 8th ed. Vol. 2. New York: Norton, 2006.

"Brian Friel's *Dancing at Lughnasa*." Playbill. Abbey Theatre, Dublin, Feb. 1 to Apr. 4, 2000.

"Brian Friel's *Translations*." Program. Lyric Theatre, Belfast, Apr. 21 to May 16, 1998.

Brown, Terence. "'Have We a Context?': Transition, Self and Society in the Theatre of Brian Friel." In *The Achievement of Brian Friel*, edited by Alan J. Peacock, 190–201.

———. *Ireland: A Social and Cultural History, 1922–2002*. New York: Penguin, 2004.

Burke, Patrick. "'As If Language No Longer Existed': Non-Verbal Theatricality in the Plays of Friel." In *Brian Friel: A Casebook*, edited by William Kerwin, 13–22.

———. "Friel and Performance History." In *The Cambridge Companion to Brian Friel*, edited by Anthony Roche, 117–28.

Calinescu, Matei. *Rereading*. New Haven, CT: Yale University Press, 1993.

Campbell, Hugh. "Modern Architecture and National Identity in Ireland." In *The Cambridge Companion to Modern Irish Culture*, edited by Joe Cleary and Claire Connolly, 285–303.

Carlson, Marvin. "*Molly Sweeney*. By Brian Friel." Review, *Theatre Journal* 47, no. 3 (Oct. 1995): 423–24. Accessed Aug. 9, 2012.

Casey, Edward S. *Getting Back into Place: Toward a Renewed Understanding of the Place-World*. Bloomington: Indiana University Press, 1993.

———. "How to Get from Space to Place in a Fairly Short Stretch of Time: Phenomenological Prolegomena." In *Senses of Place*, edited by Steven Feld and Keith H. Basso, 13–52. Santa Fe, NM: School of American Research Press, 1996.

———. *Imagining: A Phenomenological Study*. 2nd ed. Bloomington: Indiana University Press, 2000.

———. *Remembering: A Phenomenological Study*. Bloomington: Indiana University Press, 1987.

Cathcart, Rex. *The Most Contrary Region: The BBC in Northern Ireland, 1924–1984*. Belfast: Blackstaff, 1984.

Cave, Richard Allen. "Friel's Dramaturgy: The Visual Dimension." In *The Cambridge Companion to Brian Friel*, edited by Anthony Roche, 129–41.

———. "Questing for Ritual and Ceremony in a Godforsaken World: *Dancing at Lughnasa* and *Wonderful Tennessee*." In *Brian Friel's Dramatic Artistry*, edited by Donald E. Morse, Csilla Bertha, and Maria Kurdi, 181–204.

Cavell, Stanley. *Contesting Tears: The Hollywood Melodrama of the Unknown Woman*. Chicago: University of Chicago Press, 1996.

———. "Opera and the Lease of Voice." In *A Pitch of Philosophy: Autobiographical Exercises*, by Stanley Cavell, 129–69. Cambridge, MA: Harvard University Press, 1994.

Chaudhuri, Una. *Staging Place: The Geography of Modern Drama*. Ann Arbor: University of Michigan Press, 1995.

Clear, Caitríona. *Social Change and Everyday Life in Ireland, 1850–1922*. Manchester: Manchester University Press, 2007.

Cleary, Joe. "Introduction: Ireland and Modernity." In *The Cambridge Companion to Modern Irish Culture*, edited by Joe Cleary and Claire Connolly, 1–21.

Cleary, Joe, and Claire Connolly, eds. *The Cambridge Companion to Modern Irish Culture.* Cambridge: Cambridge University Press, 2005.

Clutterbuck, Catriona. "Lughnasa after Easter: Narrative Treatments of Imperialism in Friel and Devlin." In Special Issue on Brian Friel, *Irish University Review,* edited by Anthony Roche, 111–18.

Cohen, Anthony, and Katsuyoshi Fukui. "Introduction." In *Humanizing the City? Social Contexts of Urban Life at the Turn of the Millennium,* edited by Cohen and Fukui, n.p. Edinburgh: Edinburgh University Press, 1993.

Conolly, Leonard. "A Tale of Two *Hedda Gablers*: The Shaw Festival, Niagara-on-the-Lake, July 28–September 29, 2012, The Old Vic Theatre, London, September 12–November 10, 2012." *Ibsen News and Comment* 32 (Jan. 1, 2012): 12–15.

Cooper, Lydia. "The Gospels of Frank: Theatrical Salvation in Brian Friel's *Faith Healer.*" *The Explicator* 71, no. 4 (2013): 240–43.

Corbett, Tony. *Brian Friel: Decoding the Language of the Tribe.* Rev. and updated ed. Dublin: Liffey Press, 2008.

Corcoran, Neil. "The Penalties of Retrospect: Continuities in Brian Friel." In *The Achievement of Brian Friel,* edited by Alan J. Peacock, 14–28.

Corringe, T. J. *A Theology of the Built Environment: Justice, Empowerment, Redemption.* Cambridge: Cambridge University Press, 2002.

Coult, Tony. *About Friel: The Playwright and the Work.* London: Faber, 2003.

Crawley, Peter. "Brian Friel: Seven Key Plays." *The Irish Times,* Oct. 3, 2015. https://www.irishtimes.com/culture/brian-friel/brian-friel-seven-key-plays-1.2376245. Accessed Oct. 5, 2015.

Crompton, John. *The Life of the Spider.* Boston: Houghton Mifflin, 1951.

Cronin, Nessa. "Lived and Learned Landscapes: Literary Geographies and the Irish Topographical Tradition." In *Irish Contemporary Landscapes in Literature and the Arts,* edited by Marie Mianowski, 106–18.

Crotty, Derbhle. "Brian Friel: A Dramatic Life." *Friel @80 Supplement. The Irish Times,* Jan. 10, 2009. http://www.irishtimes.com/indepth/brian-friel/delving-deep-into-divided-donegal-landscape.html. Accessed May 9, 2011.

Csicsila, Joseph. "'Isn't It the Stupidest Thing You Ever Heard?': The Everyday Human Struggle in Brian Friel's *The Freedom of the City.*" In

A Companion to Brian Friel, edited by Richard Harp and Robert C. Evans, 15–22.

Csikai, Zsuzsa. "Brian Friel's Adaptations of Chekhov." *Irish Studies Review* 13, no. 1 (2005): 79–88.

Cullingford, Elizabeth Butler. "British Romans and Irish Carthaginians: Anticolonial Metaphor in Heaney, Friel, and McGuinness." *PMLA* 111, no. 2 (1996): 222–39.

———. "Gender, Sexuality, and Englishness in Modern Irish Drama and Film." In *Gender and Sexuality in Modern Ireland*, edited by Anthony Bradley and Maryann Gialanella Valiulis, 159–86.

Daly, Mary E. "'Oh, Kathleen Ni Houlihan, Your Way's a Thorny Way': The Condition of Women in Twentieth-Century Ireland." In *Gender and Sexuality in Modern Ireland*, edited by Anthony Bradley and Maryann Gialanella Valiulis, 102–26.

Daly, Nicholas. *Literature, Technology, and Modernity, 1860–2000.* Cambridge: Cambridge University Press, 2004.

Dantanus, Ulf. *Brian Friel: A Study.* London: Faber & Faber, 1988.

Davidson, Donald. "A Mirror for Artists." In *I'll Take My Stand: The South and the Agrarian Tradition*, 28–60. 1977. Reprint, Baton Rouge: Louisiana State University Press, by Twelve Southerners, 1995.

Davis, Colin. "*Etát Présent*: Hauntology, Spectres, and Phantoms." *French Studies* 59, no. 3 (2005): 373–79.

Day, Christopher. *Places of the Soul: Architecture and Environment.* London: Thorsons, 1999.

Deane, Ciarán. "Brian Friel's *Translations*: The Origins of a Cultural Experiment." *Field Day Review* 5 (2009): 7–47.

Deane, Seamus. "Brian Friel: The Double Stage." In *Celtic Revivals: Essays in Modern Irish Literature, 1880–1980*, 166–73. Wake Forest, NC: Wake Forest University Press, 1985.

———. "Brian Friel: The Name of the Game." In *The Achievement of Brian Friel*, edited by Alan J. Peacock, 103–12.

———. "Introduction." In *Brian Friel: Plays 1*, 11–22. London: Faber & Faber, 1996.

———. "Introduction." In *The Diviner: The Best Stories of Brian Friel*, 9–18. Dublin: O'Brien Press, 1983; London: Allison and Busby, 1983.

———. "Introduction." In *Selected Stories: Brian Friel*, 9–15. Loughcrew, Ireland: Gallery Press, 1979.

———. *Strange Country: Modernity and Nationhood in Irish Writing since 1790*. Oxford: Oxford University Press, 1997.

Deharme, Paul. "Proposition for a Radiophonic Art." *La Nouvelle Revue Francaise* 30 (1928): 413–23. Reprint, *Modernism/Modernity* 16, no. 2 (Apr. 2009): 406–13.

Delaney, Paul, ed. *Brian Friel in Conversation*. Ann Arbor: University of Michigan Press, 2000.

DeVinney, Karen. "Monologue as Dramatic Action in Brian Friel's *Faith Healer* and *Molly Sweeney*." *Twentieth-Century Literature* 45, no. 1 (Spring 1999): 110–19.

Derrida, Jacques. *Specters of Marx: The State of the Debt, the Work of Mourning, and the New International*. New York: Routledge, 1994.

De Valera, Eamon. "The Undeserted Village Ireland." In *The Field Day Anthology of Irish Writing*, edited by Seamus Deane, 747–50. Vol. 3. Derry: Field Day, 1991.

Devitt, John. *Shifting Scenes: Irish Theatre-Going, 1955–1985*, edited by Nicholas Grene and Chris Morash. Dublin: Carysfort Press, 2008.

Dixon, Stephen. "Mapping Cultural Imperialism." In Delaney, *Brian Friel in Conservation*, 135–37.

Donoghue, Denis. *Speaking of Beauty*. New Haven: Yale University Press, 2004.

Dowling, Joe. "Staging Friel." In *The Achievement of Brian Friel*, edited by Alan J. Peacock, 178–89.

Duffy, Enda. *The Speed Handbook: Velocity, Pleasure, Modernism*. Durham, NC: Duke University Press, 2009.

Duffy, Patrick J. *Exploring the History and Heritage of Irish Landscapes*. Dublin: Four Courts, 2007.

Dupré, Louis. "Ritual: The Divine Play of Time." In *Play, Literature, Religion: Essays in Cultural Intertextuality*, edited by Virgil Nemoianu and Robert Royal. Albany: SUNY Press, 1992, 199–212.

Eagleton, Terry. *Heathcliff and the Great Hunger: Studies in Irish Culture*. London: Verso, 1995.

Elliott, Marianne. *The Catholics of Ulster: A History*. London: Basic Books, 2001.

————. *When God Took Sides: Religion and Identity in Ireland—Unfin-ished History*. Oxford: Oxford University Press, 2009.

Evans, E. Estyn. *The Personality of Ireland: Habitat, Heritage, and His-tory*. Dublin: Lilliput, 1996.

Everett, Matthew A. "Review—*The Home Place*—Guthrie—5 Stars." Ty-rone Guthrie Theater, Minneapolis, Nov. 18, 2007. http://www.matthew aeverett.com/columns/detail.php?articleID=1291. Accessed Aug. 11, 2012.

Fallon, Brian. *An Age of Innocence: Irish Culture, 1930–1960*. Dublin: Gill & Macmillan, 1998.

"Families 'Need to Know' Soldiers' Names." *The Irish Times*, June 15, 1999. http://www.ireland.com/newspaper/ireland/1999/0615/north15 .htm. Accessed June 16, 2000.

Fanon, Frantz. *Black Skin, White Masks*, translated by Charles Lam Mark-mann. New York: Grove Press, 1967.

Ferriter, Diarmaid. *The Transformation of Ireland*. Woodstock, NY: Over-look Press, 2004.

Fitzpatrick, David. "Ireland since 1870." In *The Oxford Illustrated His-tory of Ireland*, edited by Roy Foster, 213–74. Oxford: Oxford Univer-sity Press, 1989.

Flaherty, Rachel, Simon Carswell, and Ronan McGreevy. "Meryl Streep on Brian Friel: 'Tender Dramatist Lovely Man.'" *The Irish Times*, Oct. 2, 2015. https://www.irishtimes.com/news/ireland/irish-news/meryl-streep -on-brian-friel-tender-dramatist-lovely-man-1.2376034. Accessed Oct. 4, 2015.

Foster, John Wilson. "The Brightest Candle of the Gael." In *Colonial Con-sequences: Essays in Irish Literature and Culture*, 3–18. Dublin: Lil-liput Press, 1991.

————. *Forces and Themes in Ulster Fiction*. Dublin: Gill & Macmillan, 1974.

Foster, Roy. *Modern Ireland 1600–1972*. London: Penguin, 1988.

Freshwater, Helen. *Theatre and Audience*. New York: Palgrave, 2009.

Friel, Brian. "After *Philadelphia*: Interview with John Fairleigh." In *Con-versations with Brian Friel*, edited by Paul Delaney, 47–50.

————. *Bannermen*. Seamus Deane Papers, Stuart A. Rose Manuscripts, Archives, and Rare Book Library, Emory University.

———. "Brian Friel." Museum number 2222. Transmission date Sept. 19, 1982. BBC Northern Ireland Radio Archives, Cultra, Northern Ireland.

———. "Brian Friel: Dramatist and Short Story Writer." Museum number 2959. Interviewed by John Boyd. Transmission date Aug. 2, 1970. BBC Northern Ireland Radio Archives, Cultra, Northern Ireland.

———. *Brian Friel: Plays 1: Philadelphia, Here I Come!, The Freedom of the City, Living Quarters, Aristocrats, Faith Healer, Translations.* London: Faber & Faber, 1996.

———. *Brian Friel: Plays 2: Dancing at Lughnasa, Fathers and Sons, Making History, Wonderful Tennessee, Molly Sweeney.* London: Faber & Faber, 1999.

———. *Brian Friel: Plays 3: Three Sisters, A Month in the Country, Uncle Vanya, The Yalta Game, The Bear, Afterplay, Performances, The Home Place, Hedda Gabler.* London: Faber & Faber, 2014.

———. "Brian Friel's First Book." *Belfast Telegraph*, Feb. 25, 1963, 3.

———. "Broadway? Who Cares!" Interview with Ronan Farren, 1980. In Delaney, *Brian Friel in Conversation*, 123–26.

———. *Dancing at Lughnasa.* London: Faber & Faber, 1990.

———. "*Dancing at Lughnasa* (1990): Background Research & Manuscripts." The Brian Friel Papers, National Library of Ireland, MS 37,104/2.

———. *The Enemy Within.* 1979. Reprint, Oldcastle, Ireland: Gallery Press, 1992.

———. "Extracts from a Sporadic Diary (1976–78): *Aristocrats*." In *Brian Friel: Essays, Diaries, Interviews: 1964–1999*, edited by Christopher Murray, 63–69.

———. "Extracts from a Sporadic Diary (1995–96): *Give Me Your Answer, Do!*" In *Brian Friel: Essays, Diaries, Interviews: 1964–1999*, edited by Christopher Murray, 166–72.

———. "Extracts from a Sporadic Diary (1992–94): *Molly Sweeney*." In *Brian Friel: Essays, Diaries, Interviews: 1964–1999*, edited by Christopher Murray, 153–65.

———. "Extracts from a Sporadic Diary (1979): *Translations*." In *Brian Friel: Essays, Diaries, Interviews: 1964–1999*, edited by Christopher Murray, 73–78.

———. "*Faith Healer* Comes to New York." *Princeton University Library Chronicle* 68, nos. 1–2 (2006): 516–18.

———. "*Faith Healer*: original notes (May 19, 1975)." The Brian Friel Papers, National Library of Ireland, MS 37,075/1.

———. "*Faith Healer*: original notes (May 22, 1975)." The Brian Friel Papers, National Library of Ireland, MS 37,075/1.

———. "*Faith Healer*: original notes (May 29, 1975)." The Brian Friel Papers, National Library of Ireland, MS 37,075/1.

———. "*Faith Healer*: original notes (July 19, 1975)." The Brian Friel Papers, National Library of Ireland, MS 37,075/1.

———. "*Faith Healer*: original notes (Oct. 1975)." The Brian Friel Papers, National Library of Ireland, MS 37,075/1.

———. "*Faith Healer*: original notes (Oct. 17, 1975)." The Brian Friel Papers, National Library of Ireland, MS 37,075/1.

———. "*Faith Healer*: original notes (Nov. 8, 1978)." The Brian Friel Papers, National Library of Ireland, MS 37,075/1.

———. "Field Day: An Introduction." In *Field Day Theatre Company and Publishing House*. Dublin: Nicholson & Bass, 1987.

———. "1ˢᵗ Notes on *Philadelphia*, Undated." The Brian Friel Papers, National Library of Ireland, MS 37,047/1.

———. Foreword to *The Big Chapel*, by Thomas Kilroy, 1. Dublin: Liberties Press, 2009.

———. "*The Freedom of the City* (1973): Manuscripts." The Brian Friel Papers, National Library of Ireland, MS 37,066/1.

———. "*The Freedom of the City*: Program." Abbey Theatre Production. World Premiere. Feb. 20, 1973. Seamus Deane Papers, Stuart A. Rose Manuscript, Archives, and Rare Book Library, Emory University.

———. "Friel's Sense of Conflict." Interview by Michael Sheridan, 1986. In *Brian Friel in Conversation*, edited by Paul Delaney, 195–96.

———. "Friel Takes Derry by Storm." Interview by Ulick O'Connor, 1981. In *Brian Friel in Conversation*, edited by Paul Delaney, 158–60.

———. *The Gentle Island*. 1973. Reprint, Oldcastle, Ireland: Gallery Press, 1993.

———. "The Giant of Monaghan." *Holiday* (May 1964): 89, 92, 94–96.

———. "The Green Years: A Talk by Brian Friel." In *Brian Friel in Conversation*, edited by Paul Delaney, 14–19.

————. *Hedda Gabler* (after Ibsen). Oldcastle, Ireland: Gallery Press, 2008.

————. *The Home Place*. Oldcastle, Ireland: Gallery Press, 2005.

————. "Interview with Brian Friel: Lewis Funke, 1968." In *Brian Friel in Conversation*, edited by Paul Delaney, 51–71.

————. "In Interview with Des Hicky and Des Smith (1972)." In *Brian Friel: Essays, Diaries, Interviews: 1964–1999*, edited by Christopher Murray, 47–50.

————. "In Interview with Desmond Rushe (1970)." In *Brian Friel: Essays, Diaries, Interviews: 1964–1999*, edited by Christopher Murray, 25–34.

————. "In Interview with Eavan Boland (1973)." In *Brian Friel: Essays, Diaries, Interviews: 1964–1999*, edited by Christopher Murray, 57–60.

————. "In Interview with Fintan O'Toole (1982)." In *Brian Friel: Essays, Diaries, Interviews: 1964–1999*, edited by Christopher Murray, 105–15.

————. "In Interview with Graham Morrison (1965)." In *Brian Friel: Essays, Diaries, Interviews: 1964–1999*, edited by Christopher Murray, 4–14.

————. "In Interview with Laurence Finnegan (1986)." In *Brian Friel: Essays, Diaries, Interviews: 1964–1999*, edited by Christopher Murray, 123–34.

————. "In Interview with Mel Gussow (1991)." In *Brian Friel: Essays, Diaries, Interviews: 1964–1999*, edited by Christopher Murray, 139–49.

————. "In Interview with Paddy Agnew (1980)." In *Brian Friel: Essays, Diaries, Interviews: 1964–1999*, edited by Christopher Murray, 84–88.

————. "In Interview with Peter Lennon (1964)." In *Brian Friel: Essays, Diaries, Interviews: 1964–1999*, edited by Christopher Murray, 1–3.

————. "In Interview with Victoria Radin (1981)." In *Brian Friel: Essays, Diaries, Interviews: 1964–1999*, edited by Christopher Murray, 92–95.

————. "Interview with Ulick O'Connor." *The [Dublin] Sunday Tribune*, Sept. 6, 1981, 2.

————. "Ivan Turgenev (1818–1883)." In *A Month in the Country (after Turgenev)*, 9–11. 1992. Reprint, Oldcastle, Ireland: Gallery Press, 2006.

———. "Letter to Seamus Deane." Nov. 21, 1979. Seamus Deane Papers, MSS 1210, box 1, folder 10. Stuart A. Rose Manuscript, Archives, and Rare Book Library, Emory University.

———. "Letter to Seamus Deane." Oct. 3, 1980. Seamus Deane Papers, MSS 1210, box 1, folder 11. Stuart A. Rose Manuscript, Archives, and Rare Book Library, Emory University.

———. "Letter to Seamus Deane." July 17, 1982. Seamus Deane Papers, MSS 1210, box 1, folder 11. Stuart A. Rose Manuscript, Archives, and Rare Book Library, Emory University.

———. "Letter to Seamus Deane." Oct. 28, 1982. Seamus Deane Papers, MSS 1210, box 1, folder 11. Stuart A. Rose Manuscript, Archives, and Rare Book Library, Emory University.

———. "Letter to Seamus Deane." June 21, 1984. Seamus Deane Papers, MSS 1210, box 1, folder 11. Stuart A. Rose Manuscript, Archives, and Rare Book Library, Emory University.

———. "Letter to Seamus Deane." Mar. 17, 1989. Seamus Deane Papers, MSS 1210, box 1, folder 9. Stuart A. Rose Manuscript, Archives, and Rare Book Library, Emory University.

———. "Making a Reply to the Criticisms of *Translations* by J. H. Andrews (1983)." In Murray, *Brian Friel: Essays, Diaries, Interviews: 1964–1999*, 116–19.

———. "Meet Brian Friel." *Irish Press*, Apr. 29, 1962, 10.

———. *The Mundy Scheme.* In *Crystal and Fox* and *The Mundy Scheme*, 149–317. New York: Farrar, Straus, & Giroux, 1970.

———. "Philadelphia, Here the Author Comes!" In *Brian Friel in Conversation*, edited by Paul Delaney, 40–46.

———. *Philadelphia, Here I Come!* Motion Picture. Dir. John Quested. American Film Theatre, 1975. 2003 DVD by Kino Video.

———. "Plays Peasant and Unpeasant (1972)." In *Brian Friel: Essays, Diaries, Interviews: 1964–1999*, edited by Christopher Murray, 51–56.

———. "The Saturday Interview: Brian Friel." Elgy Gillespie, 1981. In *Brian Friel in Conversation*, edited by Paul Delaney, 153–57.

———. *The Saucer of Larks.* Garden City, NY: Doubleday, 1962.

———. "'Secular Prayers' for the New Lyric Theatre, Belfast." Edited and introduced by Marilynn Richtarik. *New Hibernia Review* 19, no. 3 (Fall 2015): 17–19.

———. *Selected Stories.* Loughcrew, Ireland: Gallery Press, 1996.

———. "Self-Portrait (1972)." In *Brian Friel: Essays, Diaries, Interviews: 1964–1999*, edited by Christopher Murray, 37–46.

———. "Seven Notes for a Festival Programme (1999)." In *Brian Friel: Essays, Diaries, Interviews: 1964–1999*, edited by Christopher Murray, 173–80.

———. "Theatre for Derry." The Brian Friel Papers, National Library of Ireland, MS 37193/5–7.

———. "The Theatre of Hope and Despair (1967)." In *Brian Friel: Essays, Diaries, Interviews: 1964–1999*, edited by Christopher Murray, 15–24.

———. "Where We Live." Preface to *Ordnance Survey Letters: Donegal. Letters Containing Information Relative to the Antiquities of the County of Donegal Collected during the Progress of the Ordnance Survey in 1835*, edited and introduction by John O'Donovan and Michael Herity, vii–ix. Dublin: Four Masters Press, 2000.

Friel, Brian, John Andrews, and Kevin Barry. "*Translations* and *A Paper Landscape*." *Crane Bag* 7, no. 2 (1983): 118–24.

Friel, Brian, Fergus Linehan, Hugh Leonard, and John B. Keane. "The Future of Irish Drama." *Irish Times*, Feb. 12, 1970, 14.

Fulton, Helen. "Hegemonic Discourses in Brian Friel's *The Freedom of the City*." In *Language and Tradition in Ireland: Continuities and Displacements*, edited by Maria Tymocyko and Colin Ireland, 62–83. Amherst: University of Massachusetts Press, 2003.

Gagné, Laurie Brands. "Three Dances: The Mystical Vision of Brian Friel in *Dancing at Lughnasa*." *Renascence* 59, no. 2 (Winter 2007): 119–32.

Garton, Janet. "The Middle Plays." In *The Cambridge Companion to Ibsen*, edited by James McFarlane, 106–25. Cambridge: Cambridge University Press, 1994.

Germanou, Maria. "An American in Ireland: The Representation of the American in Brian Friel's Plays." *Comparative Drama* 38, nos. 2–3 (Summer/Fall 2004): 259–76.

Gibbons, Luke. "Projecting the Nation: Cinema and Culture." In *The Cambridge Companion to Modern Irish Culture*, edited by Joe Cleary and Claire Connolly, 206–24.

Giedion, Siegfried. *Mechanization Takes Command: A Contribution to Anonymous History*. New York: Norton, 1969.

———. *Space, Time, and Architecture: The Growth of a New Tradition.* 4th ed. Cambridge, MA: Harvard University Press, 1962.

Girard, René. *Violence and the Sacred.* Baltimore: Johns Hopkins University Press, 1977.

Gleitman, Clare. "'I'll See You Yesterday': Brian Friel, Tom Murphy and the Captivating Past." *A Concise Companion to Contemporary British and Irish Drama*, edited by Nadine Holdsworth and Mary Luckhurst, 26–47. Malden, MA: Blackwell, 2008.

———. "Three Characters in Search of a Play: Brian Friel's *Faith Healer* and the Quest for Final Form." *New Hibernia Review* 13, no. 1 (Spring 2009): 95–108.

Goldsmith, Oliver. "The Deserted Village." In *Eighteenth-Century English Literature*, edited by Geoffrey Tillotson, Paul Fussell Jr., and Marshall Waingrow, 1252–57. Fort Worth: Harcourt Brace Jovanovich, 1969.

Gorringe, T. J. *A Theology of the Built Environment: Justice, Empowerment, Redemption.* Cambridge: Cambridge University Press, 2002.

Grant, Patrick. *Breaking Enmities: Religion, Literature, and Culture in Northern Ireland, 1967–97.* New York: Macmillan, 1999.

Gregory, Lady Augusta. *Cuchulain of Muirthemne.* Gerrards Cross, UK: Colin Smythe, 1993.

Grene, Nicholas. "Brian Friel and the Sovereignty of Language." *Irish Theatre International* 2, no. 1 (Aug. 2009): 38–47.

———. "*Faith Healer* in New York and Dublin." In *Politics and Performance in Contemporary Northern Ireland*, edited by John P. Harrington and Elizabeth J. Mitchell, 138–46.

———. "Five Ways of Looking at *Faith Healer*." In *The Cambridge Companion to Brian Friel*, edited by Anthony Roche, 53–65.

———. "Friel and Transparency." In Special Issue on Brian Friel, *Irish University Review*, edited by Anthony Roche, 136–44.

———. *The Politics of Irish Drama.* Cambridge: Cambridge University Press, 1999.

Hamon, Denis. "Landscape, *Senchas*, and the Medieval Irish Mind." In Mianowski, *Irish Contemporary Landscapes in Literature and the Arts*, 26–38.

Harp, Richard, and Robert C. Evans, eds. *A Companion to Brian Friel.* West Cornwall, CT: Locust Hill Press, 2002.

Harrington, John P., ed. *Irish Theater in America: Essays on Irish Theatrical Diaspora*. Syracuse: Syracuse University Press, 2009.

Harrington, John P., and Elizabeth J. Mitchell. "Introduction." In *Politics and Performance in Contemporary Northern Ireland*, edited by John P. Harrington and Elizabeth J. Mitchell, 1–6.

Harrington, John P., and Elizabeth J. Mitchell, eds. *Politics and Performance in Contemporary Northern Ireland*. Amherst: University of Massachusetts Press, 1999.

Harris, Claudia W. "The Engendered Space: Performing Friel's Women from Cass McGuire to Molly Sweeney." In *Brian Friel: A Casebook*, edited by William Kerwin, 43–75.

Heaney, Seamus. "Brian Friel and Field Day." Interview with *Raidio Telefís Éireann* of Field Day Theatre Company. Directors Brian Friel, Seamus Deane, David Hammond, Heaney, Stephen Rea, and Tom Paulin. In *Brian Friel in Conversation*, edited by Paul Delaney, 178–91.

———. "For Liberation: Brian Friel and the Use of Memory." In *The Achievement of Brian Friel*, edited by Alan J. Peacock, 229–40.

———. *Opened Ground: Selected Poems 1966–1996*. New York: Farrar, Straus, & Giroux, 1998.

———. "The Regional Forecast." In *The Literature of Region and Nation*, edited by R. P. Draper, 10–23. New York: St. Martin's Press, 1989.

———. "Sparks in the Tin Hut." In *Irish Theatre on Tour*, edited by Nicholas Grene and Chris Morash, 1–5. Dublin: Carysfort Press, 2005.

———. *Spelling It Out: In Honour of Brian Friel on His 80th Birthday*. Oldcastle, Ireland: Gallery Press, 2009.

———. "Vision." Program for *Molly Sweeney*. Gate Theatre, Dublin, 2011.

Hewitt, Rachel. "The Ordnance Survey in Ireland: A Bloody Military Operation?" Playbill for June 23–Aug. 13, 2011 Abbey Theatre production of *Translations*. Dir. Conall Morrison.

Holy Bible. New International Version. Grand Rapids, MI: Zondervan, 1993.

Holy Bible. New Revised Standard Version. Oxford: Oxford University Press, 1990.

Ibsen, Henrik. *Hedda Gabler*. In *A Doll House, The Wild Duck, Hedda Gabler, The Master Builder*, translated and with a foreword by Rolf Fjelde, 217–304. Vol. 1 of *Four Major Plays*. Rev. ed. New York: Signet, 1992.

————. *Hedda Gabler.* In *Four Major Plays: A Doll House, Ghosts, Hedda Gabler, The Master Builder,* translated by Jens Arup, 165–264. New York: Oxford World's Classics, 1998.

————. *Hedda Gabler.* In *Ibsen's Selected Plays,* selected and edited by Brian Johnston, translated by Rick Davis and Brian Johnston, 288–356. Norton Critical Editions. New York: Norton, 2004.

Isherwood, Charles. "Cherry Jones's 'Faith Healer' Performance Illuminates an Artist's Struggle." *New York Times,* Aug. 13, 2006. https://www.nytimes.com/2006/08/13/theater/13ishe.html. Accessed July 17, 2019.

Jones, Cherry. "Keeping the Faith." Interview by Brian Scott Lipton. *Theater Mania,* Apr. 12, 2006. http://www.theatermania.com/new-york-city-theater/news/04–2006/keeping-the-faith_8044.html. Accessed Oct. 1, 2014.

Jones, Nesta. *Brian Friel.* London: Faber & Faber, 2000.

Joyce, James. "Letter to Stanislaus." In *Dubliners: Text, Criticism, and Notes,* edited by Robert Scholes and A. Walton Litz, 255–56. New York: Penguin, 1976.

Kearney, Richard. "Language Play: Brian Friel and Ireland's Verbal Theatre." In *Brian Friel: A Casebook,* edited by William Kerwin, 77–116.

————. "Memory in Irish Culture: An Exploration." In *The Famine and the Troubles,* edited by Oona Frawley, 138–51. Vol. 3 of *Memory Ireland.* Syracuse: Syracuse University Press, 2014.

Keating, Sara. "Delving Deep into Divided Donegal Landscape." *Friel @80 Supplement, The Irish Times,* Jan. 10, 2009. http://www.irishtimes.com/indepth/brian-friel/delving-deep-into-divided-donegal-landscape.html. Accessed May 9, 2011.

————. "*Molly Sweeney.*" Review, Gate Theatre, Dublin, June 28–July 23, 2011. *Irish Theatre Magazine.* http://www.irishtheatremagazine.ie/Reviews/Current/Molly-Sweeney. Accessed Aug. 9, 2012.

Kennedy, Dennis. *The Spectator and the Spectacle: Audiences in Modernity and Postmodernity.* Cambridge: Cambridge University Press, 2009.

Kerrigan, John C. "Swimming in Words: *Molly Sweeney'*s Dramatic Form." In *A Companion to Brian Friel,* edited by Richard Harp and Robert C. Evans, 151–61.

Kerwin, William, ed. *Brian Friel: A Casebook.* New York: Garland, 1997.

Kiberd, Declan. *After Ireland: Writing the Nation from Beckett to the Present.* Cambridge, MA: Harvard University Press, 2018.

———. "Brian Friel's *Faith Healer*." In *Brian Friel: A Casebook*, edited by William Kerwin, 211–26.

———. "*Dancing at Lughnasa*: Between First and Third World." In *Ireland on Stage: Beckett and After*, edited by Horoko Mikami, Minako Okamuro, and Naoko Yagi, 153–76. Dublin: Carysfort Press, 2007.

———. *Inventing Ireland*. Cambridge, MA: Harvard University Press, 1996.

Kilroy, Thomas. "The Early Plays." In *The Cambridge Companion to Brian Friel*, edited by Anthony Roche, 6–17.

———. "Theatrical Text and Literary Text." In *The Achievement of Brian Friel*, edited by Alan J. Peacock, 91–102.

Kimmer, Garland. "'Like Walking through Madame Tussaud's: The Catholic Ascendancy and Place in Brian Friel's *Aristocrats*." In *Brian Friel: A Casebook*, edited by William Kerwin, 193–210.

Kopytoff, Igor. "The Cultural Biography of Things: Commoditization as Process." In *The Social Life of Things: Commodities in Cultural Perspective*, edited by Arjun Appadurai, 64–91. Cambridge: Cambridge University Press, 1986.

Krause, David. *The Profane Book of Irish Comedy*. Ithaca: Cornell University Press, 1982.

Kress, Simon B. "The Music of the Sentimental Nationalist Heart: Thomas Moore and Seamus Heaney." *New Hibernia Review* 15, no. 1 (Spring 2011): 123–37.

Kurdi, Maria. "An Interview with Richard Pine about Brian Friel's Theatre." In *Brian Friel's Dramatic Artistry*, edited by Donald E. Morse, Csilla Bertha, and Maria Kurdi, 301–24.

Lahr, John. "In *Dancing at Lughnasa*, Due on Broadway This Month, Brian Friel Celebrates Life's Pagan Joys." In *Brian Friel in Conversation*, edited by Paul Delaney, 213–17.

Lanters, José. "Brian Friel's Uncertainty Principle." In Special Issue on Brian Friel, *Irish University Review*, edited by Anthony Roche, 162–75.

———. "Queer Creatures, Queer Place: Otherness and Normativity in Irish Drama from Synge to Friel." In *Irish Theatre in Transition from the Late Nineteenth to the Early Twenty-First Century*, edited by Donald E. Morse, 54–67. New York: Palgrave, 2015.

Leavy, Adrienne. "Brian Friel One Year On: A Critical Overview." *The Irish Times*, Oct. 2, 2016. https://www.irishtimes.com/culture/books

/brian-friel-one-year-on-a-critical-overview-1.2813558. Accessed Oct. 5, 2016.

Leeney, Cathy. "*Dancing at Lughnasa.*" Abbey Theatre Program for *Dancing at Lughnasa*. 2000.

Ling, Ruth. "Faber and Irish Literature." In *The Irish Book in English, 1891–2000*, edited by Clare Hutton and Patrick Walsh, 562–75. Vol. 5 of *The Oxford History of the Irish Book*. Oxford: Oxford University Press, 2011.

"Living Lines: Friel's Finest Dramas." *Friel @80 Supplement. The Irish Times*, Jan. 10, 2009. http://www.irishtimes.com/indepth/brian-friel /living-lines-friel's-finest-dramas." Accessed May 7, 2011.

Lojek, Helen. "Brian Friel's Gentle Island of Lamentation." In Special Issue on Brian Friel, *Irish University Review,* edited by Anthony Roche, 48–59.

———. "Brian Friel's Sense of Place." In *The Cambridge Companion to Twentieth-Century Irish Drama*, edited by Shaun Richards, 177–90. Cambridge: Cambridge University Press, 2004.

———. *The Spaces of Irish Drama: Stage and Place in Contemporary Plays*. New York: Palgrave, 2011.

Lonergan, Patrick. "'Dancing on a One-Way Street': Irish Reactions to *Dancing at Lughnasa* in New York." In *Irish Theater in America: Essays on Irish Theatrical Diaspora*, edited by John P. Harrington, 147–62.

———. *Theatre and Globalization: Irish Drama in the Celtic Tiger Era*. New York: Palgrave, 2009.

Longley, Michael. *Tuppenny Stung: Autobiographical Chapters*. Belfast: Lagan Press, 1994.

Loveridge, Charlotte. "*The Home Place.*" Review, Comedy Theatre, London, May 31, 2005. *CurtainUp: The Internet Theatre Magazine of Reviews, Features, Annotated Listings*. http://www.curtainup.com/home place.html. Accessed Aug. 11, 2012.

Lysaght, Sean. "Contrasting Natures: The Issue of Names." In *Nature in Ireland: A Scientific and Cultural History,* edited by John Wilson Foster, 440–60. Dublin: Lilliput Press, 1997.

MacCana, Proinsias. "Early Irish Ideology and the Concept of Unity." In *The Irish Mind: Exploring Intellectual Traditions*, edited by Richard Kearney, 56–78. Dublin: Wolfhound Press, 1985.

MacLaughlin, Jim. "Donegal and the New Ireland." In *Donegal: The Making of a Northern County*, edited by Jim MacLaughlin, 283–91. Dublin: Four Courts Press, 2007.

MacNeill, Máire. *The Festival of Lughnasa*. Oxford: Oxford University Press, 1962.

Mahony, Christina Hunt. "Memory and Belonging: Irish Writers, Radio, and the Nation." *New Hibernia Review* 5, no. 1 (Spring 2001): 10–24.

Maley, Patrick. "Dwelling in Dissonance: Brian Friel's *The Freedom of the City*, Posterity, and History." *Field Day Review*, no. 9 (2013): 54–71.

Mason, Patrick. "Eggs de Valera: Reflections on *Dolly West's Kitchen* and *Dancing at Lughnasa*." Special issue on Frank McGuinness, *Irish University Review* 40, no. 1 (Spring/Summer 2010): 35–45.

Matthews, Kelly. "Brian Friel, The BBC, and Ronald Mason." In "Writing from Northern Ireland." Supplement, *Irish University Review* 47 (2017): 470–85.

Maxwell, D. E. S. *Brian Friel*. Lewisburg, PA: Bucknell University Press, 1973.

Mays, Michael. "A Nation Once Again? The Dislocations and Displacements of Irish National Memory." *Nineteenth-Century Contexts* 27, no. 2 (June 2005): 119–38.

McAuley, James W. "Cuchullain and an RPG-7: the Ideology and Politics of the Ulster Defence Association." In *Culture and Politics in Northern Ireland 1960–1990*, edited by Eammon Hughes, 45–68. Philadelphia: Open Press, 1991.

McFarlane, James. "Introduction." In *The Lady from the Sea, Hedda Gabler, The Master Builder*, edited by James McFarlane, translated by James McFarlane and Jens Arup, 1–24. Vol. 7 of *The Oxford Ibsen*. Oxford: Oxford University Press, 1966.

McGrath, F. C. *Brian Friel's (Post) Colonial Drama: Language, Illusion, and Politics*. Syracuse: Syracuse University Press, 1999.

McGuinness, Frank. *Brian Friel's Dancing at Lughnasa*. Screenplay. London: Faber & Faber, 1998.

———. "*Faith Healer*: All the Dead Voices." In Special Issue on Brian Friel, *Irish University Review*, edited by Anthony Roche, 60–63.

McKenna, Bernard. *Rupture, Representation, and the Refashioning of Identity in Drama from the North of Ireland, 1969–1994*. Westport, CT: Praeger, 2003.

McLoone, Martin. "Inventions and Re-imaginings: Some Thoughts on Identity and Broadcasting in Ireland." In *Culture, Identity, and Broadcasting in Ireland: Local Issues, Global Perspectives*, edited by Martin McLoone, 2–30. Belfast: Institute for Irish Studies, 1991.

McMullan, Anna. "*The Home Place*: Unhomely Inheritances." *Irish Theatre International* 2, no. 1 (Aug. 2009): 62–66.

Melaugh, Martin, and Fionnuala McKenna. "Violence—Details of 'the Disappeared'" at http://cain.ulst.ac.uk/issues/violence/disappeared.htm. Accessed on May 8, 2012.

Mianowski, Marie, ed. *Irish Contemporary Landscapes in Literature and the Arts*. New York: Palgrave, 2012.

Miller, Arthur. "Ibsen and the Drama of Today." In *The Cambridge Companion to Ibsen*, edited by James McFarlane, 227–32. Cambridge: Cambridge University Press, 1994.

Moi, Toril. *Henrik Ibsen and the Birth of Modernism: Art, Theater, Philosophy*. Oxford: Oxford University Press, 2006.

Moloney, Karen M. "Molly Astray: Revisioning Ireland in Brian Friel's *Molly Sweeney*." *Twentieth-Century Literature* 46, no. 3 (Autumn 2000): 285–310.

Morash, Christopher. *A History of Irish Theatre, 1601–2000*. Cambridge: Cambridge University Press, 2002.

Morse, Donald E., Csilla Bertha, and Maria Kurdi, eds. *Brian Friel's Dramatic Artistry: "The Work Has Value."* Dublin: Carysfort Press, 2006.

Mullan, Don. *Bloody Sunday: Massacre in Northern Ireland*. Niwot, CO: Roberts Rinehart, 1997.

Mumford, Lewis. *The City in History: Its Origins, Its Transformations, and Its Prospects*. New York: Harcourt Brace, 1961.

Murray, Christopher, ed. *Brian Friel: Essays, Diaries, Interviews: 1964–1999*. London: Faber & Faber, 1999.

———. "Friel and O'Casey Juxtaposed." In Special Issue on Brian Friel, *Irish University Review*, edited by Anthony Roche, 16–29.

———. "Friel's 'Emblems of Adversity' and the Yeatsian Example." In *The Achievement of Brian Friel*, edited Alan J. Peacock, 69–90.

———. "Introduction." In *Brian Friel: Essays, Diaries, Interviews: 1964–1999*, edited by Christopher Murray, vii–xxii.

———. "Introduction." In *Brian Friel: Plays 2*, vii–xxiii. London: Faber & Faber, 1999.

———. "Introduction." In *Brian Friel: Plays 3*, vii–xxxi. London: Faber & Faber, 2014.

———. *The Theatre of Brian Friel: Tradition and Modernity*. London: Bloomsbury, 2014.

———. *Twentieth-Century Irish Drama: Mirror Up to Nation*. Manchester, UK: Manchester University Press, 1997.

Myerhoff, Barbara G. "A Death in Due Time: Construction of Self and Culture in Ritual Drama." In *Rite, Drama, Festival, Spectacle: Rehearsals toward a Theory of Cultural Performance*, edited by John J. MacAloon, 149–78. Philadelphia: Institute for the Study of Human Issues, 1984.

Niel, Ruth. "Disability as Motif and Meaning in Friel's Drama." In *Brian Friel's Dramatic Artistry*, edited by Donald E. Morse, Csilla Bertha, and Maria Kurdi, 205–27.

Nietzsche, Friedrich. *The Birth of Tragedy: Out of the Spirit of Music*, translated by Shaun Whiteside and edited by Michael Tanner. London: Penguin, 1993.

Nightingale, Benedict. "Brian Friel, Irish Playwright of Poetic Beauty, Dies at 86." *New York Times*, Oct. 3, 2015. A18.

Northam, J. R. *Ibsen's Dramatic Method: A Study of the Prose Dramas*. London: Faber & Faber, 1953.

O'Brien, George. *Brian Friel*. Dublin: Gill & Macmillan, 1989.

———. "Meet Brian Friel: The *Irish Press* Columns." In Special Issue on Brian Friel, *Irish University Review*, edited by Anthony Roche, 30–41.

———. "The Late Plays." In *The Cambridge Companion to Brian Friel*, edited by Anthony Roche, 91–103.

O'Clery, Conor. "Bloody Sunday Victims Can 'Rest in Peace.'" *Global Post*, June 15, 2010. http://www.globalpost.com/print/5560402. Accessed Sept. 3, 2010.

O'Connor, Frank. *The Lonely Voice: A Study of Short Fiction*. Dublin: Macmillan, 1963.

O'Connor, Ulick. *Brian Friel: Crisis and Commitment: The Writer and Northern Ireland*. Dublin: Elo Press, 1989.

O'Donoghue, Bernard. "Borders in Brian Friel's *Translations*." *English Language and Literature* 59, no. 6 (2013): 927–37.

O'Malley, Aidan. *Field Day and the Translation of Irish Identities: Performing Contradictions*. New York: Palgrave, 2011.

O'Neill, Declan. "Ancient Red Hand Symbol of Ulster Still Has Power to Divide Northern Ireland." *Belfast Telegraph*, Apr. 26, 2010, n.p.

O'Siadhail, Michael. *The Five Quintets*. Waco, TX: Baylor University Press, 2018.

O'Toole, Fintan. "Celebrating the Life and Genius of Brian." *The Irish Times*, July 19, 2008. n.p.

————. "*Collected Plays* by Brian Friel Review: 29 Survivors of Their Maker's Culls." *The Irish Times*, Dec. 10, 2016. https://www.irishtimes.com/culture/books/collected-plays-by-brian-friel-review-29-survivors-of-their-maker-s-culls-1.2876896. Accessed July 8, 2017.

————. "The 'Eerie Afterlife' of Donal McCann." *The Irish Times*, Dec. 19, 2009. https://www.irishtimes.com/culture/tv-radio-web/the-eerie-afterlife-of-donal-mccann-1.793148. Accessed July 17, 2019.

————. "Friel Does More Than Simply Translate Ibsen's Classic Play, He Makes It Better." *The Irish Times*, Sept. 13, 2008. 6.

————. *The Lie of the Land: Irish Identities*. London: Verso, 1999.

————. "Modern Ireland in 100 Artworks: 1979—*Faith Healer*, by Brian Friel." *The Irish Times*, Feb. 6, 2016. https://www.irishtimes.com/culture/modern-ireland-in-100-artworks-1979-faith-healer-by-brian-friel-1.2522733. Accessed July 17, 2019.

————. "Tracing a Rocky Path from the Past." *Friel @80 Supplement. The Irish Times*, Jan. 10, 2009. http://www.irishtimes.com/indepth/brian-friel/delving-deep-into-divided-donegal-landscape.html. Accessed May 9, 2011.

Parker, Michael. "Forms of Redress: Structure and Characterization in *The Freedom of the City*." In *Brian Friel's Dramatic Artistry*, edited by Donald E. Morse, Csilla Bertha, and Maria Kurdi, 271–300.

Paulin, Tom. *A New Look at the Language Question*. Field Day Pamphlet, no. 1. Derry: Field Day, 1983. Reprint, *The Routledge Language and Cultural Theory Reader*, edited by Lucy Burke, Tony Crowley, and Alan Burke, 293–301. New York: Routledge, 2000.

Peacock, Alan, ed. *The Achievement of Brian Friel*. Gerrards Cross, UK: Colin Smythe, 1993.

————. "Translating the Past: Friel, Greece and Rome." In *The Achievement of Brian Friel*, edited by Alan Peacock, 113–33.

Pelletier, Martine. "'Creating Ideas to Live By': An Interview with Stephen Rea." *Sources: Revue d'études anglophones* 9 (Fall 2000): 48–65.

———. "From Moscow to Ballybeg: Brian Friel's Richly Metabiotic Relationship with Anton Chekhov." In *Adapting Chekhov: The Text and Its Mutations*, edited by J. Douglas Clayton and Yana Meerzon, 180–99. New York: Routledge, 2013.

———. "'New Articulations of Irishness and Otherness' on the Contemporary Irish Stage." In *Irish Literature since 1990: Diverse Voices*, edited by Scott Brewster and Michael Parker, 98–117.

———. "*Translations*, the Field Day Debate, and the Re-imagining of Irish Identity." In *The Cambridge Companion to Brian Friel*, edited by Anthony Roche, 66–77.

Pike, Frank. "Letter to Michael O'Brien." Aug. 17, 1982. Gallery Press/ Peter Fallon Collection, Stuart A. Rose Manuscript, Archives, and Rare Book Library, Emory University.

Pine, Emilie. "The Music of the Tribe." *Irish Theatre Magazine* 8, no. 36 (Winter 2008): 32–38.

Pine, Richard. *Brian Friel and Ireland's Drama*. London: Routledge, 1990.

———. "Coming Home to the Truth." Program for *Faith Healer*. Donmar Warehouse, London, June 23 to Aug. 20, 2016.

———. *The Diviner: The Art of Brian Friel*. Dublin: University College Dublin Press, 1999.

———. "Friel's Irish Russia." In *The Cambridge Companion to Brian Friel*, edited by Anthony Roche, 104–16.

Pringle, Peter, and Philip Jacobson. *Those Are Real Bullets: Bloody Sunday, Derry, 1972*. New York: Grove Press, 2000.

Raban, Jonathan. "Icon or Symbol: The Writer and the 'Medium.'" In *Radio Drama*, edited by Peter Lewis, 79–90. New York: Longman, 1981.

Rafferty, Oliver P. *Catholicism in Ulster, 1603–1983: An Interpretative History*. Dublin: Gill & Macmillan, 1994.

Rattigan, Dermot. *Theatre of Sound: Radio and the Dramatic Imagination*. Dublin: Carysfort Press, 2002.

Rayner, Alice. *Ghosts: Death's Double and the Phenomena of Theatre*. Minneapolis: University of Minnesota Press, 2006.

Richards, David. "Now Starring in Dublin: A Poetic Friel Heroine." *New York Times*, Sept. 7, 1994. http://www.nytimes.com/1994/09/07/arts /critic-s-notebook-now-starring-in-dublin-a-poetic-friel-heroine.html ?pagewanted=all&src=pm. Accessed Aug. 10, 2012.

Richards, Shaun. "Brian Friel: Seizing the Moment of Flux." *Irish University Review* 30, no. 2 (Autumn/Winter 2000): 254–71.

Richtarik, Marilynn J. *Acting between the Lines: The Field Day Theatre Company and Irish Cultural Politics 1980–1984.* Oxford: Oxford University Press, 1994.

———. "Brian Friel and Field Day." In *The Oxford Handbook of Modern Irish Theatre,* edited by Nicholas Grene and Chris Morash, 357–71. Oxford: Oxford University Press, 2016.

Ricoeur, Paul. *Memory, History, Forgetting,* translated by Kathleen Blamey and David Pellauer. Chicago: University of Chicago Press, 2004.

Roach, Joseph. "'All the Dead Voices': The Landscape of Famine in *Waiting for Godot.*" In *Land/Scape/Theater,* edited by Elinor Fuchs and Una Chaudhuri, 84–93. Ann Arbor: University of Michigan Press, 2002.

Robinson, Tim. *Setting Foot on the Shores of Connemara and Other Writings.* Dublin: Lilliput Press, 1996.

Roche, Anthony. *Brian Friel: Theatre and Politics.* Houndmills, UK: Palgrave Macmillan, 2011.

———. *Contemporary Irish Drama.* 2nd ed. New York: Palgrave, 2009.

———. *Contemporary Irish Drama from Beckett to McGuinness.* Dublin: Gill & Macmillan, 1994.

———. "Friel and Synge: Towards a Theatrical Language." In Special Issue on Brian Friel, *Irish University Review,* edited by Anthony Roche, 145–61.

Roche, Anthony, ed. *The Cambridge Companion to Brian Friel.* Cambridge: Cambridge University Press, 2006.

———. Special Issue on Brian Friel. *Irish University Review* 29, no. 1 (Spring/Summer 1999): 1–215.

Roche, Mark William. *Why Literature Matters in the 21st Century.* New Haven, CT: Yale University Press, 2004.

Roche-Tiengo, Virginie. "The Voices of the Dead and the Silence of the Living in Brian Friel's Drama." In *Silence in Modern Irish Literature,* edited by Michael McAteer, 201–12. Leiden: Brill/Rodopi, 2017.

Rotman, Brian. "Automedial Ghosts." In *Profession,* 118–22. New York: Modern Language Association of America, 2011.

Russell, Richard Rankin. "Brian Friel's Short Fiction: Place, Community, and Modernity." *Irish University Review* 42, no. 2 (Fall/Winter 2012): 298–326.

———. "Deprovincializing Brian Friel's Drama in America, 2009 and 2014: *Dancing at Lughnasa* in Fort Myers, Florida, and *Faith Healer* in Houston, Texas." In Special Issue, "Mirror up to Theatre: Essays in Honor of Christopher Murray," *Irish University Review* 45, no. 1 (Spring/Summer 2015): 103–16.

———. "Home, Exile, and Unease in Brian Friel's Globalized Drama since 1990: *Molly Sweeney, The Home Place,* and *Hedda Gabler* (after Ibsen)." *Modern Drama* 56, no. 2 (Summer 2013): 206–31.

———. "The Liberating Fictional Truth of Community in Brian Friel's *The Freedom of the City*." *South Atlantic Review* 71, no. 1 (Winter 2006): 42–73.

———. "The Play between Text and Intertext." Review of *The Theatre of Brian Friel: Tradition and Modernity,* by Christopher Murray. *Hungarian Journal of English and American Studies* 21, no. 2 (Fall 2015): 448–53.

———. *Poetry and Peace: Michael Longley, Seamus Heaney, and Northern Ireland*. Notre Dame, IN: Notre Dame University Press, 2010.

———. "Seamus Heaney's Creative Work for BBC Northern Ireland Radio, 1968–71." *Irish Studies Review* 15, no. 2 (May 2007): 137–62.

———. "'Something Is Being Eroded': The Vanishing Agrarian Epistemology of Brian Friel's *Translations*." *New Hibernia Review* 10, no. 2 (Summer 2006): 106–122.

Saunders, Timothy. "Classical Antiquity in Brian Friel's *Translations*." In Special Issue, "The Island and the Arts," *Nordic Irish Studies* 11, no. 1 (2012): 133–51.

Scarry, Elaine. *On Beauty and Being Just*. Princeton: Princeton University Press, 1999.

Schrank, Bernice. "Politics, Language, Metatheatre: Friel's *The Freedom of the City* and the Formation of an Engaged Audience." In *Theatre Stuff: Critical Essays on Contemporary Irish Theatre,* edited by Eamonn Jordan, 122–44. Dublin: Arts Council, 2000.

Smyth, Gerry. *Space and the Irish Cultural Imagination*. New York: Palgrave, 2001.

Snodgrass, Mary Ellen. *Brian Friel: A Literary Companion*. Jefferson, NC: McFarland, 2017.

Sontag, Susan. *Regarding the Pain of Others*. New York: Picador, 2003.

Spencer, Charles. "Friel Falls Short of the Russian Master." Review of *The Home Place*, Comedy Theatre, London. *The Telegraph*, May 26, 2005. http://www.telegraph.co.uk/culture/theatre/drama/3642670/Friel-falls -short-of-the-Russian-master.html.

Steiner, George. *Grammars of Creation*. New Haven: Yale University Press, 2002.

Strain, Margaret. "'Renouncing Change': Salvation and the Sacred in Brian Friel's *Faith Healer*." *Renascence* 57, no. 1 (Fall 2004): 63–73.

Sweeney, Bernadette. *Performing the Body in Irish Theatre*. New York: Palgrave, 2008.

Tacitus. *The Agricola and the Germania*. Translated and introduction by H. Mattingly. Revised translation by S. A. Handford. New York: Penguin, 1970.

Taylor, Charles. *Sources of the Self*. Cambridge, MA: Harvard University Press, 1989.

Taylor, Peter. *Loyalists*. London: Bloomsbury Press, 1999.

Teachout, Terry. "Great Play, Great Player." *Wall Street Journal*, May 19, 2006. n.p.

———. "'The Home Place' Review: Friel Returns to Irish Rep." *Wall Street Journal*, Oct. 12, 2017. https://www.wsj.com/articles/the-home-place -review-friel-returns-to-irish-rep-1507840174. Accessed July 10, 2019.

———. "Remembering Brian Friel (1929–2015): A Poet of the Particular." *Wall Street Journal*, Oct. 2, 2015. https://www.wsj.com/articles /remembering-brian-friel-1929–2015-a-poet-of-the-particular-144381 2843.

———. "The Very Best We Have." *Wall Street Journal*, Jan. 26, 2007, W7.

Thompson, Spurgeon. "Edmund Burke's *Reflections on the Revolution in France* and the Subject of Eurocentrism." *Irish University Review* 33, no. 2 (Autumn/Winter 2004): 245–62.

Thornton, Weldon. *The Antimodernism of Joyce's Portrait of the Artist as a Young Man*. Syracuse: Syracuse University Press, 1994.

———. *J. M. Synge and the Western Mind*. Gerrards Cross, UK: Colin Smythe, 1979.

Toíbín, Colm. "Colm Toíbín on a Time of Theatrical Miracles for Brian Friel." *The Irish Times*, Oct. 2, 2015. https://www.irishtimes.com/culture /brian-friel/colm-tóibín-on-a-time-of-theatrical-miracles-for-brian-friel-1 .2376210. Accessed Oct. 4, 2015.

Toulmin, Stephen. *Cosmopolis: The Hidden Agenda of Modernity.* Chicago: University of Chicago Press, 1990.

Tracy, Robert. "Brian Friel's Rituals of Memory." *Irish University Review* 37, no. 2 (Autumn/Winter 2007): 395–412.

———. "The Russian Connection: Friel and Chekhov." Special Issue on Brian Friel, *Irish University Review,* edited by Anthony Roche, 64–77.

Tuite, Patrick. "'Walking in the Steps of Your Forefathers': Locating the Actor and the Audience in Derry's Siege Pageant." In *Audience Participation: Essays on Inclusion in Performance,* edited by Susan Kattwinkel, 167–84. Westport, CT: Praeger, 2003.

Turner, Victor. *Dramas, Fields, and Metaphors: Symbolic Action in Human Society.* Ithaca, NY: Cornell University Press, 1974.

———. *The Ritual Process: Structure and Anti-Structure.* Chicago: University of Chicago Press, 1969.

———. *From Ritual to Theatre: The Human Seriousness of Play.* New York: Performing Arts Journal Publications, 1982.

Wallace, Kathleen R., and Karla Armbruster. "Introduction: Why Go Beyond Nature Writing, and Where To?" In *Beyond Nature Writing: Expanding the Boundaries of Ecocriticism,* edited by Armbruster and Wallace, 1–25. Charlottesville: University Press of Virginia, 2001.

Walsh, Martin. "Ominous Festivals, Ambivalent Nostalgia: Brian Friel's *Dancing at Lughnasa* and Billy Roche's *Amphibians.*" *New Hibernia Review* 14, no. 1 (Spring 2010): 127–41.

Watkin, William. *On Mourning: Theories of Loss in Modern Literature.* Edinburgh: Edinburgh University Press, 2004.

Watt, Stephen. "Friel and the Northern Ireland 'Troubles' Play." In *The Cambridge Companion to Brian Friel,* edited by Anthony Roche, 30–40.

Weaver, Richard M. *Ideas Have Consequences.* 1948. Reprint, Chicago: University of Chicago Press, 1984.

Welch, Robert. *The Cold of May Day Monday: An Approach to Irish Literary History.* Oxford: Oxford University Press, 2014.

———. "Sacrament and Significance: Some Reflections on Religion and the Irish." In Special Issue, "The Endless Knot: Literature and Religion in Ireland," *Religion and Literature* 28, nos. 2–3 (Summer/Autumn 1996): 101–13.

Whelan, Kevin. "The Bases for Regionalism." In *Culture in Ireland—Regions: Identity and Power: Proceedings of the Cultures of Ireland*

Group Conference, 27–29 November, 1992, edited by Proinsias O'Drisceoil, 5–62. Belfast: Institute of Irish Studies, 1993.

———. "Between: The Politics of Culture in 'Translations.'" Playbill for June 23–Aug. 13, 2011 Abbey Theatre production of *Translations*. Dir. Conall Morrison.

———. "The Cultural Effects of the Famine." In *The Cambridge Companion to Modern Irish Culture*, edited by Joe Cleary and Claire Connolly, 137–54.

White, Harry. *Music and the Irish Literary Imagination*. Oxford: Oxford University Press, 2008.

Wilson, Gordon. "Gordon Wilson: I Have Lost My Daughter. . . . I Shall Pray for Those People Every Night." *Consolatio*, Nov. 8, 2007. https:// www.consolatio.com/2007/11/gordon-wilson-i.html. Accessed July 19, 2019.

Wilson, Thomas M., and Hastings Donnan. *The Anthropology of Ireland*. New York: Berg, 2006.

Winkler, Elizabeth Hale. "Brian Friel's *The Freedom of the City*: Historical Actuality and Dramatic Imagination." *Canadian Journal of Irish Studies* 7, no. 1 (June 1981): 12–31.

Wirzba, Norman, ed. *The Art of the Commonplace: The Agrarian Essays of Wendell Berry*. Washington, DC: Shoemaker & Hoard, 2002.

———. "Placing the Soul: An Agrarian Philosophical Principle." In *The Essential Agrarian Reader: The Future of Culture, Community, and the Land*, 80–97. Lexington: University of Kentucky Press, 2005.

Wittgenstein, *Philosophical Investigations*. Translated by G. E. M. Anscombe. 3rd ed. New York: Macmillan, 1968.

Woodworth, Paddy. "Reasons for Having a Field Day." *Irish Press*, Nov. 1, 1982, n.p.

Worth, Katharine. "Translations of History: Story-telling in Brian Friel's Theatre." In *British and Irish Drama since 1960*, edited by James Acheson, 73–87. New York: St. Martin's Press, 1993.

Worthen, W. B. "Homeless Words: Field Day and the Politics of Translation." *Modern Drama* 38, no. 1 (Spring 1995): 22–41.

———. *Modern Drama and the Rhetoric of Theater*. Berkeley: University of California Press, 1992.

Wyse, Bruce. "Traumatizing Romanticism in Brian Friel's *Faith Healer*." *Modern Drama* 47, no. 3 (Fall 2004): 446–63.

York, Richard. "Friel's Russia." In *The Achievement of Brian Friel*, edited by Alan J. Peacock, 164–77.

Zapf, Hubert. "The State of Ecocriticism and the Function of Literature as Cultural Ecology." In *Nature in Literary and Cultural Studies: Transatlantic Conversations on Ecocriticism*, edited by Catrin Gersdorf and Sylva Mayer, 49–69. New York: Rodopi, 2006.

Index